Yearbook 2013

The Professional Handbook of Educators in Ireland

Edited by
Dr. Tony Hall

Published by Education Matters
www.educationmatters.ie

Printed in Ireland by
Walsh Colour Print,
Castleisland, Co. Kerry.

Contents

Foreword *by the Minister* — iii

Editor's Welcome — vi

Introduction *by Brian Mooney* — viii

1. Early Childhood — 1
2. Primary — 33
3. Post-Primary — 81
4. Third Level — 142
5. Fourth Level — 200
6. Further Education & Lifelong Learning — 216

Afterword *by the Minister* — 241

National Learning Network
Investing in People, Changing Perspectives
A Rehab Group Company

We can help you open the door to employment

If you or someone you know has had difficulties getting employment due to injury, illness, learning difficulties or mental ill-health, National Learning Network can offer a fresh start.

In partnership with FÁS and the HSE, National Learning Network has a wide range of accredited training programmes available across Ireland.

In 2012, over 90% of those who completed our programmes progressed to employment or further education and training.

If you'd like more information and a prospectus, call us on 1890 283 000, email info@nln.ie or visit www.nln.ie

Foreword by Minister for Education & Skills Ruairí Quinn T.D.

I'm very pleased to be once again invited to write a foreword for Education Matters and I hope that you enjoy this latest edition.

On previous occasions, I have written about the economic situation that our country faces and the challenges that reductions in public expenditure bring to the administration of the education budget.

This year, I want to take a different approach. I want to give a brief overview of the improvements that are being introduced to our education system. These improvements should not be viewed in isolation, but rather as a set of interconnected developments that will lead to a better future for children and a better future for teachers.

I also want to convey my appreciation of the contribution those involved in the management of schools make, including board members and school leaders. The quality of the education we provide to our young people is very strongly linked to the leadership of school principals, and to the support provided by boards of management to the work and life of each school.

Literacy and Numeracy
In July 2011, I published the National Literacy and Numeracy strategy to prioritise literacy and numeracy. The strategy sets out a significant range of new developments and the first benchmark against which our efforts will be measured are the forthcoming PISA results, due to be published by the OECD in December 2013.

Implementation to date has been encouraging. Over the last twelve months, the amount of time devoted to literacy and numeracy in our classrooms has increased.

The investment in CPD for our teachers has also been significant. In 2013, we will spend an additional €6.5 million on continuing to implement in full the Literacy and Numeracy Strategy.
Finally, the new primary language curriculum will be ready for children from junior infants to second class in September 2014.

Fully implementing the Literacy and Numeracy Strategy will be central to achieving our ambition to rank among the best performing countries in the world.

School Self Evaluation
One of the biggest changes unveiled since last year's edition of Education Matters has been the introduction of School Self-Evaluations, or SSE.

We have known for some time that Ireland lags behind other countries in the frequency and depth of self-evaluation processes in schools. Complemented by external inspections, the introduction of SSE will improve the quality of schooling.

It will also reinforce the professionalism of teachers. In addition, it will increase both the autonomy and accountability of our principals, teachers and boards of management.

I recognise that SSE is bringing about a considerable change in culture in our schools. This can be challenging for both teachers and principals alike as greater openness is required to ask challenging questions about practice and standards.

School self-evaluations will also introduce a higher level of transparency for the school community, which is to be welcomed. I believe the roll-out has been planned in a reasonable, limited way, allowing the school system time to adjust to these changes.

In the first four years, schools will focus on literacy, numeracy and one other area – with the emphasis in particular on teaching and learning in those areas.

We are supporting the change through guidelines for schools, evidence-collecting tools for school staff, checklists for boards of management, a dedicated website, and training for school leaders. I also want to acknowledge the positive engagement of teachers and principals in this process so far. No doubt together we will continue to learn as the process is embedded in the life of our schools.

Junior Cycle reform
The Framework for Junior Cycle, published last October sets out Principles, Statements of Learning and Key Skills. I accept that realising deep educational change can only happen through teachers and school management.

I have been deeply encouraged by the strong support that seems to exist across the second-level system for the introduction of short courses. I accept that we need to work carefully to ensure that all students benefit from this innovation.

It will create interested, independent learners who will be better prepared to meet the challenges of life beyond school.

I believe these reforms will enable the educational system to deliver a junior cycle that places the needs of students at the core of quality learning and teaching.

Assessment should assist students in their learning and not be regarded as the end point. Assessment is not about "proving" but about "improving" learning outcomes.

Just as we reached a point in 1967, where there was no longer a need for a state examined Primary Certificate, I believe we have now reached that point in relation to the Junior Certificate.

The abolition of the Primary Certificate did not change primary school teachers from advocates for their students to judges of them. Instead, it lifted the dead hand of a narrow external assessment, and paved the way for the introduction of a child-centred curriculum for pupils. I genuinely believe the transformation of Junior Cycle will have a similar impact on our secondary-school system and this is to be welcomed.

Admission to Schools
The Education Act of 1998 set out quite clearly that schools are required to operate admissions policies that provide for maximum accessibility to the school. Put simply schools should be inclusive.

Most schools in Ireland, most of the time, are inclusive and welcoming of all children. The Education Act however is light touch in terms of providing ways and means of ensuring that all schools welcome all children.

Other than Section 29, which has become cumbersome for schools and parents, the current legislation does not include provisions for resolving problems when they arise.

At present we do not have any tailored measures in legislation that deal with issues around school admission. For example there is a difference between dealing with oversubscription, which means that all simply cannot be accommodated in the school of first choice, and a situation where an individual child can find no place at all.

I will shortly bring to Government draft heads of a bill. – the Education (Admission to School) Bill 2013. I will be publishing the Bill in draft form to allow a full public discussion, including inputs from the Oireachtas committee and the education partners.

I do not want to unnecessarily intrude into how schools do business. My only policy objective is to ensure that the way in which schools decide on applications is more structured, fair and transparent. The draft legislation will make it clear that some methods of controlling admissions will no longer be permitted. However, any school that is faithful to the Education Act in relation to providing maximum access will have nothing to fear from my proposals.

Conclusion
These are just some of the reforms that are underway across the education spectrum. We are also examining other parts of the education system.

Strengthening the quality of early childhood education and initial teacher education will directly lead to improvements in the teaching and learning in our schools.

The establishment of the Education and Training Boards and SOLAS will help us develop our further education and training sector.

The recently announced reconfiguration of the higher education landscape will allow us to eliminate unnecessary duplication across that sector and look towards better educational provision for third-level students.

I am privileged to serve as Ireland's Minister for Education and Skills. I approach my task with a deep conviction that our country needs an ambitious set of improvements across all levels of education. We must look towards a better future for children, and a better future for teachers. Each of the changes is designed with one purpose in mind - enhancing the educational opportunities and outcomes for all our students.

I have an enduring belief that working together we can deliver that better future for all.

FOR STABILITY, JOBS AND GROWTH.

Editor's Welcome
by Tony Hall

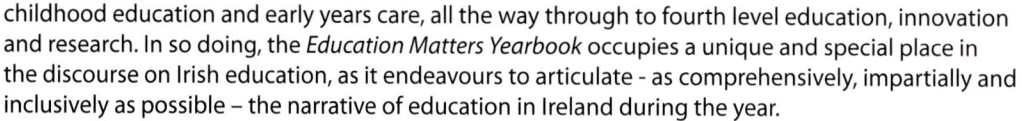

Dear Reader,

I am delighted to welcome you to the *Education Matters Yearbook 2013: The Professional Handbook of Educators in Ireland*. This is the seventh edition of the Yearbook, which affords a panoptic of key developments, innovations and issues in Irish education over the course of the year. Interleaving salient media items about Irish education with reflective, critical and informative commentary from key stakeholders in Irish education, the *Yearbook* recounts the main events in the Irish educational system, from early childhood education and early years care, all the way through to fourth level education, innovation and research. In so doing, the *Education Matters Yearbook* occupies a unique and special place in the discourse on Irish education, as it endeavours to articulate - as comprehensively, impartially and inclusively as possible – the narrative of education in Ireland during the year.

It would simply not be possible to realise the project every year without our many contributors, from across all sectors of Irish education. I would like here to thank the large number of people who have contributed to the Yearbook this year, and to pay a particular tribute to those who have contributed to, and supported *Education Matters* and the *Education Matters Yearbook* over many years now.

The compilation, design and production of the *Yearbook* annually constitute a significant editorial and educational undertaking. I would like to thank the editorial board who worked so creatively, efficiently and productively together over the year. I wish especially to thank Jackie O'Callaghan, PRO, National Parents' Council Post-Primary; Peter Mullan, Press Officer, INTO; Stiofán Ó Cualáin, Acting Principal, Coláiste na Coiribe, Galway; Rita Melia, Head, Membership Directorate Early Childhood Ireland; Caroline Loughnane, Director, Marketing & Communications, NUI Galway; Áine Lynch, CEO, National Parents' Council Primary; Michael Gallagher, Principal, Scoil Éinde Primary School, Galway and Irish National Teachers' Organisation; Virginia O'Mahony, Assistant Director, Irish Primary Principals' Network; Dr. Anne Walsh, Academic Coordinator, Open Learning Centre, NUI Galway; and Ms. Bernadette O'Sullivan, Director of the MA Journalism, NUI Galway.

Minister for Education and Skills Ruairí Quinn TD with members of the Education Matters Editorial Board at the launch of the Education Matters Yearbook in NUI, Merrion Square, Dublin in November 2012

I would especially like to thank NUI Galway for supporting *Education Matters Yearbook 2013*, all our sponsors and advertisers, and the *Irish Times, Irish Independent* and *Irish Examiner*.

I would like also to thank NUIG students Amy Haverty and Steven McElligott for their contributions to *Education Matters* and the *Education Matters Yearbook* over the year; and our talented design team, Mary Lillis and Shona Reilly of *PrintThat*, NUI Galway. I wish also to thank Dr. Attracta Halpin, Registrar, National University of Ireland (NUI), and the NUI for their support of *Education Matters* and the *Education Matters Yearbook*.

Finally, I would like to pay a particular tribute to Phyllis Mitchell, for her creativity, vision, and dedication, and without whom *Education Matters* and the *Education Matters Yearbook* would simply not be possible.

We trust that you will find this year's edition an engaging and informative read, whilst providing a repertory of the key developments, innovations and issues in Irish education in 2013.

Le gach dea-mhéin,

Anthony Hall

Tony Hall
School of Education, NUI Galway
August 2013

Professor Jim Browne, President NUI Galway, Dr Tony Hall, Editor and Minister for Education and Skills Ruairí Quinn TD at the launch of the Education Matters Yearbook in NUI, Merrion Square, Dublin in November 2012

Introduction
By Brian J Mooney

Overview of Educational Developments in Ireland: 2012-2013

Childcare and Pre-School Education
The 10th November 2012 saw the passing by referendum of the children's rights amendment, which strengthened their constitutional rights. By May of this year, the gap between constitutional aspirations and stark reality was highlighted by a "Prime Time" special on childcare centres which showed that, according to a HSE inspection report, 75% were in breach of regulations last year.

The report, which focused on the behaviour of some staff in three crèches, shocked the nation. For the 24,000 childcare practitioners, most of whom act totally professionally in their care of children, this programme cast them in a very poor light. But to what extent do we really value our childcare services? An unqualified childcare worker earns €10.10 an hour. Following a 3-year level 7 Ordinary level degree, their hourly rate goes up by €1.14. If we pay qualified childcare workers a few Euros over the minimum wage for their skills, are we surprised if their motivation level falls?

There is strong political support across all political parties for a second preschool year. However, although Minister for Children Frances Fitzgerald and others in Cabinet have raised the issue of transferring some of the funding which currently goes directly to parents to fund a second preschool year, such a transfer of resources is deeply unpopular with parents, who would see their child benefit payments cut again. Therefore, this is unlikely to be implemented.

Haddington Road Agreement
The demand from Government for savings of €1 billion through public service pay and pension cuts dominated the education debate at both primary, post primary and third level. Teachers have seen huge drops to their take home pay since cuts were introduced after the crash in 2008. The proposals under the Croke Park II agreements removed the supervision and substitution payment from all teachers, and further removed the entire income over €65,000 for those earning €69,000 - because of the way the 5.5% cut was structured back to €0 once a person's earnings went beyond €65,000.

The main category of teacher affected by these cuts is Assistant Principals, Deputy Principals and Principals. The end of the school year saw a large number of these teachers announcing their retirement, with many more to follow them by the deadline of 31 August 2014 for pensions based on pre-cut salaries.

The report from the State Examinations Commission in August 2013 on the errors which occurred in the June 2013 state examinations put some of the blame on the huge loss of senior managers - and thus corporate memory - over the past few years. What will be the effect on the quality of our education system of the sudden loss of the wisdom accumulated over many years by assistant, deputy and principal teachers? And what motivation will there be for a teacher over the next four years, who on the top of their scale at approximately €65,000, to apply for a senior management post in any school?

Croke Park II having been rejected by all the teacher unions, new proposals emerged from the LRC in May 2013 which will see the restoration of substitution and supervision payments in 4-5 years' time as part of core salary, and the full restoration of pay cuts for those earning over €65,000 by 1 January 2018.

Members of the INTO accepted the Haddington Road agreement by a two to one majority, whereas the other teachers unions rejected it without consulting their members. Their Executives were forced to reconsider this decision, and met in late August to do so. The ASTI, TUI and IFUT are going to ballot their members in early September 2013, with the ASTI recommending rejection of the proposed agreement, while the TUI is putting the proposals to their members without any recommendation. In the meantime, the more draconian terms of the Financial Emergency Measures in the Public Interest Act 2013 has been applied to teachers' salaries, other than those in primary schools, from 1 July 2013.

Given that all the other public service unions have now accepted and are operating the terms of the Haddington Road agreement, it would be pure lunacy for teachers to attempt to bring it down by engaging in industrial action. As we start into a new school year in September, I would predict that - after much huffing and puffing on the part of some teacher representatives - most classroom teachers on the ground will realise the futility of attempting to break the Government on this issue and will reluctantly accept their terms.

Primary Education
The issue of new school patronage rumbled on during the past academic year. An online survey took place in five areas, Arklow, Castlebar, Tramore, Trim, and Whitehall, to determine parents' attitudes to creating a diversity of school types within their locality, through the transfer to other patronage models of a number of existing Catholic schools. By November, it became clear that fewer than 2,000 parents had responded, making up just over a third of eligible parents.

In January 2013, the DES extended the survey to 38 other areas. The process is moving along at a snail's pace, and the task of telling any specific group of parents that their school will be relinquished from local Catholic patronage has yet to be confronted. In April 2013, the tensions came to the surface as the Minister tried to nail down agreement on the details of the transfer of 29 out of 3000 Catholic schools. In my opinion getting any local community to agree to this transfer will be far more difficult to bring about than either the Minister or the Irish Bishops may realise.

Special Needs Support
Supports for students with special needs are a relatively recent innovation within our secondary and primary school system. Even so, Minister Quinn has had to give way to the huge public resistance to his reform measures aimed at controlling the escalating costs of these supports. Having announced cutbacks in May, the Minister was forced to go to Cabinet to secure agreement for the release of 500 additional teaching posts to ensure that there would be no cut in the support for special needs children. We will see the rest of the education system paying the price of this back down when the details of the next round of education cuts are announced in October's early budget.

The compensation package agreed during the year with former residents of the Magdalene laundries will also necessitate further cuts to areas of current education spending. Given that we spend only

4.6% of GDP on education in the first place, compared to the 7% spent by more enlightened OECD countries, the year on year cutbacks are beginning to do serious long term damage to the very fabric of our education system at all levels.

Cyber bullying
The issue of cyber bullying, more than any other, grabbed the national consciousness during the past year. A series of tragic deaths, including that of two sisters in Donegal, meant that the topic was never out of the national media for more than a few weeks. Now that the ownership and daily use of smart phones have become commonplace among children, protecting them from accessing inappropriate online content or becoming the subject of cyber bullying is getting progressively more difficult. As online technology becomes more and more central to the way that teaching and learning take place in our schools, and text books are replaced by electronic devices, maintaining any barrier between our children and the potential destructiveness of anonymous online communication is next to impossible.

At second level, the loss of a specific guidance counselling allocation led to many Principals removing Guidance Counsellors from both their offices and their service of providing one-to-one counselling to students experiencing distress. When tragic incidents occurred in our schools in the past year, either as a result of cyber bullying or other trigger factors, Principals have been left in the impossible situation of attempting to withdraw the Guidance Counsellor from the teaching duties assigned to them in September 2012, to deal with the fallout from such incidents. One Guidance Counsellor in Kerry, who had been re-assigned to subject teaching duties, had to deal with three tragic deaths in a twelve week period while still striving to provide undisrupted teaching and learning of examination subjects for the classes which had been assigned to her.

Many Principals only came to realise the nature of the one-to-one counselling work, which has been taking place completely under the radar in Guidance Counsellors' offices for many years now, when they found themselves dealing with a constant stream of deeply distressed students arriving at their office doors. They very quickly realised that they had neither time, nor training, nor skills to provide counselling support to students. When Minister Quinn suggested at a press conference in Marlborough Street that the caretaker or cleaner could be the person to provide appropriate support to a distressed student, he drew some very sharp responses from a lot of people – including myself.

Junior Cycle Reform
The framework for Junior Cycle reform was launched in October 2012 following years of work within the NCCA. The teacher unions had cooperated in the consultations and development of proposals but were shocked when the Minister decided that, as part of the implementation of this reform process, the Junior Certificate - a mini Leaving Certificate as we know it - would be abolished.

The Minister defended his decision by referring to the fact that the Primary School Certificate was abolished in the 1960s without causing any problems, so why not the Junior Certificate. Having sat the Primary Certificate myself in 1966, I would ask the Minister whether we would have had the same level of literacy and numeracy deficiencies, which we are now attempting to address in Junior Certificate reform, if large numbers of children were seriously underperforming in a primary school terminal examination over the past fifty years?

By removing the overview which the Junior Certificate gives of the quality of the teaching and learning of our teachers, are we running the risk that some of the poor professional practices that have crept into the teaching methods of those with Transition Year classes will now spread into the three years of the Junior Cycle?

It is also certain that many teachers will use the freedom that locally designed and moderated Junior

Cycle curriculum gives them to improve the quality of teaching and learning in their classrooms.

On balance, I believe that an externally controlled terminal examination at age 15-16 provides a rigor and discipline which children of that age require, quite apart from the motivation which it provides for their teachers.

The long term future of private fee-charging schools
The debate on the future of our private fee paying schools continued all year. Minister Quinn increased the pupil teacher ratio to 23:1 from September 2013, thus reducing the number of teachers who will be funded by the State. These schools have seen teachers retiring in June 2013 being replaced by teachers funded out of the school's own resources, paid out of parents fees, or where sufficient retirement did not occur to bring the State funded number down to the new 23:1 ratio, some teachers being redeployed to Sate funded non-fee-paying schools.

Higher Education
There are three major issues dominating the third level agenda at the moment; (i) the rationalisation of our college structure; (ii) how they are to be funded into the future; (iii) the rationalisation of the over 1400 courses into more broad based programmes at undergraduate level.

Rationalisation of our Third Level Colleges
In May 2013 Minister Ruairí Quinn announced a major re-organisation of the country's higher education sector that includes provision for the creation of new Technological Universities. This announcement follows recommendations made by the HEA calling for consolidation of the Institute of Technology (IT) sector; the creation of a small number of technological universities; the formation of regional clusters between universities and stronger ITs; implementation of recommendations to rationalise teacher education; as well as increased sustainability and capacity in the higher education system.

The Minister instructed the HEA to begin to implement the report's recommendations that will result in the consolidation of three groups of institutes of technology to progress towards attaining Technological University status. The three are:
- Dublin Institute of Technology, Institute of Technology Tallaght and Institute of Technology, Blanchardstown
- Cork Institute of Technology and Institute of Technology, Tralee
- Waterford Institute of Technology and Carlow Institute of Technology.

The next stage for each of the applications will be the preparation of a plan to meet the criteria for Technological University status. The plan must be based on a legally binding memorandum of understanding between each consortium of institutions describing their consolidation into a new single institution. The plans will be evaluated by an independent expert international panel that will decide if the applicant can meet the agreed criteria in the proposed timetable and can proceed to the final stage.

In addition, the Minister is asking the HEA to establish regional clusters of institutions in three identified regions, Dublin/Leinster, the South/South East and West/Mid West. All seven universities and 14 ITs will be grouped as follows:

South/South East - University College Cork, Cork IT, IT Tralee, Waterford IT and IT Carlow;
West/Mid/North West - University of Limerick, Mary Immaculate College, Limerick IT, Galway-Mayo IT, IT Sligo, Letterkenny IT and NUI Galway (St Angela's and Shannon College incorporated into NUI Galway);

Dublin/Leinster Pillar I - University College Dublin, Trinity College Dublin, National College of Art and Design, Marino Institute of Education, Dun Laoghaire Institute of Art, Design and Technology; Dublin/Leinster Pillar II – Dublin Institute of Technology, IT Tallaght, IT Blanchardstown, Dublin City University (incorporating linked colleges), National College of Ireland, Dundalk IT, NUI Maynooth, Athlone IT and Royal College of Surgeons in Ireland.

Heads of institutions in these clusters will now develop regional plans, eliminating unnecessary duplication of provision and establishing clear pathways of transfer and progression for students in the region. Emerging alliances between universities and institutes of technology will be strengthened and promoted - developing critical mass and centres of excellence in undergraduate, postgraduate and research provision.

College Funding to be based on Performance
A further key development in higher education has been the announcement in mid-August that funding in the sector will presently be linked to performance. HEIs will be rated on how well they perform in a number of important contexts.

As it is, the State contributes approximately €1.1bn annually to higher education. It is proposed that there will be penalties for those HEIs who fail to meet targets, and resources potentially diverted to those institutions that excel and outperform.

Writing on the 12 August 2013 in the Irish Independent, Education Editor Catherine Donnelly outlined the situation as follows:

"Universities and other third-level colleges face the prospect of having up to 10pc of their state funding withheld if they fail to reach new performance targets.

"It is part of a revolutionary change to how higher education is funded, which will – for the first time – link how much colleges receive in state grants to how well they perform.

"The new 'stick and carrot' approach will rate colleges under a number of different headings, such as student retention, research and matching graduates to the needs of industry."

The new system will be rolled out next year, affecting "the seven universities, the 14 institutes of technology and the teacher-training colleges."

"Initially, the Higher Education Authority (HEA) will reserve 5pc of the annual grant allocated for each college subject to a review of how well it meets its targets."

Supporting a better transition from second level to Higher Education
At a conference organised by the HEA and NCCA in June 2013, the Minister addressed the issue of supporting a better transition from second level to Higher Education. One of the three strands of this commitment is to: (i) significantly reduce the number of programme offerings for a broader undergraduate entry to level 8 honours bachelor degree programmes in the universities; (ii) to review level 8 programme provision in the institutes of technology to ensure a mixed portfolio of programmes with denominated and generic entry.

The intention is that the new arrangements will begin to be implemented on a phased basis with the first stages for those students commencing fifth year of second level in September 2014. Details of the timing of implementation will form part of the announcement of the full set of new arrangements to be made before the end of 2013. There are only 70 courses in the CAO system offering over one hundred places and yet we now have almost 1400 programmes on offer.

The huge increase in programme numbers over recent years is all part of the struggle between universities and institutes of technology, along with private colleges, to attract the brightest students onto their campus. The courses offered at undergraduate level need to be far more broadly based, so that students are able to identify broad areas of interest at the end of second level education and rationalise them as they progress through their undergraduate degrees.

Higher Level Research
A 2010 OECD report (main science and technology indicators) used data from 2007-8 to provide the percentage of higher education R&D financed by industry in OECD countries. This report was discussed in an article by Prof Brian Mac Craith, President of Dublin City University, published in The Irish Times, August 2013.

At 3.9 per cent, the value for Ireland is below the OECD overall value of 6.6 per cent and is well below the value for Germany (14.2 per cent), but is above the values for Japan (3.0 per cent), France (1.6 per cent) and, interestingly, Singapore (1.3 per cent).

A more recent BERD (Business Expenditure on R&D) report published by the Central Statistics Office in 2011 states that almost a fifth of enterprises in Ireland engaged in joint research with higher education institutions in Ireland in 2009. While it is clear Ireland could do better, it is by no means at the bottom of the table.

Given the economic tumult that has taken place since 2008, it is important to examine the current situation in the Irish R&D landscape. Science Foundation Ireland places a strong emphasis on industry engagement and, in February this year, announced a landmark investment in scientific research which is closely aligned to industry needs. Some €200 million of exchequer funding will be invested in seven research centres in Irish universities over the next six years. In addition, more than €100 million in cash and in-kind contributions will come from 156 industry partners, making it our largest ever State-industry research co-funding announcement.

Enterprise Ireland plays a key role in supporting industry-academic research collaboration through its industry-led technology centres on university campuses, its Innovation Partnership and Innovation Voucher schemes. In 2012, 525 Innovation Vouchers and 40 Innovation Partnerships were supported.

Through its Enterprise Partnership Scheme (EPS), the Irish Research Council has engaged over 200 companies to co-fund research in Irish universities in recent years. Since 2010, EPS has generated over €6 million in direct research funding from industry partners.

A key issue that is often cited as a barrier to industry-university research collaboration is the difficulty and inconsistency in agreeing contracts, especially in the context of intellectual property rights. In a partnership between the Irish Universities Association and Enterprise Ireland, a new central technology transfer office has been established and it is expected to lead to greater consistency in industry-academic relationships.

As a result of sustained exchequer investment, the research performance of Irish universities has soared dramatically in recent decades with the result that Ireland is now ranked globally in the top 20 and in the top five for some specific areas of science and technology. A high quality education and research system will be central to Ireland's social and economic recovery. It is evident that flourishing industry-university partnerships can play a key role in this. While current indicators are reasonably positive, there is room to improve our performance. The onus is on both sides to address this.

Developments in the Further Education and Training Sector
As I outline in an article within this year's Yearbook, the Further Education and Training (FET) sector is being revolutionised. The establishment of sixteen Education and Training Boards (ETB's) through the amalgamation of the existing VEC's, and the integration of the FÁS Training Centres into the ETB structure, means that the delivery of education and training will be the responsibility of the ETB's, under the guidance of SOLAS, which will have a strategic policy and funding role for the Further Education and Training sector.

Furthermore "Quality and Qualifications Ireland" was established on 6th November 2012 under the Qualifications and Quality Assurance (Education and Training) Act 2012. QQI was created by an amalgamation of four bodies that have both awarding and quality assurance responsibilities: the Further Education and Training Awards Council (FETAC), the Higher Education and Training Awards Council (HETAC), the National Qualifications Authority of Ireland (NQAI) and the Irish Universities Quality Board (IUQB). QQI has assumed all the functions of the four legacy bodies while also having responsibility for new or newly-statutory responsibilities in particular areas.

In an article in this yearbook Stan McHugh, Consultant in Qualifications and Quality Assurance in Education and Training, and former Chief Executive of FETAC, points out that formal registration with the Teaching Council under Regulation five is now required of teachers involved in Further Education. Previously the main national providers included the VEC'S, FÁS, CERT and Teagasc, and a range of private trainers and the Community /Voluntary sector. The certifying bodies included the NCVA, City and Guilds, Ed Excel, FÁS/Department of Education, the NTCB, and Teagasc. Each certifying body had its own way of assuring standards for its own sector, but that none of them had a direct say in the professional standards of teaching or training.

Stan in his article points out that there is a significant cohort of tutors, trainers and instructors delivering programmes at Levels 1 to 6 on the Framework who are not recognised Teachers under the auspices of the Teaching Council. He states that this is not tenable into the future from a quality perspective, and needs to be addressed by the provision of appropriate programmes to facilitate the necessary upskilling of personnel and through the Recognition of Prior Learning, if the sector is to successfully contribute to the National Skills Strategy. Recognition of prior learning (RPL) is also discussed in depth by Dr. Cathal de Paor, Director of CPD in the Faculty of Education, Mary Immaculate College in the Further Education & Lifelong Learning section of this book.

The upskilling of tutors/teachers presents great challenges at a whole range of levels, both from a human resource management and a labour relations level. Achieving a fully recognised teaching workforce within FE at a time of ongoing cuts in the terms and conditions of all public sector workers is a real challenge.

Chapter 1
Early Childhood

Contents

		Page
1.	**A Momentous Year in Early Childhood Education** *Irene Gunning*	4
2.	**ECCE Services: Facts & Figures** *Toby Wolfe*	8
3.	**Government-funded Programmes** *Joe Rynn*	10
4.	**Partnership with Parents Programme** *Marijka Walsj*	15
5.	**Evidence-based practice and student wellbeing** *Dr Brian Merriman*	17
6.	**Achieving SIOLTA validation** *Margaret Brown*	19
7.	**The Aistear in Action Initiative in Tipperary and Cork** *Dr Mary Daly*	22
8.	**Activators of Learning: The Role of the Artist** *Orla Kenny*	26
9.	**Literacy: 'Help my Kid Learn' Website** *Margaret Murray*	29
10.	**Professional Development for Early Childhood Educators** *Mary Ryan*	30
11.	**Going to 'Big School'** *Áine Lynch*	31
12.	**Who's Who** *Dr. Geoffrey Shannon*	32

Introducing the Early Childhood Chapter

by Tony Hall, *Editor*

2013 was a very significant year for early childhood education in Ireland, a year in which a first children's referendum was held in the State.

The aim of the Education Matters Yearbook is to provide a panoptic of Irish education over the year, represented by key educational stakeholders, the educational media and educational research. Our first section of the Education Matters Yearbook includes articles from key stakeholders in the early childhood sector in Irish education, affording an insight into this key, early years sector in the educational system in Ireland.

Our first keynote article, by Irene Gunning, Director of Early Childhood Ireland, provides an overview of the salient developments in early childhood education and care over the last year.

As discussed in Ms Gunning's article and later in this section of the Yearbook, the free preschool year entered its second year, with over 65,000 children availing of the free preschool year in 2012-2013, constituting 95% of the eligible cohort. 2013 also marked the further implementation of Síolta ('Seeds'), the quality framework for early childhood education in the State, and the Aistear ('Journey') curriculum for early childhood. The chapter features, amongst others, articles on professional education/CPD (continuing professional development) for early childhood educators; the key facts and figures for the sector this year; a support guide to parents whose children are in the transition from an early years setting to primary school; and literacy and art education in early childhood education and care.

As is a foundational theme throughout the Yearbook, this section also contains a selection of the key media articles pertaining to early childhood education and care in Ireland this year, including the 'Prime Time Investigates' documentary, and response to the programme from key stakeholders in the sector.

The section concludes, with this year's 'Who's Who' profile, featuring Dr. Geoffrey Shannon, Solicitor, and Rapporteur on Child Protection and Chairman of Adoption Authority of Ireland.

Early Childhood

A Momentous Year in Early Childhood Education

Irene Gunning *CEO of Early Childhood Ireland*

2013 was a year in which we recognised children as young citizens with rights.

On 10 November 2012, the Irish people went to the polls and voted in favour of the 31st amendment to the Constitution to strengthen the constitutional rights of children. Early Childhood Ireland is delighted with the result as this amendment makes certain that legislation will have the widest possible interpretation for children's rights.

At a practical level, the **amendment to the constitution** accentuates young children's right to quality early childhood care and education experiences. Early childhood professionals are best placed to provide such provision in partnership with parents. An example of one such partnership with parents, a project developed by Barnardos, is described in this chapter.

Transitions need careful handling when children move from one setting to another with parents, teachers and early childhood professionals all playing their part. This is another project included in the chapter, one that started in 2012 when the National Parent's Council Primary and Early Childhood Ireland developed a leaflet for parents to assist them in preparing their child for the transition from preschool to primary school. This leaflet was distributed to over 30,000 parents and has now become an annual project.

The **free preschool year** entered its second year and a significant number of children - over 65,000 - accessed early childhood education representing 95% of the eligible cohort. Consequently it was good to have some quality initiatives specifically investigating quality of provision. The first group of services implementing Síolta, the national quality framework, had their validation visits under the guidance of the Early Year's Education Policy Unit, Department of Education and Skills. This quality mentoring programme has supported early years educators to reflect, evaluate and implement changes to their early childhood care and education services, providing enhanced quality experiences for young children.

Curriculum also became a priority during 2012-13. Early Childhood Ireland was delighted to work in collaboration on the first pilot project in early childhood education services "Aistear in Action" with the National Council for Curriculum and Assessment (NCCA). There is more about Aistear, the National Curriculum Framework for children aged 0-6 years and this pilot programme later in the chapter. As a framework, Aistear recognises the importance of play for young children's holistic learning and development.

Language and literacy was another great focus of 2012-13, crossing all ages but finding a new emphasis in early childhood. The Department of Children and Youth Affairs (DCYA) commissioned the National Adult Literacy Association (NALA) to develop a programme to support parents with their children`s literacy skills. Details of the programme are highlighted in this chapter.

In conclusion, 2012-13 was a momentous year for early childhood education with the introduction and implementation of the above quality initiatives many of which are discussed in this chapter. As early childhood professionals we welcome these measures, anticipating that they will further enhance early education experiences for young children which in turn will have lasting positive effects. *"Mol an óige agus tiocfaidh sí."*

A Global Gathering for Early Childhood will take place at the Aviva Stadium, Dublin 4

16 – 19 October 2013

Keynote Speakers will include:
- Professor Margaret Carr, Director of Early Years Research Centre, University of Waikato, New Zealand.
- Ms. Wendy Lee, Co-Director of Early Childhood Learning and Exemplar Project with Professor Margaret Carr.
- Stuart Shanker, Distinguished Research Professor of Philosophy and Psychology at York University.
- Dr. Stuart Brown, medical doctor, psychiatrist, clinical researcher, and Founder of The National Institute for Play in California.

The Social Programme will include:
- A Gala Dinner in the historic St George's Hall at Dublin Castle
- A traditional Céilí Night at the Clyde Court Hotel

For further details about conference programme, registration and accommodation visit www.earlychildhood2013.ie/index.html OR Telephone Sarah at +353 1 296 7257 Email sarah@conferencepartners.ie

EDUCATION IN THE MEDIA

Inequality of opportunity remains

September 12, 2012

Governments need to spend more on early childhood programmes, a new OECD report states.

The 'Education at a Glance' 2012 report says that, at the same time, governments need to maintain reasonable costs for higher education to reduce inequality, boost social mobility and improve people's employment prospects.

"Countries need an increasingly educated and skilled workforce to succeed in today's knowledge economy," said OECD secretary-general Angel Gurría.

"Investing from an early age is crucial to lay the foundations of later success. High quality education and skills have to be among the number one priorities for governments, for economies and for societies. Supporting the poorest and ensuring equal access is another important pillar in an inclusive education policy strategy."

'Education at a Glance 2012' points up stark differences between countries in terms of the opportunities they offer young people to enter higher education, especially in the case of children of poor families or whose parents have had a limited education.

Australia, Finland, Ireland and Sweden have the highest success rates in the OECD for young people with poorly-educated parents attaining a tertiary degree.

www.publicservice.co.uk/news_story.asp?id=20865

Angel Gurría, Secretary General OECD

EDUCATION IN THE MEDIA

Blokes needed as early role models

September 12, 2012

Blokes teaching in early childhood education are "rare", says Wendy Ure, manager of New Zealand Early Childhood Education Centre and head of Ormond Kindergarten.

New Zealand has one of the lowest rates of male early childhood teachers in the OECD, at around 1 percent. This makes early childhood teaching one of the most gender-segregated occupations in the NZ labour force, even more so than fire-fighters, says Mrs Ure.

Colleague Jeff Ruston says that while there are not many guys in early childhood, the ones who are there stand out in a positive light. Neil Aitkenhead is a case in point.

Neil grew up on the streets of Belfast, Northern Ireland, during the 1970s-80s. The idea of men in early childhood education was an alien concept, he says.

Neil's mum is a teacher, but as far as he was concerned education started when you were five years old.

This mindset changed when he had children of his own. Now living in Gisborne, New Zealand, Neil has recently graduated with a Bachelor's degree in Early Childhood Education.

Jeff Ruston says there is a need for more male ECE teachers.

"It is definitely of benefit having men in the sector. We bring a different set of skills and life experiences which are good for the overall development of the children."

But Neil Aitkenhead says, adding that bad press involving historic cases of men in the industry has discouraged men from considering ECE as a career path.

"Mud does stick, especially when they are high-profile negative cases."

In 2008. the 167 male preschool teachers in New Zealand (out of a total of more than 15,000) formed EC Men NZ with the aim of boosting male representation within the profession to 10 percent within the decade.

www.gisborneherald.co.nz/article/?type=article&id=29379

Lecturer says referendum wording is 'ambiguous'

September 20, 2012

While the announcement of the children's rights referendum has been broadly welcomed, concerns are being raised about a possible lack of clarity in the wording.

Frances Fitzgerald TD

Children's Minister Frances Fitzgerald officially announced the wording yesterday ahead of the November 10 vote.

Article 42A provides for, among other things, the voice of the child to be heard and the interests of the child to be pursued. However, the wording of the referendum deviates from that which was recommended by a 2010 Oireachtas committee, chaired by Mary O'Rourke.

Conor O'Mahony

Conor O'Mahony, who is a lecturer in constitutional law at University College Cork, says he is concerned that the wording is ambiguous.

Meanwhile, another lecturer from the Department of Law in UCC said yesterday that the childrendsreferendum.ie website should also be available in Irish due to the 'huge constitutional importance' of the language.

www.irishexaminer.com/breakingnews/ireland/lecturer-says-referendum-wording-is-ambiguous-567606.html

EDUCATION IN THE MEDIA

Full text of the children's referendum

September 19, 2012

Thirty-First Amendment of the Constitution

Article 42A

1. The State recognises and affirms the natural and imprescriptible rights of all children and shall, as far as practicable, by its laws protect and vindicate those rights.

2. 1° In exceptional cases, where the parents, regardless of their marital status, fail in their duty towards their children to such an extent that the safety or welfare of any of their children is likely to be prejudicially affected, the State as guardian of the common good shall, by proportionate means as provided by law, endeavour to supply the place of the parents, but always with due regard for the natural and imprescriptible rights of the child.
    2° Provision shall be made by law for the adoption of any child where the parents have failed for such a period of time as may be prescribed by law in their duty towards the child and where the best interests of the child so require.

3. Provision shall be made by law for the voluntary placement for adoption and the adoption of any child.

4. 1° Provision shall be made by law that in the resolution of all proceedings—
    i brought by the State, as guardian of the common good, for the purpose of preventing the safety and welfare of any child from being prejudicially affected, or
    ii concerning the adoption, guardianship or custody of, or access to, any child, the best interests of the child shall be the paramount consideration.
    2° Provision shall be made by law for securing, as far as practicable, that in all proceedings referred to in subsection 1° of this section in respect of any child who is capable of forming his or her own views, the views of the child shall be ascertained and given due weight having regard to the age and maturity of the child.

www.irishtimes.com/news/full-text-of-the-children-s-referendum-1.737558

Burton keen to extend preschool scheme to two years

October 13, 2012

Minister for Social Protection Joan Burton wants the provision of free early childhood education extended for a second year.

At present more than 60,000 children take part in the scheme, getting one year of preschool care at a cost of €166 million per year, but Ms Burton has said she wants to extend the scheme to cover two years.

Since 2010, children between the ages of three and four have been entitled to one year's free nursery or Montessori education under the Early Childhood Care and Education (ECCE) scheme. The State pays a weekly capitation fee of €62.50 over 38 weeks to playschools and daycare services to provide the one-year preschool service.

Ms Burton said she had been impressed by the impact of the scheme.

"I think that we should seek to expand that. To that end there is an interdepartmental working group between my department and Frances Fitzgerald's department [of children] and we have to have more discussions with Brendan Howlin about how we do this."

Ms Burton has just returned from a two-day trip to Sweden where free childcare is provided for every child aged between three and five. The Scandinavian childcare model grew out of the banking crashes in those countries in the mid 1990s, she said.

"People there set targets for things that should be fundamentally reformed and among those was helping women, regardless of relationship status, to be active in the workforce, to boost their own income and their families' incomes."

Ms Burton made her comments at a pre-budget forum attended by more than 30 charities and non-governmental organisations.

www.irishtimes.com/news/burton-keen-to-extend-preschool-scheme-1.551598

ECCE Services: Facts & Figures

Toby Wolfe, *Acting Director, Start Strong*

There are approximately 4,500 early care and education services in Ireland, with just over 4,300 delivering the Free Pre-School Year in 2012.

The number of children participating in the Free Pre-School Year is approximately 65,000 (95% of the eligible cohort). The average size of early care and education services is 33.5 places (of which on average 30.5 are filled) and 5.5 staff.

Early care and education workforce
The total number of practitioners working in early care and education services is approximately 24,000. Qualification levels of the early care and education workforce are as follows:

- 76% of all staff in early care and education services is qualified to FETAC Level 5 or higher.
- The proportion of services with one or more staff qualified to FETAC Level 5 or higher is 96%.
- The proportion of services with one or more staff qualified to graduate level (HETAC Level 7 or higher) is 34%.

The proportion of services delivering the Free Pre-School Year that received the higher capitation grant (for services with a graduate leader delivering the Free Pre-School Year and with assistants qualified to FETAC Level 5) was 14.6% (in 2011).

The average wage for early care and education practitioners:
- For unqualified staff: €10.10 per hour.
- For staff qualified to FETAC Level 5: €10.85 per hour.
- For staff qualified to HETAC Level 7: €11.24 per hour.

Fees
The average fees charged for services outside the Free Pre-School Year:
- Full day-care place: €166 per week.
- Part-time place: €85 per week.
- Sessional place (3 hours per day): €59 per week.

International comparisons
Total public investment in early care and education services (data from 2009):
- Ireland = 0.4 % GDP (including expenditure on 4 and 5 year olds at primary school).
- OECD average = 0.7 % GDP.
- New Zealand = 1.0 % GDP.
- Finland = 1.1 % GDP.

The Economist Intelligence Unit in 2012 published the Starting Well Index, comparing the quality, affordability and availability of early education for 3-6 year olds:
- Ireland's score was 67.4 out of 100, ranking 18th out of the countries surveyed.
- New Zealand's score was 73.9 out of 100, ranking 9th.
- Finland's score was 91.8 out of 100, ranking 1st.

Costs to parents of early care and education services as a % of average family income:
- Ireland: 29% of average family net income.
- OECD average: 13 % of average family net income.

Toby Wolfe is Acting Director of Start Strong. Start Strong is a coalition of organisations and individuals seeking to advance children's early care and education in Ireland. Start Strong works from a children's rights perspective, and bases its advocacy work on research and evidence from national and international experience.

Sources and further reading:
Central Statistics Office (2009) QNHS – Special Module on Childcare *(http://www.cso.ie/en/media/csoie/releasespublications/documents/labourmarket/2007/childcareq42007.pdf)*

Department of Children and Youth Affairs (2012) State of the Nation's Children 2012 *(http://www.dcya.gov.ie/documents/research/StateoftheNationsChildren2012.pdf)*

Early Childhood Ireland (2012) Salary Survey 2012 *(http://www.earlychildhoodireland.ie/policy-advocacy-and-research/salary-survey-2012/)*

Economist Intelligence Unit (2012) Starting Well: Benchmarking Early Education Across the World *(http://www.lienfoundation.org/pdf/publications/sw_report.pdf)*

OECD Family Database *(http://www.oecd.org/els/soc/oecdfamilydatabase.htm)*

Oireachtas Library & Research Services (2012) Spotlight: Early Childhood Education and Care *(http://www.oireachtas.ie/parliament/media/housesoftheoireachtas/libraryresearch/spotlights/spotEarlyEd180412.pdf)*

Pobal (2012) Pobal Annual Survey of the Early Years Sector 2011 *(https://www.pobal.ie/Publications/Documents/Pobal%20Annual%20Survey%20of%20the%20Early%20Years%20Sector%202011.pdf)*

UNICEF (2008) Report Card 8: The Child Care Transition: A League Table of Early Childhood Education and Care in Economically Advanced Countries *(http://www.unicef-irc.org/publications/pdf/rc8_eng.pdf)*
Start Strong, *(http://www.startstrong.ie)*

EDUCATION IN THE MEDIA

'No' group tells parents not to be hoodwinked

October 18, 2012

A NEW lobby group has warned that parents are being "hoodwinked" into betraying their offspring by voting Yes in the children's referendum.

The warning came after Tanaiste Eamon Gilmore expressed his fear that there could be a low turnout because there was not the "same degree of controversy" over the referendum.

But the newly-formed Parents For Children announced its opposition to the forthcoming referendum with a series of controversial claims. It said that if passed the amendment to the Constitution could lead to the state taking special needs children into care if their parents felt "under pressure".

It also claimed that parents could be forced to vaccinate their children and allow a teenage daughter to have an abortion.

Spokeswoman Maria McMenamin confirmed that none of these scenarios was possible under the law at present, but said the new amendment would allow them.

The group is printing 26,000 leaflets in its campaign for a "No" vote. Its members include Fr Brian McKevitt, editor of the Catholic newspaper 'Alive'.

He accused the state of engaging in a "confidence trick" to become the "parent-in-chief", and said: "We are being asked to buy an expensive second-hand car from a very shady dealer without even getting a look at the product."

www.independent.ie/irish-news/no-group-tells-parents-not-to-be-hoodwinked-28820505.html

Government-funded Programmes

Joe Rynn, *Manager, Dublin City Childcare Committee*

Ireland's decade-long investment in childcare can provide the basis for quality services for children and families.

Prior to 2000, there was limited availability of childcare places in the childcare sector. However, over the decade 2000 to 2010, the State, initially in partnership with the EU, invested €425 million capital funding to create childcare places throughout Ireland. About 65,000 extra places were created. Due to this investment, Ireland has a good infrastructure for childcare which can provide the basis for quality services that meet the needs of children and families.

Government-funded Childcare Programmes:

- **Early Childhood Care and Education Programme (ECCE)**
  In January 2010 a universally available preschool year (ECCE programme) was introduced. The programme is provided in both community and private crèches and about 4,500 settings participate. The State invests about €175 million each year in the scheme.

- **Community Childcare Subvention Programme (CCS)**
  Participation in the CCS programme is restricted to community/not-for-profit childcare services. The CCS Programme supports disadvantaged parents and provides support for parents in low paid employment and training or education by enabling qualifying parents to avail of reduced childcare costs at participating community childcare services.

- **Childcare Education and Training Support (CETS)**
  The CETS programme was introduced in September 2010, This programme provides qualifying FAS and VEC students with childcare places for the duration of their course. There are currently 2,800 CETS places which benefit some 7,000 children. (This reflects the fact that many courses are of relatively short duration so places are used by more than one child over the year.) (Source: DCYA website. Accessed 07-06-2013)

What is the Early Childhood Care and Education Programme?
The Early Childhood Care and Education Programme (ECCE) is designed to give children access to a free Pre-School Year of appropriate programme-based activities in the year before they start primary school. A good quality preschool helps get your child ready for Primary School.

The ECCE programme provides a pre-school session of 3 hours per day, 5 days per week, 38 weeks per year, for which parents will not be charged anything. ECCE capitation fees will be paid at the rate of €62.50 over 38 weeks to the childcare provider.

What is the Community Childcare Subvention Programme?
The Community Childcare Subvention Programme (CCS) is a support programme for community-based childcare services to provide quality childcare services at a reduced rate to parents. It is a programme which enables

Community Childcare Services to give parents in receipt of certain social welfare payments (the majority of which are covered under the CCS Programme), Family Income Supplement, and holders of medical cards and GP visit cards, a reduction in their childcare fees.

The amount of CCS funding that a childcare service will qualify for will depend on the number of children attending the service whose parents/guardians qualify for one of the CCS subvention rates. The service will use the subvention funding to operate a tiered fees policy based on the cost of the service(s) less the various subvention rates.

Childcare Education Training Support Programme (CETS)
The Childcare Education Training Support Programme (CETS) programme is managed by the Department of Children and Youth Affairs on behalf of FÁS and the VECs. The purpose of the programme is to benefit parents on eligible FÁS and VEC courses. Parents who are doing a CETS approved VEC or FÁS course may be eligible for a childcare place under this programme. Rules of eligibility and terms and conditions of the programme are determined by FÁS and the VECs in conjunction with the Department of Education and Skills.

Depending on the course, parents may be able to access one of either a Full Day Place, a Half Day Place, or an After School Place. Eligibility does not guarantee a place. Places are allocated on a "first come, first served" basis.

After School Scheme
The subsidised after-school child care scheme is a new initiative, financed through the Department of Social Protection and managed by the Department of Children and Youth Affairs. The scheme supports low-income and unemployed persons to return to the workforce. To be eligible for this scheme, you must:
- Be in receipt of Jobseeker's Allowance (JA),
- Have been in receipt of JA or a combination of the One-Parent Family Payment (OFP) followed immediately by JA, for a minimum of one year immediately before applying for a subsidised after-school childcare place,
- Take up either full-time or part-time employment opportunity, or increase the number of days of your existing employment, or start on a Community Employment (CE) or Tús scheme, AND
- Have one or more children aged between 4 and 13 years who are attending primary school.

NOTE: Eligibility does not guarantee a place. Places are allocated on a "first come, first served" basis. The scheme is not open to self-employed JA recipients.

Joe Rynn, Manager Dublin City Childcare Committee and John Lonergan, Former Governor of Mountjoy Prison

EDUCATION IN THE MEDIA

Referendum passed amid low turnout

November 11, 2012

Taoiseach Enda Kenny has welcomed the passing of the children's referendum by 57.4 per cent to 42.6 per cent.

"The passing of this amendment will help make childhood a good, secure and loving space for all our children," Mr Kenny said in a statement. "It will also give hope, reassurance and confidence to parents, foster parents and vulnerable children."

...More than 3.1 million people were eligible to vote, but the low-key campaign failed to capture the public imagination. The turnout was just 33.5 per cent.

Despite the low turnout, Minister for Children Frances Fitzgerald said it was a "historic day" for children's rights in Ireland.

... Leo Varadkar, Fine Gael's director of elections for the referendum, said he would have liked the turnout to have been higher.

"We did expect the margin to be a little bit wider but we've had plenty of low turnouts before in referenda and we've had a lot of referenda that were a lot tighter and in the fullness of time people forget those details," he said.

"What history will record is that the Irish people voted today to enshrine children's rights in our constitution and that makes it a historic day and a day for celebration."

Three of the 43 constituencies in the State voted No: Donegal North East, Donegal South West and Dublin North West.

Total votes: 1,066, 239
Invalid: 4,645
Valid: 1,061,594
Yes votes: 615,731 (57.4%)
No votes: 445,863 (42.6%)
Turnout: 33.5%

Asked about the low turnout, Taoiseach Enda Kenny said that in some countries it was compulsory to vote but this was a democracy and people couldn't be forced to vote. He added that holding a referendum on a Saturday made little difference.

www.irishtimes.com/news/children-s-referendum-passed-amid-low-turnout-1.748197

Results of referendum challenged

November 20, 2012

The Government has been left embarrassed after two women began a legal challenge aimed at overturning the result of the children's referendum.

The women — Joanna Jordan, of Dún Laoghaire, Co Dublin, who campaigned for a no vote, and Nancy Kennelly, a nursing home resident in Askeaton, Co Limerick, who voted yes — claim that the Coalition's use of public money to fund an unbalanced information campaign wrongfully affected the outcome.

The opposition said the legal challenge had been all but inevitable given the Government's failure to mount an impartial information campaign.

The women are challenging the result based on the Government's misuse of public money on its information campaign. The women's petition was supported by journalist and no campaigner John Waters, who said the Government's information could not but have influenced people to vote yes.

Reacting last night, Fianna Fáil TD Robert Troy said the challenge was "probably inevitable".

Sinn Féin's Caoimhghín Ó Caoláin, whose party also supported the amendment, agreed that a challenge had always been a possibility.

"However, given the yes majority of almost 170,000, it would be my earnest wish that the decision of the electorate would stand."

www.irishexaminer.com/ireland/women-challenge-result-of-childrens-referendum-214538.html

EDUCATION IN THE MEDIA

Supreme Court hands down Children's Referendum judgment

RTE News, 11 December 2012

The Supreme Court has handed down the full judgment in its ruling that the Government acted wrongfully by spending €1.1m on its own information campaign for the Children's Referendum.

In a unanimous judgment, the five-division court ruled that parts of the campaign were not fair, equal or impartial.

Senior Counsel Richard Humphreys, acting for the successful challenger, Mark McCrystal, said they would be applying for costs in the case but would need to read the judgments first.

He said the application would go above and beyond the usual because of what he said happened after the litigation began, although he did not expand on this point.

Chief Justice Susan Denham said the applications for costs would be heard next month with submissions from the appellant by 18 January.

She ruled that the Government placed the rights of those in favour of the Children's Referendum above those against when it put together its information campaign.

Ms Justice Denham

In her written judgment, Ms Justice Denham said this breached the McKenna principles, which hold that public monies should not be used to sway one side of a referendum over the other.

She said the public purse was used to espouse views anathema to those of some citizens even though they had contributed to it.

She said this was wrong, was a breach of democratic process and must stop.

Ms Justice Denham said two slogans - "protecting children" and "supporting families" - used in the campaign - were not neutral.

The positive, happy images of children were also partial and there was an admitted error by the Government, which was not brought to the attention of the public. Colm MacGeehan, solicitor for Mr McCrystal, said they were fully vindicated by the judgments and would be applying for their full costs.

He said the Government information campaign was propaganda and had called for a Yes vote in everything but name.

Mark McCrystal

Mr McCrystal said the rules were crystal clear and there was a clear disregard for the McKenna principles.

Patricia McKenna said there was a need for a permanent Referendum Commission which would put forward yes and no arguments while Kathy Sinnott said the Government must pay back the money it used.

Speaking in the Dáil, the Taoiseach said the Government was carefully studying the judgement which clarifies how the Government can make information available to the public during a referendum.

He said the Court found the Government methods, in attempting to inform the people, had strayed beyond the bounds of providing information to the electorate but that it also found the Government had acted in a bona fide manner.

He said the Government was committed to working within the parameters set down by the Court.

www.independent.ie/irish-news/government-failed-test-of-being-fair-on-childrens-referendum-says-supreme-court-28946117.html

EDUCATION IN THE MEDIA

Seminar on Childcare: 'Green Shoots'

April 24, 2013

"We don't need a Scandinavian model in childcare, what we need is a uniquely Irish model that meets needs of children," Minister Frances Fitzgerald said.

The seminar on Childcare, hosted in Dublin this month by Early Childhood Ireland, was opened by Minister for Children Frances Fitzgerald.

Speaking to an audience of 150 childcare professionals, students and policy makers from around the country, the Minister emphasized the big questions:
- the scale of national investment in childcare,
- the ongoing work of the Minister and her department on a second year in the free preschool scheme
- the building blocks for a second free preschool year, such as the training and development of the workforce.

She also highlighted childcare for under-ones as an "area of concern", given that parents in Ireland are faced with less time off and a consequent need for more choice and support in their childcare options.

Irene Gunning, CEO of Early Childhood Ireland said: "Children's lives matter and so do the adults who work closely with them. What we need is a training fund and a workforce that is not only qualified to do the job but is also paid properly to do it."

Early Childhood Ireland represents over 3,300 preschool, day-care (crèche) and afterschool centres nationwide supporting over 100,000 children and their families.

Other speakers at the seminar were psychology professor and author Ian Robertson from Trinity College Dublin and Professor Ferre Laevers, internationally renowned early years advocate, author and researcher, from the University of Leuven.

Pictured at the Early Childhood Ireland's "Green Shoot" seminar which took place at the Herbert Park Hotel, Dublin (l to r): Iliot and Eoghan Lane (20 months) from Newbridge, Co. Kildare with Minister for Children Frances Fitzgerald and Senator Jillian Van Turnhout, Chairperson Early Childhood Ireland.

Partnership with Parents Programme

Marijka Walsh, *Best Practice Officer, Barnardos*

Partnership with Parents is an individual, home-based programme for parents who require support to develop their ability to parent effectively.

The programme was designed to strengthen the parent-child relationship and improve the quality of the parenting, thereby improving the lives of children and families. The programme, designed by Barnardos Ireland, is evidence informed and has been used extensively within Barnardos services since 2011.

Partnership with Parents (PwP) is informed by evidence of 'what works' in order to ensure that it has the best chance to succeed and make a real difference. It is tailored to meet the specific needs of children from 0-18 years of age and their families, and is suitable for parents who feel overburdened.

The outcomes that the programme aims to achieve are:

- Improving parent-child communication
- Increasing parental understanding of and ability to manage their child's behaviour
- Improving the child's social development
- Introducing consistent routines
- Increasing parental involvement in the child's education
- Ensuring the child's physical needs are met
- Increasing parental ability to manage crises effectively

The child is at the centre of the PwP programme and all work completed with parents is focused on achieving outcomes for their children. PwP establishes a partnership between the parent and worker which is connected, facilitative, purposeful and supportive. Ghate and Hazel (2002) found that parents want services that allow them to feel in control and meet their self-defined needs. Fahlberg (1993) notes that every effort must be made to treat parents and children as collaborative partners in the identification of problems, in planning and in treatment. It is widely accepted that if parents identify the issues and solutions, they are much more likely to perceive them as relevant and act upon them (Tones & Tilford, 2001).

Certain skills and qualities of the worker are necessary to create this collaborative partnership. In PwP we define staff qualities (e.g. warmth, respect, patience); interpersonal skills (e.g. communication skills, awareness of self and others); and approach (e.g. flexibility, reflection).

These skills and qualities must be consciously and actively demonstrated in order for the parents to experience them.

The PwP programme consists of six optional modules or plug-ins: Parent-child relationship, Behaviour, Social development, Routines, Education and Physical development. Parents are offered one or multiple plug-ins depending on their needs. The programme also includes a crisis management tool and practical support approach. Each plug-in consists of a parent's activity booklet and related staff guidance, which informs the worker how to complete the activity with the parent and relevant background information.

Parents have found the programme has helped them to:

- Understand their child's needs more
- Develop confidence in their ability to parent
- Improve their relationships with their children and other family members such as grandparents and partners
- Have child-centred conversations rather than ending up in conflict (separated parents)
- Be proactive in relation to bringing children to appointments and arranging meetings with the school
- Resume the parenting role after children have been cared for by others
- Furthermore, staff have observed warmer, more supportive relationships between parents and children, with the children reporting:
- 'There is not as much shouting in our house anymore.'
- 'I can go out with my friends and not be afraid that my Mum will be gone when I get back.'
- 'My relationship with Mum is great now, we talk and communicate.'

For further information on PwP contact Barnardos, Christchurch Square, Dublin 8
Telephone: 01-4530355

Bibliography:
Fahlberg, V. (1993). Working with parents. In P. Marsh, & J. Triseliotis (Eds.), Prevention and reunification in childcare: policy and practice. London: Batsford Publishers.

Ghate, D., & Hazel, N. (2002). Parenting in poor environments: stress, support & coping. London: Jessica Kingsley Publishers.

Pinkerton, J., Dolan, P., & Canavan, J. (2004). Family Support in Ireland – Definition & Strategic Intent: A Paper for the Department of Health & Children. Dublin: Stationery Office.

Tones, K., & Tilford, S. (2001). Health education: effectiveness, efficiency and equity. London: Chapman & Hall

EDUCATION IN THE MEDIA

'Building blocks' for second free preschool year

May 19, 2013

A nationwide consultation process regarding a second free preschool year, led by Early Childhood Ireland, kicked off in Dublin on May 15.

Early Childhood Ireland, the representative group for over 3,300 preschools and full day-care centres nationwide, has started a countrywide consultation process regarding what it calls the "building blocks" for a second free preschool year.

Sixty childcare professionals attended the Dublin meeting on May 15 and further meetings are scheduled for Cork and Galway this week.

Teresa Heeney, Chief Operations Officer, Early Childhood Ireland said:

"Consultation with the childcare sector is key and we are conducting this 'ThinkTank' with members to discuss the building blocks for a second free preschool year. We will be sharing the findings with Ministers Fitzgerald, Burton and Quinn.

"Investing in children's early years should be an 'economic imperative' and we hope this aspiration is reflected in the reality of the budget later this year. "The question of whether the sector is ready for a second preschool year is being asked and we see the key building blocks for the discussion as qualifications, capacity, curriculum, capitation.

"Children's lives matter and so do the lives of adults who work closely with them. Measures to support quality assurance and workforce development must go hand-in-hand with any extension of the free preschool year.

"What we need is a training fund and a workforce that is not only qualified to do the job but is also paid properly to do it. This is in line with the 2010 Workforce Development Plan and we call on the Government to implement this plan.

www.educationmatters.ie/2013/05/19/building-blocks-for-second-free-preschool-year/

Evidence-based practice and student wellbeing

Dr Brian Merriman, *Research Fellow, Children's Research Network*

Through research we now know the factors that foster or foil development

Where previously there had been relatively little systematic research in this country, the demand for evidence-based practice from policy makers, service providers, and parents has in recent years prompted considerable investment in research and evaluation. The return on these investments in research and evaluation is clear and this article lists some of the main developments, particularly bearing in mind their impact on children's well-being.

Child well-being encapsulates numerous dimensions including physical and mental health, relationships and emotional development, and positive interactions with society. Current scholarship in the area emphasises peer and family relationships. From the United Nations Convention on the Rights of the Child to the Irish National Children's Strategy, child well-being is a central principle of policy and practice in Early Childhood Care and Education (ECCE).

Síolta - the framework of principles and standards - refers repeatedly to the importance of child well-being in the areas of positive relationships, play, and a stimulating environment. Well-being is also one of the four themes of Aistear, the Early Childhood Curriculum Framework.

Growing Up in Ireland – the National Longitudinal Study of Children is tracking the development of more than 11,500 infants and recently published the first results at age three.

The Prevention and Early Intervention Programme (PEIP) consists of three projects which were set up to examine innovative approaches to improving outcomes for children: (i) Preparing for Life (PFL), (ii) Tallaght West Childhood Development Initiative (CDI), (iii) youngballymun. Each project operates a range of programmes from pre-natal to school-age, including early childhood education. Each programme has been rigorously evaluated with respect to cognitive, social, and emotional developmental outcomes.

Tallaght West Childhood Development Initiative (CDI) recently published the evaluation of its Early Years Programme, which found that the intervention was associated with improved peer relationships and pro-social behaviour.

Preparing for Life (PFL) reported on the impact of its parenting intervention at 12 months, with favourable outcomes in some communication and motor domains, as well as resilience to social and emotional difficulties.

The youngballymun 3, 4, 5 Learning Years programme is specifically focused on early childhood care and education. Evaluation of the programme implementation found that 33% of staff had FETAC Level 5 qualification, 12% Level 6, and 15% Level 7 or above, though 20% had no qualification.

Another youngballymun programme is **Incredible Years**, a social skills curriculum for children aged four and five years and their teachers and parents. Teachers observed decreases in hyperactivity and peer problems, as well as increases in pro-social behaviour, although there was no comparison to children who were not in the programme.

Knowledge increases effectiveness
Extensive evaluation of early years components in the PEIP and the broad scope of these evaluations means that we now know more about the factors that foster or foil development, the economics of early intervention, and the impact of early childhood education. Expanding the locally-tailored PEIP model, the Department of Children and Youth Affairs is spending €14.85 million between 2013 and 2016 on the Area-Based Responses to Child Poverty Initiative.

Providers can take confidence from the positive impact of early childhood education reported in the PEIP projects and can continue to make a case for the value of their work by building on the rigorous monitoring and evaluation methods used. The Children's Research Network for Ireland and Northern Ireland is currently engaging with its members in the Early Years sector to include monitoring and evaluation as a core element of services. In this way, service providers can maintain, renew, and refine the evidence base for early childhood education. 1The Prevention and Early Intervention Programme for Children (PEIP) is Government funded from the Dormant Accounts Fund linked to matching investment by The Atlantic Philanthropies, amounting to €36 million in total. The programme is managed jointly by the DCYA and The Atlantic Philanthropies and examines innovative methods for improving outcomes for children in an integrated way.

The projects conclude this year (2012-13). The findings from the programme will inform the formulation of policy and services for children and families, in particular in relation to services for disadvantaged children. http://www.dcya.gov.ie/viewdoc.asp?fn=%2Fdocuments%2Fpolicy%2Fprevproject.htm

Project websites:
www.childrensresearchnetwork.org
www.growingup.ie
www.preparingforlife.ie
www.twcdi.ie
www.youngballymun.ie

Pictured last September at the 2012 Conference of the Children's Research Network for Ireland and Northern Ireland were L to R: Prof Richard Layte (ESRI), Prof Catherine Comiskey (TCD and Chair of the Children's Research Network for Ireland and Northern Ireland), Dr Dominic Richardson (OECD), and Brian Merriman formerly of Children's Research Network for Ireland and Northern Ireland and now researcher at St Patrick's College Drumcondra.

Achieving SIOLTA validation

Margaret Brown *Owner, Luttrellstown Tots Preschool, Castleknock Dublin*

I had been operating my preschool for over 12 years and was eager to keep current with new developments in childcare

Having completed a Montessori diploma and Fetac level 5 and 6, I felt that SIOLTA was a wonderful project and that getting involved would improve the quality of my service.

What is SIOLTA?
Siolta is the national quality framework for early childhood care and education services. It is a quality assurance programme, where a service undergoes a programme to look at their preschool, policies, procedures and practices.

In total there are 16 standards of quality. These are: the rights of the child, environments, parents and families, consultation, interactions, play, curriculum, planning and evaluation, health and welfare, organisation, professional practice, communication, transitions, legislation and regulation, and community involvement.

Based on the principles of quality which represent Siolta, the service then reflects on its own policies, procedures, practices and incorporates changes to enrich the lives and families of the children availing of the service and the professional practice of the adults.

What was involved
I spent approximately a year and a half attending Siolta Information Seminars with Carol Duffy, my Siolta Co-ordinator from Early Childhood Ireland. This has been a fantastic experience, and a long road with a lot of hard work from everyone involved. Initially I was quite daunted by the amount of paperwork, but I realised I had already been doing all of the necessary things, and it has allowed me to see that I am operating at a high standard.

I compiled a folder of evidence of the quality in my preschool. This included policies and procedures, photographs, video clips, samples of work and all documentation relating to my service.

Changes
I have made positive changes for everyone involved in the preschool. My biggest change to date has been implementing my play based emergent curriculum based on the principles of Aistear (early childhood curriculum).

I plan and produce themed weekly plans with the children and allow for the children's current and emerging interests. This allows me to follow a structure that has plenty of content but still allows for personalised learning as appropriate.

The children show great interest in projects in which they have had an input and they show fantastic imagination and knowledge when they plan their play. This play engages the children and it is very beneficial to them because it is based on their current interests.

I love to share the wonderful stories each day with families and parents, and I am very proud to show them all their children's work, words, marks, video clips and learning stories. This really allows parents to feel part of their child's day. Sharing this throughout the year gives a true honest picture of their child's development and in this way parental involvement in their child's learning experiences is made real in the preschool.

My confidence has grown in my work and I am much more open to welcoming parents, community members and prospective students into my preschool. I realise how enriching and important it is to stay in contact with other services and Early Childhood Ireland. Overall I have really enjoyed the journey, and the changes I have made, along with their impact on my service. I do feel I have put a tremendous amount of work into this very worthwhile, challenging project.

I was thrilled to receive a quality rating of 4 in my service in all the standards and believe that Siolta will greatly improve the standards of childcare in the country, enriching children's lives and the professional practice of adults working in the area of childcare.

Margaret Brown is owner of Luttrellstown Tots Preschool.

EDUCATION IN THE MEDIA

Conduct at Irish crèches called into question on 'Prime Time'

May 28, 2013

A HSE inspection report into childcare centres across the country shows that 75% of them were in breach of regulations last year.

The report was aired in a 'Prime Time Investigates' documentary broadcast on RTÉ tonight which revealed widespread breaches of childcare guidelines.

The programme focused on three crèches in Dublin and Wicklow, and showed footage of children being flung onto mattresses, manhandled, shouted at and strapped into their chairs sometimes for hours at a time.

The HSE inspection report expresses "grave concern" at what it describes as a "culture of light touch regulation at the expense of children's care" and a "dangerous over-emphasis on the business interests of childcare providers."

Minister for Children Frances Fitzgerald is due to make a detailed comment on the contents of the programme tomorrow.

www.irishexaminer.com/breakingnews/ireland/conduct-at-irish-creches-called-into-question-on-prime-time-595878.html

EDUCATION IN THE MEDIA

Gardaí investigating Prime Time programme on crèches

May 29, 2013

The Government has confirmed that a Garda investigation is now underway into last night's Prime Time investigation into childcare facilities.

This afternoon 11 TD's from both Government and opposition parties called on Children's Minister Frances Fitzgerald to act. She said there is now a very detailed and comprehensive Garda investigation underway.

Meanwhile, the Taoiseach Enda Kenny has said the Government will also consider withdrawing State funding from any crèches found guilty of breaches of care.

"The Minister for Children is going to supervise and monitor this," he said.

"As I said in the Dáil this morning, it's not just about regulations, it's not just about inspections, it is about quality and standards and they need to be applied on a national scale, on a national basis."

www.irishexaminer.com/breakingnews/ireland/gardai-investigating-prime-time-programme-on-creches-595998.html

---

Early Childhood Ireland issues statement following Primetime programme

May 29, 2013

"As the representative group for 3,330 preschool, full daycare (crèche) and afterschool providers supporting over 100,000 children nationwide, we are both disturbed and saddened by the Primetime Investigates programme. There are no excuses to justify such poor practice.

"Our thoughts go out to the children and parents directly affected but also to the thousands of childcare professionals across the country who deliver great experiences for children every day who are feeling vulnerable following this programme.
"It is important to take action now to help restore confidence in the early childhood care and education sector and there are a number of urgent steps to be taken:

"We urge the government and HSE to enhance both the approach and the numbers of inspectors for the early education sector and we welcome the commitment given last week to put inspection reports online as a matter of urgency.

"We welcome the fact that the HSE has already committed to introducing a registration system for early childhood service and we would urge them to accelerate this process.

"We reiterate our call on Minister Fitzgerald to introduce mandatory levels of training for the sector and to set a very clear timetable for achieving this, which must be accompanied by the right level of funding. Now more than ever the regulations need to be changed to require minimum qualification standards.

"All of these elements will require additional investment. This crisis is our opportunity as a nation to define the ideal model of early childhood care and education in Ireland, the quality levels we require on behalf of our children, and the investment needed to make this happen.

"To the parent body across the nation who drop their precious children to crèche or playgroup each working day, who may have seen the programme, we advise them to talk to their crèche or playgroup manager as soon as possible. Be upfront about expressing your concerns and make it your business to find out more about quality assurance in your child's place of care and education. Don't keep these worries bottled up.

"These incidents are not reflective of the high standard of early childhood care and education happening every day across this country. We have a great curriculum in Aistear that deserves to be implemented. We urge everyone to visit our website and to read some of the learning and innovation stories from across the nation.

"We encourage our members and their staff to meet parents and to explain to them how quality assurance happens in their setting.

"As we've said before real engagement between parent and practitioner is key. Parents must understand the preschool curriculum at the centre of their child's learning and experience and be confident in this.

Parents should be welcome to drop into an early childhood care and education setting at any time, and should be encouraged to do so."

The 'Aistear in Action' Initiative in South Tipperary and North Cork

Dr Mary Daly, *Education Officer, NCCA*

An alliance between Early Childhood Ireland, the NCCA and seven services in South Tipperary and North Cork.

It ran across two pre-school years from November 2011 to June 2013. The 24 practitioners involved in the initiative used Aistear: the Early Childhood Curriculum Framework (NCCA, 2009) to develop the curriculum they provide for children aged 3-5 years. The resources from the initiative will be published in the Aistear Toolkit (www.ncca.ie/aisteartoolkit) in the coming months to support other practitioners in using Aistear to develop an exciting, fun and interesting curriculum for young children. The table below summarises the design of the initiative.

Participants	24 pre-school practitioners
Design	Inquiry-based developmental project Supporting self-reflection and action
Learning together	Monthly on-site visits Cluster meetings Termly seminars IT- documentation and reflection
Aistear Toolkit	Videos, photos, stories

The practitioners have worked with all aspects of Aistear in developing their practice - the principles, the themes (*Well-being, Identity and Belonging, Communicating,* and *Exploring and Thinking*) and the guidelines on partnerships with parents, interactions, play and assessment. Self- and group-reflection followed by action has greatly enhanced the curriculum provided for the 3-5 year old children in the seven services.

Changes to practice

Each service has made significant changes over the course of the initiative. For two of the services a large portion of the first year was spent making changes to the indoor environment.

For another service there was a strong focus on making their outdoor environment more natural (it had a high fence and safety surface but lacked natural elements like plants and trees).

They added planting and digging areas, flowers and plants, chalk boards, mirrors, old tyres and pieces of wood to create richer outdoor learning opportunities for children.

An Environmental Audit Tool (which is available on the Aistear Toolkit) was developed to help services make a more exciting learning space for the children.

Almost every service reorganised the daily routine and made more time for child-initiated time. The daily routine became more flexible and if children were engrossed and wanted to spend more time on what they were doing this was facilitated.

Changes in planning also occurred. Services no longer choose the topics in advance that form the curriculum. Instead they listen to and observe the children and incorporate materials, resources and activities that follow on from their interests. The short-term planning template (available on the Toolkit) was developed to support this type of planning.

Services do still plan around the seasons and celebrations but in addition, children learn about topics when they are of interest to them. For example, in one service a child visited the natural history museum in London with his mum. This became a huge topic of interest and children built dinosaur worlds and learned words like fossils, palaeontologist and extinct in a meaningful way.

Learning and enjoyment through working with the soil

As most of the services are based in rural areas farming-related issues are nearly always of interest, depending on the time of year there can be baby lambs being born, vets doing caesarean sections, silage harvesting or milking parlours that are fully operational!

Conclusion

Reflecting on their experience of the initiative, the practitioners noted, Aistear has been a tool to help then change the way they look at the children and their learning. They also say it has highlighted for them the need to respect the individuality of children, their families, cultures, interests, likes, dislikes and abilities. I think one practitioner really summed up Aistear in Action when she said, we are now seeing the positive results – happy, confident children with a thirst for learning.

Find out more about the practitioners' work with Aistear by visiting the Aistear Toolkit (www.ncca.ie/aisteartoolkit).

Throughout the Aistear in Action Initiative, staff in the services, were supported by Máire Corbett and Lucy Connolly from Early Childhood Ireland, and Mary Daly from NCCA.

References

National Council for Curriculum and Assessment, (2009) Aistear: The Early Childhood Curriculum Framework, Dublin, Government Publications, www.ncca.ie/earlylearning

EDUCATION IN THE MEDIA

State paid millions to three crèche firms in RTE spotlight

May 29, 2013

THE crèche companies at the centre of the ongoing controversy over childcare have received millions of euro in state funding.

In the past two years, a total of €3.6m of taxpayers' money was paid to the companies running the three crèche chains highlighted on the RTE Primetime documentary. The money was paid as part of the Early Childhood Care and Education (ECCE) programme, under which every child is entitled to a free pre-school year in a crèche.

The level of funding paid to each crèche depends on parental choice, with the money following the child. If a parent decides to move their child to another crèche, the fee is also transferred.

All of the three companies highlighted appear to be in good financial health. However, the pay for staff at such crèches remains modest. According to the last available set of accounts for one of the crèche chains, staff was paid €18,200 on average.

www.independent.ie/irish-news/state-paid-millions-to-three-creche-firms-in-rte-spotlight-29303920.html

---

Just 15 of 4,300 childcare centres assessed

June 03, 2013

Education standards have been assessed at just 15 of the 4,300 childcare centres paid more than €600m to provide a free pre-school year since 2010.

It also has emerged it will be next year at the earliest before new national education standards are applied and inspected, even though a framework for an early learning curriculum has been in place since 2009. Education Minister Ruairi Quinn was told when he took office in March 2011 that pilot inspections of learning would take place that autumn, in records seen by the Irish Examiner.

EDUCATION IN THE MEDIA

"There has not as yet been a focus on accountability for educational outcomes in ECCE [early childhood care and education] commensurate with the level of investment in early years' education by the State," said a previously unpublished briefing note from senior Department of Education officials.

The evaluations only took place in the first half of last year, carried out by Department of Education and HSE inspectors in 15 centres.

Ms Fitzgerald told the Irish Examiner that systems for quality and curriculum in early childhood education, in place since 2006 and 2009 respectively, will have to be followed under new national standards to be published in a few months.

Meanwhile, Gordon Jeyes, who will be chief executive of the Child and Family Agency, apologised that childcare inspection reports had not previously been published. He said historic reports would be put online soon, as well as reports of all new inspections which, following last week's RTE Prime Time documentary, Ms Fitzgerald promised would happen within weeks.

Mr Jeyes said the agency should have greater powers than the HSE has when childcare providers are in regular breach of regulations, as three or four prosecutions a year is not good enough, when accidents in crèches have led to child deaths.

www.irishexaminer.com/ireland/just-15-of-4300-childcare-centres-assessed-233096.html

---

Extra pre-school year 'on hold' over scandal

Irish Independent, June 03, 2013

A second free pre-school year has been ruled out until at least 2014 following revelations of mistreatment of children in crèches.

Currently, some 68,000 children avail of schooling through the Early Childhood Care and Education scheme (ECCE), which costs €175m a year.

But Children's Minister Frances Fitzgerald said that not until higher standards were in place in all childcare facilities - with all staff were qualified, new standards introduced and a "more robust" inspection regime implemented - would parents be offered a second year of pre-school education.

"That's going to happen, and we're going to have to plan for that from mid-2014," Ms Fitzgerald told the Irish Independent.

"We'll be negotiating the contracts to make sure we have qualified people.

"I'm going to put that into the contract and work with the sector to move towards it. We will have to have training, but the key point is it has to be a statement of what we want in the sector.

"It's not that I'm ruling it out. I am for this year's Budget, but it's really important we work towards it. These are the steps we need to take, and it would save parents up to €3,000 a year because we will provide 3.5 hours of care every day."

The move to introduce a second year of pre-school education is strongly backed by Education Minister Ruairi Quinn.

Early Childhood Ireland, which represents 3,300 crèches and childcare facilities, said many members were ready to provide high-standard care.

"The investment in childcare by the State is far short of what it should be and we need proper debate followed by targets, timelines and responsibilities to make this happen," the organisation said in a statement.

"However, pushing that State investment decision two or three years down the line won't work while at the same time asking the sector and hard-pressed parents to pay hefty registration fees to fill the shortfall in the meantime."

www.independent.ie/irish-news/extra-preschool-year-on-hold-over-scandal-29314983.html

Early Childhood

EDUCATION IN THE MEDIA

New organisation launched to represent childcare professionals

June 7, 2013

The Association of Childhood Professionals (ACP) has been established to be the voice of an estimated 22,500 childhood professionals across the country. The association was formally launched on 7 June 2013 by the Minister for Children and Youth Affairs Frances Fitzgerald.

Speaking at the launch, ACP Chairperson Marian Quinn said:
"Our objective is for the early years sector to become a fully developed professional sector in its own right – similar to teaching, medicine or law. We have a strong mandate from the grassroots to progress this agenda.

"We are calling for an initial statutory minimum requirement for all childhood professionals of a FETAC level 5 Childcare qualification together with a national register - with only those who are qualified and registered being eligible for employment.

"This should apply for both those working in childcare centres and pre-schools and also for professionals who are contracted to care for children in the home.

"This qualification is currently required for professionals delivering the ECCE programme (free pre-school year), but not for other age groups of children in childcare settings.

"The ACP is also calling for a standard childhood sector contract to be developed which includes permanent contracts in pre-schools to improve continuity in the work place and bring greater job security for staff. It should also allow for non-contact time (admin work) and for continuous professional development (CPD), as is the norm in other professions.

"The sector also needs accessible progression routes for training, a proper career path and remuneration structure. For example, a room leader in a crèche would require a certain level of additional training and experience compared to an entrant, and a crèche Manager would need further training and experience to be eligible for that role.

Pictured at the launch of the Association of Childhood Professionals (ACP) were Prof. Noirin Hayes ACP Patron, Marian Quinn Chairperson ACP, Minister Fitzgerald, ACP Committee

People can find out more at www.acpireland.com.

Activators of Learning: The Role of the Artist

Orla Kenny, *Artistic Director, Kids' Own*

What it is that the artist brings that is unique to the early years setting?

What is the difference between art and play? And what added value do the arts bring to a child's development and learning experiences?

These are just some of the questions that were investigated during a cross border project that took place in late 2012 and was funded by the Department of Foreign Affairs Reconciliation Fund. It was devised and delivered by Kids' Own, in partnership with Early Childhood Ireland[2] and Early Years, the Organisation for Young Children, Northern Ireland.

The broad aim of the project was to "develop a north-south interagency framework that supports and celebrates creativity, diversity, inclusion and family learning and to build a network that supports a culture of mutual respect and understanding within the home and wider community." Working with parent & toddler groups on both sides of the border, our intention was to engage parents in the creative process alongside their children and to really impact on family and community approaches in this way, by creating a triad between artist, child and parent.

Four artists worked with four parent & toddler groups over a 7-week period and the emphasis was on exploration and creative play. As a pilot there were no predefined outcomes, and artists kept a blog of their work over the course of the project on www.practice.ie – Ireland's online network of artists working with children & young people.

An important aspect of this project was a piece of independent research that was conducted retrospectively by Researcher Áine McKenna, which sought to draw out a number of key questions from the project. Among the areas that were explored was the consideration of how the varying approaches of the artists involved impacted on

(a) parents' deep learning in terms of directive and non-directive approaches; and

(b) long-term community approaches. Among the findings, McKenna stated that "this evidence suggests that arts workshops delivered by professional artists within Parent & Toddler group settings may provide a context to facilitate adaptive changes in family learning dynamics."

Within the research report (http://issuu.com/practice.ie/docs/kids_own_opening_the_door_full_research_report?e=1981449/3077536), she also states:

"Artists are perfectly placed in communities to facilitate the shift towards the 'pedagogy of mutuality' (Bruner) both within families and learning communities. They also understand how 'aesthetic vibration' which encompasses sensory perception, pleasure and the power to seduce can become an 'activator of learning".

"Artists who listen to children intuitively understand how to design environments that

Early Childhood

entice children to engage with them. This approach nurtures children's creative expression, children's sense of agency, as well as their sense of empathy, which is characterised by the ability to imagine the perspective of another.

"Artists who work in the Early Years utilise 'aesthetic vibration' to facilitate visual investigations using process based approaches that utilise intersubjectivity, collaboration and a co-construction of meaning during the learning journeys."

With further funding Kids' Own hopes to develop this project in 2013-14 and is excited about the possibilities of establishing deeper and more long-term relationships in border communities between artists, parents and young children.

Our new book, "Opening the Door" shares case studies and the research from the Being & Belonging project. Copies available by emailing info@kidsown.ie

EDUCATION IN THE MEDIA

Providers about inconsistencies in inspection process

July 15, 2013

Early Childhood Ireland survey shows level of concern from childcare providers about inconsistencies in inspection process

The survey also shows that many inspection reports are out of date and don't include right to reply from the crèche or preschool involved

One in four (25%) preschools and crèches around the country have not been inspected since 2011, according to an Early Childhood Ireland survey published on July 15, 2013 which involved 1,078 respondents from crèches and preschools across the country.

According to the survey which was conducted in early July, 82% of respondents welcome inspections going online, but only 34% submitted a right of reply in their most recent inspection report. Many members complained that they had not been offered their right to reply and 75% said that if given the opportunity they would submit their right to reply before their inspection report goes online.

According to Teresa Heeney, Chief Operations Officer of Early Childhood Ireland:

"Given the fact that 25% of respondents have not had an inspection visit since 2011, it is reasonable to assume that the service has changed in that time. Putting these out of date reports online without a right of reply serves no-one's interests.

Teresa Heeney, Chief Operations Officer of Early Childhood Ireland

"A more consistent, robust and regular inspection process is good for everyone, especially children. This survey has been sent to the Minister for Children & Youth Affairs with a view to highlighting the flaws within the existing inspection process and the urgent need to make the reports which are going online more consistent, transparent and fair.'

EDUCATION IN THE MEDIA

Study shows clearly first three years of life are crucial

June 27, 2013

By Richard Layte, researcher at the ESRI

High quality preschool can be particularly important for children from poor families

Over the past seven years researchers from the ESRI and Trinity College Dublin have been following almost 20,000 children as they grow and develop. The study is called "Growing Up in Ireland" (GUI) and is Government-funded. The data is providing important insights into the factors that promote healthy, happy child development and educational success.

The new analysis shows, conclusively, that a child's environment in the first three years of life is crucial. It leaves an indelible mark, affecting the risk of obesity, level of educational development and psychological well-being. The GUI research adds to a growing international evidence base that shows children's early life environments determine not only their physical health, but may also contribute to childhood and adult criminality, educational failure, family breakdown and mental health.

Further evidence is provided by recent findings from the Irish Longitudinal Study of Ageing (TILDA), that the risk of a number of diseases among adults over the age of 50 was linked to their experience of childhood adversity.

Foundations
It will come as no surprise to most people that the foundations of all aspects of human development – physical, psychological, social and emotional – are laid down in early childhood. What might be news is that infancy and childhood are often a "critical period", after which remedial treatment can be less effective and increasingly expensive.

In the words of a recent UK report, "If people keep falling off a cliff, don't worry about where you put the ambulance at the bottom. Build a fence at the top and stop them falling off in the first place".

What policy implications do these results have? Each year Ireland spends millions of euro dealing with the health and social consequences of child deprivation. We should invest instead in early childhood, during the 'critical period' of early life before age three. New evidence from the UK shows that high quality preschool is beneficial for all children, but is especially important for deprived children. It acts to 'inoculate' them against poor circumstances later in childhood. As recent events have highlighted, our model of preschool provision needs to change from one of child-minding to one of high quality and better funded preschool education.

Public health nurse
Studies show that families who get regular visits from a public health nurse from before the birth of their child enjoy better child health, development and behaviour for up to two decades afterwards, compared with families who don't.

The public health nurse system in Ireland is poorly funded, yet expansion of the service would be a relatively cheap and efficient way to get concrete improvements in child outcomes in both the short and long-term. Regular public health nurse visits would benefit all sections of Irish society, but targeting deprived areas initially would be a more effective use of scarce resources.

With a tight national budget we need to think carefully about investing for the future. Our prosperity depends on having an educated, creative and competitive workforce. By investing in early childhood we will be developing healthier, happier and more productive adults for all our tomorrows – and saving money in the process. Can we afford not to?

www.irishtimes.com/news/social-affairs/investment-in-child-development-at-an-early-stage-leaves-an-important-positive-legacy-1.1443638

First published in the Irish Times, June 27th 2013

Literacy: 'Help My Kid Learn' website

Margaret Murray, *Literacies Development, NALA*

The new website is aimed at the parents, guardians and minders of children aged 0-12

Launched in September 2012, this website provides many creative ideas for activities that adults can do with their children to improve their child's speaking, reading, writing, and maths skills. The website highlights the way children learn as part of their everyday lives, especially the things they can learn at home and when they are out and about with the significant adult(s) in their lives.

What's on the website?
www.helpmykidlearn.ie mixes the old with the new - from card games and hopscotch that help practice maths, to e-books that can be read out to the child and "apps" you can download to a smart phone. Information is broken down into five age groups: 0-2 years, 3-4 years, 5-7 years, 8-9 years and 10-12 years. Activities are organised into five areas: Talk, Play, Read, Write and Count. The website is updated regularly and includes video content to support parents who have literacy difficulties themselves and links to other websites.

Why was the new website developed?
The National Adult Literacy Agency (NALA) developed www.helpmykidlearn.ie as part of the Department of Education and Skills' (DES) National Strategy to Improve Literacy and Numeracy among Children and Young People 2011-2020. It is part of a campaign to raise awareness of the important role that parents and the community can play in building children's literacy and numeracy skills. 'The Family Project' TV series on RTE 1 on Mondays at 7.30pm is another part of this campaign. NALA developed the website with forty stakeholders, including Early Childhood Ireland. Stakeholders gave ideas and are now helping to promote the website.

Promoting the website
A national "Literacy and Numeracy Working Group" made up of the Early Years Policy Unit, DES, national childcare organisations, county childcare committees and NALA also looked at how best to promote and make the most out of the website. In May 2013, county childcare committees undertook to disseminate a total of 98,180 www.helpmykidlearn.ie bookmarks, 13,745 fliers, 20,000 posters to parents, guardians and childminders in crèches, parent and toddler groups and registered childminders. Libraries also promoted the website with parents and guardians through a national day in the libraries on June 11, 2013.

You can help
1. Encourage childminders and parents to see www.helpmykidlearn.ie as a resource. Childminders could let parents know about it when giving feedback to parents at the end of the day or in "parent teacher" meetings.
2. Share the website with colleagues and friends with Facebook and Twitter. You can also look at http://www.facebook.com/helpmykidlearn.
3. Put a link on your organisation's website.
4. Include information in newsletters, ezines and in correspondence with parents.
5. Sign up for more tips and NALA will send you one email per month.

Professional Development for Early Childhood Educators at Limerick College of Further Education

Mary Ryan, Head of School of Childcare, Healthcare and Science at Limerick College of further Education describes the work and mission of the School.

Limerick College of Further Education is the largest centre of further education in the Mid West region. Its School of Childcare, Healthcare & Science is very dynamic in delivering full time day courses to 9 groups covering all disciplines.

On the full-time day courses, there are two groups taking the FETAC Certificate in Early Childhood Care & Education, level 5, and one group studying the FETAC Advanced Certificate in Early Childhood Care & Education, level 6.

The Adult Education/ night programmes offer both level 5 and level 6 components of Childcare, giving the learner an opportunity to study for the FETAC Full Award on a part-time basis. The learner can choose what components s/he wishes to study, over a time scale that fits into their working lives.

The staff/teachers in the School of Childcare have a wealth of knowledge and experience between them. Their qualifications include Degrees in Montessori, Early Childhood Studies, Nursing/midwifery, Social Studies and general B.A. in Arts. Two teachers previously had their own Childcare business, and their experience is invaluable in supporting the learners in the practical application of the theory of their components.

City of Limerick VEC is very supportive of all teachers doing Continuous Professional Development on an annual basis. This includes general training/ education for the teaching profession, as well as specific training/ education to keep up to date with latest research of the Childcare profession.

Early Childhood Ireland is proactive in the professional development for all childcare professionals and Limerick College of Further Education is a member. Under the Leonardo programme, the organisation gave two teachers the opportunity to travel - one to Scotland and another to Italy - to see at first hand the policies and practice of excellent childcare. This influenced the teaching of international practice to the learners. All teachers have completed training on the Aistear and Siolta programmes of good practice, and this knowledge is passed on to the learners with confidence of practical delivery.

Limerick College of Further Education, in conjunction with both the City and County Childcare Committees, organises an annual seminar including workshops on different topics relating to childcare.

Last year the school held a professional Forum in the college with a wide range of speakers from varied walks of life.

These were available at different work stations for learners who wished to talk to them about their individual needs.

Under FETAC guidelines, all learners of the Childcare programmes must complete a minimum of 120 hours/20 days on work experience placement. Limerick College of Further Education has allocated hours for a teacher to visit the learners in their placement as they are timetabled to attend one day each week. This facilitates great relationships between the childcare supervisors, learners and the College. Discussion takes place on each visit on promoting good practice and encouraging the learner to become active in her own learning.

This is the one part of the programme that all learners enjoy as it supports their understanding of theory being put into practice.

Going to 'Big School'

Áine Lynch, *CEO National Parents Council Primary*

A useful "go to" guide is available to help parents in preparing their child for primary school

Transition from primary to post primary school is often seen as a key milestone in children's lives and research has shown it is a significant period which - if navigated well - can be central to the child's future success.

What has possibly had less attention, however, is the **transition from home or early childhood settings into primary school.** Recent research has shown that this is a vital transition period not only for children but for families also. In fact Smart et al 2009 states that "Societies benefit when children and families view school as a positive place to be and when education is regarded as valuable, relevant and attainable. A positive start to school, leading to greater and ongoing connection with school, has been identified as a factor disrupting cycles of social and economic disadvantage and in promoting resilience among young people".

This said, it is vital that the initial introduction from the early years setting is made in the most **positive and supported way**. If children and families do not transition into primary education well, this can have an impact on their entire education career.

The process of transition is not a one-off event. It is not just about the first day of 'big school', it **occurs over time.** It should begin well before children start school and continue until children and their families feel a sense of belonging at school and also, importantly, until the school staff can recognise that sense of belonging in the children and their families.

A child's transition into primary education requires **a team approach.** Effective partnerships between families, educators, other professionals and the community will ensure that children are given the best possible start to their journey through education, one which hopefully will lead to lifelong learning pathways for all children.

In this spirit of partnership, the National Parents Council (Primary) and Early Childhood Ireland began **to collaborate closely** in an effort to support parents in their role of supporting their child through the transition period leading up to and starting primary school. This collaboration is in the early stages of what both organisations hope will become a permanent feature of their work, which will grow year on year. We are delighted that it has already borne fruit in the form of a joint publication **"Going to Big School".** This leaflet has been produced as a useful "go to" guide for parents during the transition period. It gives support on preparing your child for school, being confident that the school is ready for your child, first day tips, and more.

The publication was very well received in its first year and was circulated to both Early Childhood Ireland and National Parents Council members as well as being available for download from the respective websites*. This leaflet has now become part of both organisations' suite of resources and joint promotion and circulation of the annual activities.

*www.earlychildhoodireland.ie and www.npc.ie

WHO'S WHO

The WHO'S WHO Profile introduces people who are making an important contribution to education in Ireland today.

Meet Geoffrey Shannon

OCCUPATION: Solicitor, Rapporteur on Child Protection and Chairman of Adoption Authority of Ireland

Where did you grow up?
Galway

What is your earliest childhood memory?
The sea, rain and being curious.

How many siblings have you?
Four.

Where did you go to school/college?
National University of Ireland Galway.

To what extent did your education shape who you are today?
Education was a key part of my personal development.

What attracted you to work in Child Protection?
I had always a strong sense of social justice.

What makes you particularly suitable for your current work?
I would like to think that my approach to all matters has been child-centred and I have pursued that approach fearlessly throughout my professional career.

What are the main responsibilities and challenges of your position?
It is balancing the rights of all parties but always with the best interests of the child as the first and paramount consideration.

What does a typical workday involve for you?
It is very varied but usually starts early and ends late!

What do you enjoy most about your work?
Results. I am a task driven person and always judge my success in terms of output.

What do you enjoy least about your work?
Sometimes, the slow pace of progress.

What would you most like to change?
Inequality in Irish society.

What do you do to relax?
I am an avid runner and also enjoy reading a good novel, though I rarely have the time to achieve the latter.

Have you a message for educators?
Teach young people that education is the key to overcoming disadvantage and the only boundaries are set by their own imagination.

Have you a message for policy makers?
Policy makers should be cognisant of the fact that policy decisions will have a very significant impact on the individual citizen.

Chapter 2
Primary

Contents

	Page
1. **From Croke Park to Haddington Road** Sheila Nunan	36
2. **A Year for Strategy** Áine Lynch	39
3. **A Watershed Year** Dr Fionnuala Waldron	42
4. **Induction for Newly Qualified Teachers (NQTs)** Billy Redmond	46
5. **Primary principals hit hard** Michael Gallagher	50
6. **'Value for Money' Review of Small Schools** Ken Fennelly	56
7. **School Self Evaluation (SSE) in Primary Schools** Carmel Hume	60
8. **Teaching Religion** Deirdre O'Connor	64
9. **Mental Health Difficulties** Carmel Browne	66
10. **Student Well Being** Dr Mark Morgan	72
11. **'Cyberbullying' – why is it different?** Dr Sharon McLaughlin	76
12. **Who's Who** Noel Ward	79

Introducing the Primary Chapter

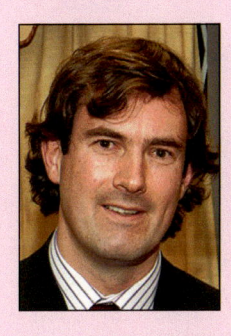

by Tony Hall, *Editor*

The narrative of Irish education since 1831 and the Stanley Letter, which effectively began the foundations of a formal educational system in Ireland, has been characterised by change. Throughout the system, significant developments are currently taking place.

In this section of the Yearbook on primary education, we feature articles from the key stakeholders in the sector. The chapter opens with a keynote commentary from the Irish National Teachers' Organisation (INTO), the largest teachers' union in Ireland, by its General Secretary, Sheila Nunan. Ms Nunan discusses the key developments in conditions of primary teachers over the year, up to and including the voting by INTO members to accept the Haddington Road Agreement in June last. Michael Gallagher, Principal in Galway City, and member of the Yearbook's editorial committee, identifies in his article, and discusses the pressures under which primary schools and their principals are trying to operate.

The primary section of the Yearbook also looks at teacher education this year, and the changes taking place in this important dimension of the Irish education system.

Dr. Fionnuala Waldron, Dean of Education in St. Patrick's College, Drumcondra outlines the significant changes taking place in initial teacher education and the preparation of teachers for the primary sector; and Billy Redmond, National Coordinator for the Induction Programme for Teachers, discusses induction within the continuum of lifelong teacher education.

This year's Yearbook also focuses on a set of key themes in Irish education, including crucially the well-being of both students and teachers. Therefore, the section includes articles on both of these salient topics. A particularly timely article, in the contemporary context, given the increasing ubiquity of technology in society and education, is the article by Dr. Sharon McLaughlin, Letterkenny Institute of Technology, on 'cyberbullying', and how we can mediate, enhance and support young people's optimal use of the web and online, mobile and portable technologies.

The 'Who's Who' profile for the primary sector this year is Mr. Noel Ward, Deputy General Secretary of the Irish National Teachers' Organisation (INTO).

Primary

From Croke Park to Haddington Road

Sheila Nunan *General Secretary of the Irish National Teacher's Organization (INTO)*

The Croke Park Agreement was working but it still fell victim to the Government's economic strategy.

Throughout 2012, the Croke Park Agreement was implemented in schools across the country by teachers. In June of that year, the Implementation Body tasked with overseeing its progress issued its second report on the workings of the Agreement and concluded that the Agreement was delivering reform and change across the Public Service and significant exchequer savings on pay.

In the education sector, specific reforms were noted including the redeployment of more than 200 secondary and 950 primary level teachers in the 2011-12 school year, which eliminated the need to recruit teachers, thereby delivering substantial savings. The report noted that school inspection outputs for 2011 were 15% ahead of the previous year and that a new contract for special needs assistants had been agreed which provided greater flexibility.

Positive signs ignored
However, in spite of these positive signs and of repeated warnings from the trade union movement that the government's policy of austerity was not working, the government persisted with its economic strategy. The growth targets set for the economy failed to materialise so it was clear that adjustments to the national finances would be made. A lightning rod for this was the perceived failure of government to meet a planned reduction of €75m from a review of allowances.

This resulted in the agreement being attacked relentlessly by politicians, members of the public and parts of the media for protecting the majority of allowances to serving public servants.

Demand for additional savings
In October 2012, the Minister for Public Expenditure and Reform Brendan Howlin met the Public Services Committee (PSC) of ICTU and demanded additional savings from the public service pay and pension bill, a message reiterated by An Taoiseach Enda Kenny some days later. An Taoiseach, while supportive of the Agreement, indicated that further savings would have to be achieved by 2015.

Threat of legislation failing agreement
The following month, public service unions were invited to enter discussions with representatives of public service management in order to seek agreement on additional reductions to the overall pay and pensions bill.

By the new year it was made clear that, in order to meet its commitment to reduce the deficit below 3% of GDP by 2015, government was determined to seek a further reduction of €1 billion on public pay and pensions, and that it would do this by legislation if no agreement was possible.

Croke Park II
Talks on an extension or revision to the Croke Park Agreement began in January 2013, brokered by the Labour Relations Commission (LRC). At the initial meeting, management outlined its proposals which included increased working hours, cuts to payments like supervision and substitution, changes to redeployment, modernisation, performance management, pay reductions at certain levels and a review of allowances.

The union agenda for the talks included measures to eliminate the two-tiered workforce, progress on the moratorium on filling promotion posts, casualization and outstanding third party recommendations including benchmarking.

Most difficult talks ever
The talks were the most difficult negotiations ever undertaken. Among the outcomes to the talks that emerged at the end of February were measures to tackle the 'two-tier' pay scales introduced when the previous Government imposed an additional 13% cut in pay scales for new entrants and the current government introduced a pay scale that subsumed academic allowances.

Improved pay scale for entrant teachers
A new improved pay scale for new entrant teachers with improvements at the bottom and the top was a key outcome of the talks for the teacher unions. The unions successfully moved management from its opening position for an extra five hours a week which would have increased the school day/ year.

The proposals provided for reduced substitute cover for some absences such as self-certified sick leave. The lunchtime supervision payment was to cease from the 2013-14 school year.

Increments
The unions moved management from an opening position of seeking to freeze all increments until the end of 2016. Instead what emerged was a proposal for a three month increment freeze for staff earning up to €35,000, two three-month increment freezes for staff earning between €35,000 and €65,000.

Earners over €65,000
The government decided to impose pay cuts on staff earning over €65,000. A cut of 5.5% was proposed for staff earning over €65,000 but less than €80,000; Earnings between €80,000 and €150,000 were to be reduced by 8%. In addition staff earning more than €65,000 per year would have a three-year freeze on increments.

The percentage pay cut would not reduce any employees' earnings below €65,000.

The teacher unions succeeded in getting the effect of the pay cut mitigated to take account of the loss of lunchtime supervision payment for those in receipt of it.

Ballot
The INTO issued the proposals to primary teachers without a recommendation, recognising the potential gains for newly qualified teachers but noting that all teachers, especially those earning over 65,000, were negatively affected. The Executive of the union was also clear about the government's intention to impose cuts and changes by way of legislation.

Teachers, at both primary and post-primary level voted, voted overwhelmingly to reject the LRC proposals. Immediately, the three teacher unions decided to ballot for industrial action, which teachers at both levels supported.

Haddington Road Agreement
Towards the end of May, an invitation to new talks was issued by the LRC to all unions and the INTO agreed to accept. Among the changes to the proposals that emerged in a set of proposals to be called the Haddington Road Agreement were:

- A provision for the restoration of supervision and substitution allowance by inclusion in the salary scale;

- Changes to the original proposals on providing substitute cover for absent colleagues on certified sick leave and bereavement leave,

- Alleviation measures in relation to multiple absences, particularly in small schools.

- The new proposals retained the grace period whereby those retiring by 31 August 2014 will have their pension and lump sum calculated on the basis of their current salary.

- For those earning over €65,000, the Agreement provided for full restoration of pay cuts by 1 January 2018 and the payment of increments due (the first on its due date with any subsequent increments being subject to a delay of 6 months).

- The HRA also provided for an Expert Group to consider and report on fixed-term and part-time employment, having regard to the importance of employment stability and security. This group will first report on reducing the qualification period for a CID from 4 years to 3 years from the 2014-15 school year. Arrangements will be made for those entering their fourth year in September 2013 with a view to the early application of this provision.

Following careful consideration of the proposals and the implications of not having an agreement, the INTO decided to recommend acceptance to members in a ballot. In June 2013, primary teachers voted by nearly two to one to accept the Haddington Road Agreement.

EDUCATION IN THE MEDIA

Schools asked to cut uniform cost

September 08, 2012

The cost of school uniforms is to be the basis of a hearing of the Dáil select committee on education.

Surveys published during the summer suggest the average cost of sending a primary-level and second-level student back to school this month is over €1,100, when uniforms, books and other costs are added.

"When I see the costs of uniforms in some of the recent surveys, that certainly isnít the case in many schools," said Joanna Tuffy, chair of the Dáil education committee.

Joanna Tuffy

"It can be done much cheaper by schools, they donít have to go with the branded uniform, when a badge or logo could be put on a generic uniform."

"They can give parents more choice about where they buy uniforms, particularly with the speed at which children grow up and some may be needing to replace the entire uniform during the school year."

Minister Quinn has made repeated calls for uniform policies that are easier on parents' dwindling budgets. But he said this week that he has no powers to force schools to act. However, Ms Tuffy claimed that increased pressure from politicians and parents can have an effect.

Meanwhile, the Department of Social Protection has already paid the Back to School Clothing and Footwear Allowance to almost 160,000 families and another 25,500 applications have to be processed.

Payments for primary-aged children have been cut this year from €200 to €150 and children aged 2-4 years are no longer covered.

www.irishexaminer.com/archives/2012/0908/world/tds-to-tell-schools-cut-uniform-cost-206901.html

A Year for Strategy

Áine Lynch *CEO National Parents' Council Primary*

National Parents Council Primary launched their new Strategic Plan in Autumn 2012

Over the last number of decades there has been a wealth of research which shows the difference parental involvement can make in educational outcomes for children. As the National Parents Council for children in primary school, this research is of vital importance to us in charting our way forward over the next five years, and at a time of constrained budgets, it is even more important that we prioritise the activities that will make the biggest difference for children, as highlighted by the research.

NPC's Strategic Plan, Supporting Parents Supporting Children, represents our commitment and determination to strengthen parental involvement in children's education to ensure that children have the best possible opportunities for their success in life.

During the consultation phase NPC sought input from members, non-members, strategic stakeholders, children, the general public and the NPC staff and Board. In total over 580 voices and opinions were heard and have contributed to developing a strategy that will drive all NPC activities over the next five years.

NPC has developed six strategic objectives to guide it over the lifetime of this strategy. These objectives, developed using Joyce Epstein's (2009) framework for parental involvement, are: Parenting, Communicating, Volunteering, Learning at Home, Decision Making and Collaborating with the Community.

While strategy is vital to ensure common goals and clarity of direction for an organisation, time however does not stand still whilst strategising is happening and there were many important issues for parents in 2012-13.

Patronage and Pluralism Forum

The advisory group to the Patronage and Pluralism Forum concluded its work and reported to the Minister for Education and Skills on their findings and recommendations. In June of 2012 the Minister held a briefing session, in which he responded to the report and set out an action plan to address the advisory group's recommendations. The NPC made a number of submissions to the advisory group during their work and were also invited by the Minister to speak at the briefing session. NPC's submission called for parent involvement to be a core feature in all decisions at all levels, especially on issues relating to patronage for new schools and in the case of an existing school changing its patron.

Following the Minister's briefing session, the NPC welcomed the fact that for the first time the preferences of parents were to be taken into account both in areas where there is demographic growth and a need for new schools and, in areas of stable population, where the need for diversity will be met from the existing school provision.

Anti-Bullying Forum
A Forum on Anti-Bullying took place on the May 17, 2012 at the Department of Education and Skills, to explore ways to tackle the problem of bullying in schools.

The Forum brought together a range of experts, support groups and representatives of the schools sector including parents and students. The Forum considered what changes to existing practices and policies in schools were needed in order to effectively tackle bullying.

The NPC made a presentation to the Anti-Bullying Forum and followed this up with a submission to the working group established to develop an action plan on bullying.

The priorities for tackling bullying in schools as set out in the NPC submission were:
- developing and implementing a shared definition of RESPECT;
- building positive relationships for students, staff members, parents and all members of the school community;
- the empowerment of children and building of their resilience;
- responding positively to negative behaviours;
- consultation on the development of the school anti-bullying policy.

Referendum on Children's Rights
On Saturday, November 10, 2012, the people of Ireland voted in favour of the 31st amendment on the Constitution Bill 2012 and legal history was made for children. The Irish Constitution will now have a new article, 42A, entitled "Children" which will greatly strengthen the rights of children in Ireland.

Many organisations worked together to support the yes vote for the passing of this Constitutional amendment and the NPC played its part in the campaign.

Looking back over the year - a year fraught with economic crisis and cutbacks - it is reassuring to note such advances are being made to support children and families to exercise their core rights for respect and protection.

PINE FOREST ART CENTRE
GLENCULLEN, KILTERNAN, DUBLIN 18

Telephone 01 2941220 | Fax 01 2941221 | Email: info@pineforestartcentre.com | www.pineforestartcentre.com

Junior and Senior Summer Camps/ Courses:
Junior 5-12 years; Senior 13-16 years.
Two weeks at a time, during July and August,
Monday-Friday, 10.00am-4.00pm.

Private buses from various South Dublin pick-up points are available if required to transport children and young people to and from Art Centre.

Portfolio Preparation Course: Ages 16-19.
This Course programme is structured to assist students in developing a comprehensive portfolio for application for entry to 3rd level institutions and/ or preparing for Leaving Certificate. An individual programme is organised for each member of the group consisting of tuition in drawing, painting and participation in craft groups, according to each person's requirements.
2-week and 4-week courses throughout August.

The Easter Camp is held in the week before Easter Sunday.
Ages: Junior 5 -12; Senior 13 -16.
Times: 10am-4.00pm.

Also available
Workshops during Hallowe'en and Christmas holidays.
School Art and Craft Activity Days from March to June

Primary

EDUCATION IN THE MEDIA

Teacher college mergers proposed

September 06, 2012

An international review group, chaired by Pasi Sahlberg from Finland, has suggested that the 19 publicly funded teacher education colleges be merged into six specialist education centres. This plan has been approved by Education Minister Ruairi Quinn.

The focus of the review, commissioned by the Higher Education Authority (HEA) on behalf of Minister Quinn, was on improving pre-service training for primary and second-level teachers rather than cutting costs.

The recommendations include moves to have students of some smaller colleges take lectures in nearby larger colleges, while changes to overall governance may also occur.

The review says the standard of applicants for teacher training courses is among the highest in the world, but a lack of jobs may deter top people from applying in future.

"Where there is an oversupply of teachers, with the consequent reduction in opportunities for employment, it may not be possible to continue to attract high calibre entrants into teaching," the review panel writes.

The report of the review group also recommends use of more full-time research-focused lecturers over experienced teachers hired as part-time lecturers.

Minister Quinn has already sanctioned the extension of degrees for primary teaching from three to four-years and the postgraduate course for second-level teaching from one year to two.

Many of the proposed groupings are already in talks about mergers and some within the six recommended partnerships have strong existing ties.
Proposed connections

Dublin City University, St Patrick's College Dublin, and Mater Dei Institute of Education (in talks with Church of Ireland College of Education).
Trinity College, Marino Institute of Education, University College Dublin, National College of Art and Design.
NUI Maynooth and Froebel College, Dublin.
University of Limerick, Mary Immaculate College, and Limerick Institute of Technology.
University College Cork and Cork Institute of Technology.
NUI Galway and St Angela's College Sligo.

www.irishexaminer.com/archives/2012/0906/world/teacher-college-mergers-aim-to-maintain-standard-206588.html

Music Conference tackles inclusion

September 26, 2012

A National Music Education Conference, held in Trinity College on September 26, looked at issues influencing inclusion and participation in music of children in Ireland.

A wide range of musicians, researchers and experts in the field of music education attended the conference, which discussed ways of increasing inclusion in music education so that all children and young people could benefit from this type of personal development, engagement with communities, and participation in society.

The conference was organised by a coalition of partners: Music Generation, St Patrick's College Drumcondra, Mary Immaculate College Limerick, Trinity College Dublin and Irish Music Education.

Keynote speaker **Dr Emer Smyth**, co-author of the ESRI report on the effect music education can have across all aspects of children's lives, said:

"Research has shown that access to cultural activities – including music – within and outside of school enhances children's development.
"Participation in the cultural life of their community is every child's right. However, children's access to cultural activities often depends on their socio-economic background and on where they live.

"It is vital to enhance children's access to these activities so that they have the opportunity to flourish."

Rosaleen Molloy, Director of Music Generation said: "The conference has highlighted the benefits of bringing music into the lives of children and young people in 21st century Ireland"

www.educationmatters.ie/2012/09/26/music-education-conference-tackles-inclusion-and-participation/

A watershed year

Dr Fionnuala Waldron *Dean of Education in St Patrick's College, Drumcondra.*

Change and transformation in primary initial teacher education in Ireland

This year has seen the implementation of profound and transformational change in the teacher education sector in Ireland, at programme level and at structural level.

Having sought the extension of the Bachelor of Education programme from three to four years for over a decade, its announcement as national policy in 2010 as part of the draft literacy and numeracy framework, which was finalised in 2011, was universally welcomed within the teacher education sector (DES, 2011). It was followed by a raft of policy documents relating to teacher education along the continuum, including new guidelines and criteria for initial teacher education (Teaching Council, 2011a, b). Many elements of the new criteria were both expected and welcome:
- the extension of school placement to 30 weeks;
- the emphasis on reflection and research;
- recognition of the importance of diversity, inclusion and equality-related issues;
- the renewed emphasis on early childhood and on areas such as digital learning;
- the increased emphasis on areas of national priority, including literacy, mathematics and the teaching of Irish.

The creation of the new programmes across the sector gave rise to a period of intense engagement with the practice of teacher education. Teacher educators welcomed the opportunities to develop new courses which captured both the learnings gained from their own research in an Irish context and from international good practice.

Last summer the new programmes, having undergone university accreditation, were presented to the Teaching Council for professional accreditation. The accreditation process proved to be both rigorous and fair; it should work well as a mechanism for maintaining the quality of provision in initial teacher education into the future once it has been applied across all programmes.

Last summer also witnessed the structural review of the state-funded initial teacher education sector, led by Finnish educationalist Pasi Sahlberg. As well as recommending a re-organisation of the sector which reduced the number of discrete providers, the review endorsed a model of university-based initial teacher education and research-based practice and highlighted the pressing need for a regulated supply model if the 'high calibre of entrants to ITE in Ireland' was to be maintained (International Review Panel, 2012, p. 19).

Having spent over a year designing, writing and accrediting the new BEd programme, last September saw the first cohort of undergraduate students coming through the doors. While the programmes offered by the five colleges of education who provide undergraduate primary teacher education in Ireland all meet the same criteria and share their underlying principles and pedagogical approaches, each provider has created its own unique blend of programme

B Ed students interact with children in the classroom during their teaching practice placements

elements, offering diversity and a spread of expertise across the system.

In St Patrick's College, we worked to embed a range of practices across our programme. The extension of the programme to four years allowed us to adopt a spiralled model which, similar to the structure of the primary curriculum, enables student teachers to revisit concepts and develop skills in ways that are increasingly complex and in greater depth as they progress through the programme.

Thus, the programme begins with two foundational years, where students are introduced to core knowledge, ideas and competences across areas of learning relevant to children's lives and to how they engage with the world.

Student teachers develop their understanding of how children learn across a range of key areas such as mathematics, literacy and language and in a range of diverse contexts. Using approaches such as enquiry-based learning, experiential learning and co-operative learning, student teachers spend much of their time engaging in interactive, dialogical seminars where approaches to teaching and learning are modelled, experienced, analysed, practised and discussed. Understanding and promoting children's creativity across the curriculum and through arts-based education provide an important focus in this formative stage of the programme.

A new feature of our programme is the scaffolding of student teachers' reflective capacities through small-group tutorials in the first two years, and through online collaborative communities of learning in later years. As they progress through the programme, student teachers will deepen and develop their knowledge and understanding, building a wide and flexible repertoire of skills, an orientation towards enquiry-based practice and an appreciation of the complexity of teaching.

Over the course of the four years, their understanding of themselves as students, student teachers and emerging professionals will grow, responding to and shaping their experiences in schools and classrooms and in the many reflective and collaborative spaces which they will experience in college.

The extension of school placement to 30 weeks in schools provides increased opportunities for students to engage in school life, to become part of school communities and to make strong and dynamic connections between their experiences in college and the real life contexts of classrooms.

This immersion in the lives of schools is premised on the idea of schools as partners in the process of teacher education. St Patrick's College has been engaged in developing partnerships with schools over many years and we are deeply appreciative of the support offered to us in our work as teacher educators.

For our students, having the guidance and expertise of experienced teachers as mentors and role models is invaluable. Conscious of the complexity of school life, and of the increasingly demanding environment in which schools operate, we acknowledge the ongoing support of our partners in teacher education and their whole hearted and generous engagement with the potential of this new model.

Another important feature of the new programme is the opportunity offered to students to specialise in areas of their own choice. According to the Teaching Council criteria, up to 20 per cent of the programme could be in the form of elective components. In St Patrick's College, we had an existing tradition of humanities subjects taken to degree level as part of the BEd and of education-based electives. In the new programme, the College is offering a broader range of education and humanities major specialisms, as well as the more traditional electives in education which are now termed minor specialisms.

The new major specialisms in education are in areas such as Physical Education, Early Childhood Education, Biology and Science Education, Human Development and Special and Inclusive Education. These specialisms will offer new expertise to the system in the years to come. In addition, staff members are research-active and new learning and insights into children's learning, teacher education and school contexts which emerge from that research are factored into our programmes on an ongoing basis, ensuring that all elements of the programme are responsive to the needs of schools, children and society.

We are engaged currently in keeping a critical eye on how student teachers respond to new modules and practices, monitoring the impact of increased opportunities for reflection and research offered by the extended programme. This ongoing monitoring and review is essential to maintain the quality and relevance of all programmes.

Rolling out extended programmes in a context where the resources for teacher education and for schools have been seriously reduced has presented a significant challenge for all providers. The level and pace of change across the education sector has exacerbated that challenge. Yet, at its heart, education as a practice is future-oriented, constructive and optimistic. Despite the constraints, we remain hopeful for the years ahead.

References
Department of Education and Skills (2011). *Literacy and Numeracy for Learning and Life: The National Strategy to Improve Literacy and Numeracy among Children and Young people 2011-2020.* Dublin: Author.
International Review Panel (2012). *Structure of Initial Teacher Education Provision in Ireland:Review conducted on behalf of the Department of Education and Skills.* Dublin: DES.
Teaching Council of Ireland (2011a). *Policy on the continuum of teacher education.* Dublin: Author.
Teaching Council of Ireland (2011b). *Initial teacher education: Criteria and guidelines for programme providers.* Dublin: Author.

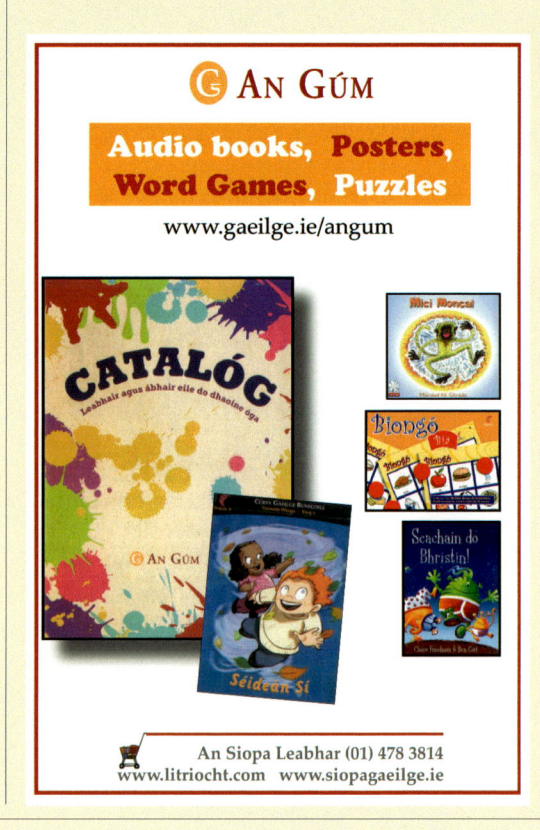

Primary

EDUCATION IN THE MEDIA

Teaching college plans for expansion

September 29, 2012

THE LARGEST teacher training college in the State will provide the very best teachers to all the schools of the nation: Catholic, Protestant, dissenter and multi-denominational, according to its new president.

In his inauguration address, Dr Daire Keogh, president of St Patrick's College, Drumcondra, also warned of the "fatal tendency" in the current climate to focus narrowly on the utility of education – and a failure to appreciate the difference between an "education society" and an "education economy".

He noted how the college – managed by Archbishop of Dublin Dr Diarmuid Martin – was first to offer an ethics and education course as an alternative to the denominational pathway to the bachelor of education.

"We are pleased to offer a certificate in ethical and multi-denominational education in partnership with Educate Together, which addresses the needs of teachers working in, or wanting to work in the growing multi-denominational sector."

Dr Keogh, a noted historian, said the college was determined to press ahead with plans to join with Dublin City University (DCU) and Mater Dei in creating a new Institute of Education under the umbrella of DCU at Drumcondra.

He was pleased that the Church of Ireland College of Education was also engaged in the process. He said the scale and capacity of the institute would be unequalled in Ireland and the UK.

Including all parties, the DCU institute at Drumcondra will have an academic staff of 100, 3,000 undergraduate students, 600 on masters track and 90 doctoral students.

www.irishtimes.com/news/teaching-college-plans-for-growing-sector-1.540610

First Communion to switch to parishes

October 01, 2012

MAJOR CHANGES in how children are prepared for First Communion in Dublin will see a shift from the school to the parents and parish. A new Catholic Church policy document to be published today also seeks to curb the excessive spending and celebrations surrounding the event.

Greater parental involvement will mean more regular attendance at Sunday Masses for families during the preparatory year and mandatory production of a child's baptismal certificate by the previous September 30th. It is also likely that smaller groups of children will receive their First Communion, and at Sunday Mass in their own parish.

The new policy will root First Communion and First Reconciliation (Confession) more firmly in the parish and will, in general, take place at Sunday Mass. This is to stress First Communion is not a private celebration but a welcome to the parish liturgical community.

Parishes will also actively encourage families to avoid extravagance in the celebrations.

www.irishtimes.com/newspaper/ireland/2012/1001/1224324667468.html

Archbishop Diarmuid Martin launches new guidelines on First Communion

Induction for Newly Qualified Teachers (NQTs)

Billy Redmond, *National Co-ordinator for the Induction Programme for Teachers*

The programme offers professional, pedagogical and personal support to NQTs in the first year of teaching

The National Induction Programme for Teachers (NIPT) was established in 2010 to support Newly Qualified Teachers (NQT) as they enter the teaching profession at primary and post-primary levels.

From its beginning as a pilot project in 2002, the programme has developed significantly over the years, and in 2011 became a cross-sectoral programme encompassing both primary and post-primary strands. The objective of the Induction Programme for newly qualified teachers is to offer systematic professional, pedagogical and personal support to NQTs in their first year teaching.

Structure
The NIPT is under the auspices of the Teacher Education Section in the Department of Education and Skills (DES) and is managed by a cross-sectoral consultative group and a management committee. The work of the NIPT is supported on three levels; by mentors at school level, by facilitators at Education Centre level and by Associates (who are facilitators and mentors) who undertake school visits and develop resources and materials.

People
Billy Redmond, Post-Primary, (the author of this article) and Mary Burke, Primary, are National Co-ordinators of the NIPT. The programme is cross-sectoral with Billy and Mary working collaboratively to ensure a sharing and exchange of knowledge, skills and experience across both sectors. The professional dialogue, engagement and reflection on practice, within the cross-sectoral context, facilitate and enrich the teaching and learning experiences for all involved with the programme.

Support
The NIPT provides support in five different ways:
1. School-Based Support - support at school level by a trained mentor
2. Workshop Programme - now a Teaching Council requirement towards full registration
3. School Visits - support for NQTs, mentors and principals by NIPT Associates
4. Website Support - www.teacherinduction.ie
5. Professional Support Groups - additional forums to develop and reflect on the content of a workshop or to provide support in a particular area identified by an NQT/s.

The first year
Induction is seen as a critical phase in the professional life of a newly qualified teacher (NQT) between Initial Teacher Education (ITE) and Continuing Professional Development (CPD) on the continuum of teacher education. According to the Teaching Council (Ireland) the continuum of teacher education can be described as:

'The formal and informal educational and developmental activities in which teachers engage, as life-long learners, during their teaching career. It encompasses initial teacher education, induction, early and continuing professional development and, indeed, late career support. (Teaching Council, 2011, p. 5).

Many NQTs experience challenges in their first year teaching, particularly in relation to mapping the theory from college to practice at classroom level. Amongst the areas that present challenges are classroom management, motivation, student evaluation and assessment and dealing with individual differences amongst pupils. (Aitken & Harford, 2010; Veenman, 1984; Vonk H., 1991; Grant, Carl, & Zeichner, 1981). The OECD report, The Teaching and Learning International Survey (TALIS), published in 2012, presents findings from new teachers in 2008 and noted:

'On average nearly one third of new teachers reported that they had a high level of need for professional development aimed at student discipline and behaviour problems, in addition, 22% of new teachers reported that they have a high level of need for professional development to improve their classroom management skills' (Jenson, 2012, p. 40).

TALIS went on to discuss the professional development needs of new teachers, referring to "the greater development needs of new teachers compared to more experienced teachers, particularly in the areas of student discipline and behaviour problems and classroom management" (Jenson, 2012, p. 50).

A whole school approach
The linking of the process of induction to the whole school is central to an effective programme of induction. The report on the pilot programme of teacher induction in Ireland notes "unless these issues are addressed in the overall context of the profession, induction provision will be an isolated form of support" (Killeavy, et al., 2006, p.3).

This support must, however, be contextualised because as Aitken and Harford (2010, p. 354) have noted "adopting a whole school approach to reducing the emotional vulnerability of NQTs in particular, and to lessening the anxiety, fear and isolation of teachers generally, is essential".

When considering the process of induction, the needs of the NQT should be central to the provision of a structure which links the learning and experiences of ITE to the classroom 'reality' and prepares a practice of CPD which will be a solid foundation for the duration of a teacher's career. This is reflected in the views of NQTs on CPD as seen in TALIS. The report notes that when thinking about CPD new teachers responded that they 'considered their professional development to have a large impact on their development as a teacher; this justifies the resources invested into professional development and provides a rationale for further investments into the development of new teachers' (Jenson, 2012, p. 39).

The report on the Pilot Programme of Teacher Induction in Ireland (2006) echoed many of these findings and went on to stress the need for a fundamental link between ITE and induction, noting that;

'Many of the needs of NQTs that emerged during the induction process arose primarily from problems associated with their transition from pre-service to classroom teaching, rather than deficiencies in their pre-service professional preparation' (Killeavy, et al., 2006).

School-based Mentor
One of the key supports for NQTs in the whole induction process is the school-based mentor. The role of the mentor in providing support for NQTs is critical in facilitating the induction process at school level. Mentors are nominated by the school principal, have a minimum of five years teaching experience and engage in a twenty-hour initial mentor training module with NIPT. Mentors provide opportunities at school level for NQTs to observe other teachers teaching, to be observed and to engage in a range of other school-based induction activities. In 2013-2014 Mentor Professional Networks will form part of the CPD Programme for the mentor in their local Education Centre on a termly basis, thus affording the mentor opportunities to engage in professional dialogue with other mentors, on the whole area of mentoring and induction.

Workshops in Education Centres
The Workshop Programme at Education Centre level facilitated by experienced teachers is another key support for NQTs. It delivers

twelve workshops to NQTs throughout the country in collaboration with the Association of Teacher Education Centres Ireland (ATECI). Four workshops are delivered on a cross-sectoral basis (to both Primary and Post-Primary teachers) and uniquely provide NQTs with opportunities to meet and share experiences with other NQTs from both sectors. The remaining eight workshops are sector-specific. All the workshops have a practical focus and the facilitators, who are experienced teachers, are NIPT trained. Many facilitators are school-based mentors which enriches their role in facilitating the workshops. In all workshops NQTs participate in a wide range of activities from role-plays to scenario-based discussion and reflection on professional practice and other related workshop activities. At each workshop NQTs receive and use a reflective workbook which has been specially developed by the NIPT to accompany each presentation. From July 2012 attendance at the NIPT Workshop Programme became a requirement for all NQTs, as a result of a decision taken by the Teaching Council in May 2012. In April 2013 the Teaching Council announced that NQTs must attend 10 out of the 12 workshops to fulfil this requirement. The role of the facilitator in facilitating the workshop programme at Education Centre level is integral to the effectiveness of the Workshop Programme.

Co-operative, sustained and embedded in school system

Looking at CPD in the 21st century, Schollaert discusses the different levels that CPD needs to operate from for it to be effective, and describes it as: 'Teacher led, a continuous process of on the job learning, inextricably linked to pupil learning, grounded in reflection, a sustained co-operative effort and embedded in institutional development' (Schollaert R. , 2011, p. 26).

The facilitators currently are part of a three-year support and training structure that involves peer observation, reflection and feedback, target setting and local, national and online CPD for all. Both school-based mentoring and facilitating workshops offer experienced teachers an opportunity to grow and develop whilst also sharing their knowledge and experience with NQTs.

Spark inspiration.

Promethean helps engage minds and inspire ideas with ingenious technologies that transform the way we learn, teach and collaborate.

For more information please visit: www.PrometheanWorld.com

EDUCATION IN THE MEDIA

Public sector numbers must "fall faster"

October 12, 2012

Taoiseach Enda Kenny warned that public sector numbers needed to be reduced at a faster rate and payroll costs significantly cut in order for the Government to meet its budget target next year.

Mr Kenny made the comments to trade union leaders yesterday and said further moves to cut the public sector bill would include fast-tracking changes to work practices in health as well as reforms in local government.

Union leaders and managers were told of the measures after Mr Kenny convened a meeting of the Croke Park implementation body.

The talks came as departments examined proposals by Public Expenditure Minister Brendan Howlin to abolish nearly 90 allowances for workers which are not considered value for money or are outdated.

An Taoiseach Enda Kenny

Unions immediately indicated they would fight the proposed cuts, which in some cases will only deduct a few euro from workers. But other allowances are viewed as core pay, such as those for gardaí and teachers.

The categories of teacher allowances to be prioritised for elimination currently cost almost €8m a year, including the €2.4m claimed by most principals for their role as board of management secretary, ranging from over €500 to almost €1,600. Almost €3m a year is paid to 1,850 teachers for teaching through Irish, and almost 800 teachers may lose a €3,063 allow-ance for working in Gaeltacht areas.

The Croke Park talks last night concluded with no definitive figure or timeline given to both sides about the Government's renewed savings effort.

A Government spokesman said ...the Government was now facing "extraordinarily difficult choices to meet its expenditure targets for the 2013 budget".

"The Government will only be able to meet these targets if it can significantly reduce payroll costs in 2013 by fully maximising the potential of the agreement."

Unions were also told that talks on cutting allowances "must be brought to a swift conclusion".

Both sides were told that employee numbers needed to be reduced at a faster rate, including through a new round of redundancies. State bodies would be amalgamated or closed, unions were also told.

However, unions will oppose the allowances being axed. The Irish National Teachers' Organisation general secretary Sheila Nunan said allowances were part of core teacher pay. "Unilateral action by government on core pay would be a breach of the agreement," she said.

Public allowances facing the chop

EDUCATION

- Allowances to be cut relate to claims and expenses for uniforms, a shoe allowance, and a clothing allowance, among others.

- Teaching through Irish: €1,583, paid to 1,634 primary and 220 secondary teachers. It cost €2.9m in 2011.

- Stocktaking allowance: Paid to VEC staff who do an annual stocktake of equipment.

- Telephone allowance: Paid to general operatives toward cost of phone if needed to return to the workplace out-of-hours.

- July provision scheme preparatory: Paid to special school and class teachers to prepare summer programme for children with autism and pupils with learning difficulties.

- Allowance for principals who act as secretary to board of management postprimary: Paid since 2007 but not claimed by all principals. Can claim €523 to €1,572: Total cost €455,000 in 2011.

www.irishexaminer.com/ireland/kenny-public-sector-numbers-need-to-fall-faster-210628.html

Primary Principals hit hard

Michael Gallagher *Principal, Scoil Einde, Galway*

Staffing, funding and legislative changes make life difficult for Primary Principals

Principal teachers in Ireland face an ever more demanding workplace ranging from instructional leadership, through personnel and human resource management, to the administration of ever diminishing resources.

In most cases all of these responsibilities land on the desk of the principal along with an ever increasing number of administrative and managerial tasks.

At the same time, principals are being urged to focus more on the educational leadership aspect of their role. Such demands are generally made without reference to (and probably without any knowledge of) the range of duties that already fall to the principal and with little acknowledgement of the limited time, guidance, support or backup to enable principals to carry out any of these duties.

No workable solution yet found
As a result, increasing numbers of principals report workload pressures and stress because of their inability to cope with such demands. They detail anxiety about being held accountable for workload over which increasingly they have less and less control, which in turn leads to a general negativity about the role of school leadership. It has to be said that such reports are not unique to Ireland but are found in many countries. A second thing that these countries appear to have in common is that no one has yet found a workable solution to the increasing demands on principals.

Unfair all round
This is obviously unfair to the individuals concerned but equally, given the recognised importance of principal teachers to the education system, the effective administration of the education system is compromised by this overloading of key individuals in the process.

Lack of role definition
At the core of this problem is a lack of role definition for the Principal teacher enforceable by a contract of employment, and a lack of support/resources to enable the job of leadership to be effectively undertaken. Principals find themselves operating in an arena dominated by government attempts to reduce spending on education. As a result they are increasingly forced to give more and more time to the position.

Insufficient training for volunteer management board
Each primary school has a Board of Management yet all Board members, except the principal, are volunteers. There is no requirement to hold particular expertise or skills in order to serve on a board, and training for BOM members is inadequate. The responsibilities of Boards have increased dramatically in volume and in complexity in recent years leading to some reluctance to volunteer or become involved. The result of this reluctance is that there are significant and growing responsibilities and pressures on principal teachers to be experts in all areas of school governance.

Fundraising a necessary component of Principal's job

Spending per pupil at primary level is inadequate and this has a significant effect on the working lives of principal teachers who must regularly seek additional funding at local level through fundraising or voluntary contributions and make scarce resources stretch while maintaining services to pupils and local communities. Compensating for inadequate and decreasing state funding across all areas of school income/expenditure is a significant workload issue for all school leaders and an increasing source of stress. Increasingly, principal teachers find themselves devoting time to juggling the payment of key operating costs and explaining or even defending the non-replacement or non-purchase of key educational resources.

Explosion of legislation has changed role of Principal

The recent past in Irish education has been characterised by an explosion of legislation covering almost every aspect of the system. The Education Act (1998), the Education (Welfare) Act (2000) and the Education for Persons with Special Educational Needs Act (2004) are pieces of complex detailed legislation governing key aspects of school life. In addition, schools now operate under other significant pieces of legislation including the Health and Safety Act, Equality legislation, data protection and child protection measures.

All of these have significantly changed the role of school principal. A key point is that most legislation not only requires compliance but written policies or statements and/or written records of proof of compliance. Responsibility for the oversight and very often, because of staffing cutbacks, the direct operational responsibility lies with the school leaders.

Increased quality assurance mechanisms and accountability

The quality assurance aspect of school leadership has increased significantly in recent years. Schools are now held accountable through a number of external and internal evaluations. Among the quality assurance mechanisms imposed on schools in recent times are School Development Planning, School Self Evaluation, Whole School Evaluations, Incidental Evaluations, Thematic Evaluations, National Assessments, International Assessments and Standardised Assessments. These developments mirror other countries where there has been a move away from a single form of quality assurance of schools towards a range of internal and external measures. In Ireland in recent years there has been a significant increase in the high stakes nature of the forms of accountability brought about primarily through the publication of school reports.

Mountain of paperwork relating to special needs education

There have been significant developments in the area of special education. Twenty per cent of primary schools have special classes or units attached catering for pupils with physical, sensory, emotional or learning disabilities. In addition, there are more than 10,000 pupils with special needs integrated into ordinary classes who are provided with additional teaching resources. Most of the resources - while welcome - are not automatically given to schools but must be negotiated usually by the principal teacher. Behind every extra hour of special needs support is a veritable mountain of paperwork.

More diverse teaching staff to be managed

Principals have responsibility to lead more diverse and specialised teaching teams as well as a significant number of non-teaching staff such as special needs assistants. There is no additional school management support for principal teachers required to manage these staff numbers and leadership allowances do not reflect these increased numbers. In addition, government does not provide additional funding to schools for pupils with special needs who are mainstreamed leaving schools to source additional learning material from regular budgets.

The burden on Teaching Principals

Approximately two thirds of primary schools are led by a principal who also has a full-time teaching responsibility. This is perhaps the major challenge facing school leadership in Ireland today as ever increasing leadership, administrative and management responsibilities have to be undertaken against a full-time teaching responsibility.

The job of Teaching Principal is undertaken in addition to the full time teaching responsibilities, preparation of work, assessment and marking of pupils work, extra-curricular activities and engaging with parents as every other teacher. For this work the principal of a 4 teacher school gets an annual allowance of €9,328.

Nor can this work be easily shared among colleagues. The moratorium on posts of responsibility is having a significant effect on many primary schools. In March 2009 about 53% of teachers had posts of responsibility. This has since reduced to about 39%. Responsibility for much of this work falls back on the principal teacher and includes increasingly complex administrative, managerial, pastoral, leadership, educational demands.

Funding
Many Irish primary schools are experiencing a funding crisis. In this and subsequent school years, many will find it very difficult to make ends meet due to a 12 per cent reduction since 2009/'10 with further reductions planned. This does not include the minor repairs grant paid annually to schools to allow for basic repair and maintenance.

All of these funding cuts come at a time when schools face further increases in running costs including gas, oil, electricity and insurance, the imposition of water charges, fire & intruder alarm monitoring & servicing etc. Primary schools already on a very tight budget are facing a financial crisis.

Conclusion
Given the above set of circumstances, it is easy to see where the workload pressures are coming from and how they impact on principal teachers. What is less obvious is what action the Department of Education and Skills - which ultimately bears responsibility - will take.

EDUCATION IN THE MEDIA

Retired teachers still getting the jobs

October 13, 2012

Despite strict new rules designed to ensure that substitution work goes to unemployed, newly qualified teachers, retired teachers are still being employed in primary schools.

Since the start of the school year -- only six weeks ago -- at least 140 retired teachers have covered absences such as maternity leave and sick leave.

The substitutes may be employed for as a little as a day, but it denies opportunities to newly qualified teachers who rely on substitution work to get on the career ladder.

Strict new regulations oblige principals to use retired teachers only if they have made every effort to find an unemployed graduate to fill the post.

The rules were tightened to ensure that any available work was given to the 1,800 new primary teachers graduating each year. There were about 600 new primary teaching jobs this year.

Education Minster Ruairi Quinn said it was "disappointing that boards of management in some schools continue to hire retired teachers instead of unemployed or newly qualified teachers".

He said the department directive on the matter was "unequivocal".

Mr Quinn said a department circular set out the position clearly and also outlined the very limited circumstances in which an unqualified or retired teacher may be hired.

Shortages
The Irish Primary Principals Network (IPPN) said despite the oversupply of teachers nationally, there were often shortages of qualified teachers in some pockets of the country and some schools were left with no option but to employ retired teachers.

Mr Quinn provided the figure on the retired teachers in response to a parliamentary question from Fianna Fail education spokesperson Charlie MacConalogue.

www.independent.ie/lifestyle/education/retired-staff-still-getting-jobs-ahead-of-new-teachers-28892923.html

AWARD WINNING HEALTHY SCHOOL LUNCHES

WINNER OF THE Q MARK FOR HYGIENE & FOOD SAFETY FOR IRISH FOOD PRODUCERS

WINNER OF THE Q MARK FOR QUALITY MANAGEMENT SYSTEMS FOR IRISH FOOD PRODUCERS

GLANMORE FOODS
Healthy Lunches

A FAMILY BUSINESS, IRISH OWNED, IRISH SUPPLIED, IRISH DELIVERED

PROMOTING IRISH EXCELLENCE, SUPPORTING IRISH JOBS, THE MARK OF QUALITY

guaranteed irish
Proud Member of Guaranteed Irish

We produce a wide variety of products on site daily, ensuring freshness, quality and the best variety in our children's lunch bags

All pastas are cooked fresh daily.

All bakery products are baked fresh daily.

All sandwiches/rolls are made fresh daily.

All sliced fruit packs are prepared fresh daily.

Glanmore Foods: Unit 3, Northwest Business Park, Blanchardstown, Dublin 15.
Tel: 01 897 6026 Fax: 01 897 6269 Email: sales@glanmorefoods.ie
www.glanmorefoods.ie

EDUCATION IN THE MEDIA

New school patrons 'by September'

October 23, 2012

PRIMARY SCHOOLS could be under new patronage by next September if sufficient numbers of parents decide they want it, Minister for Education Ruairí Quinn has said.

Parents in five areas where there are a considerable number of primary schools will be given that choice through an online survey.

The parents of both preschool and primary-school children in Arklow, Castlebar, Tramore, Trim and Whitehall are being asked to identify their preferred school patron. They will be asked to complete surveys stating their preferences for the type of local school they would like their children to attend.

Minister for Education and Skills Mr. Ruairí Quinn

The results will be presented to the Catholic Church, which has said that if enough parents in certain areas decide they want a different patron for a school, they will hand over that patronage.

The move is the first step in a process in which schools in 44 areas could be divested of the control of the Catholic Church. The areas in question are those where there is a stable population and a clear demand for a greater diversity of school types.

The other 39 areas will be surveyed from next month. Mr Quinn said the purpose of the survey of the five areas was to ensure the online process was carried out properly before it was extended to other areas.

He expects the results will be available by the end of the year and the first change of patronage will happen "next September or the following September" if everything goes according to agreed procedures.

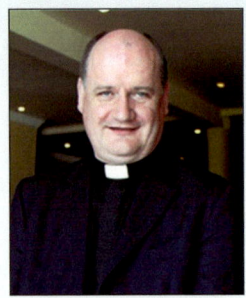

Fr Michael Drumm Chariman of the Catholic Schools Partnership

Fr Michael Drumm, chairman of the Catholic Schools Partnership, said they would abide by the survey results, even though they would have preferred a paper rather than an online survey because many parents do not have access to the internet.

"We would of course facilitate change where there is real demand for it," he told RTÉ Radio's News at One programme.

He said that if only a small number of parents respond to the survey, the partnership would take that as a signal that the rest were happy with the status quo. He also stressed the survey could not be regarded as a plebiscite or a vote on future patronage.

The National Parents Council urged parents to participate in the survey so the results could truly reflect the wishes of the local communities.

The bodies which have expressed interest in becoming patrons of divested schools in the five areas are An Foras Pátrúnachta, the patron body for Gaelscoileanna in Ireland; Educate Together; VECs; the National Learning Network; and the Redeemed Christian Church of God.

The survey process will be overseen by the independent New Schools Establishment Group.

www.irishtimes.com/newspaper/ireland/2012/1023/1224325578365.html

---

Patrons subject to strict rules

October 23, 2012

PATRON bodies vying to take over primary schools from the Catholic Church will be subject to strict rules about how much they spend on their campaigns, what they can say about each other and where they say it.

A limit of €300 has been set for spending on a campaign by an individual patron in any single area, while an overall ceiling of €4,000 for each patron applies. They have been warned that no subjective statements about, direct commentary on or description of schools under other forms of patronage should be made. The code also bans door-to-door calls on parents and other direct canvassing means of communications.

www.independent.ie/national-news/patrons-subject-to-strict-polling-rules-3266783.html

EDUCATION IN THE MEDIA

Teachers protest outside Dáil over new wage structure

October 24, 2012

THOUSANDS of protesting teachers have warned they would fight further education cuts that target the most vulnerable.

Students and newly qualified men and women also joined the rally (which was organised by the INTO, ASTI and TUI) at the Dail to demand equal pay for equal work after the government slashed their starting salaries.

Gerry Breslin, president of second-level school union ASTI, told about 2,000 supporters that education cuts affect children and young people's lives today and in the future.

"They affect student well-being and student attainment," he said. "They hinder economic recovery. They hurt the vulnerable the most.

"Our children, our young people, our young teachers are being hurt. It is essential that we send a clear message today. There can be no more cuts to education."

Anne Fay, president of the Irish National Teachers' Organisation (INTO), said primary schools were already on the breadline.

"Education funding has fallen off a cliff in recent years while the system is coping with more and more pupils every year," she said.

"The school system is at breaking point and we need to send a message to government today that education cuts don't heal."

The unions - backed by several politicians - criticised failings to tackle teacher unemployment and cuts to the pay of new teachers and allowances of others.

Yvonne Rossiter, a newly qualified teacher, said the treatment of new teachers is everyone's concern.

"If we devalue the work of one teacher we short change every student and every teacher in our schools," she said.

Elsewhere TUI President Gerry Craughwell warned education cuts don't heal.

"Any further cuts to the education system will have a profound effect on our society, on our young people and on our chances of economic recovery," he added.

"We currently have a situation whereby many of our talented, enthusiastic new teachers and lecturers are attempting to survive in part-time positions, with mere fragments of jobs.

"They are struggling to build a career on incomes which don't provide a basic standard of living."

www.independent.ie/irish-news/teachers-protest-outside-dail-over-new-wage-structure-28823091.html

Newly qualified teachers demand equal pay for equal work after government slashes their starting salaries

'Value for Money' Review of Small Schools

Dr Ken Fennelly *Secretary General, Synod Board of Education and Education Officer, Republic of Ireland.*

Anxiety generated in 2011 by announcement of 'vfm' review has proved well founded

Although it is the case that "value for money" reviews are a feature of the on-going review of operations in all government departments, the announcement in January 2011 that a value for money review (or "vfm") of "small schools" caused much anxiety across the Irish primary education system.

In the first instance it was noted that an expenditure review of the Small and Rural Schools Initiative and Permanent Accommodation Initiative was published as recently as 2006. That Report reviewed the Department of Education and Skills initiatives regarding devolved funding which, beginning in 1997, devolved "authority and responsibility on the SMAs for capital investment, and it was well received by the school authorities". It also stated that "the approach of the Department of Education and Science to small primary schools is based on current Government policy: that one-teacher schools with twelve pupils should be allocated a second teacher. The clear import of this policy is that the existing network of small schools should be supported and maintained where possible".

This policy was given practical support through the Small Schools Initiative (SSI) whereby funding was allocated (€5 million in 2005) and autonomy given to schools of four teachers or less to carry out works of necessity. The announcement of a vfm on "small schools" in January 2011, coming as it did so soon after the 2006 Report (and in the wake of the "McCarthy" Report), caused concerns to arise that the Government was of a mind to review this policy of supporting "small schools".

Budget 2012
These fears were well founded. The Budget statement of 5th December 2011 outlined reforms to the teacher allocation schedule. This provision of Budget 2012 incrementally increased the thresholds by which schools receive their second and subsequent teachers based on pupil numbers. Its effect has been to create a situation whereby a school with nineteen pupils or less will only receive one teacher. This marks a clear reversal of Government policy in relation to the support of smaller schools.

Budget 2012 also withdrew the "minor works" grant which was the key component of the devolved funding initiatives mentioned above. This also marked a reversal of Government policy in relation to granting "authority and responsibility" to schools regarding funding and maintaining the school building.

Economic factors are the driving force
Funding is therefore the major driver for the Minister for Education and Skills and his Department officials in relation to the future of small schools. Indeed there is no doubt that the costs related to small schools are significant. The Department of Education and Skills estimates the annual cost of educating a child in a one teacher school as €13,080 per annum

as compared to €2,973 per annum in a four teacher school. These costs are significant and it would be disingenuous to ignore them. It is worth highlighting however, that these or similar costs were known in 2006 when Government policy was to support one, two and three teacher schools. Clearly the economic climate had cooled significantly in the intervening period but the shift in policy demonstrates that economic factors are the driving force in policy formulation in relation to primary education, rather than seeking to provide accessible primary education and a high quality reflected in a low pupil teacher ratio.

Yet, a report published in April 2012 by the Inspectorate of the Department of Education and Skills indicates that there is no significant difference in learning outcomes for pupils in smaller as compared to larger primary schools.

The case for small schools

"Should 'small' schools continue to be supported?" will likely be a key question that will be addressed in the vfm Report on small primary schools which, it is understood, will be published during the summer period of 2013. While it is obvious that the vfm Review will answer this question from a financial perspective, it could be argued that the answer to that key question regarding small primary schools very much depends upon perspective.

As mentioned above, from a learning outcomes perspective, the Inspectorate concluded that pupils learning outcomes are not adversely affected by the fact that they attend a school with a lower pupil teacher ratio. Nor are their learning outcomes affected by the likelihood that their class will be a multi-grade class.

From an educational perspective therefore, a smaller class size optimises the level of attention that the pupil can receive from the teacher and in that regard it is not difficult to understand why parents of children in smaller schools are happy with the levels of education their children receive and also it is not surprising to find this evidenced in reports of the Inspectorate.

Benefits for the community

From a community perspective the importance of retaining the primary school in the locality are obvious in terms of community cohesion. The primary school forms the backbone of the locality, along with the church, post office, Garda station, shop and petrol station. The community aspect of having a school is no doubt extremely important to local communities in areas where a school provides the life-blood to whole host of other community activities such as sports clubs and other leisure activities. As a support to the community and society in general, the value for money of having that school in its locality should not be underestimated or indeed under-valued based on a cold monitory rationalised basis. Rural communities are entitled and have an expectation of a level of services equal to those provided to urban based communities.

Minority religious situation

There is another perspective and it is that of the members of minority religious traditions within the State. The nature of religious minority communities is that they are small and, in the case of the mainstream Protestant denominations, contain the significant characteristic of being spatially dispersed across the country.

Note: You can read Dr Ken Fennelly's presentation to the Joint Committee on Education and Social Protection on July 3, 2013, on the subject of Small Schools and the Value for Money review, at dail.ie/parliament/media/.../K-Fennelly-Presentation--3-July-2013.doc

EDUCATION IN THE MEDIA

Educate Together pupils 50% Catholic

October 25, 2012

About half of pupils in schools managed by the multidenominational group Educate Together are Catholic.

That's according to a new Economic and Social Research Institute report, which also shows mothers in multidenominational schools are "as likely to describe themselves as very religious or spiritual" as mothers in Catholic schools.

A sizeable (30 per cent) Catholic intake was also found in minority faith (mostly Church of Ireland) schools. The report, 'School Sector Variation Among Primary Schools in Ireland', by ESRI researchers Merike Darmody, Professor Emer Smyth and Dr Selina McCoy, was published jointly by the ESRI and Educate Together. It provides new insights into the growing diversification of types of schools at primary level in Ireland.

It concludes that primary schools in Ireland have remained predominantly denominational, chiefly Catholic, in both ownership and management, despite demographic changes in recent decades.

At the same time, it states, increased diversity in the Irish population has contributed to a growing demand for new types of school that are multidenominational in character.

The report shows that while the population has become more diverse in recent years, student intake in the Catholic schools is still predominantly Catholic. It also finds school choice is constrained by the availability of places in the school of parents' choice. While there has been growth in pupil intake, this growth has been more marked in multi-denominational schools. Schools of patrons such as Educate Together are more likely than other school types to be oversubscribed, it says.

The report shows how the various primary school types differed in terms of social class background and maternal education levels. It says minority faith and multi-denominational schools had higher proportions of children from professional, managerial and technical backgrounds than Catholic schools.

Maternal education levels were higher in multidenominational schools than in minority faith or Catholic schools. This factor had a stronger impact on school selection than social class.

The research found most children liked their school and their teacher. Furthermore, pupils who were particularly positive about the school and teachers came from a variety of backgrounds.

www.irishtimes.com/newspaper/ireland/2012/1023/1224325578426.html

---

Low response to patronage survey

November 15, 2012

Fewer than 2,000 parents have responded to surveys on local school patronage in five areas where the possibility of handing over Catholic primary schools is to be considered.

Although official figures on the number of children in the areas are unknown, the responses to the Department of Education survey probably represent between one quarter and one third of those eligible to take part in Arklow, Co Wicklow; Castlebar, Co Mayo; Tramore, Co Waterford; Trim, Co Meath; and Whitehall in Dublin.

Education Minister Ruairi Quinn said the level of interest from parents was encouraging after the figures were released. The survey was open and to be completed online for three weeks up to last Friday.

The parents of 3,776 children answered the survey on current provision, whether they would prefer greater choice of school types, and, if so, which patron they would prefer for their children's school.

This represents about 40% of the 9,859 children attending schools in the five areas but the department said it does not know the numbers of children of pre-school ages whose parents were also open to taking part in the survey.

Comparing participation just to existing enrolments, the response rates range from 34% in Tramore to 41% in Castlebar.

Minister for Education Ruairí Quinn claimed the results in the five pilot areas showed a strong demand for change.

However, Fr Michael Drumm of the Catholic Schools Partnership said only a small percentage of parents in some areas favour changes to school patronage.

EDUCATION IN THE MEDIA

He claimed that only 25 per cent of relevant parents surveyed responded.

Fr Drumm said he could not understand why the Department of Education could not publish the exact statistic on the percentage of parents who participated. "I think people should look at the real figures. Take Arklow – those who want change are parents of 80 children in a school population of 1,965. That is only 4 per cent."

Mr Quinn's officials will now prepare a report on the outcomes and seek feedback from the patrons offering to run schools in these areas before deciding if any changes to the survey process are needed.

www.irishexaminer.com/archives/2012/1115/world/low-response-to-patronage-survey-214018.html

---

Patronage survey rolled out to 38 areas

January 14, 2013

The Department of Education is to extend the survey on school patronage to 38 areas around the country.

Parents will be asked what kind of primary school they want for their children as part of plans to divest a number of schools from the Catholic Church.

At present, 96% of primary schools are under church patronage, with more than 90% or approximately 3,000 schools under the remit of the Catholic Church.

If parents indicate they would like a wider choice of patron, then the Department of Education and Skills (DES) will ask existing patrons to come up with a plan to transfer some schools to other patron bodies.

The 38 areas being surveyed have 311 primary schools between them, or an average of around eight each. But the Department of Education says there are no primary schools in most of them besides those under the control of the local Catholic bishop or other religious patrons, and there is insufficient population growth for new schools to be built.

Kildare town has been removed from the list of areas being surveyed as an Educate Together school opened there in 2011 and a new gaelscoil is to be set up after evidence of demand put forward by all-Irish schools patron An Foras Pátrúnachta.

Both groups expressed interest in taking over any divested Catholic schools in most or all of the 38 remaining areas, with city or county vocational education committees interested in running primary schools in all of them.

Parents in three towns — Clonmel, Longford, and Monaghan — who would like more choice will also have the option of picking Rehab Group's National Learning Network as an alternative patron. The Redeemed Christian Church of God, a Nigerian-founded church, is interested in running schools in Cobh, Dublin 6, Longford, and Shannon.

The bodies which have indicated that they would like to become patrons of any divested schools in the identified areas are the VECs, An Foras Pátrúnachta, Educate Together and, in a small number of areas, the National Learning Network and the Redeemed Christian Church of God.

A wider information campaign is planned to promote the survey after the mixed response to the trial survey before Christmas.

The Department of Education will send leaflets to every home in each of the 38 towns and suburbs where they want to find out how much demand there is for alternatives to the current provision of primary schools almost exclusively under religious patronage.

A more extensive campaign of radio and newspaper advertising is also planned.

List of 38 areas to be surveyed
Ballina; Ballinasloe; Ballyfermot/ Chapelizod/ Palmerstown/ Cherry Orchard; Bandon; Birr; Buncrana; Carrick-on-Suir; Carrigaline; Celbridge; Clonmel; Cobh; Dublin 6; Dungarvan; Edenderry; Enniscorthy; Fermoy; Kells (Ceanannas); Killarney; Leixlip; Longford; Loughrea; Malahide; Monaghan;Nenagh; New Ross; Passage West;Portmarnock; Roscommon;Roscrea; Rush; Shannon; Skerries; Thurles; Tipperary; Tuam; Westport; Wicklow;.Youghal

www.irishexaminer.com/breakingnews/ireland/school-patronage-survey-rolled-out-across-38-areas-581081.html

www.irishexaminer.com/archives/2013/0114/world/efforts-to-boost-school-patronage-poll-awareness-219468.html

School Self Evaluation (SSE) in Primary Schools

Carmel Hume *Principal of Presentation National School, Terenure, Dublin.*

The School Self Evaluation process places trust in the professionalism of teachers

In October 2012 the Department of Education and Skills launched guidelines on school self-evaluation. These guidelines are designed to give schools a framework against which teachers can evaluate their work and improve teaching and learning.

The initiative had its roots in the Programme for Government (2011-2016) which contained a commitment to introduce self-evaluation into schools which would require schools to evaluate performance and publish information across a range of criteria. The National Literacy and Numeracy Strategy published a year previously requires schools to engage in self-evaluation and set targets for improvement.

In summary, over the next four years schools are expected to review three curriculum areas (literacy and numeracy being two) and draw up and implement a school improvement plan (SIP). As part of this review each school is expected to gather evidence from a number of sources such as standardised test results, other assessments and/or the views of teachers, parents and pupils. This is an important distinction between this process and school evaluation processes in other countries which are centred or focussed around the outcomes of standardised tests only.

Out of this process schools are required to develop a plan of action that recognises the schools strengths and areas where improvement is needed. The guidelines are flexible to enable account to be taken of local circumstances.

Respect for professionalism of teachers

A preliminary analysis of the guidelines is that the process places trust in the professionalism of teachers in different school settings. Every school is different and therefore schools are empowered to adapt or modify any tools they choose to use from the guidelines. It is not seen as a one size fits all exercise. Indeed in some schools, SSE will be significantly advanced and there will be no need for these guidelines.

SSE is a long term project made up of small manageable steps involving the whole school community. It is important to get the process working successfully rather than quickly. This measured approach is welcome given the scale of the work involved and the need to make sure the process of school self-evaluation gets off to a good start. Much education reform all over the world has floundered because schools were asked to bite off more than they can chew.

The guidelines explicitly advocate that SIPs are short documents and there appears to be general agreement that paperwork be kept to a manageable level. Schools have been warned about the danger of data overload.

The initiative is a little different from the usual prescriptive ones that land regularly on school principals' desks. In the first place the guidelines for schools are not a prescription of practice for every school but rather respects the professionalism of teachers.

School self-evaluation asks schools to look at their own teaching and learning, at what they do well and at what they need to work on to bring about improvement. It doesn't ask them to impose some externally determined artificial achievement targets to be met by a certain date.

Challenge of scarce resources
This work is well underway in many schools, particularly disadvantaged schools which have been doing this very well for years. But they did have advice and hands-on support from the Department, something that is less than generous in this initiative. Schools have suffered budgetary cutbacks. There is less money, fewer promoted teachers and less training for teachers. The Minister needs to make sure that schools have enough resources to do this job properly.

Case study
In my own school we began by examining numeracy and within that prioritised money as an area needing attention. We are now taking a more detailed look at where and why children are not doing so well when it comes to money numeracy. This involves all teachers testing children in aspects of money.

We also surveyed both parents and children about mathematics and got some very useful feedback. Most children like maths. Parents wanted suggestions from the school about games apps tips that they could use to help their children. They saw rote learning, especially tables, as important in developing maths skills. Pupils wanted to see more group work or co-operative learning in maths classes.

This work, and it is substantial, is being done in our school as part of the Croke Park Agreement where in all primary schools, teachers are working hours above and beyond their teaching day. More of the work is being done in the classrooms as part of teaching and learning.

None of this is to suggest that this is easy. Most schools are struggling with the moratorium suppressing promotion which impacts on the introduction of initiatives such as this. School self-evaluation must be small enough to fit into a school's Croke Park hours along with every other demand and hidden curriculum issues like bullying which all compete for limited teacher time.

System reform and investment needed
Like all initiatives its success will depend on system reform and investment in schools and teachers for the benefit of the children. This means issues like class size reductions and Early Childhood Education must be prioritised. There must be learning support for all children that need it especially in Mathematics. School budgets do not have adequate resourcing for classroom equipment and too much depends on parental contributions.

Nothing typifies this lack of support more than the poor state of schools ICT infrastructure.

Success will also be determined by how much the Department of Education and Skills steps up to the plate. There must be on-going research into what works and what doesn't and a sharing of that research. The over-crowded curriculum must be tackled and account taken of the hidden curriculum that schools must deal with every day.

If this is done then trust between schools and central administration will be established which will be good for the process.

Getting the focus right
As long as the focus remains on children and not compliance all will be well. A process that prioritises professional judgement over informed prescription will be welcomed.

So far, what we have learned is not to be over-ambitious. If improvement is going to be effective it must be realistic and achievable. There is a danger that in some schools, strengths could become overshadowed by weaknesses. Were this to happen it would defeat the whole purpose. Every school has significant strengths and areas of excellence which deserve to be recognised and celebrated.

Although we are only starting out on this journey we have already learned that the most important thing is to take small steps. School improvement - if it is to be successful - is not a sprint but a marathon.

EDUCATION IN THE MEDIA

New Action Plan on Bullying launched

January 29, 2013

New Action Plan on Bullying, launched in Dublin today (January 29) by Ministers Ruairí Quinn and Frances Fitzgerald, is welcomed by unions.

The Action Plan follows the Anti-Bullying Forum jointly held in May 2012 by Minister for Education and Skills Ruairí Quinn and Minister for Children and Youth Affairs Frances Fitzgerald. As part of that Forum Minister Quinn sought submissions from interested parties and established a working group to prepare an action plan on preventing and tackling bullying in schools.

Today's report from the Anti-Bullying Working Group makes it clear that preventing and tackling bullying requires support from parents and wider society and is not a problem schools can solve alone.

The Plan sets out twelve actions to help prevent and tackle bullying in primary and second level schools, which include the following:

- Support a media campaign focused on cyber bullying specifically targeted at young people as part of Safer Internet Day 2013;
- Establish a new national anti-bullying website;
- Begin development immediately of new national anti-bullying procedures for all schools. These will include an anti-bullying policy template and a template for recording incidents of bullying in schools. These should be in place by the start of the next school year;
- Devise a co-ordinated plan of training for parents and for school boards of management;
- Provide Department of Education and Skills support for the Stand Up! Awareness Week Against Homophobic Bullying organised by BeLonG To Youth Services;
- Review current Teacher Education Support Service provision to identify what training and Continuous Professional Development teachers may need to help them effectively tackle bullying;

As well as implementing the Action Plan, Minister Quinn announced that the Department of Education & Skills will be supporting a revision of the Stay Safe Programme for primary schools. The revised programme will address new forms of risk, including cyber bullying, and incorporate new research and best practice in the area of safeguarding children as well as changes and developments in the educational context in terms of policies, provision and curriculum.

At the launch of the Action Plan, Minister Quinn said he broadly accepted the proposed actions in the report and has requested his officials to ensure that work on implementation begins immediately in consultation with teachers, parents and management bodies at first and second-level.

He has ring-fenced €500,000 to support the implementation of the Action Plan on Bullying in 2013.

INTO general secretary Sheila Nunan also welcomed the report. She said that not all bullying happens in schools but most people look to schools to resolve it. Primary schools have shown they can be part of the solution, she said, but active involvement by others is also needed.

"This report sets out the need for others, particularly policy makers and parents, to be actively involved in tackling the problem. Recommendations in the report, if implemented and resourced, could improve the situation."

The Irish Secondary Students' Union (ISSU) added its voice in welcoming the report. The union has been strongly involved in developing the Action Plan and Equality Officer Mark Caffrey, member of the Anti-Bullying Working Group, is looking forward to its full implementation.

"Bullying is something which we know affects our students hugely – around one quarter of students are likely to have experienced some form of bullying in the past couple of months, and I'm delighted that an action plan to tackle this head on has been launched today. Bullying is a serious problem, so it needs to be taken seriously," Mark said.

"Schools need to be given the necessary supports in order to manage and prevent bullying in all forms, and we need to make sure that parents are aware of the role they can play in both preventing bullying, and intervening in an appropriate way where it is occurring. "Tackling homophobic bullying and cyber bullying are key focuses of this action plan, and we look forward to working with other partners to see it implemented".

The Plan is available to download at www.education.ie

EDUCATION IN THE MEDIA

New campaign – 'Put Education First'

February 09, 2013

A campaign is being launched aimed at changing legislation which "allows schools to discriminate against children and teachers on basis of religion."

The legislation in question is Section 7.3 (c) of the Equal Status Act 2000 and Section 37 of the Employment Equality Act.

According to the Integration Centre, the first of these laws allows schools to refuse children entry because of their parents' religious beliefs and can prevent children from going to school in their own neighbourhoods; while the second enables schools to hire and fire teachers based on their religion.

The Integration Centre points out that, as of the last twelve years, many schools have incorporated a 'Catholics First' stance into their admissions policy. This discrimination is unconstitutional, the Centre says, and contravenes international human rights law – yet it is protected by the legislation mentioned above.

The Integration Centre is calling on the Minister for Education & Skills Ruairí Quinn, who is clearly "committed to progressive reform", to change these laws.

www.educationmatters.ie/2013/02/05/new-campaign-put-education-first/

Report on primary school patronage

April 02, 2013

The report on the survey of parental preferences for primary school patronage was published today by the Department of Education.

Catholic bishops in 23 areas across the State have six months to provide detailed proposals on how they plan on divesting primary schools of their patronage.

Minister for Education Ruairí Quinn said this morning he expected Catholic bishops to cooperate in identifying suitable primary schools for the transfer of patronage. The Department of Education will send surveys to the patrons seeking an initial response after three months and a final response in six months, he said.

"I would hope and expect during that period a suitable school will be identified by them within the various towns and arrangements will be made for the orderly transfer of the patronage of that school back to the Department of Education," Mr Quinn said on RTÉ Radio. Mr Quinn said he expected cooperation from the Catholic Church because patronage had been identified as an issue by Archbishop of Dublin Diarmuid Martin. It was about "parental choice" not a "general election", Mr Quinn said.

Out of 38 survey areas selected according to specific demographic criteria, 23 have demonstrated demand for "an immediate change in the existing school patronage", according to a Department of Education statement.

The majority of parents who took part in the survey named Educate Together as their preferred patron, chosen in 20 of 23 areas.

Fr Michael Drumm, chairman of the Council for Education of the Irish Bishops' Conference, said there was a "measurable small demand" for change in school patronage in certain areas and parents should have a choice. He claimed however that demand for choice was "lower than anticipated" and pointed out that attention must be given to the "large majority" of parents who expressed no interest in change.

He said the report raised the issue of "displacement" in trying to cater for the views of a minority who wanted change.

The problem on the ground was that numbers displaced could be greater than numbers catered for, he said. In Celbridge Co Kildare, for example, some 100 parents desired a different type of school but the smallest Catholic school was 300 children, he said.

It was about getting the "balance right", he added. He also said that the survey showed a "very strong affirmation" of Catholic schools with no real interest in change from 15 of the 38 areas.

Educate Together said in a statement that they were "delighted" and "honoured" that many communities had selected them as a preferred patron. The results were "significant" and showed "demand for diversity", the organisation said.

Teaching Religion

Deirdre O'Connor *Senior Official and Equality Officer, INTO*

What do primary teachers think?

Research on teachers views' on the teaching of religion was carried out this year and was presented at the INTO Equality Conference in March 2013. This research followed on from similar research carried out in 2002. The results reflect the views of the primary teachers who are at the interface of home, school and community in the important and ongoing debate about the place of religion in Irish primary schools.

The INTO survey was sent to almost 1000 INTO members, and there was a 38% return. The returned surveys came from a broadly representative sample of members, both in terms of the profile of the teachers and the schools in which they worked. When compared to the sample for the 2002 survey, the changes in the patronage of primary schools were reflected, with an increase in respondents working in schools under the patronage of Educate Together and An Foras Patrúnachta.

Teachers' attitudes

Teachers' attitudes to teaching religion were explored by asking them to choose which statement from a range best reflected their attitude to the teaching of religion. The most frequent response was "I teach religion willingly", with 49% choosing this statement. This statement was chosen more frequently by older teachers. In 2002, 61% of respondents chose this statement. 20% of respondents chose "I am not opposed to teaching religion". 10% of teachers chose the response, "I would teach broad religious education programme willingly, but would prefer not to teach religious instruction in a particular faith". 7% of respondents chose the statement "I would prefer if I didn't have to teach religion". 2% stated that they would like to opt out of teaching religion, and less than 1% stated that they had opted out.

Religion in schools

60% of respondents agreed that religion should be taught in school hours, compared to 80% who agreed with this statement in 2002. However, only 47% agreed that children should be prepared for the sacraments in primary schools, with 55% stating that the family should have the main responsibility for these preparations. Teachers also pointed to the additional time (apart from allocated religion time) spent in their schools in preparing for the sacraments with 71% saying that additional time was taken up. This was a huge increase on the 18% who stated this in 2002.

71% of teachers agreed that Education about Religion and Beliefs (ERB) should be part of the curriculum in schools, with 51% stating that it should be part of the religious education programme. The NCCA has recently begun work on developing a curriculum and Guidelines for schools on ERB and Ethics, a proposed in the Report of the Forum on Pluralism and Patronage.

When asked about school ethos, and how this permeates the school, 79% of teachers referred to the presence of religious pictures and icons in their school (up from 69% 10 years ago), 79% referred to visits by clergy (up from 67%) and 75% to Mass or religious services in the school. These increases seem to point to a more visible religious ethos in schools compared to 2002.

School Type
There has been much debate on the patronage of schools in the past few years, in particular since the establishment by Minister Ruairí Quinn of the Forum on Pluralism and Patronage. In the survey, teachers were asked to indicate what type of school most schools should be. 28% responded that most schools should be denominational, while almost 49% favoured multi- denominational schools. 10% favoured non-denominational schools, even though no such primary schools are currently available in Ireland.

Teacher Education
The role of religion in teacher education and qualifications has also been the subject of debate. Currently, all the state funded primary teacher education colleges in Ireland are denominational. Only 15% of teachers agreed that this should be the case, down from 36% in 2002. Almost 60% of respondents said that a qualification for teaching religion should be separate from the general qualification.

Conclusion
Primary teachers' views on the teaching of religion, and the patronage of schools, are changing over time, reflecting the changes and demands of society. Teachers largely accept the place of religion in schools, while expressing support for the wider availability of multi-denominational and non-denominational schools. The religious ethos in denominational schools appears to have become more visible over the past ten years. Teachers are concerned about the time being spent on sacramental preparation, and believe that this preparation should fall primarily to the parents and the parish.

Over the coming ten years, there will be further demands for change, which will impact on teachers' professional practice and employment. The broad goodwill towards the teaching of religion and the place of religion in schools should not be overlooked or damaged in developing the primary education system for Ireland today.

Full details of the survey can be found at www.into.ie

EDUCATION IN THE MEDIA

Principals' network wants change in schools admission policies

April 25, 2013

A web-based system of application for school admission would standardise the enrolment process and cut down on nepotism, the director of the Irish Primary Principals Network (IPPN) said.

Sean Cottrell proposed a web-based system that would allow parents to rank schools in their order of preference.

Children would be allocated their first, second or third choice place in a school, depending on supply and demand factors, in a method similar to the CAO application process for college, he said.

Parents' PPS number would be used and parents would be giveen a pick of 5-10 schools.

Preference would be given to those who lived near to the school or who had siblings in the school, Mr Cottrell advised.

There would be the option to select between an all-girls school, an Irish language school or a Catholic school, depending on availability.

Securing a place would not be influenced by whether or not the child's parents were past pupils or teachers, according to Mr Cottrell.

"Neither should benefactors of the school, scholarships, multi-annual waiting-lists, booking deposits and aptitude screening be among the criteria, official or otherwise, required for enrolment in any school."

Under the new national enrolment policy, Mr Cottrell proposed that funding for schools would be proportionate to the number of children enrolled and a capitation weighting would apply in the case of Traveller children, new Irish children, children from designated disadvantaged areas, and children with special education needs.

"The technology is there," the IPPN director added.

Mental Health Difficulties

Carmel Browne MA, *Teacher, Melview National School, Longford.*

Experiences of Teachers - Summary Research Report

Keywords: mental health, primary school teachers, reasonable accommodation, raising awareness.

The research findings are based on the perceptions and experiences of six primary school teachers with mental health difficulties. The main issues related to work related stress in schools are identified. Findings show that early diagnosis of a mental health difficulty is paramount to its successful treatment. While respondents identified a number of early signs of stress and anxiety which colleagues could look out for in schools, the findings indicate that raising awareness of mental health difficulties could make it easier for teachers to detect early symptoms.

Bearing in mind that statistics indicate that 1 in 4/5 suffer from a mental health difficulty at some point in their lifetime early warning signs that individuals can look out for in their own lives are identified. There is a consensus of opinion that talking about your mental health difficulty is very helpful.

Participants feel that things are improving with regard to the way people perceive mental health difficulties. However they agree that there is still a stigma attached and therefore a need to raise awareness levels and provide more education on the broad spectrum of mental health difficulties that exist. A key finding is that participants in general were able to successfully return to work. In some cases this was accommodated by management. The participants' belief in the need for and value of good communication in schools is highlighted.

Introduction
In conducting this research the INTO Equality Committee sought to get the lived experiences of teachers with regard to their mental health difficulties, in order to raise awareness of mental health difficulties in teaching. The overall aim of the research was to examine the nature of personal experiences of primary school teachers with mental health difficulties.

Subsidiary objectives were to:
- ascertain the perceived impact which mental health difficulties have had on teachers' professional lives;
- identify ways in which teachers with a mental health difficulty can be reasonably accommodated in the workplace.

Once volunteers to participate in the research were identified, one to one semi-structured interviews were conducted and recorded with the permission of the participants. Verbatim transcripts of all interviews were prepared. Based on evidence from literature (Caeilli et al. 2000; Braun and Clarke 2006; Petrie 2010) a thematic analysis method was applied to this study on the basis that it is a flexible tool which can provide a rich, detailed account of the data. The issues presented in this article are not a comprehensive representation of all the data collected but they represent the recurring central themes and key findings that emerged following its thematic analysis. Pseudonyms are used throughout to ensure confidentiality and anonymity. This article includes quotes from the participants as it is important for their voices to be heard by fellow educators.

Research Findings

Types of mental health difficulties experienced

In general, participants in this study indicated that their mental health difficulties were related to stress and anxiety with the resultant diagnoses of depression. There is agreement among the participants that there were a number of different underlying causes of their stress and anxiety but for the purposes of this article the focus is on the overarching common themes relevant to the workplace.

In commenting about how they became aware they had a mental health difficulty respondents suggest that one of the first indicators that there was something not right was their inability to sleep while they also identified stomach problems, exhaustion and low energy levels as key early signs. There was a consensus of opinion among participants that everything became an ordeal and that focusing on ordinary daily tasks was difficult:

"Everything was an ordeal I couldn't make decisions. It would take me half an hour to decide what clothes to wear… When I went to the shop I couldn't think of what I wanted to buy… I'd try to put a wash on but I couldn't decide dark/white, what temperature? I just couldn't do it…" (Avril).

Some respondents also indicated that they experienced panic attacks:

"I got night time panic attacks. When I had depression there were mornings when I was driving to school when I had panic attacks. I had to pull over onto the hard shoulder and I had to breathe and talk to myself. I thought to myself if I can only get to school, if I can get through the door, if I can start teaching I will be alright" (Susan).

When commenting on what they perceived as work related triggers to stress and anxiety attacks respondents indicated that on reflection they felt changes to their work practices including change of class had been a factor:

"The first time anxiety came was when I had a big change …. When I was going back from job sharing to full time teaching, it was going to be a huge jump to go back into the classroom because when you are out of the classroom like that for a while it is difficult because you feel as if you are not going to be able to go back in and I let that feeling take over and that is what happened" (Cáit).

Jane and Áine had similar experiences. Jane explained:

"It was gradually creeping up on me… I had been doing learning support for thirteen years and then I was put back in the classroom that was a huge shock I wasn't able to cope. The job contributed to my depression I was back in the classroom in a position I was not familiar with after thirteen years out and then there was the new curriculum" (Jane);

While Áine felt change also had a huge impact on her mental health:

"I had been in RTT for three years then I applied for a job as a home school liaison teacher, I was hoping that was the road I was going to go down, I didn't get that job, I was devastated, I was really really gutted. I found it very hard to come back into the classroom, especially infants as I hadn't been there for 17 years. I was a bit demoralised but I can say that the seeds of mental ill health started there" (Áine).

In light of the evidence from these findings it would appear that the allocation of classes needs to be given greater consideration in some schools. Respondents indicated that better communication on this matter would be beneficial.

Another contributing work related factor identified was the increased workload on teachers especially in regard to planning and paperwork:

"There is more stress… now you have to work harder than we did in the past, there's much longer hours and you're under more pressure due to large classes, too many subjects, split classes, new

technology and the demand for extra-curricular activities" (Susan).

Somewhat surprisingly participants felt that pressure of planning lessons often caused stress during holiday periods or time off.

It is apparent from these and other comments that there needs to be a review of planning policies in schools in order to eliminate stress. The evidence from this research suggests that facilitating collaborative planning in schools would be helpful as that would eliminate the feelings of isolation experienced by some:

"Well I suppose I am very lucky because I work on a staff where once a week we have a group meeting in infants, a number of colleagues working in the same area so we can share ideas and it takes a huge amount of pressure off planning, it really does" (Cáit).

General impact on working lives
While opinions differed on the impact of diagnosed mental health difficulties on the respondent's classroom management and their relationship with their pupils, the analysis of respondents' replies suggests that the main impact of mental health difficulties on their working lives is that they had feelings of worthlessness and not being able to cope:

"I kept thinking I was useless I convinced myself that I was no good at teaching… I thought I just can't go in and stand in front of a class… I just felt I wasn't as confident… I didn't feel confident in my ability to do the job and then when I came home I'd always be second guessing everything 'did I do/say the right thing?'…." (Avril).

This is akin to Marian's experiences:

"I couldn't concentrate so it was very hard to do a lesson with the kids… sometimes if I was doing a long passage I wouldn't be able to take it in myself…" (Marian);

Response of Principal and Board of Management, Reasonable accommodation
Evidence from empirical research indicates that being in work is generally beneficial to mental health. Work provides a sense of identity and belonging which are important in promoting good mental health. (OECD, 2011). Research shows that people can and do make a full recovery from mental health difficulties, or learn to manage them so that they can fully participate in work. All the participants in this research responded that they have had to take time off work. In all but one case the participants have returned to work. Susan is of the belief that it is helpful to be working when you have a mental health difficulty because it helps you to focus on someone or something else:

"Even when I was suffering from depression, I used to welcome going to work because I could lose myself in somebody else. Once you go in [to school] there are children in front of you and they have needs so it takes you out of yourself for a while you forget about it your own life" (Susan).

Cáit explained that initially taking time off work was detrimental to her wellbeing:

"I felt I was helpless no use at home and no use in school so I literally didn't sleep so I made the decision to take time off work and then BANG I got really depressed the minute I stopped work" (Cáit).

In this instance the success or otherwise of participant's return to work was influenced by supports in place in their respective schools. Although respondents did not allude to direct involvement by their Board of Management, a positive finding is that the majority of respondents expressed the opinion that their principal was very supportive and discreet. In some cases a return to work was facilitated by a phased return to full time teaching or a job sharing role. While in other cases a change of class was offered. Principals in general also made provision to allow the teacher take sufficient time off to give her/him time to recover. However it is worth noting that respondents alluded to the fact that it is quite likely that they might need time off work again in the future therefore they observed that the new sick leave arrangements could have a huge impact on them.

In stark contrast in situations where principals

were not as supportive a return to work proved very difficult. Respondents are in agreement that they would benefit from a more flexible system of employment being available. Noting this evidence now might be an appropriate time to further explore the proposal on the partial resumption of duties.

Participants' perspectives on treatment received
Participants strongly suggest that once you become aware that something is not right it is important to talk to someone and to seek professional help as quickly as possible as early intervention is crucial:

"Now I'd definitely say deal with it. Go to a doctor and get help and deal with it right away. Talk to a friend about it…If you don't talk about it [stress and anxiety] it will become more difficult for yourself if you are able to talk about it, it is much better than hiding it" (Cait).

All respondents stated that medication in the form of anti-depressants and sleeping tablets. was prescribed. The majority of participants responded that were referred to a psychiatrist which resulted in a variety of therapies being recommended along with medication. In general participants agree that this holistic approach to treatment has worked well for them. Beneficial treatments alluded to included yoga, meditation, counseling reflexology, Cognitive Behaviour Therapy and WRAP (Wellness Recovery and Action Plan) programmes.

Some participants also expounded the positive effects of exercise while Susan found art very therapeutic: *"Art has been great …getting back in touch with art"*. All participants expressed the opinion that a key component for well being is to ensure that you set aside time for yourself for relaxation, while Cáit and Jane agree that it doesn't help to dwell on stressful events. They suggest it is important to live in the moment:

"It is good to deal with stress at the moment then leave it and move on, don't let it build up. There is no point taking it with you because that's not going to solve it" (Cáit);

"We often spend time thinking about the past and worrying about the future. If we do that there is no happiness in the now. It is important to try and live in the now and focus on good stuff, try not to worry about what's happened or what might happen" (Jane).

In most cases respondents were referred to Medmark. In the main they found that was a positive experience. However evidence gleaned from the data indicates that Medmark's only role was in deciding whether or not respondents were fit to return to work. There is no evidence to show that they were in any way proactive in trying to provide reasonable accommodation. Surely providing reasonable accommodation to facilitate a return to work should be a key role of an occupational health provider?

Perceived stigma often associated with mental health difficulties
There is general agreement among the participants that there is still a stigma attached to having a mental health difficulty, in particular in rural Ireland. Participants felt that they didn't want colleagues, friends and sometimes even family to know what was wrong with them. They agreed that people go to extreme lengths at times to cover up the fact that they have a mental health difficulty. Participants expressed the opinion that the problem is exacerbated by the fact that they are teachers as it is particularly difficult for teachers to disclose that they had a mental health difficulty due to fears about how parents might react. However respondents did suggest that there needed to be more openness by all concerned suggesting people who have a mental health difficulty need to be able to talk about it themselves before they can expect empathy.

Creating awareness
It is apparent from comments made by the participants that there is a need to develop knowledge and create awareness about mental health difficulties among teachers and principals. Participants expressed the opinion that it would be helpful if teachers and principals were more aware of the early signs often associated with mental health difficulty.

Some even suggested that teachers, especially those in management positions, should receive specific training in identifying early signs of mental health difficulties:

"There should be some education for staff on mental health. They should be aware of symptoms… It would be helpful if teachers could understand the condition." (Marian)
"I think in every school there should be inservice on mental health… the common difficulties, the signs to look out for…" (Áine).

Information gleaned from the research indicates that some common early warning signs to watch out for in colleagues in school would include: Not going to staffroom for break; isolating themselves from the staff; being more irritable than normal; spending more time on paperwork; change in personality-acting out of character; stepping back from responsibility.

Respondents also stated clearly that colleagues should be proactive if they identify early signs or feel a member of staff is struggling to cope. Áine's comments on how colleagues should react if they identify early signs of a mental health difficulty are particularly clear:

"Yes they should definitely talk to them. They should certainly ask and keep asking are you ok? Are you sure you are ok? Are you doing ok"? (Áine).

Empirical research has found that 1 in 4/5 suffer from a mental health difficulty at some point in their lives cited HSE (2007). A stark reality of those statistics is that in every medium-to-large primary school in the country there are a number of our colleagues experiencing mental health difficulties. Bearing this in mind early warning signs that individuals can look out for in their own lives were also identified. Symptoms to watch out for include: having difficulty sleeping; problems with eating; unexplained weight loss (in some cases more severe problems like anorexia or bulimia); lower energy levels than normal; or feeling that you are unable to cope with everyday things that you have no control or are finding it difficult to make decisions.

Agenda of issues arising
In concluding it is important to note that respondents felt that it was empowering to have participated in this research. In the main they were delighted to get the opportunity to have their voices heard.

There is a consensus of opinion among participants that in order to reduce or eliminate the stress and anxiety associated with working in schools the following supports should be put in place:
- There should be a more collaborative approach to planning;
- There is a need for more ongoing professional development for teachers in newer subject areas e.g. science, as well as technology;
- Break times should be sacred, a time to relax – not an opportunity for mini staff meetings and 'shop talk';
- Be wary of 'scare mongering' about things like WSE and incidental inspections;
- Colleagues and staff should be aware that a teacher working in a prefab away from the main building could feel isolated;
- There could be greater consideration given to allocation of classes in some cases;
- All staff especially principals should receive specialist training in the area of mental health difficulties in particular the signs and symptoms to watch out for;
- A successful return to work for a person suffering a mental health difficulty can be facilitated by a flexible approach to staffing in schools e.g., Providing the opportunity to job share or work as part of a resource team;
- The possibility of a return to work on a part time basis (partial resumption of duties) should be further considered and explored;
- A support group for teachers experiencing mental health difficulties be established.

Cáit summed up the way you can feel when you have a mental health difficulty:

"you feel there are two you', there is the one who is energetic and ok and the other one who is trying to pull you down, I was always trying to get out of this person but I couldn't" (Cáit).

EDUCATION IN THE MEDIA

Parents welcome new involvement of Ombudsman

April 11, 2013

By Lorraine Dempsey, Chairperson of Special Needs Parents Association

On 5 April, it was announced that the National Council for Special Education would come under the investigative remit of the Children's Ombudsman.

This announcement – which followed a long campaign by TDs, parents and representations by the Ombudsman for Children Emily Logan – necessitated an amendment to The Ombudsman for Children Act, 2002 which set out the responsibilities and duties of the Ombudsman for Children and what organisations the Ombudsman could investigate.

While the Department of Education, primary and post primary schools were amongst those establishments which could be investigated following a complaint to the Ombudsman for Children, up until now the NCSE was exempt from such processes.

Ombudsman for Children Emily Logan

Complaints in relation to allocation of SNAs

In the past few years, the Ombudsman for Children has reported an upsurge in the number of complaints made by parents of children with special needs, particularly in relation to the allocation of Special Needs Assistants. The increase in complaints appeared to coincide with the reductions in the numbers of Special Needs Assistants sanctioned by the Department of Education from 2009 onwards and the cap on overall SNA posts for the past two year at 10,575.

New role of Children's Ombudsman

Up until this point in time, such complaints could not be dealt with and had to be redirected to the NCSE itself. From the 30th of April 2013, any complaints made by a child under the age of 18 years, or adult on their behalf, in relation to the NCSE, can now be pursued by the Children's Ombudsman.

In relation to the NCSE, the Ombudsman would work independently on complaints about SNAs and would see if there had been maladministration of the scheme and if there had been an adverse effect on the child involved. It would then look to see if the NCSE was following its own policy and, if not, had the child been negatively affected as a result.

Benefits for parents

For parents, this represents a significant move towards having an independent method of appealing a decision. Prior to this, if a Senior SENO agreed with the allocation sanctioned by a Local SENO, the parent had no further recourse available to them in cases where they felt the level of support would not meet their child's needs to enable them to fully participate in an educational environment, and reports provided by healthcare professionals were felt to not have been given sufficient weighting by NCSE officials.

Needs of the child come first

It is important for parents to have faith that there is transparency and consistency in decision making processes in relation to SNA allocations and that allocation decisions are solely based on meeting the needs of the child with special needs and not influenced by pressures to keep within predefined resources as set out by the Department of Education.

Complaint procedure a last resort

In particular, we would envisage that complaints in relation to SNA allocations would only be made once all other avenues have been exhausted by the parents and school staff to increase SNA support and where a child is unable to fully participate in an inclusive and safe manner in their school despite evidence of other interventions being implemented.

Insufficient SNA allocations not acceptable

Parents do not find it acceptable that their child with special needs should miss out on opportunities to participate fully in all school activities due to difficulties with the more common phenomenon of 'Shared Access' to SNA support. It is also not acceptable that Special Needs Assistants, teaching professionals and children are unnecessarily put at risk of injury due to insufficient SNA allocations to meet the collective needs of all the children with low incidence disabilities in the school in order to prove that an increase in SNA allocation is justified.

Student Well Being

Dr Mark Morgan *Cregan Professor of Education and Psychology at St. Patrick's College, Dublin and Co-director of 'Growing Up in Ireland'*

Adverse Events in Childhood: Protective and Aggravating Factors

Based on the data from 'Growing up in Ireland' (the national longitudinal study), a report on the kinds of adversity experienced by 9 year olds was completed last November. The study by Mark Morgan and James Williams was concerned with the negative happenings that occur to Irish 9 year olds, together with an examination of the significant influences that protect children from negative effects or indeed magnify the impact. While it has been known for some decades that there are lasting consequences of traumatic, painful consequences including adjustment problems in adolescence and adulthood, the factors that aggravate such experiences are less well understood. The present study showed that having more than one adverse event greatly increased negative social and emotional outcomes, while a range of assets including social-support and social background enhanced resilience. The study has important implications for child development and for education particular in drawing attention to the importance of school success for helping cope with negative experiences.

Background

While there is a consensus that adverse events in childhood can have long-term consequences, even in the case of traumatic experiences, from which the post-traumatic stress syndrome (PTSS) might be expected to ensue, there are major differences in the extent to which negative outcomes actually occur. For example, there is also evidence that children exposed to human-generated traumatic events carry a higher risk of developing PTSS than those who are exposed to other kinds of events e.g. accidents and natural disasters. The other interesting outcome of the research on PTSS is that children and adolescents who have a high degree of social support both before and after a traumatic event are less likely to be vulnerable to the development of the syndrome.

A relatively recent development in this area is around the suggestion that that adverse events can have positive consequences. For example, following negative events, the process of 'benefit finding' results in a positive adjustment some time later e.g. following a bereavement or a major loss. The strongest claim for benefit finding has been made by researchers who claim to have found evidence linking the growth of 'wisdom' as an outcome of trauma. This can happen because a feature of wisdom is uncertainty, and trauma shatters our fundamental assumptions about the world, thus resulting in an enhancement of wisdom. However, no research has been carried out on the cost of acquiring such wisdom and whether this 'wisdom' has the same benefits as that acquired in other.

Growing up in Ireland

The study 'Growing up in Ireland involves two groups or "cohorts" of children – an older and younger group. From the perspective of the present study the relevant group is the child group (aged 9 at data collection), involving nearly 9,000 children as well as their parents/

carers, teachers and school Principals. The children were in 910 primary schools and were selected randomly thus giving a representative sample.

The data gathered was extremely comprehensive and included information from main caregivers on health, social development as well as school engagement and achievement. From the present perspective, a central feature was the report of the main care-giver on the adverse experiences that the child had encountered until age 9 years. Because this list was quite exhaustive, the main events reported on are shown in Table 1 together with the percentage who reported that the children did indeed have the experience in question.

Table 1: Adverse Events Experienced by 9-Year Olds (Sample of Events)

Death of a parent	2.5
Death of a grandparent	28.3
Death of a sibling	1.1
Death of an uncle/aunt	7.0
Illness or injury	4.7
Illness or injury - family member	13.3
Divorce/separation of parents	14.7
Conflict between parents	12.3
Moving country	10.3

Table entries are percentages of children experiencing the event in questions

Outcomes and Resilience

The outcomes of the adverse events were measured largely through a rating of various negative social and emotional outcomes including anxiety, peer problems, conduct disorders and hyperactivity. The most important outcome was that while there were differences between different kinds of events, there was a tendency for adverse events to have negative outcomes on the social-emotional outcomes. It was especially striking that while a single adverse event did not have a major impact, two or more events had a relatively greater effect and any one event. This is in line with previous research that shows that while children can manage one episode of adversity, they have major problems with repeated episodes. It is worth noting that there is a built in connection between some of the adverse events, e.g., conflict between parents can result in separation or divorce.

The other interesting point that emerged was that children who had various assets were more likely to be able to get over an adverse event without too much difficulty in contrast to those who did not have such assets. This extended to social background including factors like mother's education as well as income-related influences. It is interesting that the same general pattern has emerged in international studies of adverse experiences; for example children who are doing well in school are found to overcome the effects of their parents' divorce and separation much better than children who are struggling in school.

Implications

The study has important implications for education and child-rearing. It is inevitable that children will have some setbacks in their lives. However, if the resulting 'knock-on' effects can be prevented, then the more serious consequences can avoided. The related important implication is that success in school in any domain (academic, sport or other extra-curricular area) has an importance beyond the domain in question since it can cushion a student against the consequences of adversity.

These findings in turn relate to another body of recent research that shows the importance of the teacher-pupil relationship for academic achievement; liking school is not only a discretionary bonus but affects engagement with school which in turn influences achievement.

If there is any dominant theme emerging from 'Growing up in Ireland', it is the finding that effects carry over into aspects of behaviour that might not be expected, as is illustrated in the case of adverse events. The emphasis on 'full and harmonious development' that was central to the 1971 primary curriculum was not misplaced.

EDUCATION IN THE MEDIA

Rift between Quinn and church over pace of school handovers

April 15, 2013

A gulf is opening between Education Minister Ruairi Quinn and the Catholic bishops over the pace at which 29 of their 3,000 primary schools will be handed over to different patrons.

The historic transfers, which follow parental surveys in 43 areas, is a step in reducing the Catholic Church's dominance in primary education and to give greater choice of school ethos.

Mr Quinn wants the bishops to provide the names of schools to be transferred by the end of this year, to allow time for arrangements for them to open under new patronage in September 2014.

But a church education spokesperson said the situation varied from one community to another and said "practical problems" were emerging in some areas.

Fr Michael Drumm, executive chairperson of the Catholic Schools Partnership (CSP), said in this situation "there is no one size that will fit all" and there would be a need for a creative response to complex situations.
Fr Drumm outlined the church's substantive response to the minister's initiative in an address to the Catholic Primary School Managers' Association (CPSMA) over the weekend.

He stressed that "in all of this, it is imperative to reassure local communities that no change will be implemented without widespread support in the area".

The areas involved have between three and 16 primary schools, predominantly Catholic, and the bishops have been asked to hand over one in each area, generally to allow for the opening of a multi-denominational school.

In practical terms, it would mean the direct handover of an existing school – likely to be met with strong resistance in local communities – or two schools amalgamating first in order to free up a building.

Fr Drumm said that in seeking to respond to the limited request for change in different areas, "attention must be given to the large majority who have expressed no such interest.

"An issue that will arise in many of these areas is the level of displacement that may be required in trying to cater for the views of a minority who want change," he said.

He said the best way forward was through amalgamations.

He would not be drawn on how many schools he thought would be under new patronage by September 2014, but said in areas of high demand for change, plans could definitely be in place by then, but where demand was low, a creative response would be needed.

Fr Drumm said that in the individual areas surveyed, between 0.6pc (Roscrea, Co Tipperary) and 8pc (Portmarnock, Co Dublin) of parents with children in schools said they would avail of another form of patronage.

He pointed to Ballina, Co Mayo, where parents of 44 children, or 2.2pc of pupils currently in primary school, said they would avail of a multi-denominational school if one was available.

"Anyone can see that responding to this level of demand will not be easy because these 44 children are probably scattered across 16 schools. This situation is replicated in many other areas".

http://www.independent.ie/irish-news/rift-between-quinn-and-church-over-pace-of-school-handovers-29195834.html

---

New proposals to obliged schools to accept special needs students

May 18, 2013

Major changes are planned for the allocation of learning support teachers to schools

The findings of a major review by the National Council for Special Education are likely to have far-reaching consequences on how education services are provided to future generations of children with special needs.

One of its key proposals is to change the way 10,000 learning support teachers are allocated to mainstream schools.

In future, these posts should be based on the individual

EDUCATION IN THE MEDIA

needs of students rather than the number of class teachers or students in a school, the report says.

Overall, as many as one in four children in the education system have some difficulties learning due to conditions or disabilities ranging from dyslexia to autism.

While funding for special education services has increased over the past decade, the council's report says there is still room for improvement.
The State body says its proposals will help ensure supports are used to maximum effect to drive improved outcomes for children with learning difficulties.

Among the report's key recommendations include:
- Every child with special needs be guaranteed access to their nearest school that is resourced to meet their needs, regardless of enrolment policies
- A school must enrol a student with special needs if directed by officials, on the basis that the school will be provided with resources
- A new model for allocating teaching resources in mainstream schools based on the profiled needs of students, rather than on the number of class teachers or students in a school
- The full implementation of the Education for Persons with Special Educational Needs Act (2004) - which gives rights to children and parents - as soon as resources permit.

At a press conference today, the national council's chief executive Teresa Griffin said the needs of students were at the heart of the report's proposals.

"We want all children with special education needs to be welcome to enrol in schools where teaching resources are already in place and where teachers can focus on each student's individual needs," she said.

Minister for Education Ruairí Quinn said he would take on board all of the report's proposals, in particular the recommendation to change the way resources are allocated.

However, some of the report's proposals have drawn sharp criticism from the Irish National Teachers' Organisation.

It said changes to the allocation of resources could dismantle two decades of progress integrating special needs children in mainstream schools.

The union said the current system was introduced to reduce waiting times for children needing extra help.

"If implemented, bureaucracy will once again become the barrier to children getting resources. Additional paperwork will be demanded of class teachers already struggling with some of the largest classes in the EU," the union said, in a statement.

Mr Quinn also said he was not satisfied with the delays facing parents in getting assessments of their children by health authorities.

The outcome of these assessments currently guides a child's access to education and other services.
New figures show that hundreds of children are waiting in excess of six months for assessments, in breach of legal time-limits.

www.irishtimes.com/news/education/schools-to-be-obliged-to-accept-special-needs-students-under-new-proposals-1.1397450

Quinn reverses planned cuts to supports of special needs pupils

June 25, 2013

Minister for Education Ruairi Quinn has reversed planned cuts to special needs supports following a public backlash.

He said today he had secured agreement at Cabinet to release 500 additional teaching posts which means special needs children will not have cuts to their supports.

He said the move was a once-off budgetary measure. In the meantime, he said he has established a working group to develop a new model to allocate resource teachers in schools.

Mr Quinn appointed Eamon Stack, a former chief inspector in the department, to chair the working group. Established by the National Council for Special Education (NCSE), the group will include parents and will report back to the Minister in September.

"Parents can be assured that their children will not be disadvantaged while we are moving towards a new model that will ensure greater fairness and quality of education for children with special educational needs," Mr Quinn said.

www.irishtimes.com/news/education/quinn-reverses-planned-cuts-to-supports-of-special-needs-pupils-1.1442100

'Cyberbullying' – why is it different?

Dr Sharon McLaughlin *Law Lecturer, Letterkenny Institute of Technology, and member of EU Kids Online*

Schools must ensure that parents and students in particular are actively involved in formualting the anti-bullying policy

Schools are charged with considerable responsibility when it comes to managing bullying behaviour. Cyberbullying poses unique challenges in this regard. It is not reasonable to expect schools to manage incidences of cyberbullying that occur when students are no longer under their care. However, there are aspects of the existing bullying management system which, if properly harnessed, could impact far beyond the schoolyard.

Cyberbullying has rarely been out of the spotlight in recent months and, with the Joint Oireachtas Committee on Transport and Communication shortly due to publish its report on tackling the abuses of social media, it looks set to remain centre stage for quite some time to come. Bullying – in all its various manifestations – is a societal issue and, as such, requires a concerted societal response. Schools, however, are charged with considerable responsibility when it comes to managing bullying behaviour. Cyberbullying poses unique challenges in this regard.

'Cyberbullying' – what is it?
The term 'cyberbullying' – also variously referred to as 'online bullying', 'e-bullying' and 'digital bullying' – is used to refer to the misuse of information and communication technology (ICT) to harass, intimidate, pester and embarrass others. Cyberbullying is a generic term encompassing an array of online behaviours such as 'exclusion' (intentional social ostracisation of an individual from an online group or community) and 'denigration' (posting online of belittling, disrespectful comments about an individual or group).

Cyberbullies have a vast technological arsenal at their disposal – mobile phones, email, instant messaging, chat rooms, blogs, bulletin boards, social networking sites, and so forth – all of which are capable of being misused to engage in bullying behaviour.

'Cyberbullying' – why is it different?
Cyberbullying is but a digitised version of an age-old behaviour – an 'old snake in new skin' – however, it differs from more conventional forms of bullying in four main ways:
1. Anonymity: some online forums permit users to operate under a cloak of anonymity thus making cyberbullying a much more insidious form of bullying;
2. Access: cyberbullying is particularly ceaseless and intrusive because cyberbullies are not subject to constraints of time and place but rather are afforded round-the-clock access to victims;
3. Accountability: ICT allow users to act impulsively and instantaneously and, as physical proximity to the victim is not a prerequisite to engaging in cyberbullying behaviour, cyberbullies often feel detached from their actions and lack any real sense of accountability;
4. Audience: ICT afford cyberbullies the opportunity to reach a sizeable, potential global audience and create electronic cliques of like-minded individuals with relative ease.

Prevalence of cyberbullying
Between 2009 and 2011, EU Kids Online II, a thematic research network funded by the EC Safer Internet Programme, conducted original empirical research across 25 participating European countries into children's (9-16 years old) and parents' experiences and practices regarding use, risk and safety online (www.eukidsonline.net). Arising from this pan-European survey and subsequent report, a national report presenting the findings specific to Irish children was published in 2011.

In relation to bullying, almost one in four (23%) of Irish 9-16 year olds reported that someone had acted in a nasty or hurtful way towards them in the previous twelve months, above the European average of 19%. Bullying in person (face-to-face) was reportedly the most common form of bullying experienced by Irish children – 15% of 9-16 year olds said that someone had acted in a nasty or hurtful way towards them face-to-face compared with 4% who said that this happened to them on the internet or by mobile phone calls or messages.

It follows that, when it comes to addressing bullying behaviour, the focus should be directed at the behaviour itself rather than the medium used to carry it out. Moreover, 14% of Irish respondents said that they had acted in a nasty or hurtful way towards others in the previous twelve months – highlighting the importance of viewing children as both victims and perpetrators of risk activities and behaviours.

Cyberbullying – Whose responsibility is it anyway?
While in their capacity as students, the behaviour of children and teenagers is rightly and necessarily subject to regulation by school authorities. A school's authoritative remit inarguably extends to the regulation of a student's expressive activities (offline and online) where such activities occur while the student is under the care of the school. In circumstances where a student: (a) misuses the schools ICT facilities in some way; (b) misuses his/her mobile telephone (or other personal communication device) while on-campus; or (c) misuses his/her mobile telephone (or other personal communication device) off-campus but during a school-sponsored or school-sanctioned excursion, the school authority does not infringe the student's rights by reprimanding such misuse, provided the sanction imposed is proportionate to the level of misuse.

The difficulty, however, arises where the expression at issue originates online and off-campus – outside school hours, off school grounds and without using the school's ICT facilities – that is, in circumstances where the student is no longer the responsibility of the school. This on-campus/off-campus distinction is a complex one – and one with which US courts have begun to grapple in recent years.

Putting these complexities of origin and responsibility aside, there are aspects of the existing bullying management system which, if leveraged and deployed to maximum capacity, could impact far beyond the schoolyard.

Maximising the impact of codes of behaviour
The formulation of a code of behaviour is one of the primary means through which schools seek to regulate the behaviour of students.

In Ireland, the Education Welfare Act 2000 (section 23) requires the Board of Management of every recognised school to develop a code of behaviour in respect of its students. As part of this code, schools are required to specify the standards of behaviour to be observed by students, as well as the measures to be taken when students fall short of these standards.

The Department of Education's 1993 Guidelines on Countering Bullying Behaviour (currently under review) recommend that 'the prevention of bullying should be an integral part of a written Code of Behaviour and Discipline in all primary and post-primary schools.' While the broad wording of section 23 provides a solid legal framework within which to formulate a code of behaviour addressing all types of bullying conduct, there is an argument for the insertion of a provision into the legislation expressly stipulating that a school's code of behaviour must include an anti-bullying policy.

The 1993 Guidelines encourage school authorities to adopt an all-inclusive approach to the development of anti-bullying policies; an approach involving all factions of the school community – teaching staff, non-teaching staff, parents and pupils. Two decades later, this approach maintains its relevance. In order to be truly inclusive, school must endeavour to ensure that parents and, in particular students themselves, are actively and meaningfully involved in the processes leading to the development of their schools' anti-bullying policy. In light of the fact that the fundamental objective of any school anti-bullying policy is to create an environment in which students (as well as school personnel) are empowered to manage incidents of bullying behaviour, it follows logically that students themselves should be involved in the creation of such policies. In addition, student involvement will increase student awareness and understanding of the final policy document, as well as increasing its legitimacy among the student populus.

In other words, because of their direct involvement in its realisation, it is likely that students will view their school's anti-bullying policy as something other than an attempt by the school authority to regulate their behaviour.

In short, school authorities must endeavour to ensure that the process leading to the development of their school's anti-bullying policy is truly inclusive and, in this regard, must pay more than mere lip-service to student involvement in the formulation of such policies.
The awareness and understanding created as a result of participating in this policymaking process will extend far beyond the schoolyard.

References:
Aitken , R., & Harford, J. (2010). Induction Needs of a Group of Teachers at Different Stages in a School in the Republic of Ireland: Challenges and Expectations. Teaching and Teacher Education 27, 350-356.
Britton, E., Paine , L., Pimm , D., & Raizen , S. (2003). Comprehensive Teacher Induction: Systems for Early Career Learning. Dordrecht : Kluwer Academic Publishers.
Grant, Carl, A., & Zeichner, K. M. (1981). Inservice support for First Year Teachers: The State of the Scene. Journal of Research and Development in Education 14(2), 99-111.
Jenson, B. e. (2012). The Experience of New Teachers: Results from TALIS 2008. Paris : OECD .
Killeavy, M., Harford, J., Walsh, B., Murphy, R., Ní Áingléis, B., & Ó Díomasaigh, S. (2006). National Pilot Project on Teacher Induction. Dublin: Stationary Office, Department of Education and Skills.
Schollaert, R. (2011). Continuing professional development for the 21st century: setting the scene for teacher induction in a new era. In P. Picard, & L. Ria, Begining Teachers: a challenge for education systems - CIDREE Yearbook (pp. 9-28). Lyon, France: ENS de Lyon, Institute francais de l'Education .
Smith, R., & Coldron, J. (2002). Thinking About the Sort of Teacher You Want to Be. In A. Pollard, Readings for Reflective Teaching (pp. 336-338). London: Continuum .
Teaching Council. (2011). Policy on the Continuum of Teacher Education. Maynnoth: The Teaching Council.
Veenman, S. A. (1984). Perceived Problems of Beginning Teachers. Review of Educational Resarch 54 (2), 143-178.
Vonk, H. (1991). Some Trends in the Development of Curricula for the Professional Preparation of Primary and Secondary School Teachers in Europe: A Comparative Study. British Journal Of Education Studies xxxix: 2, 117-137.
Wong, H. K., Britton, T., & Ganser, T. (January 2005). What the World Can Teach Us About New Teacher Induction. Phi delta Kappan Vol 86, No 5, 379-384.

Minister for Education and Skills, Ruairí Quinn, T.D., Minister for Children and Youth Affairs, Frances Fitzgerald T.D., Deputy Aodhán Ó Riordáin T.D. marking the launch of 'Action Plan on Bullying'

WHO'S WHO

The WHO'S WHO Profile introduces people who are making an important contribution to education in Ireland today.

Meet
Noel Ward

OCCUPATION: Deputy General Secretary, Irish National Teachers' Organisation

Where did you grow up?
In Abbeyfeale, west Limerick (I could literally throw a stone across the River Feale into Kerry from the back of the house).

What is your earliest childhood memory?
I recall a minor crash, when in the back of our Morris, with a Cadbury van when (as I'm told) I was only two.

How many siblings have you?
Two (another brother died in an accident some years ago).

Where did you go to school/college?
Abbeyfeale BNS, secondary school in Abbeyfeale (Coláiste Íde Naofa), and later to St. Pat's Drumcondra and UCD.

To what extent did your education shape who you are today?
To some extent: beyond schooling, my reading and involvement in campaigns were strong influences. I never had an intention to become a teacher - economics (affordability) dictated it, but it's not a direction I have ever regretted taking.

What attracted you to work in INTO?
I had been on the INTO Executive as a young teacher and after some years away I felt that I could contribute ideas and commitment to INTO so I applied for and was appointed as a Senior Official in 2002. My current position (Deputy General Secretary) is one to which I had the honour to be elected by INTO members at the end of 2009.

Have you worked outside education?
Yes – I was appointed as a Programme Manager with the "Rainbow" government (1994-1997) where I was directly responsible to Pat Rabbitte as a Cabinet Minister and was one of two such Managers with the smallest party in a 3-party Coalition. That was tough but fascinating work and the experience has stood to me. While with INTO I was seconded for eighteen months from ICTU to the Second Benchmarking Body which reported in 2008. That Report was not well timed; our Principals and Deputy Principals are still due their money from the exercise.

What makes you particularly suitable for your current work?
My 25 years in the classroom, as well as experience in administration and campaigning, are among suitability factors.

What are the main responsibilities and challenges of your position?
The big challenge is to work with head office colleagues and our CEC to safeguard all we can of teachers' conditions and education resources against the onslaught of austerity and the Troika. In addition, I am General Treasurer of INTO and have responsibility for managing the union's resources.

What does a typical work day involve for you?
No such thing exists really as the schedule responds to demands as they arise. I try hard to

put aside some time for reading and reflection on policy issues in the education and union areas. Some landmarks – CEC meetings, our end-year accounts/audit, and INTO Annual Congress – require particularly targeted work and preparation.

What do you enjoy most about your work?
The sense that what INTO does really matters for teachers but also for the quality of education. And the good humour of colleagues in Parnell Square!

What do you enjoy least about your work?
The lack of planning/reflective time or sessions; we make serious efforts to develop policy proposals and plans but the urgent demands often win out.

What would you most like to change?
The economic background!

Are you a workaholic?
Don't think so, but I do work long hours and regularly do some work seven days a week. So maybe?

What do you do to relax?
I cycle and am still an occasional runner. Reading, a little Guinness, some more wine, can help. Not sure this is a healthy mix.

Do you like living in Dublin?
Yes but I think I could adapt to most surroundings.

Are you married?
To Joan, for quite a few good years now.

What plans have you for the future?
To think younger as I get older.

Have you a message for educators?
Teaching is an important role, a great job. The spending pressures of today will pass but the effects of high quality education will last in students' lives and in Irish social, economic and cultural life.

Have you a message for policy makers?
Early Childhood Education is still the best investment, in every sense.

Chapter 3
Post-Primary

Contents

		Page
1.	**Gearing up for Junior Cycle Change** *John Hammond*	84
2.	**Huge Appetite for Change** *Clive Byrne*	88
3.	**A Framework for Junior Cycle** *Dr Pádraig Kirk*	92
4.	**JC2.0 - Doing it our way** *Noel Malone*	96
5.	**School Self-Evaluation** *Deirdre Matthews*	100
6.	**Literacy improvement and SSE** *Stiofán Ó Cualáin*	104
7.	**Embracing ICT to enhance teaching and learning** *Seán Gallagher*	108
9.	**Modern Languages in Post-Primary Education** *Karen Ruddock*	113
10.	**Galway EC partners with UCD Confucius Institute** *Bernard Kirk*	115
11.	**The Irish Curriculum at Primary and Post-Primary Levels** *Muireann Ní Mhóráin*	117
12.	**The Challenges for Voluntary Secondary Schools in 2013** *Ferdia Kelly*	120
13.	**Teachers' Personal Wellbeing** *Dr Joe O'Connell*	124
14.	**Young professionals with nowhere [attractive] to go** *Pat King*	128
15.	**Contradictory policy messages about student welfare** *Bernie Judge*	132
16.	**A 2020 Vision for Education** *Jim Moore*	136
17.	**Some flourish but some don't** *Bernadette O'Sullivan*	138
15.	**Who's Who** *Joan Crowley O'Sullivan*	141

Introducing the Post-Primary Chapter

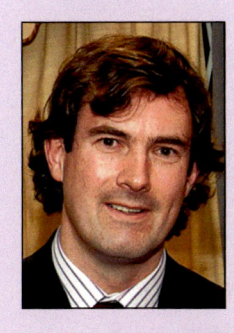

by Tony Hall, *Editor*

It is now approaching the fiftieth anniversary of the introduction of the Free Education Scheme by then Minister for Education, Donogh O'Malley. In the intervening years, the post-primary/secondary sector has experienced very significant development. 2013 has been a significant year in the post-primary/secondary sector in Ireland. This chapter features several articles on the key topic of the Junior Cycle Reform, including a focus that contextualizes these changes in relation to broader educational reform concerns. John Hammond, Deputy Chief Executive of National Council for Curriculum and Assessment outlines how the changes will be implemented as we approach the full rollout of the new curriculum. Clive Byrne, Director of the National Association of Principals and Deputy-Principals discusses how there is very significant motivation – throughout the educational system – for the reform of the Junior Cycle.

Dr Pádraig Kirk CEO of County Louth VEC and Director of Junior Cycle for Teachers Support Service (JCT) outlines the mission, vision and scope of the JCT, in particular how it will aim to support teachers through the change process. This chapter also includes an article by Mr. Noel Malone, Principal of Coláiste Chiaráin, Croom, Co. Limerick on the implementation of the new Junior Cycle in situ, in his school. The post-primary section of this year's Yearbook contains articles from the educational unions, both from Pat King, Association of Secondary Teachers Ireland and Bernie Judge, Teachers' Union of Ireland, on the key changes and challenges for post-primary teachers in 2013. Ferdia Kelly, General Secretary of the Joint Managerial Body/Association of Management of Catholic Secondary Schools outlines the challenges faced by voluntary secondary schools in 2013.

A continuing theme in the Yearbook this year is teachers' and students' well being; Dr. Joe O'Connell's article looks in particular at the issue of teachers' personal wellbeing. The section also features an article by Deirdre Matthews, Assistant Chief Inspector, Department of Education and Skills, on School Self-Evaluation: an enabling process for educational change in schools. Preceding the section on languages, including Gaeilge, Stiofán Ó Cualáin, Principal, Coláiste na Coiribe, Galway, and member of the editorial committee looks at literacy improvement measures and School Self-Evaluation (SSE).

In the section on languages at post-primary, Bernard Kirk, Director of the Galway Education Centre, describes the interesting partnership between Galway Education Centre and UCD's Confucius Centre; and Muireann Ní Mhóráin Chief Executive Officer of COGG, An Chomhairle um Oideachas Gaeltachta & Gaelscolaíochta, discusses the imperative of a coherent and integrated approach to Irish language and culture education.

As well as a selection of relevant media items from the year in post-primary education, the section also features Jim Moore on the Post Primary Education Forum; and an article by Bernadette O'Sullivan, NUI Galway on how education should be conceptualised, inspired by the ideas of education and creativity scholar and innovator, Prof. Ken Robinson.

The 'Who's Who' profile for post-primary this year is Joan Crowley O'Sullivan, National Director of the Professional Development Service for Teachers (PDST).

Post-Primary

Gearing up for Junior Cycle Change

John Hammond
Deputy Chief Executive of National Council for Curriculum & Assessment (NCCA)

In 2014, first year students in all schools will commence the new Junior Cycle Programme

The school year we're just entering, 2013-14, represents something of a watershed in Irish education; the final year before the new Framework for Junior Cycle is introduced and the year in which the education system gears up for that change.

The Framework for Junior Cycle was launched in October, 2012 by the Minister for Education and Skills, Ruairí Quinn. It followed extensive discussion and consultation around two NCCA papers on junior cycle, Towards a Framework for Junior Cycle (2011) and Innovation and Identity: Ideas for a new Junior Cycle (2010). These and related background documents are all available for reading and download at www.juniorcycle.ie.

In 2014, first year students in all schools will commence a junior cycle programme planned within the new Framework. What does this involve? What are the main features of the developments at junior cycle that the Framework facilitates?

Learning and skills
The developments, first and foremost, are focused on:

- enhancing learning in junior cycle;
- linking learning progress closely with assessment activity;
- engaging teachers directly in these contexts.

Because the student and their learning is the central focus of junior cycle education, the Framework establishes and clarifies what should be learnt at junior cycle. That learning is set out in 24 statements around which schools build their programme, select their subjects and design other learning activity.

The statements of learning suggest a different kind of core from the one we're used to. At the moment when we think of what is 'in the core' and what isn't we usually think in terms of compulsory, national examination subjects. The core requirements of the new junior cycle are set out in the statements of learning.

The skills of **literacy and numeracy** and six other key skills, Managing information and thinking | Working with others | Managing myself | Communicating | Staying well | Being creative are also emphasised in the Framework. All skills will be embedded in the learning outcomes of every junior cycle subject and short course – they won't be taught separately as such! There is considerable detail on each of the key skills in the Framework and there are toolkits to assist teachers using key skills in their classrooms on the junior cycle website. Overall, the level of detail and the toolkit supports give teachers a very clear picture of what a student who is developing the key skill should be able to do. They are the kinds of skills that have been identified in most countries as important for 21st century learning and living – skills that support students in understanding and getting to grips with learning and that contribute to preparing them well for senior cycle and life after school.

Curriculum and programme planning
There are significant features of the Framework related to curriculum and programme planning. It is important to stress that it is a Framework more than a set of rules. It allows the school to review its junior cycle programme and adjust it, reform it or plan a new one depending on what it sees as needed. It offers the school considerable flexibility and autonomy in this context.

It is envisaged that subjects will remain a central part of the junior cycle programmes of schools – none of the existing junior cycle subjects have been removed from the range of options available. In addition to subjects, there are two new curriculum components available for schools to use on an optional basis – short courses and priority learning units. Some short courses will be developed and specified by the NCCA. Currently, nine courses are being developed. They will be available to schools from September, 2014. But, for the first time, schools can also develop their own short courses locally and these can feature in junior cycle certification.

The priority learning units (PLUs) are specifically designed to be used with students with a particular level of special educational need, as part of a Level 2 Learning Programme (L2LPs).

Further information about these programmes, including a toolkit to assist teachers in developing programmes for individual students, is available on the junior cycle website.

Assessment
Arguably the most significant feature of the changing junior cycle is in the area of assessment. The most fundamental change in this context is the decision to discontinue the Junior Certificate and to introduce school-based assessment on a widespread basis at junior cycle. All short courses and most subjects will be assessed in the school. In the subjects English, Irish and Mathematics, 40% of the overall marks will be based on a component assessed in the school.

This change involves building a new assessment culture in schools and a new set of assessment arrangements for the education system. There is existing practice, knowledge and experience within schools and beyond to draw upon in this context but it nonetheless represents a challenge of considerable proportions that will take time, resources and supports, in the areas of professional development, quality assurance and quality control, to embed.

These are some of the features that can contribute to introducing new assessment arrangements successfully:

- Increased emphasis on formative assessment and on feedback to students about how to progress learning and performance;
- Linking the outcomes of formative assessment into summative assessment tasks like portfolios of work, presentations and interviews ;
- Clear learning outcomes and expectations for learners in the specifications for subjects and short courses;
- Including examples of student work, marked and annotated by teachers, that show those expectations for learners being realised;
- Clear description of the assessment tasks (for certification) involved in each subject and short course and the Features of Quality criteria (set out grade by grade) that teachers use to discuss and mark student work;
- A process of school-focused moderation where teachers have the opportunity to discuss how they apply standards in marking student work using the material above and, through this discussion, achieve consistency and comparability of judgement

in how standards are applied to the work of students;
- A toolkit of assessment materials and guidance to support teachers in their work on assessment;
- Professional development and other practical supports;
- The retention of State Examinations in English, Irish and Mathematics and the provision of Final Assessments in all other subjects by the State Examinations Commission for the foreseeable future;
- The monitoring of the assessment results of schools by the Department of Education and Skills.

Certification and reporting

A final noteworthy feature of the developing junior cycle is the introduction of a new School Certificate and School Report. Certification of achievement at junior cycle will now be school based. It will be available at two levels, aligned with Levels 2 and 3 of the National Framework of Qualifications. A final decision has yet to be taken on what the certificate will be called but the title will be used by all schools. Level 3 is the level at which the current Junior Certificate is placed. The Level 2 certificate is new and is designed to recognise the learning achievements of those students with special educational needs who have followed a Level 2 Learning Programme in junior cycle.

The certificate will be will be generated and issued by the school. It will include the results of the student in the subjects they have taken or in a combination of subjects and short courses. A student can include up to a maximum of 10 subjects on the Level 3 certificate. If they include up to the maximum of 4 short courses, then the number of subjects decreases e.g a certificate can include 8 subject and 4 short courses or 9 subjects and two short courses.

It's also envisaged that schools, at the end of junior cycle, will also issue a School Report that may include, on an optional basis, elements such as participation and attendance, personal and social development, a key skills profile of the student, their achievement in subjects and short courses additional to those included on the certificate, and a student reflection on their junior cycle. The report will be assembled using an online reporting tool similar to that currently used in primary schools.

What's next?

The Framework for Junior Cycle places students and learning at the centre of the educational experience and, through the developments and change associated with it, is aimed at enabling young people to be active, resourceful and confident learners in junior cycle, onwards into senior cycle and beyond into all aspects and stages of their lives. The work involved in developing junior cycle and introducing the Framework is extensive and multi-faceted.

Minister for Education and Skills, Ruairí Quinn T.D., marking the Junior Certificate Reform with students

Some key developments to watch out for over the school year 2013/14 are tabled below.

Developments	Timeframe
Specification for Junior Cycle English	Consultation: June to September 2013 Online publication: Autumn 2013 Introduction in schools: September 2014
Specifications for Junior Cycle Business Studies, Irish and Science	Consultation on the background paper and brief for the review of these subjects: September to October 2013 Development of specification: 2013/14 Consultation on specification: April-June 2014 Online publication: Autumn 2014 Introduction in schools: September 2015
Specifications for NCCA short courses in Level 3 Artistic Performance Chinese Language and Culture Civic, Social and Political Education (CSPE) Digital Media Literacy Physical Education (PE) Programming and Coding Social, Personal and Health Education (SPHE) Level 2 Personal Project: Caring for Animals Exploring Science	Consultation: Autumn 2013 Online publication: Early 2014 Introduction in schools: September 2014
Assessment and Moderation Toolkit	Initial online publication (material will be added on a regular basis): Autumn 2013
Toolkit for Level 2 Learning Programmes	Currently available on www.juniorcycle.ie Refined and published online: Early 2014
Template and Guidelines for developing short courses	Currently available on www.juniorcycle.ie Refined and published online: Autumn 2013

EDUCATION IN THE MEDIA

Teaching Council unable to hire staff out of its own resources

September 29, 2012

The Teaching Council is unable to hire an extra 16 staff out of its own resources because it is subject to the public sector recruitment embargo. It is a self-funded body and most of its income comes from subscription fees paid by the 77,000 registered teachers in the State.

The council, under new director Tomás Ó Ruairc, has said it has a requirement of 48 staff.

Under the Government moratorium and the employment control framework, however, it is not allowed to employ more than 32 staff irrespective of having the resources to employ 48 staff without drawing anything from the State purse.

In a statement, the council contended that this anomaly must be revisited for self-funding bodies such as itself. The extra staffing resources would allow it to tackle a backlog in Garda vetting and assessing foreign qualifications, and also allow it to carry out new functions.

"The public sector staffing moratorium has placed significant pressure on the staff complement of the Teaching Council," said the statement. "As the council's functions expand over the coming two years with the implementation of outstanding sections of the Teaching Council Act, the capacity and resources of the organisation will need to grow accordingly to ensure it remains fit for purpose."

The council made a submission to the Department of Education in June 2011 and is still awaiting a decision. The department, in response to queries from The Irish Times, said the employment control framework applied across the public sector.

It said Minister for Education Ruairi Quinn was aware of the situation and that there had been ongoing discussions with the Department of Public Expenditure about the matter. The department said while the council paid the staff, the pensions were funded by the Department.

"The possibility of outsourcing some Teaching Council functions is being examined by the department," said a spokeswoman.

www.irishtimes.com/newspaper/Ireland/2012/0929/1224324604416.html

Huge Appetite for Change

Clive Byrne *Director of the National Association of Principals and Deputy Principals (NAPD)*

Junior Cycle Reform is aimed at shaping independent learners who can think for themselves

In the interests of our long-term development as a society, Ireland urgently needs a generation of creative, bright, self-directed, confident, entrepreneurial, creative, innovative young people. That is less likely to happen with an educational model that values teaching to the test, rote learning, passive classrooms and with a terminal exam focus.

Over the next eight years, the traditional Junior Certificate will be replaced by a curriculum that aims to shape independent learners who can think for themselves. The objective is to get students used to analysing critically and problem-solving, rather than just learning off by heart. Teacher-dominated, passive classrooms with passive learners accepting pre-digested material will be replaced with active classrooms with self-directed learners who can make choices about what and how they learn.

Our current system leads to teaching-to the-test, rote learning, memorization and competition within and between schools and, of course, league tables. The new Junior Certificate will encourage teacher-supported self-directed learning and will encourage innovation, experimentation, self-discovery and collaboration within and between schools.

The role of the teacher will fundamentally change within the new Junior Certificate – the teacher will be less a transmitter of facts and more a facilitator of student learning. Classrooms will have less teaching and more learning. The big challenge for Principals will be to lead teachers in the WHY and the HOW of this paradigm shift.

Stephen Covey's model of change has three dimensions – the WHY, the WHAT and the HOW.

The WHY of the new Junior Certificate will take intelligent persuasion. The challenge for Principals will be to convince teachers, parents and students of the need for change.

Explaining the WHAT will be relatively easy – a thinner curriculum, short course and a new pedagogy that will offer teachers opportunities to inspire, excite, challenge and provoke learning.

The HOW will be the greatest challenge for Principals. Teachers will need to engage with the new pedagogy and how it will change classroom practices and improve the nature and quality of learning.

Since Ireland has little history of inter-school collaboration - mainly due to local competition for student enrolment - developing collaboration between and within schools will be both a challenge and an opportunity.

With our current system, the Department decides what is to go into the students' heads (curriculum), gives it to teachers to "deliver" (pedagogy) and then creates tests to see if it's in there (examinations). The classroom is often a place where 30 students go to watch a teacher working. The new Junior Certificate will make learning the activity of the learner. The learner will be active in constructing sense from the classroom environment and not passively receiving it. Teachers will be encouraged to collaborate with learners about the sequence of topics in the curriculum and to collaborate with learners on how they learn most effectively. Our current system is oriented towards scores, grades, exam results and believes that ability alone leads to success (you either have it or you don't). In effect, our current system is about proving competence which leads to assessment of learning. By contrast, the new Junior Certificate is about improving competence; about assessment for learning; is oriented towards learning and has at its heart a belief that effort leads to success.

The Junior Certificate is no longer a terminal exam because about nine out of 10 children who start school stay there to complete the Leaving Certificate. It is important that, before we embark on system-wide reform at senior cycle, parents and educators are assured that the reforms proposed in junior cycle work. We can afford to be imaginative in our reforms, provided school leaders are adequately resourced to deliver the new model.

The Minister's reassurance that adequate resourcing will be provided is welcome, because reform is long overdue. Research from the Economic and Social Research Institute has shown that students in their first year of secondary school make little or no progress in reading and maths. In second year, many become disengaged and rarely reconnect with school.

In our eagerness for reform, we must not lose sight of what is working within the system. Ireland has talented teachers and school leaders who care about our children and who have demonstrated creativity and innovation in straitened circumstances. Our current system restricts teachers' professional autonomy, judgement, creativity and passion with packed prescribed curricula. The new Junior Certificate will allow schools to develop their own programmes and make best use of the passion and creativity of staff.

There is currently confusion about the multiplicity of mandated changes - Junior Certificate, School Self-Evaluation and the Literacy & Numeracy Initiative. In reality, these initiatives are three legs of the one stool. Principals must be helped to understand, and in turn help teachers, students and parents understand, why Junior Certificate reform must be prioritised – it is the key reform that everything else can successfully hinge on. Reform is deliverable, provided it is supported by proper resources

In all this, we must ensure that the integrity of our education system is upheld and standards are not dumbed down. By trusting our teachers and challenging pre-conceptions, we can aspire to a second-level system that is responsive to societal needs and stands on its own educational merits.

There is a broad base of support for Junior Cycle Reform. There is huge appetite for change, for reform that will rekindle the innate enthusiasm and grá of everybody involved in the education process.

Clive Byrne, Director NAPD with Bridget McManus, Chairperson NCCA and Kay O'Brien, President NAPD at this year's NAPD Symposium on Curricular Reform.

EDUCATION IN THE MEDIA

ASTI: Changing status of fee-paying schools could cost State €40m a year

October 08, 2012

The Association of Secondary Teachers Ireland is claiming that if every fee-paying school went non-fee, the State would be forced to fork out an extra €30m to €40m a year to fund them.

Over the weekend, Minister of State Alan Kelly called for the amount of Government support to private schools to be revisited as part of plans to cut €77m from the education budget. When fee income and State support is combined, private schools receive €277m annually.

Pat King, General Secretary of the ASTI, said fee-paying schools miss out on many subsidies from the State.

"In a fee-paying school, the number of teachers is smaller, paid for by the State. They don't get a capitation grant for students, they don't get science grants, economics grants and there are other capital grants they don't get.

"So if every fee-paying school in the country in the morning decided to become non fee-paying, the State would have to find and extra €30 to €40m a year to fund them."

www.irishexaminer.com/breakingnews/ireland/asti-changing-status-of-fee-paying-schools-could-cost-state-40m-a-year-569756.html

---

'We are no worse off financially since we cut tuition fees'

October 10, 2012

ONE well-known Protestant school says it is better off since it stopped charging tuition fees a year ago. Adrian Oughton, principal of Wilson's Hospital School, Multyfarnham, Co Westmeath said: "We are no worse off financially and we are better off in terms of the pupil-teacher ratio."

The school, with 440 day and boarding pupils, negotiated a deal with the Department of Education to enter the free education scheme.

Its pupils pay for services, such as accommodation (in the case of boarders), meals and supervised study. "We charge day pupils for what the State does not provide; those things are entirely optional but we have a very high uptake" said Mr Oughton.

The school is now allowed one teacher for every 19 pupils, compared with one for every 21 pupils in fee-paying schools.

It also qualifies for various grants the department pays to schools in the free education scheme.

www.independent.ie/lifestyle/education/we-are-no-worse-off-financially-since-we-cut-tuition-fees-28891572.html

---

ICT literacy among teachers needs to be improved – Jobs Committee report

October 10, 2012

There is a need to boost the level of ICT-literacy among teachers if Ireland is to prepare a workforce with relevant skills for a knowledge economy, according to a new report A review of the ICT skills demand in Ireland from the Committee on Jobs, Enterprise and Innovation. There is a significant gap between the ICT skills which are taught in our schools and those that are required to take up job opportunities in the technology sector, the report found.

Report author and Committee member, Senator Deirdre Clune, said: "Only 25% of post-primary teachers rated themselves as having 'intermediate' or 'advanced' IT skills according to a 2008 inspectorate report. It will be impossible to further the development of computing within schools unless we have teachers who are capable of showing their students how to engage with the creative use of ICT."

Inadequate resources and broadband in schools are also making the implementation of ICT strategies more difficult, the report said.

The Committee notes the decision to include the option of studying short courses in computer programming as part of a new curriculum to replace the Junior Cert at schools. However, its report recommends making programming and/or computer science as much a part of the curriculum as French or German.

EDUCATION IN THE MEDIA

"Our students must have the opportunity to learn the global languages of programming such as Java and C++. There are already transition year programming modules on stream including the NCCA-approved Lero programme, Gem Pool's module and Coder Dojo. However, these efforts need to be supported and supervised.

The aim should be to create a single compulsory transition year programming module with uniform implementation. Yet, we must not rest there. A one-off module for transition year is not sufficient to create the swell of ICT literacy which is needed. At present, there is no stand-alone computer science subject at either Junior or Senior Cycle. It is imperative that alongside the integration of ICT into other subjects, the option of taking computer programming as an exam subject is available to students."

The report found that the European Computer Driver's License, the programme used by 54% of schools in terms of having ICT on the curriculum, does not offer any significant insight into the creative use of ICT equipment.

A high-level of proficiency in mathematics is an essential part of technology courses, according to the report. While the increase in students taking higher level maths is a very positive step, it is also important to monitor the uptake of higher level maths to ensure that the increased numbers taking the exam and the increase in those securing honours grades this year is sustained. In tandem with this, the new Project Maths curriculum should also be closely monitored to ensure it is delivering on its goals and that students are leaving school with the requisite problem solving skills, it said

The importance of creating an accreditation system for ICT professionals was also highlighted.

"The benefits of creating an accreditation system within the Irish technology sector include providing greater clarity for those who wish to pursue careers within the ICT sector, assuring a standard for companies investing in Ireland and raising the standard of the entire industry," said Senator Clune.

Read the report at http://bit.ly/SP3zrL

Schools seek to offer free education

October 10 2012

THREE Protestant schools have approached the Department of Education about changing their fee-paying status.

The move has been forced by cuts in state support for the country's 55 fee-paying schools, expected to continue in December's Budget.

Protecting
The exploratory talks could see the three schools enter the free education scheme, which means they would no longer charge for tuition.

However, they could charge for other services such as meals and supervised study and, in the case of boarders, accommodation. They would operate along the lines of a model introduced in Wilson's Hospital School, Multyfarnham, Co Westmeath, a year ago.

Being in the free education scheme would mean the department would pay the €518 per pupil to cover day-to-day running costs and caretaker and secretarial services.

They would also have their building costs covered by the department instead of paying for them themselves. While the State is committed to protecting minority ethos schools, it is also legally constrained from discriminating in their favour. This means it cannot exclude them from cuts.

Protestant schools are predominantly boarding schools as they provide an education in their minority religious ethos for families scattered over a wide geographic region.

There are no Protestant schools in 13 of the 26 counties, demonstrating the lengths many pupils have to travel to get their education of choice.

Many of the pupils come from families that are not well-off, and 30pc of Protestant parents receive financial help in sending their children to school.

Chris Woods, principal of Wesley College, Dublin, said research done by the Protestant schools showed that 15pc of pupils were from households where the income was less than €40,000 a year, while in 5pc of cases the income was below €20,000.

www.independent.ie/lifestyle/education/cuts-prompt-protestant-schools-to-seek-talks-on-offering-free-education-28891573.html

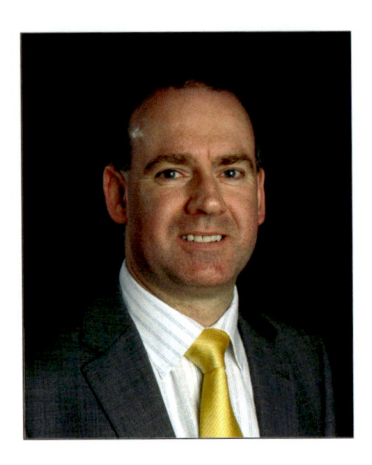

A Framework for Junior Cycle

Dr Pádraig Kirk *CEO of Co. Louth VEC and Director of Junior Cycle for Teachers Support Service (JCT)*

DES has established a dedicated CPD Service: Junior Cycle for Teachers

A *Framework for Junior Cycle*, published by Minister Ruairí Quinn in October 2012, is widely regarded as one of the most significant reforms of post-primary education since the foundation of the State.

The *Framework* sets out the principles, key skills and statements of learning for the new Junior Cycle. It also highlights the need for fundamental changes in our approach to learning, teaching, assessment and curricular planning if we are to improve the quality of students' learning experiences and outcomes.

The implementation of the *Framework* is set to commence in schools in September 2014. Through a commitment to the implementation of all aspects of the Framework, the education system will be able to deliver a Junior Cycle that places the needs of students at the core of learning and teaching.

Necessity of leadership and support
Comprehensive implementation of the *Framework* will improve the quality of the learning experiences and outcomes of all students. This will require leadership and support not only from the Department of Education and Skills (DES), National Council for Curriculum and Assessment (NCCA) and the State Examinations Commission (SEC), but from school management in particular.

It will also require the commitment of teachers and the support of parents in realising high expectations for all students.

As envisioned throughout the *Framework* document, schools will need to be supported in implementing change:
...... the *"new focus on assessment, particularly on 'assessment for learning' as well as on 'assessment of learning' will be a challenge for schools and will require significant Continuing Professional Development (CPD) for principals and teachers"*, (p.3)
.... *"supports will include detailed subject and short course specifications, an assessment and moderation toolkit for teachers and schools that will include samples of student work exemplifying a range of standards, a new reporting system for Junior Cycle and also include formative and summative resource material for use by schools. Principals and teachers will have access to CPD"*, (p. 19)
........*"Principals and Deputy Principals in their leadership role will receive comprehensive professional development in curriculum leadership, educational assessment, including moderation and change management"* (p. 26)

Dedicated Professional Development Service
As a response to the scale of the task of implementing the Framework in schools, the DES has established a new dedicated continuing professional development (CPD) service – Junior Cycle for Teachers. The aim of this new service is to support schools in their implementation of the Framework through the provision of appropriate high quality continuing professional development for school leaders and teachers,

and the development of suitable resources. This support will remain in place for the lifetime of the implementation phase of the Framework. Junior Cycle for Teachers support service (JCT) The Junior Cycle for Teachers (or JCT) support service will commence formally in July 2013, well over one full year in advance of the implementation of the first subject in the new Junior Cycle in schools, namely English. It was announced in January 2013 that I (Pádraig Kirk) would act as the Director of this new support service, having previously served as Chief Executive Officer of Co. Louth VEC and Senior Inspector in the Department.

Secondment to JCT
In May this year a recruitment drive commenced to fill other posts in the service on a secondment basis. Soon, two Deputy Directors will join the team, one with a specialism in school leadership, the other in student assessment. In its first year the service will also recruit a cohort of Advisors (English). The administrative base for JCT is Monaghan Education Centre and the service will work collaboratively on an on-going basis with all of the other twenty Education Centres around the country, with NCCA, SEC and with existing DES support services including the Professional Development Service for Teachers and the Special Education Support Service.

Phased implementation of subjects
The *Framework* outlines a schedule for the phased implementation of subjects. There are four phases in all, commencing with the introduction of English to 1st year students in the 2014/2015 school year, with other subjects introduced in the following years. CPD will be provided for subject teachers a year in advance of the implementation of the subject in schools. So, for example, while science will be introduced to 1st year students in the 2015/16 school year, the provision of CPD for teachers of science will commence in the 2014/15 school year. This principle applies across all of the Junior Cycle subjects.

National database of teachers
In order for the new support service to ensure that all teachers are provided with the opportunity to engage in relevant CPD, it is important that the service has knowledge of who the teachers are. For this reason JCT will compile a national database of teachers. Work is already underway in the case of teachers of English. In the final term of the 2012/2013 school year all post-primary school principals were requested to register their schools' English teachers online at www.metc.ie. The response was tremendous, and while it is necessary to follow up with a small number of schools, it is clear that schools are keen to ensure that their teachers are involved. The Junior Cycle is also provided in certain non-school settings (e.g., Youthreach) and the same registration process must take place in the case of these settings also. This will ensure a comprehensive register of teachers.

Dedicated CPD for school leaders
The successful implementation of the Framework in schools will require effective leadership. School leaders will be provided with dedicated CPD provision to support them in this role. In the last term of the 2012/2013 school year, all school leaders were invited to an information seminar on the new Framework. These seminars were extremely well attended nationally and provided opportunities for principals and deputies to gain further insights into the Framework itself, including its implementation, and to offer constructive feedback. The views of participants were recorded and will feed into the design and delivery of national CPD provision.

Mix of delivery modes for CPD
Implementing the Framework is not without its challenges. Notwithstanding the fact that many schools already implement most, if not all, of the initiatives espoused in the Framework, the Framework will require schools to implement them on a more formal basis. There are a number of elements that stand out, for example, the new specifications for subjects, short courses and Priority Learning Units, student assessment practices, moderation, standardised testing and reporting of student progress. These necessitate that CPD, in order to be relevant, must focus on these areas, while simultaneously ensuring that other key areas are catered for also. This will be done through a mix of delivery modes provided both during and outside of school time. All teachers will be provided with the opportunity

to engage with no less than three full days of CPD during school time across the roll out of their particular subject area. These days will take the form of facilitated CPD sessions, and for the first time on such a wide scale, some in-school teacher-led sessions for which the DES will provide appropriate substitution cover. A wide range of elective CPD opportunities that will be provided outside of school time, including after school and at weekends, will also be available. On-line support will be a key feature of the supports provided for schools with a new one-stop-shop website currently being planned for all things JCF related – www.juniorcycle.ie.

CPD for school leaders and English teachers
The first CPD sessions for school leaders will commence early in the next school year (September/October 2013). These will be followed by CPD sessions for teachers of English which will commence after the October mid-term break. Subsequent years will see an intensive period of CPD for teachers at post-primary level as all of the new subjects are rolled out across schools.

Many teachers, however, will have a second teaching subject and these teachers will find that many of the new skills and practices picked up during the CPD engaged in within the context of their first teaching subject will automatically transfer across to their other teaching subject(s).

While the provision of CPD is vital, it must then be reflected in the changing approaches adopted by the school through the leadership of school management and the classroom practices of teachers. We all have a role to play in ensuring that the new Framework makes the difference that we want it to make.

Making it work
JCT will discharge its functions with the utmost efficiency. The new service will display high standards of professionalism and will undertake its work in accordance with best national and international practice. As Director of JCT, I look forward to working collaboratively with all the education partners in supporting schools in implementing the JCF and to gaining their trust, cooperation and confidence.

EDUCATION IN THE MEDIA

Dundalk teacher critical of the Junior Certificate reforms plan

October 17, 2012

THE Junior Cert reforms announced last week have been criticised by Dundalk teacher Elaine Devlin, a representative of the Association of Secondary Teachers (ASTI) and a member of the Teaching Council of Ireland.

Ms Devlin, a Maths teacher at De La Salle College, said teachers welcome reform, but the relationships between teachers, pupils and parents will now be drastically changed.

"Effectively, teachers will spend up to four years assessing students.

"The current Junior Cert has public confidence," she added, pointed out that details of the Minister's plans were a surprise.

"At meetings we had with the National Council for Curriculum and Assessment (NCCA) we were told that the terminal Junior Cert exam would stay. It seems that the Minister has gone behind the backs of the NCCA. "It's worrying. Essentially, this is a political decision made due to the lack of funds. It costs €20 million to operate the Junior Cert."

Last week Minister for Education Ruairi Quinn announced the most radical shake-up of the junior cycle programme since the ending of the Intermediate Certificate and Group Certificate examinations in 1991. Minister Quinn has broadly accepted proposals put forward by the National Council for Curriculum and Assessment to introduce a new junior cycle programme.

Local Oireachtas members were among the first to welcome the initiative.

Senator Mary Moran said such a move is long overdue and will ensure that students, rather than examinations, are at the centre of the three year Junior cycle.

Her Labour Party colleague deputy Gerald Nash said the Junior Cert has been tinkered with for years but it is essentially the same structure today as it was in the past.

www.dundalkdemocrat.ie/news/local/dundalk-teacher-critical-of-the-junior-certificate-reforms-plan-1-4347807

EDUCATION IN THE MEDIA

Teachers shouldn't fear marking own students – Quinn

October 20, 2012

TEACHERS have nothing to worry about in assessing their own students for the new-style Junior Cert, Education Minister Ruairi Quinn has insisted.

He said they would only be doing what they are already doing for pupils in non-exam years, such as second and fifth year.

There has been hostile reaction from teacher unions to the scale of change involved and concerns have been expressed about the extra workload, training and the implications for pupil-teacher relations.

Mr Quinn siad that teachers could be "absolutely assured" that taking on the role of assessor of their own students would not damage the teacher-pupil relationship.

"I am only asking them to do in third year what they currently do in second year and fifth year," he told the Irish Independent.

Speaking earlier at the annual conference of the National Association of Principals and Deputy Principals, he said the phrase 'continuous assessment' was misleading and hard to sell to people who "fear the workload involved".

He said it should be more accurately called 'periodic work-programme assessment', similar to what already happens with portfolios at third level.

www.independent.ie/lifestyle/education/latest-news/teachers-shouldnt-fear-marking-own-students-quinn-3265534.html

---

Parents to get assessments on schools' performance

October 20, 2012

SECOND-LEVEL schools are set to give parents an annual report based on the school's own assessment of teaching and learning in the school.

Minister for Education Ruairí Quinn said the new school self-evaluations would place the school principal "at the centre of developing a culture of quality, improvement and accountability in their schools".

Addressing the annual conference of the National Association of Principals and Deputy Principals (NAPD) in Galway, Mr Quinn explained how the new system would complement the work of Department of Education inspectors in school evaluations.

The new school self-evaluations would, he said, "give schools and school leaders more autonomy in setting the agenda for school improvement. Providing a clear framework in which school leaders and their staffs can focus on 'making learning better' is the key objective of school self-evaluation . . .

"You are being empowered, as school leaders, to manage the teaching and learning in your schools and to focus, with your teachers, on educational improvement in your schools."

Mr Quinn also announced that new rules for school admission, designed to ensure greater transparency in the allocation of places, will be introduced next year. He said legislation allowing for a new regulatory framework for enrolments would be published in 2013.

This should improve openness, consistency and equity in enrolment processes.

The new rules are likely to be controversial. They could, for example, force schools to abandon admissions policies that favour the siblings of current or past pupils. In 2006, a Department of Education audit found some schools were using restrictive admissions policies to exclude certain categories of students, including Travellers, those with special needs, children of immigrants and low academic achievers.

Mr Quinn told the conference there would be a rise of more than 20,000 pupils in the post-primary sector over the next five years.

The Minister also announced the establishment of a new group in his department that will oversee changes in the transition by students from Leaving Cert to higher education.

The new transitions reform steering group – chaired by secretary general of the Department of Education Seán Ó Foghlú – also includes representatives from the third-level colleges.

www.irishtimes.com/newspaper/ireland/2012/1020/1224325506270.html?via=rel

JC2.0: Doing it our way

Noel Malone *Principal, Coláiste Chiaráin, Co Limerick*

It has utterly transformed the educational experience of our first years

One of the most revolutionary and striking innovations in my fourteen years as principal of Coláiste Chiaráin has taken place over this past academic year, with the introduction in the school of what we call the 'Super Options'.

Coláiste Chiaráin has developed a track record over the past decade in terms of ICT and curriculum development, so when the opportunity presented in 2012 to participate in the Framework for Junior Cycle, we felt we were well positioned to pilot the new programme.

Having applied to become one of the initial lead schools, we were delighted to learn that we had been chosen to participate. Although 2014 was identified as the year in which the first new junior cycle subjects would be launched officially, we decided to begin the introduction of our version of the 'short courses' in September 2012.

Since then, I can honestly say that it has utterly transformed the educational experience of our first years and has radically refocused teaching and learning across the wider curriculum in the school. We have of course worked closely with our colleagues in the National Council for Curriculum and Assessment, following their guidelines and providing support where possible to other schools that were considering similar moves.

Eight examinable subjects

One of the first key decisions we made was to scale down to eight examinable subjects for our incoming first years. This was not as difficult a challenge as had been initially envisaged. It did in fact provide a solution to a long-standing concern of subject overloading at junior level. Up to this, our students studied up to 12 or 13 subjects for the Junior Certificate and by all accounts we knew that this was unsustainable and probably counterproductive educationally. The decision was pretty easy in the end.

All students from September 2012 now study **Irish, English, Mathematics, Science, a modern language, and one each from a range of 3 optional lines.** We also strategically made sure that History, Geography and Business were available repeatedly on each of these lines so as to ensure their on-going viability and this has indeed worked to our satisfaction. We also now deliver the CSPE and SPHE programmes in a cross-curricular approach, probably in a much more effective manner than the conventional approach.

'Super Options'

In addition to these eight examinable subjects, each student now has a choice of 2 from up to 12 new 'Super Options'. Drawing on the talents and skills of our staff, we designed these initial new 'Super Options', which we presented to all the key stakeholders - including parents, teachers and students. The response was extremely positive, so we embarked on a programme of NCCA workshops, in-house training and development courses, and most importantly, the establishment of education partnerships with industry and third level institutions. The response from both these sectors has been tremendous, and the establishment of an educational and/or career context for each Super Option gives the programme both authority and credibility.

196 Hours

These two Super Options are studied over the three-year Junior Cycle – with three class periods each per week. These Super Options were designed to follow the same guidelines as the NCCA short course templates, but we extended the duration to 196 hours, as opposed to 100 hours. Outside of this time, we encourage at least 4 'workshop' opportunities over each of the 3 school years. We worked very closely with the NCCA to ensure that all our new courses faithfully fulfilled the requirements of the Framework for Junior Cycle document, which was published by the Minister for Education and Skills, in October 2012.

Advantages of Super Options

The reason we decided to opt for this particular approach was that we felt that taking 'short courses' as currently defined by the NCCA would in some way limit the opportunity for students to fully engage and 'achieve' in a very real and tangible manner. Taking two of these 'Super Options' over three years gives a real chance for teachers to move the subject to a much higher plain than the alternative 'short courses' model, which in our view runs the risk of being too disparate and 'bitty'. We wanted real 'substance' and achievement. We also chose carefully the range of these 'Super Options', with the essential proviso that they would enhance, in a very real way, the body of knowledge and learning skills for the students in preparation for the current Leaving Certificate and indeed the wider third level sector. There is a direct relationship therefore between each of these subjects and potential choices for our students at senior cycle.

Innovative new areas of study

I am happy that we chose well and the progress to date has been very gratifying. The 'Super Options' include an array of innovative new areas of study, ranging from Television & Radio Broadcasting, to Experimental Science Investigations, to Innovation & Creative Entrepreneurship. They are delivered in conjunction with a variety of third level education and business partnerships, including RTÉ, the University of Limerick, University College Cork and the Institutes of Technology, specifically through our link with the Limerick Institute of Technology.

The 'Super Options' are designed to help students develop their own creativity, confidence and decision-making skills, as well as introducing them at an early stage to what we believe are exciting career options.

Lights, camera, action!! Junior cycle students at Coláiste Chiaráin get creative with TV broadcasting.

Creative entrepreneurship at Coláiste Chiaráin

Three additional programmes

Having completed the first year of the Super Options syllabus, from September 2013, we added three new programmes, Chinese Language and Culture, European and World Studies and Digital and Print Journalism. Each of these programmes originates from the talents of our teachers and the needs of the students. It has engendered a whole-school impact, which I would never have imagined.

Increased professional collaboration

Another key consideration in year 2 was the issue of sustainability, especially in terms of capacity building. We encouraged each of the first year teachers to move on with their class into second year and largely replaced them in the new first year with different personnel from amongst the other staff members. This has further encouraged a level of professional collaboration not seen in the school heretofore.

Positive change in teaching and learning

These are difficult times for all of us in education, but I have to say that now that we are well into the programme, we are confident that we have established a syllabus that will facilitate positive change both in the way we as educators teach, and how our students learn. Most importantly, teachers, parents, third level institutions and industry are working together to provide the very best opportunities for each and every student in our school.

I would passionately urge my colleague principals and deputy principals to make a start as soon as possible. The train is on the track and we all need to be on it or we run the risk of being left behind.

EDUCATION IN THE MEDIA

Teachers stage protest over cuts

Oct 24, 2012

Several thousand teachers protested in Dublin this evening against cuts to pay for new entrants and continuing cuts to the education sector.

The protest march - organised by the three teacher unions - comes after changes to new entry grades. In 2009, new entrants to the profession earned about €41,000. But a raft of budget and other cuts has cut the starting salary to €32,000. The cuts have already been imposed on at least 3,000 teachers. Two thousand more - due to graduate from teacher training college next year - also face this cut.

The Valuing Education protest at the Dáil was supported by hundreds of student teachers and recently qualified teachers.

Yvonne Rossiter, a newly qualified teacher, said the treatment of new teachers is everyone's concern: "If we devalue the work of one teacher we short-change every student and every teacher in our schools."

www.irishtimes.com/news/teachers-stage-protest-over-cuts-1.744913

The 'Valuing Education' Protest in Dublin, October 2012

EDUCATION IN THE MEDIA

Garda probe into abuse of teachers on Facebook page

November 17, 2012

Gardai have been contacted after a social network site was used to target teachers and pupils at a secondary school.

Photographs and derogatory comments were posted on a Facebook page about some of the teachers at the all-boys Colaiste Phadraig Christian Brothers CBS school in Lucan, Dublin.

Principal Brian Murtagh confirmed the gardai had been contacted after the school was made aware of the postings on the social networking site.

"There were offences, and untrue statements were made on a Facebook page about some pupils and teachers at our school," said Mr Murtagh.

"We have had the page removed and we are trying to take all measures that we can to find out where the material was sourced and who put it up."

www.independent.ie/irish-news/garda-probe-into-abuse-of-teachers-on-facebook-page-28902492.html

---

New Croke Park talks to begin in January

November 29, 2012

The Government held preliminary discussions yesterday with the teacher unions and formal talks on a new Croke Park deal on public sector pay and reform are to begin in January. There will be ongoing contact next month and the Labour Relations Commission will also be involved.

The public sector unions are expected to use this time between now and January to consult with their executives to get agreement on entering talks.

A chairman for the negotiations is also expected to be identified.

Sources involved in the preliminary talks said Government officials set out the reasons why the Coalition felt new negotiations on extending the talks were needed and how an extra €1bn might be saved from the public sector pay bill.

Public sector unions warned they would not accept any more pay cuts for lower-paid workers.

www.independent.ie/irish-news/new-croke-park-talks-will-begin-in-january-28941055.html

---

Education Minister concerned by time spent on teaching religion and Irish

December 11, 2012

Minister for Education Ruairí Quinn has said that he would like to see more time devoted to science and maths in Irish schools, rather than Irish and religion.

"The official time allocation for religion and Irish is high relative to other subjects," he said.

"Am I personally concerned by that? Yes I am. But this is a choice that parents and teachers and the patrons of schools have to make.

"That's why we've asked for the divestment by the Catholic church of many of the primary schools that they currently have."

A new international study has found that Irish primary school students scored above the average in reading, maths and science.

However, we failed to make it into the top performing countries in any of the three - particularly maths and science.

Ireland was ranked 10th in reading out of 45 countries; 17th in maths out of 50 countries; and 22nd in science out of 50 countries.

www.irishexaminer.com/breakingnews/ireland/education-minister-concerned-by-time-spent-on-teaching-religion-and-irish-577436.html

School Self-evaluation

Deirdre Matthews *Assistant Chief Inspector at the Department of Education & Skills*

An enabling process for schools

The 2012-13 academic year saw the initial steps in the introduction of school self-evaluation as a national educational initiative in all primary and post-primary schools.

Of course, many individual schools, and indeed teachers, had developed their own reflective practices in the years preceding this initiative. In some cases, schools had engaged in very useful self-evaluation, for example by inviting students and parents to participate in surveys to identify areas for improvement, and by tracking and analysing student progress and learner outcomes.

The school self-evaluation initiative builds on these valuable practices, and gives all schools a systematic process to follow to enable them to be the agents of their own improvement.

The initiative also reframes the school development planning process, with less focus on documentation and greater emphasis on the core work of schools: teaching and learning.

The Minister for Education and Skills, Ruairi Quinn, launched the initiative in November 2012. The Department of Education and Skills has provided a range of supports to assist schools to embark on the school self-evaluation (SSE) process and to take ownership of it. Circulars 39/2012 (primary) and 40/2012 (post-primary) were issued to all schools, explaining the requirements, areas of focus, and timeframes for various stages of the process.

The Department Inspectorate developed Guidelines for primary and post-primary schools and copies were sent to all schools. In October 2012, the Chief Inspector wrote to schools inviting them to avail of a visit from an inspector to outline the process to the whole staff; between November 2012 and May 2013, inspectors facilitated SSE visits for almost 3000 schools.

As part of its continuing support for schools engaging in the SSE process, the Inspectorate maintains a dedicated web site, www.schoolself-evaluation.ie, which holds all the documents mentioned above, and a range of resources including templates for schools to use and adapt. In addition, the web site hosts an expanding repository of schools' own SSE reports and improvement plans, which schools have generously made available in the interests of sharing and further developing good practice. The Inspectorate has also produced an e-bulletin, the SSE Update, on the web site, which will appear three times a year to provide ongoing advice and information to schools.

How the SSE process works
The SSE process has a number of distinguishing characteristics. It is systematic and evidence-based. It operates at a whole-school level. It enables schools to evaluate their own teaching, learning and assessment practices in a structured way. It ensures that improvement is real and identifiable. Above all, it affirms that teaching and learning – what is happening in the

classroom – is the beating heart of every school.

A school's successful engagement with self-evaluation will be seen, not in what is put down on paper in an improvement plan, but in what is put into action in every classroom to improve learner outcomes.

The six steps of the process (see below) are intended to help schools to see clearly what is happening in their teaching and learning practices, to build on strengths and to address in a targeted way any areas of weakness they identify.

In following the process, schools will gather relevant evidence, analyse it, and make judgements regarding their own strengths and areas for development.

To provide schools with a benchmark by which to evaluate their own practice, the SSE Guidelines contain evaluation criteria and quality statements with regard to teaching and learning.

Having evaluated their current practice, schools will then record their findings, draw up their own three-year improvement plans, and implement and monitor the actions they have agreed in order to achieve the planned targets.

Schools will inform the school community about their findings and improvement plans.

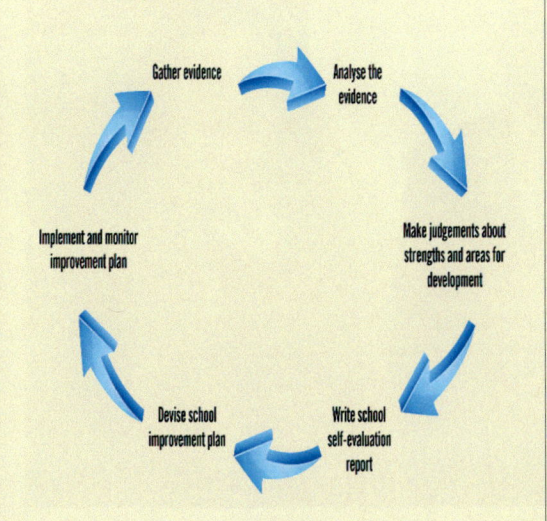

How the SSE process supports other educational initiatives

School self-evaluation is part of a natural progression towards systematising existing and developing good practice with regard to school improvement. It is also an important component of the education landscape at a time of innovation, when the educational needs of children and young people require new approaches and the setting of challenging but realisable targets.

The National Literacy and Numeracy Strategy (2011) contains such targets and commits educational stakeholders to achieving improved outcomes for all our learners. Therefore, the implementation of the Strategy has been coupled with the SSE process in the materials and supports provided.

The six steps of the SSE process will facilitate schools to ascertain learners' present levels of proficiency, set measurable targets, and identify and put into action the teaching and learning approaches best suited to achieving the targets.

Crucially, the SSE process will ensure that literacy and numeracy development is a whole-school endeavour, allowing students to learn and apply the same key skills across the curriculum.

DEIS Schools

The DEIS initiative, delivering equality of opportunity in schools, requires action planning in a number of areas. The SSE process will help DEIS schools to ensure that their action plans are soundly based, and will have an impact, wherever relevant, on teaching and learning practices and on students' learning experiences.

This focus on enhancing teaching and learning should assist DEIS schools in their ongoing efforts to improve attendance, retention, and attainment.

An Ghaeilge

Táthar ag iarraidh go mbeidh daltaí ábalta Gaeilge a labhairt agus a léamh agus a scríobh go líofa. Chun an aidhm sin a bhaint amach ní foláir do scoileanna machnamh a dhéanamh ar an gcaoi ina múineann said an teanga.

Cycle diagram: Gather evidence → Analyse the evidence → Make judgements about strengths and areas for development → Write school self-evaluation report → Devise school improvement plan → Implement and monitor improvement plan.

Ní miste freisin iniúchadh foirmeálta a dhéanamh ar an gcaighdeán a bhaineann daltaí amach sna scileanna teanga uile. Cabhróidh féinmheastóireacht scoile leo an machnamh gníomhach sin a dhéanamh ar bhonn córasach, uile scoile.

Nuair a bhaineann scoileanna úsáid as an bpróiseas féinmheastóireachta scoile beidh siad ábalta a scéal féin a insint maidir le conas a mhúintear an Ghaeilge agus cén torthaí a bhaineann daltaí amach, torthaí a thomhaistear ar dhá leibhéal, cén ghreim atá acu ar an teanga (ábhar agus scileanna) agus cén dearcthaí atá acu i leith na teanga.

Nuair atá cinntí, bunaithe ar fhianaise, déanta ag scoileanna faoi seo beidh siad in ann spriocanna cinnte don fheabhsúchán a dhearadh agus tabhairt faoin bhfeabhsúchán sin. Tá tábhacht faoi leith ag baint leis an obair laethúil, leanúnach a tharlóidh dá bharr sna seomraí ranga; sin an áit ina gcuirfear an feabhsúchán i bhfeidhm.

Má dhírítear ar an teagasc agus ar an bhfoghlaim le fuinneamh, le dea-thoil agus le dóchas ba chóir go rachadh an córas chun leasa na Gaeilge. Deis luachmhar a bheidh ann chun an caighdeán Gaeilge a ardú sna scoileanna.

Common ground
"I want the junior cycle to place the needs of our students at the core of what we do and to improve the quality of their learning experiences and outcomes."

So writes Minister for Education and Skills, Ruairi Quinn, in the foreword to A Framework for Junior Cycle (2012).

This statement firmly situates junior cycle reform in the same space as the school self-evaluation process: responding to the needs of learners and focusing on improved outcomes.

Post-primary schools can use the school self-evaluation process to gather and analyse evidence, and to draw conclusions about the strengths and areas for development in their current junior cycle. The school improvement plans arising from this work could articulate

Minister for Education and Skills, Ruairi Quinn, T.D., with students from Dominican College, Sion Hill, at launch of 'School Self Evaluation' Programme

targets in terms of the Framework's statements of learning, while the SSE Guidelines will help schools to identify the teaching and learning practices required to achieve them.

Used in this way, the SSE process will enable schools to explore the range of learning opportunities that the Framework has opened up for junior cycle students.

How school self-evaluation will develop
The Inspectorate's presentation to schools, which is available on the SSE web site, emphasises that the SSE process works best when integrated into the day-to-day life of the school. It simply becomes, for schools, 'the way we do things'.

Because teaching and learning is the core work in every school, it makes sense for this to be the initial focus of school self-evaluation.

Over time, and using the same six-step process, schools will also evaluate management and leadership, and support for pupils and students.

During the first cycle of school self-evaluation, from 2012-13 to 2015-16, all schools will use the SSE process to support their work on literacy and numeracy skills development. As a third element, primary schools will select one other curriculum area in which to develop and implement a three-year improvement plan; post-primary schools will select another aspect of teaching and learning, and may choose, as outlined above, to focus on a reformed junior cycle curriculum. Irish medium schools will have an litirtheacht Ghaeilge as a third focus.

SSE a proven practice
Work in progress in Irish schools, including DEIS action planning, has shown that school self-evaluation works. It is embedded practice in many other countries, notably those whose educational systems are seen to be very successful. The Department looks forward to continuing to work in partnership with schools as they engage with this process and make it their own, for the benefit of all our children and young people.

EDUCATION IN THE MEDIA

Support key to brave new world of tech in classrooms

December 13, 2012

Despite the Department of Education and Skills outlining a purchasing framework for schools investing in information and communications technology (ICT), many in the education sector claim successfully integrating technology into the classroom is done on an "ad hoc" basis throughout the Republic, often relying on "one person to take the lead" in individual schools.

Adrienne Webb, who is on the national executive of the Computers in Education Society of Ireland, says that often an individual can be left to act as ICT manager, tech support and teacher "all in one".

"There are a lot of schools up and down the country where a teacher who happens to express an interest" in ICT are handed over complete responsibility for it, she says.

Webb, who is quick to add that she's "blessed to have a principal who invests in maintenance" of technology in St Michael's Holy Faith Secondary School in Finglas, was reacting to recent UK research which claims that hundreds of millions of pounds' worth of technology is under-utilised in schools and of little use to a pupil's education.

The research, carried out by Nesta – an independent charity which promotes innovation – stated that while technology can "offer opportunities to transform learning and teaching", there was "no strong evidence of this transformation taking place".

'Very disappointed'
Here in the Republic, Clive Byrne, director of the National Association of Principals and Deputy Principals (NAPD), says he has heard of several school inspectors who have been "very disappointed" with the use of available technology such as interactive whiteboards in the classroom.

"They have the technology there but often it isn't used as much as it could be, either through reluctance of the teachers to use it in case it won't work when the inspectors are in, or they're not comfortable with the technology," says Byrne.

www.irishtimes.com/business/sectors/technology/support-key-to-brave-new-world-of-tech-in-classrooms-1.2694

Literacy improvement and SSE

Stiofán Ó Cualáin, *Acting Principal, Coláiste na Coiribe, Galway*

Many schools chose literacy as their initial area of focus for School Self Evaluation

The year saw significant progress in literacy improvement measures in second level schools, following the launch of School Self Evaluation (SSE) guidelines in November 2012. Literacy improvement at second level uses the SSE process as a framework, the first cycle of which began in 2012-13. Many schools chose Literacy as their initial area of focus for SSE.

Core teams established
In these schools core teams were established, comprising teachers from various subject areas and led by a link teacher who attended the relevant in-service support provided by the Department. These teams, guided by the SSE framework, set about gathering data in an effort to establish areas of strength and areas for improvement in their particular school.

Examples of such data gathering exercises included the use of questionnaires to explore the views and habits of students, teachers and parents on literacy related issues from their recreational reading habits to classroom practices.

Analysis of State examinations results and results of standard tests (STEN) received from feeder primary schools also provided valuable insights.

Support, in-service, review and action plan
A member of the Inspectorate visited each school between November 2012 and May 2013, to give a presentation on SSE to school staff. Much emphasis was placed on literacy and numeracy during this session which used Croke Park hours for its delivery. Principals were invited to an information session on SSE which was presented by the PDST with members of the Inspectorate present.

Link teachers were invited to two days in-service between March and April, to support them in their new roles and to provide them with relevant resources/practices to take back to their schools. The work of the core team during the year was presented to the school staff at the end of term in many instances, where agreed areas of focus and action plans for September 2013 were outlined. These objectives are the subject of each school's SSE report for the year, which represents the blueprint for action for the year ahead.

Increased awareness of literacy
There has been an explicit focus on literacy improvement in second level schools in the past year, which has raised the awareness among subject teachers of literacy and of their newly defined role in its improvement among their students. With the preparation work complete, 2013-14 promises to be an interesting year in literacy Improvement efforts in the post-primary sector.

Edco e-books

The Educational Company of Ireland

Ireland's Leading e-book Publisher
www.edcoebooks.ie

"As ICT Coordinator, I found Edco e-books excellent. The ease of deployment, support and outstanding quality of the content puts them head and shoulders above other publishers."

Frieda Crehan, Malahide Community School, Co. Dublin

Edco e-book Free Trial
To apply for a free trial, please email us at info@edcoebooks.ie

Why choose Edco e-books?

- Edco e-books make learning more engaging
- They include over 8,000 interactive videos, animations and audio clips
- The tools allow students to highlight and make notes to personalise their learning
- Edco e-books can now be rented which means reduced annual costs and savings
- With Edco e-books the days of heavy schoolbags are over

Here are some of our tools in action...

Handwriting Tool: Use your finger or stylus to write key notes or prompts on the page.

Highlighter Pen: Highlight key pieces of text on the page.

Post-it Pad: Type class notes and review them later through the post-it pad symbol.

Resources Tab: Search your current page or chapter for one of over 8,000 relevant video files, animations, audio clips, PowerPoint presentations, exam questions, solutions, and numerous partner resources.

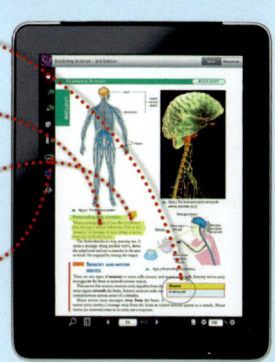

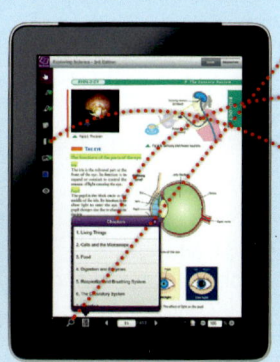

Search: Search the current page or chapter by inserting keywords.

Table of Contents: Quickly skip to another chapter within the book.

Bookmark: Bookmark a page for easy access later.

"Edco e-books are in my opinion the most advanced digital books at this time."

Colm O'Connor, Piper's Hill College, Naas, Co. Kildare

www.edcoebooks.ie

Call our dedicated e-book representative,
Alan Wright on 086 771 2978 or email awright@edco.ie

The Educational Company of Ireland
Ballymount Road, Walkinstown, Dublin 12. Phone: (01) 4299231 | Email: info@edcoebooks.ie
www.edcoebooks.ie | www.edco.ie

EDUCATION IN THE MEDIA

Croke Park extension talks begin today

January 14, 2013

Talks begin today on an extension to the Croke Park deal, covering pay and pensions in the public service. The Government is said to be targeting savings of €300m this year, and €1bn over three years.

The opening session of the Croke Park extension talks will bring together representatives from 26 worker groups before they move to the Labour Relations Commission in the coming days. It is expected topics such as increments, premium pay and overtime will all be tackled in the process.

Teachers may be asked to change the way supervision and substitution payments are made. Premium pay and overtime for gardaí and prison officers may also be looked at.

Some reports say the coalition intends to bring in compulsory redundancies in the public service for the first time, targeting workers who are unsuitable for redeployment.

www.irishexaminer.com/breakingnews/ireland/croke-park-extension-talks-begin-today-581069.html

---

New campaign: 'Put Education First'

5th February 2013

A campaign is being launched aimed at changing legislation which "allows schools to discriminate against children and teachers on basis of religion."

The legislation in question is Section 7.3 (c) of the Equal Status Act 2000 and Section 37 of the Employment Equality Act.

According to the Integration Centre, the first of these laws allows schools to refuse children entry because of their parents' religious beliefs and can prevent children from going to school in their own neighbourhoods; while the second enables schools to hire and fire teachers based on their religion.

The Integration Centre points out that, as of the last twelve years, many schools have incorporated a 'Catholics First' stance into their admissions policy. This discrimination is unconstitutional, the Centre says, and contravenes international human rights law – yet it is protected by the legislation mentioned above.

The Integration Centre is calling on the Minister for Education & Skills Ruairí Quinn – who is clearly "committed to progressive reform" – to change these laws.

Croke Park discussions continue apace

February 15, 2013

The Government has told public service unions that there will be pay cuts for higher-paid public servants, though the percentage or the threshold for those cuts has not been specified.

It is understood that the issue of increments is at an impasse and is not being discussed at present.

Headcount reductions and cuts in higher pay are expected to contribute a sizeable proportion of the savings sought.

Additional working hours are also being sought by the Government, though it is understood that they are no longer seeking five additional hours per week per employee.

The supervision and substitution payments for teachers, which cost €127m per year, are also being targeted for significant reductions and possible abolition. The requirement could be reduced by teachers working extra hours.

It is understood the unions are seeking to have a higher level of income exempt from the pension levy, and are also concerned about the emerging two-tier workforce and outsourcing.

They also want to ensure that any agreement that emerges is fair and equitable.

Discussions on how the Government proposals can be applied on a sector-by-sector basis are taking place this afternoon, starting with the health and education sectors, and will continue over the weekend.

EDUCATION IN THE MEDIA

Key elements of new Croke Park deal

February 25, 2013

A deal struck with trade unions to slash €1bn from the public servants' pay bill includes salary cuts, increased working hours and pay rise freezes. Some of the main features of the three-year agreement which would run to June 2016 are as follows:

- Those currently on a working week of less than 35 hours will in future work a minimum of 37 hours.
- Those working between 35 and under 39 hours will have to put in at least 39 hours, with additional hours helping to cut public sector numbers.
- Reduced overtime rates, down to time and half for those on less than €35,000; time and a quarter for those earning more than €35,000.
- Public servants currently on a 39-hour week will provide an unpaid hour's overtime.
- So-called "Twilight payments" – for work between 6pm and 8pm – will be abolished.
- A reduced Sunday rate of pay, down from double-time to time-and-three-quarters.
- A three-year freeze on annual pay rises for those earning more than €65,000.
- Public-sector workers with salaries between €35,000 and €65,000 will get two 15-monthly, rather than annual pay rises over the period of the agreement.
- Those on less then €35,000 will have a three-month postponement on their first due pay rise, before returning to annual increments as normal.
- Those at the top of their pay scales will have to give up six days annual leave over the next three years or offer an equivalent cash deduction from their salary.
- High-earners will have their salaries and allowances cut 5.5% for those between €65,000 and €80,000; with an extra 8% off earnings between €80,000 and €150,000; another 9% off pay between €150,000 and €185,000 euro; and 10% shaved off any earnings above €185,000.
- The cuts would mean someone on €100,000 euro salary and allowances would be down €6,000 to €94,000; someone on €160,000 would have their earnings cut to €149,100; while a top public servant on €200,000 would see their pay cut to €185,350.
- Supervision and substitution payments for teaching staff to be axed.
- Other cutbacks include changes to flexitime, work sharing arrangements, redeployment provisions, new performance management arrangements and pay-grade restructuring.

www.irishexaminer.com/breakingnews/ireland/key-elements-of-new-croke-park-deal-586085.html

---

Teacher unions urge no to Croke Park deal

February 28, 2013

The Teachers' Union of Ireland (TUI) and the Irish Federation of University Teachers (IFUT) have both advised members to ballot against accepting the terms of Croke Park II.

The executive of the Teachers' Union of Ireland, which represents second and third-level teachers, met yesterday to discuss how the €1bn in savings being sought by the Government would impact upon its 15,500 members.

Afterwards general secretary John MacGabhann said his executive believed the suite of measures proposed were "excessively draconian" and that the best way to address the financial situation was through taxation.

He also said there was a deep mistrust of the Government as people had signed up to the first Croke Park deal on the basis that it would not be revisited.

Earlier, following a meeting of its executive, the Irish Federation of University Teachers made the same recommendation as TUI to its 2,000 members.

The standing committee of the Association of Secondary Teachers Ireland met yesterday. Afterwards it said there was "deep anger" at plans to worsen pay and conditions as all second-level teachers had already taken a pay cut of 14%.

The ASTI and INTO are seeking clarifications from the Government before deciding on their recommendations to members ahead of ballots.

www.irishexaminer.com/ireland/teacher-unions-urge-no-to-croke-park-deal-224004.html

Embracing ICT to enhance teaching and learning

Seán Gallagher *Director of PDST Technology in Education (formerly NCTE)*

Technology will never replace the art of teaching but it can enhance it

ICT has infiltrated every part of our lives. Technology is used in a myriad of ways to supplement the art of teaching in Irish classrooms and with each year come new technologies and new applications. As a profession, we have embraced ICT to enhance almost all aspects of school life – administration, communication and most importantly teaching and learning.

Pedagogical use of ICT

PDST Technology in Education (formerly NCTE) aims to support teachers in their integration of ICT in teaching and learning. In line with Department of Education and Skills priorities, the focus of ICT professional development for teachers is currently on the use of ICT to support literacy, numeracy and school self-evaluation at primary and post primary levels.

The Professional Development Service for Teachers (PDST) must ensure that opportunities for teachers to experience ICT in their learning and teaching are a key element of all professional development events offered to teachers. While the technologies and their potential uses change rapidly, the focus of ICT CPD remains firmly on the pedagogical use of ICT. With that in mind, this article will explore some of the ways ICT can be used in Irish classrooms and by Irish teachers for their professional development.

Digital content for learning and teaching

Digital content, in all its various forms, provides opportunities for richer, more engaging learning experiences across all schools subjects and all learning styles. The ongoing strategy within PDST Technology in Education with regard to digital content is:

- To ensure that an adequate supply of high quality, Irish curriculum-related digital teaching and learning material is available to teachers and students at all levels
- To ensure that teachers are encouraged and supported in the creation and sharing of their own digital resources.

Britannica online

To support these objectives the www.scoilnet.ie portal website which provides teachers with access to 13,000+ classroom-focused, digital content web resources, all of which have been mapped to the Irish curriculum, will be further developed. This development will facilitate the sharing of open educational resources (OER) created by Irish teachers. The central procurement and distribution of niche digital reference content for all schools will be continued– Britannica online is now available free of charge to all Irish schools on the School Broadband network. It is also available to all pupils through the Scoilnet website.

With three reading and content levels available for pupils – Foundation, Intermediate and Advanced – pupils can access differentiated content within the same interface. The challenge for us as a profession is to assign tasks to our pupils to engage with this quality content by encouraging them to analyse it, summarise key points, choose relevant sections and choose how they will present their findings. Higher order skills will be used instead of a shallow copy and paste exercise.

Scoilnet maps

Scoilnet maps is a fantastic interactive mapping tool available to all Irish teachers. It offers a range of features that support teaching and learning, including "spotlight" and "swipe" tools that help teachers to highlight all locations in Ireland and compare aerial photos with maps (current and historical). It also features an "elevation" tool to study cross-sections, map contours, landscape and terrain. This is in sharp contrast to the past when quality maps of all locations were difficult to access.

Based on software developed by ESRI Ireland, Scoilnet maps give pupils the opportunity to experience real-world technology and develop skills that will equip them for adult life. It features an easy-to-use interface that is suitable for students of all ages. Scoilnet Maps was developed as collaboration between Scoilnet, the Professional Development Service for Teachers and the forward planning unit of the Department of Education and Skills.

Following nomination by ESRI Ireland, Scoilnet maps has received a Special Achievement award from ESRI Inc. for the use of a geographic information system (GIS) for Ireland. The awards ceremony took place on July 10th at the San Diego Convention Centre. Teachers in other countries would love to have access to this fantastic technology. If you have not already done so, register for a Scoilnet account at www.scoilnet.ie to use Scoilnet maps in your class.

Looking into other classrooms

One of the core reference books for students of teaching in recent times was 'Looking in classrooms' by Thomas L. Good and Jere Edward Brophy. It brought the reader into classrooms and explored a variety of teaching methodologies that could be employed in different situations. On entering the teaching profession, we concentrate on establishing the routines and effective methodologies for our own classrooms – often without consulting with any other teacher. This can lead to a feeling of professional isolation and yet there is tremendous potential for learning by 'looking into our own classrooms'. There is also potential for learning from our fellow teachers all over the world. Advances in technology now allow teachers and students to collaborate and communicate in a myriad of different ways. A combination of technologies and online tools/media can be used. Teachers in other parts of the world can learn from Irish teachers also.

Collaborative learning

Within Ireland, powerful communities of learning exist irrespective of geographical location where teachers can engage in professional dialogue and continue to develop professionally throughout their teaching careers. One example of a pilot project which took place in the North West this year was the Collaborative Learning Initiative (CLI). One group of teachers who took part in this project were the teachers in the island schools off the Mayo coast – Clare Island, Inisturk and Inisbofin.

Advisors from the Professional Development Service for Teachers (PDST) facilitated professional dialogue between the schools through a free online video conferencing application. The teachers collaborated on shared documents and were delighted that the feeling of professional isolation was reduced as a result. Further details of this and other communities can be viewed at http://pdstcli.wordpress.com. Advances in technology have resulted in a number of free tools for schools that allow users share and collaborate on documents/presentations/ spreadsheets in real time.

The Computers in Education Society of Ireland (CESI) have a very active online community of learners where queries relating to the use of ICT in schools are posted and solutions debated. The 2013 CESI conference, marking the 40th anniversary of CESI, was a well-attended event with inspirational inputs in a variety of presentation and workshop formats – see http://www.cesi.ie

Bringing innovation to all schools

There are many teachers using ICT brilliantly to enhance their teaching and the learning in their respective classrooms. This innovation can be shared through learning communities – face-to-face and online. They can also be showcased through the use of good practice videos – there are a variety of them on the PDST Technology in Education website – http://www.pdsttechnologyineducation.ie. The most recent videos produced focus on the use of Scoilnet maps in the classroom as well as the use of tablet devices.

Showcase learning

Students sometimes feel that the results of a terminal examination like the Leaving Certificate do not do justice to the work they have put into that subject. Understanding is demonstrated through handwritten responses to nationally agreed questions. Perhaps deeper learning could be exhibited if students could present their learning as part of a larger portfolio complete with shared reflections and notes with their teacher – a shared collaborative space.

This does not mean a series of manila folders for all subjects anymore. Electronic or eportfolios afford students the opportunity to develop various stages of their learning in a private area. Other sections of the eportfolio can be shared with their teacher and feedback and various annotations can be made. The showcase section of the eportfolio is where the student demonstrates the artifacts they have created at the culmination of a unit of work. For exam revision, the eportfolio can be used as a useful revision tool where the reflections of the students can be revisited as well as the various artifacts created.

It is crucial that students acquire the ICT knowledge, skills and attitudes and values to allow them use these tools and new methods of communication effectively. Ireland is part of a larger Eufolio project where eportfolios are being researched and will be piloted in Irish schools. This may inform the use of eportfolios as part of the reformed Junior Cycle.

Online Safety

The emergence of social media tools and their use in schools means that Media Education, as outlined in the Social, Personal and Health Education (SPHE) curriculum/syllabus at primary and post primary levels respectively, is assuming huge importance in the promotion of safe and effective use of these multi-faceted means of communication.

Interdepartmental collaborations have been established already with one particular example being the 'Garda Schools Programme', 'Webwise', 'Stay Safe programme' and the SPHE support service at post primary level all working together on the 'Connect with respect' and 'Watch your space' awareness campaigns in the area of internet safety. To mark Safer Internet Day 2013, there was an anti-cyber bullying campaign directly targeting secondary school pupils in Ireland with the key message being to empower bystanders to intervene positively in online bullying situations.

The Webwise youth panel met three times in the last year and played an active role in the Digital Childhoods seminar series and the development of the anti-cyber bullying campaign. Webwise also participated in the Department of Education and Skills' Anti-Bullying Working Group. Further supports will be developed in this way to ensure our use of digital tools is carried out responsibly.

Continuing Professional Development

International initiatives indicate that appropriate professional development and support, in tandem with teachers' personal motivation, are key factors in progressing ICT integration. Accordingly, teachers must be enabled to gain the capabilities to make meaningful use of ICT in their work, both by themselves and by their students to assist student learning. ICT is increasingly being included in teacher professional development and is being integrated in all curriculum design and development.

Access to CPD by teachers is being increased by the provision of CPD and learning resources in different formats to include face-to-face, online and blended forms of learning. These are being integrated with existing and new arrangements for CPD to enable learning both during the school day, in teachers' own time and anytime, anywhere learning.

Leading elearning at school level

Empowering leadership in the integration of ICT in schools through enhanced supports to school principals as curriculum leaders within a school is another key consideration. A key element of the e-Learning planning process is the e-Learning Roadmap that enables schools to prioritise areas for ICT development under a number of headings including teacher professional development. School-based and school-cluster based approaches to CPD often form part of this plan and will continue to be supported as part of the overall CPD provision. A module on e-learning planning developed by PDST Technology in Education has been included in all leadership programmes facilitated by PDST.

Schools broadband and services

A vision of technology-enhanced learning recognises the capacity of ICT to motivate and inspire students to engage with, and explore the world around them. To do so students need to be equipped with future proofed life-long learning skills. The emerging range of 21st century technologies increasingly facilitates this process by using online collaborative and interactive learning tools and environments to support learning.

The ICT infrastructure required by schools to support this vision needs to provide high quality access to ICT and online services for teachers and students to use and share digital resources from anywhere in the school. Cloud based services can be similarly accessed from outside the school by teachers and students to facilitate anytime, anywhere learning opportunities, and to extend collaborative learning and interaction with other learners beyond the traditional school day.
In term of priorities it is essential to continue to develop the schools broadband network into a national high quality network for all primary and post-primary schools, regardless of their location or size, and support the provision of the necessary ICT infrastructure to assist schools to access online applications and services.

Schools need relevant and high quality advice and guidance in terms of suitable technologies, processes and tools to select the appropriate technologies to support their learning needs. PDST Technology in Education will continue to provide advice to schools in these key areas. By the end of 2013, an additional 200 schools (in Dublin, Meath, Kildare and Wicklow) will receive quality 100Mbps broadband with all remaining Post Primary schools connected in 2014. The current strategy document for ICT in schools – Investing effectively in Information and Communications Technology in Schools, 2008 – 2013 will be replaced by a new ICT strategy document for schools in 2014.

Conclusion

Technology permeates every aspect of our lives. Technology must never be seen as a replacement for the art of teaching but rather a set of tools we can use to enhance our teaching. The ultimate beneficiaries will be the students in our classrooms – these classrooms can now be windows to other classrooms around the world, windows to collaborative online spaces where we can reflect on our learning and present our understanding in a variety of ways. What an exciting time to be a teacher and student.

Edco e-books: keeping students interested

By Emer Ryan and Alan Wright

Since the company's foundation over a century ago, **The Educational Company of Ireland (Edco)** has grown to become Ireland's leading educational publisher, dedicated to providing high-quality learning and teaching products to generations of primary and post-primary students and teachers.

Over the years, the company has witnessed many significant changes and trends in Irish education. One of the most exciting in recent times has been the development of digital technology and the subsequent growth in the use of ICT in the classroom.

Recognising the opportunity provided by this, we created our edcoDigital website where teachers have free access to a wide range of digital resources and activities for use in the classroom. We have also been to the forefront in creating attractive microsites, where students can practise, study and revise, reinforcing what they have learned in class.

With the rapid growth in the use of tablets and other hand-held devices, e-books were the inevitable next step. Always seeking to provide a more engaging learning experience for students, we invested considerably in the development of a unique e-book platform. Working closely with leading IT companies, including Apple, Microsoft, Samsung and Intel, we were able to ensure that our platform is best in class.

A bespoke set of tools allows students to highlight, annotate, type notes, search for key words and ultimately to synchronise these individual revision notes across a range of devices and through the web version of their app, which is located at www.edcoebooks.ie. This important student information is all kept safe and secure in our cloud-based platform, which means that students, parents and schools can be confident that their e-books and notes are securely backed-up and can be easily retrieved if a device is lost or broken.

Teachers have told us that using Edco e-books in the classroom has brought about a more engaging learning experience, with students now having daily access to a wide variety of resources, from video files and audio clips to animations and interactive activities. Over 8,500 resources are currently available.

Edco e-books are now being used by over 11,000 Irish teachers and students across a range of schools nationwide. With increasing numbers of schools expressing an interest and requesting demonstrations, we continue to invest in our platform and to take advantage of new technologies.

This year saw the introduction of a unique 'workspaces' feature to our updated iPad app, following the successful launch of the same feature to our Windows app in September 2012. Workspaces allow students to access their e-book account from any PC through any web browser. Any notes created on this temporary device can be seamlessly transferred to a student's personal device the next time the student accesses it, ensuring that all notes are kept in one place for the duration of the student's Junior Cert or Leaving Cert cycle.

Conscious of the current economic climate and the pressure on parents and schools, Edco has introduced a new and innovative scheme that allows schools and students to rent their e-books, in order to spread the payment, help reduce annual costs and save money.

Edco is proud to have been involved in Irish education for so many years. With our passion for creating high-quality educational products, and the skills and expertise of our dedicated staff, we are ready to embrace the challenges and opportunities of the future with confidence and enthusiasm.

Emer Ryan is Publisher and Alan Wright is Digital Representative at The Educational Company of Ireland (Edco).

Modern Languages in Post-Primary Education

Karen Ruddock, *National Co-ordinator of Post-Primary Languages Initiative*

French is the most studied non-mother-tongue language in Ireland.

There is almost blanket provision of French across post-primary schools in Ireland and there are historical reasons for this associated with the European religious congregations with long-established French traditions who set up so many schools in Ireland. French is not an unimportant language; it is the official language across 33 countries and is the native language of more than 130 million people across 5 continents. One could however, argue that any language is important.

German, for example, which is only taken by a quarter of the number of students who take French is the most widely spoken language in Europe. It is spoken by 100 million native speakers. Germany has the 3rd strongest economy in the world and is the third biggest export nation in the world. It is also a country with plenty of job opportunities.

Six times fewer students take Spanish than French but with some 400 million speakers in the world some people estimate that it is more widely spoken than English, it is the official language of 20 countries, and Spain is also a country with strong historical links and cultural connections to Ireland.

Sixty six times fewer students take Italian than French although Italy has the same economic output per year as France, Irish exports to Italy are as much as half the value of exports to Germany, and two-thirds the value of exports to France. Italy is also the 3rd largest importer of Irish beef.

Non-curricular and other languages

One could argue in similar ways concerning the importance of other languages and in different ways concerning the importance of the non-curricular languages, many of which are spoken as home languages in the families of our recent immigrants. Although some of these languages are taught in the complementary schools, and the Post-Primary Languages Initiative provides some classes for speakers of Russian as a home language in Dublin and Galway, for the most part these languages are not supported.

Becoming a multilingual society

In the European context the learning of these languages is seen as central to the support of social cohesion and intercultural understanding in a world where there has been vast changes in the make-up of societies which necessitate recognition of what are termed plurilingual and pluricultural identities.

The National Development Plan 2007-2013, Transforming Ireland, identifies investment in language learning as an important goal, and establishes as a priority the development and implementation of an integrated language policy in line with recommendations made in a joint publication by the Council of Europe in Strasbourg and the Department of Education and Science Ireland Language Education Policy Profile in 2007. It also identifies the strengthening and diversifying of language learning as important national objectives. The main challenge for Ireland in this regard is to move away from "an official but lame bilingualism" to become a truly multilingual society, where the ability to learn and use two and more languages is taken for granted and fostered at every stage of the education system and through lifelong education. This commitment is a logical consequence of Ireland's membership of the European Union and the Council of Europe (p.51).

Most students only study one foreign language and the number of students not taking any language at Junior and Leaving Certificate examinations is increasing year by year. This is despite Ireland having signed up to the goal of "mother tongue plus two foreign languages" at Barcelona in 2002. This is also despite more and more emphasis being placed at a global level on the importance of being able to speak a second or third world language, as English becomes the basic 'must-have' skill. This is being increasingly recognized in countries such as India and China, which are already moving beyond learning English to embrace other emerging languages of importance.

Japanese and Russian have been provided on a limited scale in post-primary schools via the Post-Primary Languages Initiative (PPLI) and the introduction of Japanese has highlighted some issues and challenges associated with diversifying the choice and provision of languages at post-primary level.

Policy on languages provision overdue
No 'languages in education' policy has been put in place so no decisions have yet been made in relation to which languages should be taught, from which starting points and to which levels; how each should be reflected in a national curricular framework; and how each should be provided with an adequate supply of teachers.

The current provision of French creates an imbalance and, in the absence of a curriculum area for language learning (as recommended by David Little in Languages in the Post-Primary Curriculum (2003), new languages must of necessity compete for space with French. The crowded curriculum in Junior Cycle, the number of French teachers in the system, and the policy in many schools to make French compulsory also mitigate against diversification of languages. There are also issues in sourcing appropriately qualified teachers.

Concern over level of language proficiency being achieved
In relation to the level of language proficiency being achieved in schools, some concerns were expressed by the Language Policy Division of the Council of Europe in Strasbourg and the Department of Education and Science Ireland in their jointly published Language Education Policy Profile in 2007. They felt that insufficient attention was being given to the oral capacities, which in some cases tend to be reduced to rote learning for the examination. They pointed out that there might be a very crucial problem in the standards of language teaching, language acquisition and teacher preparation in the universities because graduates are not coming out of the universities with a high enough level to give their students a working knowledge of the foreign language they are learning.

Feast of jobs for multilinguals
In the meantime, most jobs that require language skills in Ireland are currently being filled by those from abroad with multilingual competence. John Dennehy, project director of the Make IT in Ireland initiative, pointed out in a recent Irish Times article (http://tinyurl.com/pa9ekld) that there would be more multilingual people hired by multinational companies in the next 12 months than java developers or .net developers. A recent report produced by Forfas and Expert Group on Future Skills Needs (2012) Key Skills for Enterprise to Trade Internationally outlines in particular the need to dramatically improve our foreign language proficiency and our ability to sell into international markets.

Galway Education Centre partners with UCD Confucius Institute

Bernard Kirk *Director of Galway Education Centre*

We can no longer ignore the need to engage with and understand China and its culture

The 2012 visit to Ireland of current Chinese President Xi Jinping when he was Vice President was a hugely significant event for Ireland. The Vice President of China is allowed to select and visit only 3 countries the year before he becomes President. Xi Jinping selected the USA, Turkey and Ireland as his destinations.

This question obviously arises, why Ireland? President Xi Jinping selected the USA as all Chinese Presidents need to visit the USA. Turkey was selected as it provides insights into Europe and Asia. The visit to Ireland was based on the fact that a Chinese delegation had visited the Shannon Duty Free Zone and returned to successfully replicate it in China. Now China sees Ireland as a country which had a rural economy in the 1950s but which transformed itself to become a high tech export-led economy. China wants to replicate this.

China has become the world's second largest economy. China controls the single largest stockpile of foreign reserves and while the US, Europe and Japan invested trillions of dollars into their economies to achieve one per cent growth the Chinese economy continues to show a 9.245 % average annual growth since 1970. Yet Time Magazine last June reported 'the library of doomsday books and articles about China's impending demise is crowded'.

Whatever one wishes to believe or predict about China and its economy, and bearing in mind the view of economist JK Galbraith that 'the primary purpose of economic forecasting is to make astrology look respectable', the fact is that we can no longer ignore the need to engage with and understand China and its culture.

In the summer of 2012, Galway Education Centre began discussions with the UCD Confucius Institute of Ireland to create a partnership to benefit teachers and young people in the West of Ireland. With global partnerships already established with companies such as Medtronic, SAP, HP, LEGO, the Galway Education Centre saw the benefits of co-operation with the UCD Confucius Institute. The Galway Education Centre were greatly honoured with the designation as the first UCD Confucius Outreach Training Centre. As the Confucius Institute of Ireland is affiliated with the Chinese Ministry of Education, the endorsement was a major boost for the Galway Education Centre.

This historic occasion was marked by a launch in October 6th 2012 by the Minister of Training and Skills, Ciaran Cannon TD. Also in attendance were Wu Xiaochuang, 2nd Secretary of the Chinese Embassy and Prof. Liming Wang, Director of UCD Confucius Institute of Ireland. The development was a direct response to the increase in demand for Chinese studies in schools in the West of Ireland. Such was the interest that the need for a local venue providing cultural and linguistic training directly to teachers in the region had become imperative.

The initial focus was on the provision of Continuing Professional Development for teachers. The decision was quickly justified with 22 teachers from places as widespread as

Castlebar, Longford and Mullingar attending a 10 week basic Mandarin and Chinese teaching skills course. Twenty of the teachers completed the course and continued with a further advanced course which is currently being completed. This group will travel to China during the summer before continuing to a higher level course in the Autumn. Due to the success of the first group, a second course has been provided.

The second phase of the strategy involved the introduction of Mandarin to primary schools. Employing a locally based teacher of Mandarin allowed the students of 3 schools, St. Nicholas NS Claddagh, Galway Educate Together and St. John the Apostle NS Knocknacarra benefit from weekly lessons. The cross curricular aspects have been highly emphasised with the topics and themes for Gaeilge each week being replicated in the Mandarin classes.

The provision of in school support allows children of all social backgrounds access to future possibilities in Mardarin and Chinese Studies.

The feedback from the teachers and students has been extremely positive and encouraging.

The third phase of the strategy has been the support for Mandarin and Chinese Studies at Transition Year level. The growing number of schools participating in the excellently resourced Transition Year scheme has created a demand which is continuing to grow rapidly.

The announcement of Chinese Studies as one of the short courses being devised by the NCCA for the Reformed Junior Cycle in 2014 will certainly add to the support teachers will require. This validation and recognition of the importance of Chinese language and Culture is a major milestone in Irish education where for the first time we have a major emphasis on a non EU language and culture.

The continuing developments and evolving strategy of the partnership between Galway Education Centre and UCD Confucius Institute of Ireland will greatly benefit teachers and students in the West of Ireland for many years to come.

Pictured at the launch marking the designation of Galway Education Centre as the first UCD Confucius Outreach Center L to r: Bernard Kirk, Director of Galway Education Centre, Wu Xiaochuang, 2nd Secretary of the Chinese Embassy, Minister of Training and Skills, Ciaran Cannon T.D., and Prof Liming Wang, Director of UCD Confucius Institute of Ireland

The Irish curriculum at Primary and Post Primary levels

Muireann Ní Mhóráin *Chief Executive Officer COGG*

The Government Statement on Irish published in 2007 affirmed support for the development and preservation of the language

The statement set out 13 policy objectives. Included were 3 objectives regarding Irish in the education system:

- Irish will be taught as an obligatory subject from primary to Leaving Certificate level. The curriculum will foster oral and written competence in Irish among students and an understanding of its value to us as a people. This will be supported by enhanced investment in professional development and ongoing support for teachers, as well as in provision of textbooks and resources, and in support for innovative approaches to teaching and learning.
- A high standard of all-Irish education will be provided to school students whose parents/guardians so wish. Gaelscoileanna will continue to be supported at primary level and all-Irish provision at post-primary level will be developed to meet follow-on demand
- Irish language pre-school education will continue to be supported and third-level education through Irish will be further developed.

The statement was followed in 2010 by the 20 Year Strategy for the Irish Language 2010-2030 with the headline goal of increasing over 20 years:

- The number of people with a knowledge of Irish from 1.66 million to 2 million; and
- The number of daily speakers from approximately 83,000 to 250,000

The Strategy set out areas of action under nine headings, including education and the actions proposed in the area of education were designed to achieve the underlying principles of the Strategy to:

- enhance and extend ability in Irish more deeply and among larger numbers of people;
- reverse negative attitudes towards Irish language usage and foster positive attitudes in their place; and
- expand the available opportunities for use of Irish within the education system by extending Irish as a medium of instruction, as well as a subject, and by linking school language learning to the informal use of Irish in recreational, cultural and other out-of-school activities.

Three years on and it would appear that the crisis in the economy and developments in the education system have overtaken the Strategy. Plans to open Naíonraí wherever there is demand, additional support for Irish in Colleges of Education and in University Schools of Education, funding for scholarships, the development of an Irish language education resource centre and of language acquisition units, funding for Irish Colleges and other planned actions have been parked at best - but shelved in many cases.

Primary

However, all is not lost as many changes are in the pipeline for Irish in the education system. A new integrated language curriculum is being developed for primary schools by the NCCA, to support the development of literacy in both Irish and English and to allow for language awareness and for skill transferral from one language to the other. This approach is of particular importance in all-Irish schools with an immersion education policy. The curriculum for the junior classes will be introduced in 2014 but the development of the curriculum for 3rd-6th classes has yet to commence.

Junior Cycle

At the same time, a new post primary junior cycle is being developed with newly developed subjects and short courses, a focus on literacy, numeracy and key skills, and new approaches to assessment and reporting. Irish will be a required subject and a revised syllabus is currently being drafted, but without continuity in language integration. The English syllabus has been developed without reference to the Irish syllabus and will be introduced to schools in 2014 and the Irish syllabus will be introduced to schools in 2015, but the primary school 3rd-6th class language curriculum will not be introduced until 2016. It is difficult to understand how continuity from primary to post-primary is to be achieved in the early years of the new junior cycle.

Junior Cycle Irish will continue until 2020 to have State Exams set by SEC but only at Higher and Ordinary Level (Foundation Level will be discontinued). This will further exacerbate the problem of having the same syllabus for learners, fluent speakers and native speakers of Irish. An add-on Short Course in more advanced Irish for Irish medium schools is to be developed as an option, but schools need not choose to offer it to students.

Review of marking system introduced in 2010

An NCCA review of the effects of the changes in mark allocation and assessment of Leaving Certificate Irish has commenced. The changes were introduced in 2010 with the aim of improving oral ability in Irish. 40% of the overall marks are allocated to the oral component, a very significant increase on the previous 25%. The weighting for other components was altered as a result. Anecdotal evidence would suggest that, rather than reversing negative attitudes towards Irish language usage, the new oral exam is further ostracising young people from the language. 20 picture stories to be prepared (learnt by heart) have taken over from where the much maligned Peig left off.

The main conclusion of research carried out by COGG in 2011-2012 found that the 2012 candidates (40% oral) scored marginally less well than the 2011 candidates (25% oral) in the aural comprehension and writing components. The difference in oral competence was negligible. If similar conclusions are made in the 2012-2013 review, it would seem likely that the current syllabus and mark allocation will be amended.

Need for overall plan and continuity

Where does this leave us? It is evident that a great deal of work is being done by the Department of Education and Skills, NCCA and others but it is of concern that so many changes are being introduced without an overall plan or 'roadmap'. Developments in Irish at primary junior cycle and post-primary junior cycle are progressing in parallel with a missing bridge between them although continuity is crucial in any attempt to improve the standard of learning and teaching in our schools.

The first cohort of students will sit the new junior cycle State Exam in Irish in 2018 but the recommendations of the Leaving Certificate review will be made in early 2014 and will, hopefully, recommend a change in mark allocation to be in place for the 2016 Leaving Cert exam and it would be expected that any changes should also be reflected at junior cycle level, but decisions may be made before the review is available.

There is huge support for the Irish language amongst the people of Ireland and those who seem opposed to it are usually opposed to how they were taught and what they had to learn. It is very urgent that these problems are addressed in our schools, be they English-medium or Irish-medium schools. To improve attitudes and ability some joined up planning, co-ordination and development is needed to avoid 'an phraiseach ar fud na mias'.

EDUCATION IN THE MEDIA

ASTI urges rejection of pay deal

March 7, 2013

The union representing secondary teachers is to urge members to reject the proposed new Croke Park agreement.

At a meeting today, the standing committee of the ASTI said teachers had reacted angrily to proposals for further pay cuts and a worsening of working conditions.

"The proposals come at a time when second-level schools are reeling from the impact of the education cutbacks including significant reductions in staffing and resources," it said.

The ASTI said its standing committee had expressed the view that "as public sector workers had already taken a 14 per cent reduction in pay and had delivered additional work and substantial savings under the Croke Park Agreement, the fairer way for the Government to achieve additional savings is through a more progressive tax system."

The union said its standing committee had noted that the Croke Park Agreement gave a commitment to no further pay cuts.

The ASTI said its standing committee had agreed to put proposals for a re-negotiated Croke Park agreement, which were produced by the Labour Relations Commission last week, to a ballot of members. However, the union is to recomend that they should be rejected.

The unions said the trade union movement would be in uncharted waters if the larger unions passed the proposals but it was rejected by a significant number of other groups.

www.irishtimes.com/news/asti-urges-rejection-of-pay-deal-1.1319740

Sally Maguire, a special needs teacher from Dublin, assumed the role of the President of the ASTI on August 1, 2013. Her key priority for the coming year is "to create greater awareness of the damage caused by nearly five years of education cutbacks and attacks on the teaching profession".

INTO makes no recommendation to members on Croke Park

March 01, 2013

The INTO - country's largest teacher union - is making no recommendation to its members on how to vote in the forthcoming ballot on the revised Croke Park Agreement.

The INTO will put the latest pay proposal to its 32,000 members in the coming weeks without any recommendation.

INTO members approved the original Croke Park deal by a two-to-one margin. INTO Spokesperson Peter Mullan said that there were pros and cons for primary school teachers.

In a statement the union said the proposals offered "significant potential gains" for newly-qualified teachers, who are on pay grades significantly lower than their colleagues who entered the system before 2011.

"However, all teachers are affected by the draft proposals, who have already had pay cuts imposed over the last two years," it added.

"The proposals include changes to increments, the loss of supervision allowance, and the financial impact for members earning over €65,000."

It said that given the government's threat to legislate for pay cuts in the absence of an agreement, the deal on the table represented the best possible package of measures that could be secured via negotiation.

Ballot papers will be sent to members on March 14, and are to be returned by mid-April.

www.irishexaminer.com/breakingnews/ireland/into-making-no-recommendation-on-croke-park-proposals-ahead-of-vote-586623.html

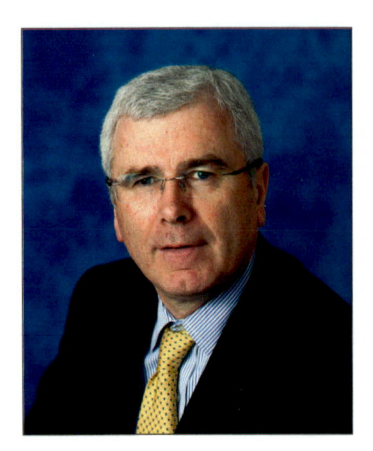

The Challenges for Voluntary Secondary Schools in 2013

Ferdia Kelly *General Secretary JMB/AMCSS*

The voluntary secondary sector plays a very significant role in the provision of education

Irish society has benefitted in so many ways from the influence of the not-for-profit or voluntary sector, especially in the areas of health and education. The voluntary sector is underpinned by a founding intention or mission and/or commitment to the common good.

Voluntary secondary schools comprising 52% of second level schools in this country, reflect all that is best in the voluntary sector.

The Ireland of today, with its more secular approach to life, presents new challenges for voluntary secondary schools in clearly articulating an identity which will be true to their founding mission and at the same time will continue to make a relevant contribution to the provision of second level education in our society.

The vast majority of Catholic voluntary secondary schools were established by religious congregations with a particular vision of education. The charism of the founder/foundress was the inspiration that led a particular movement to grow. Religiously professed sisters, brothers and priests staffed these schools and their presence provided a professional and human resource base on which secure foundations were laid.

From the 1960s onwards large numbers of similarly professional lay staff joined these schools and, over time, were employed in leadership roles. More recently, with the declining number of religiously professed personnel, many of these congregations have transferred their schools to new trustee bodies. These new voluntary organisations, with a civil and canonical identity, are now charged with giving contemporary expression to an inherited charism. A smaller group of voluntary secondary schools are continuing under diocesan, religious or lay trusteeship.

In November 2012 the Catholic Schools Partnership issued a discussion paper to trustees entitled "The future of Catholic education at second-level in the Republic of Ireland". Following feedback from the trustees, it was agreed that the Catholic Schools Partnership, in conjunction with the Association of Trustees of Catholic Schools and the Association of Management of Catholic Secondary Schools, would prepare a further discussion paper on voluntary secondary schools with a view to engaging in a public debate on the future of voluntary and denominational education in this country. It is proposed to engage a wider cross-section of stakeholders such as parents, pupils, teachers, members of boards of management and trustees in this debate.

Fee charging schools

The JMB raised serious concerns on behalf of the fifty-five fee charging schools as to the potential impact of the announcement in Budget 2013 of the increase in the pupil-teacher ratio to 23:1 for fee charging schools as and from September 2013.

The JMB believes that it is vital that the concerns for the future of fee charging schools are raised at every possible level.

In March 2013, the Department of Education and Skills published a report entitled "Fee Charging Schools – Analysis of Fee Income". The JMB highlighted significant concerns with a number of aspects of the report:

1. The reference to "discretionary income" being available to the fee charging schools, when in reality this money is used to pay for the basic upkeep of the schools such as heat, light, maintenance of buildings, insurance etc.

2. The report fails to recognise the position of parents who make a decision to pay fees to a fee charging school from their after tax income. In making a decision to send their child to a fee charging school parents are, like all parents, exercising their entitlement to parental choice. In effect, fee charging schools are an example of public private partnership.

3. The Minister for Education and Skills on behalf of the Government has promoted diversity as a key principle underpinning the education system; the attempt by Government to drive fee charging schools out of existence is, in fact, reducing the levels of diversity.

4. The JMB, working with voluntary secondary schools in both the Free Education and fee charging sectors, knows that reducing the number of teachers allocated to fee charging schools will only lead to a greater cost to the state. Children have to be educated. In order to educate children, teachers have to be employed. By increasing the pupil teacher ratio in fee charging schools the state will not save money, but in effect will lead to additional costs for the state in the form of capitation and other grants as fee charging schools close or move into the Free Education sector.

Proposed new enrolment policies
In October 2011 the Joint Managerial Body (JMB) welcomed the publication of the DES Discussion Paper on a Regulatory Framework for School Enrolment. Admissions policies and practices in voluntary secondary schools are inclusive, compliant and essentially unproblematic.

It is the position of the JMB that the results of the DES audit of enrolment policies in 2008 indicating 'no evidence of any system-wide enrolment practices that give rise to concern' should form the foundation of any discussion and that the high levels of integrity with which voluntary secondary schools have been exercising their responsibilities are recognised.

The Minister has recently indicated that he and his officials are in the process of preparing draft legislation in the area of enrolment policies.

The JMB believes that the consideration of the introduction of a new regulatory framework, as opposed to a legislatively-driven approach, would represent a more appropriate development in bringing coherence to the question of school enrolment.

Parents are the primary educators of their children and our schools continue to support the Constitutional position whereby
> *The State acknowledges that the primary and natural educator of the child is the Family and guarantees to respect the inalienable right and duty of parents to provide, according to their means, for the religious and moral, intellectual, physical and social education of their children (Article 42).*

The experience of the Section 29 appeals process on the part of voluntary secondary school management as well as parents has not been uniformly positive. Shortcomings of the process are well outlined in the DES discussion paper and require only the inclusion of 'adding significantly to the workload and anxiety-burden of school principals' to be complete.

The twin aims of reducing the number of appeals and the introduction of a simpler, more localised adjudication procedure would support both parents and schools, particularly in cases where the refusal of a place is solely demanded by virtue of oversubscription. In particular, the recommendation that enrolment policies be easily accessible to parents and an outline in simple terms of the procedures to be adopted in the event of oversubscription, should reduce the extent of recourse to appeals mechanisms. It must be acknowledged and accepted however, that any mechanism designed to address oversubscription will, by definition, disappoint a proportion of applicants. Demanding that an oversubscribed school takes a pupil requires another pupil to be refused.

The JMB recommends that an emphasis be placed on finding a solution at local level with a suggestion that the facilitator be given a more central role. The key to the success of such a role is that all admissions policies be transparent and published, so that the facilitator is in a position to identify whether the policy has been applied fairly or not.

In any event, the overarching policy of supporting 'decision-making as residing with Boards of Management' must be maintained in the emergence of any new appeals framework.

In 20% of schools where the number of applicants exceeds available places, schools are compelled to apply oversubscription criteria which must be unambiguously framed in policy, adequately disseminated, and be carried out in a fair and transparent manner. Once again, these operational decisions are, and should remain, a function of the Board of Management as contextual and ethos factors are key.

> "Kids don't remember what you try to teach them. They remember what you are."
>
> Jim Henson

EDUCATION IN THE MEDIA

Croke Park II is 'dead'

April 16, 2013

THE Croke Park II deal "is dead" after members of the country's largest union, SIPTU, voted against the agreement to slash €1bn from the state payroll over three years, despite its leaders' recommendation of a yes vote.

Given the ballot results already announced, no combination of votes by the 20 public sector unions can now get the deal over the line.

SIPTU General President Jack O'Connor appealed to the government not to go down the path of confrontation and impose pay cuts on all 290,000 public servants.

"The proposal is dead," he said. "The proposal is rejected. It cannot be accepted now."

The union leader said that people who rejected the proposals are resolved to take industrial action if the government proceeds unilaterally.

Teachers, civil and public servants and members of Siptu trade union all rejected the agreement today, throwing options for radical savings into chaos.

The Irish National Teachers' Organisation voted against the deal, while TUI and ASTI members overwhelmingly rejected it last month.

General secretary Sheila Nunan said the result reflects a justified sense of grievance over who was being asked to bear an unfair proportion of the country's financial adjustment.

ASTI leader Pat King said that teachers had taken significant pay cuts averaging 14 per cent and had made significant contributions in terms of additional work and flexibility.

"Young teachers on low incomes have been subjected to additional pay cuts," he added.

www.independent.ie/irish-news/siptus-oconnor-croke-park-ii-is-dead-29200729.html

Post-Primary

EDUCATION IN THE MEDIA

Teachers plan strike in pay battle

April 27, 2013

Teachers are drawing up plans for rolling strikes and other forms of industrial action that will cause chaos in schools as they gear up for a battle with the Government over threatened pay cuts.

Strikes could close schools for one or more days at a time, while a possible ban on parent-teacher and other meetings outside school hours would result in pupils being sent home early.

Teachers may also withdraw from, or limit, supervision and substitution work. Such a move could force schools to close on health and safety grounds because of lack of cover.

The education system would be brought to its knees very quickly if teachers vote for, and implement, the range of options now under consideration.

Second-level unions have already confirmed that there is no threat to the Leaving Cert and Junior Cert exams.

Ballots of members are being organised as the Labour Relations Commission (LRC) seeks to break the deadlock between the Government and unions.

The Government insists that the €300m savings envisaged this year – rising to €1bn in 2015 – must be achieved through pay cuts.

The teacher unions will ballot members on the possibility of industrial action in the summer when schools are closed, meaning strikes could begin in September.

Irish National Teachers Organisation (INTO) general secretary Sheila Nunan said "nothing is ruled out or in".

She said possible industrial action could include withdrawal of goodwill, ceasing additional work, a withdrawal from the terms of Croke Park I – a key feature of which was extra working hours by teachers to allow for meetings outside school time.

The three main unions will co-ordinate their action in the biggest show of strength by teachers in over 25 years.

The Irish Federation of University Lecturers (IFUT) will decide on its position at its annual conference today.

Teachers invited to talks on pay deal

May 16, 2013

The Labour Relations Commission has invited teaching unions to attend talks next week as part of the Government's plans to reduce the public service pay and pensions bill.

The four unions (Irish National Teachers' Organisation – INTO, Association of Secondary Teachers Ireland - ASTI, Teachers Union of Ireland – TUI, and Irish Federation of University Teachers - IFUT), all voted to reject the proposed Croke Park II agreement last month.

The chief executive of the Labour Relations Commission Kieran Mulvey said that 10 unions opposed to the original Croke Park II agreement were now "potentially looking at it afresh in a more positive disposition".

The teacher unions are expected to put the invitation before their executives for consideration.

The TUI faces a complication in dealing with the invitation in that its annual conference passed a motion mandating the union not to go back into any talks with the Government in relation to the Croke Park proposals.

www.irishtimes.com/news/teachers-invited-to-talks-on-pay-deal-1.1396676

Kieran Mulvey Chief Executive of the Labour Relations Commission and previously General Secretary of the ASTI

Teachers' Personal Wellbeing

Dr Joe O'Connell *Director Limerick Education Centre*

The school environment is the most significant enabler of a culture of wellbeing

In recent years significant interest has focussed on the concept of wellbeing in the Irish education system where the connection between educational activities and systems, on the one hand, and the conception of personal wellbeing, on the other hand, has come under scrutiny.

Wellbeing is primarily presented as a much desired virtue with the key ideals of self-responsibility and self-actualisation. In this short reflection I aim to provide my personal interpretation of what is in reality a complex construct often reified like other ideals, seldom fully defined for principals and teachers and perceived by many as difficult to operationalise with valid substance.

Whole school approach to wellbeing

In contemplating this reflection I have been challenged to isolate the ingredients that have, over the years, blended together to form and mould my practice as a second level teacher, school principal and education centre director.

What has risen to the forefront of my thoughts is the belief, that I know is shared by many, that the most significant purpose of education in a democratic society is to equip people to participate fully in life by enabling them to think critically and to question purposefully thus empowering them to make informed and considered decisions ultimately leading to a flourishing life. This anticipated outcome of education is I believe, aligned in many ways with the underpinning philosophy of wellbeing which advocates awareness of self in all that we do. If we accept that this is the case then the fundamental question is how can we facilitate a school environment that extolls exemplary practice in the promotion of whole school approaches to wellbeing?

Incorporating the practices of wellbeing

As is the case in many other instances, consideration of wellbeing and the role that the education system plays in realising it leads to a myriad of other questions.

- Do we, as educators, really have an active role in choosing wellbeing?
- Is it an individual or collective responsibility?
- What is the most appropriate course of action to promote discussion on these questions?
- How can we as educators assume this responsibility along with all of the other areas that we are charged with and of course the perennial question as to what resources will be placed at our disposal to fulfil this aim?

I recognise all of these as legitimate and valid questions which are, however, to my mind, subordinated by the belief that the empowerment that holistic education holds for all demands of us to reflect on and express the ideas about human wellbeing and its ingredients and to identify where and how within our autonomy as educators we can incorporate the practices of wellbeing.

Wellbeing is attitudinal
I am arguing therefore that in order to enact a culture of wellbeing the most significant enabler is the school environment which, when positively disposed to reflective practices on how things are done; seeking to uncover both what is and what is not yet working well, can be a key enriching force for wellbeing. Conversely, I believe that the non-reflective practitioner or school organisation is a major impoverishing factor on the wellbeing of the whole school community.

Wellbeing is therefore attitudinal; it is the exercise of our self-awareness and our sensitivity in relation to our actions and reactions to self and others. It is both the recognition of and acceptance of our interconnectedness and interdependence, our mutual dependency on each other as human beings within our school community.

An ongoing organic process
The achievement of wellbeing for all within the school community is not a single set of activities; moreover it is an on-going activity, an organic process heavily influenced by the many and varying encounters and experiences with a wide variety of differing people in an even wider variety of situations.

In order to be able to maintain and experience wellbeing in a school community we need to scaffold all the potential relationships we encounter, teacher-pupil, pupil-teacher, teacher-parent, parent-teacher, teacher-teacher, teacher-principal, principal-teacher etc.

The cornerstone of this scaffold is the shared belief that wellbeing is achieved through real partnership across all the relationships in the school community.

In defining real and effective partnership I place communication at its core. The school community that discusses, considers and defines specific actions as to how all parties communicate with each other is one that lays a solid foundation for wellbeing amongst the community.

For this to flourish, the emphasis must be placed on a system of communication that is both respectful of role and responsibility and meaningful in practice. In providing opportunities to all parties to be able to express what one sees as challenging and to welcome the articulation of concerns, a culture is being developed that fosters reflection on words and actions which I argue is a fundamental keystone of a nurturing partnership that promotes wellbeing.

Active dialogue and listening
The school community that cultivates active dialogue and listening between and amongst all parties is in reality facilitating the on-going journey towards wellbeing. Dialogue of this nature unveils our influencing styles, our approaches to challenging behaviour and our ability to resolve issues of disagreement.

Adopting a structured and respectful framework for such dialogue unleashes the potential of shared actions and is best placed to foster wellbeing. It is, however, easy to advocate for but important to recognise that in reality it can be challenging to develop and implement.

A reflective school community with a focus on the individual and collective wellbeing of its members requires a willingness and openness to reviewing the traditional attitudes to authority and the power structures that sustain it.

We know that in times of challenge rational thinking decreases and emotional thinking and responses heighten, hindering the possibilities of open and honest exchange.

To ameliorate this reality it is essential that we have a significant amount of professional courage to allow others' opinions to influence direction and decision making.

In pursuit of this professional courage the focus has to be placed on supporting school leaders, teachers, parents and pupils on the importance of their collective relationships and how best to optimise them.

The language register has to change to focus on what we can do together as opposed to an approach which emphasises individual roles and responsibilities. We need less attention on detailing individual responsibility and accountability and much more on developing a shared understanding and a collective response to the nurturing of everyone's wellbeing.

It is time to move away from the uncritical position that hinders development to an era of openness that welcomes dialogue and reflection as legitimate professional activities that foster positive developments and change in organisations.

Collective responsibility
Maslow encouraged us all as learners to move from the state of unconscious incompetence to one of conscious competence but this will remain aspirational in terms of personal wellbeing if the debate does not shift to one where equal importance is assigned to both personal as well as professional agency. Our critical denominator as principals, teachers, parents and pupils is that we exist in a relational world where feelings and attitudes need to be respected and understood and where effectiveness should never be subjugated by a single-minded desire for efficiency.

At all times we need to be able to intervene in events in a purposeful and considered manner in the hope that we can change the course of events. The pursuit of wellbeing is a collective responsibility developed over time and through real and meaningful dialogue.

EDUCATION IN THE MEDIA

ASTI, TUI and INTO accept invitation to attend LRC pay talks

May 18, 2013

The executive of the ASTI has decided to accept the invitation of the Labour Relations Commission to enter new talks on the Government's plans to reduce the public service pay and pensions bill.

The Irish National Teachers' Organisation (INTO) and Teachers' Union of Ireland (TUI) yesterday decided to accept the invitation to the new talks on a successor to the Croke Park deal.

The ASTI is currently balloting its members on industrial action to be taken if the Government cuts the pay or worsens the working conditions of teachers. It said the result of the ballot will be announced on Monday.

The INTO said yesterday its members overwhelmingly backed proposals for industrial action in schools, up to and including strikes, if the Government unilaterally cuts their pay. Some 91 per cent of primary teachers voted in favour of action.

The TUI said its decision to re-enter talks was taken following detailed discussion and careful consideration in order to best represent the interests of members and to negotiate on their behalf. The TUI annual conference in April had passed a motion that it would not go back into talks with the Government.

Some 85 per cent of ASTI members rejected proposed Croke Park II deal in a vote last month.

"Teachers have given a clear message. Teachers feel aggrieved that the Government is again demanding that public servants bear the brunt of the fiscal crisis. This is the context in which the ASTI is accepting the LRC's invitation to education sector talks," said Mr King.

Minister for Public Expenditure and Reform Brendan Howlin is expected to bring a report to Cabinet on Tuesday on the state of play in the talks between the Labour Relations Commission and various trade unions.

The Government is still continuing preparatory work on legislation to secure reductions in the pay bill, including pay cuts, an indefinite freeze on increments and reductions in premium and overtime rates, if there is no agreement with unions.

EDUCATION IN THE MEDIA

Successor to Croke Park II published

May 23, 2013

A successor to the Croke Park II deal - formally called the Haddington Road Agreement - has been published, containing the recommendations of the Labour Relations Commission (LRC).

The LRC - which brokered the deal - said the positions in the document represent the limit of what can be achieved by negotiation between the parties. Unions are now meeting to discuss the proposals.

Meanwhile, the Government has also today published the approved text of proposed new legislation which will give effect to public service pay cuts should the Haddington Road Agreement not be accepted by the majority of trade unions.

Second level teachers reject new pay deal

May 24, 2013

Secondary schools face the prospect of reopening in chaos in September after teacher leaders rejected the latest pay and productivity deal.

The Association of Secondary Teachers Ireland (ASTI) and the Teachers Union of Ireland (TUI) are on a collision course with the Government after refusing even to ask their members to ballot on the new proposals.

The Government has warned that it will begin to impose mandatory cuts in the pay of public sector workers in unions that reject the deal on offer.

Legislation published yesterday, the Financial Emergency Measures in the Public Interest Bill 2013, will allow for the pay and pension cuts to take effect.

The new deal, the successor to the Croke Park Agreement, was called the Haddington Road Agreement, after the address of the Labour Relations Commission office in Dublin, where the proposals were negotiated.

The two teaching unions issued a joint statement, saying there were not sufficient changes to Croke Park II – which was rejected by over eight in 10 of their members – to put the Haddington Road Agreement to a vote.

As a result, their opposition stands and if the Government goes ahead with threatened pay cuts on July 1, it will trigger the unions' mandates for industrial action when the schools return in September.

The two second-level unions are at odds with the position of the leadership of their primary-school counterparts in the Irish National Teachers Organisation (INTO), which is putting the proposals out to ballot with a recommendation to accept.

The difference in the position of unions at primary and second-levels raises the messy prospect of teachers in the different sectors being employed on different terms and conditions after July 1.

ASTI general secretary Pat King said the key reasons behind the emphatic rejection of Croke Park II by teachers remained part of the Haddington Road Agreement, including the abolition of payment for supervision and substitution work and cuts to pay.

TUI general secretary, John MacGabhann said that notwithstanding some welcome measures in regard to casualisation, the proposals did not go far enough in addressing the inequalities suffered by recent entrants to the teaching and lecturing professions.

However, SIPTU and IMPACT said the agreement would offer protection against job losses and guarantee that pay would be protected for the next three years.

Details of the pay agreement show that unions negotiated a raft of concessions from the Government. In a major concession to unions, increments will continue to be paid across most grades, but with longer periods between payments.

While no compulsory redundancies or further pay cuts are planned, the Government can revisit the agreement if economic circumstances change.

www.independent.ie/irish-news/teachers-reject-new-pay-deal-29292502.html

Dedicated young professionals with nowhere [attractive] to go

Pat King *General Secretary of the Association of Secondary Teachers in Ireland (ASTI)*

We are constantly told that the key to a good education system is the quality of its teachers

It is good teachers who inspire students, who excite them in science, history or English poetry. It is skilled and committed teachers who challenge the imagination of young students, who motivate them, who instil in them a love of learning.

Why teach?
ASTI surveys and other research demonstrate that young people choose teaching as a career because of the vocational aspects of the job – working with young people, contributing to people's lives, teaching a subject they are passionate about. Irish second-level schools seek to deliver a holistic education to their students; an education that nurtures and supports them as unique human beings, rather than focusing on academic ability alone. This is despite external pressures such as college-entry tables and demands for a results-oriented education system.

This emphasis on the whole student is one reason why talented, dedicated and exceptional young people continue to be attracted into teaching.

However, the attractiveness of second-level teaching as a career is being severely undermined due to the increasingly problematic nature of entry into the profession in the first instance and, more recently, due to the reductions in salaries and the introduction of an inferior pension scheme for new entrants to teaching.

For the last decade and more, the situation has prevailed that less than 10% of new second level teachers annually obtain full-time permanent employment positions in their first year following graduation. The majority are employed **on a temporary or contracted hours basis for at least five years.** The impact of this on the young teacher who is present in a school for less than 10 hours a week, or is employed on short-term contract after short-term contract, moving from one school to the next, cannot be overstated.

Given that the vocational aspect of teaching is key to its initial attractiveness as a career, many young teachers are faced with the paradoxical experience of being committed to their profession, but unable to make a real connection and commitment to a school community. As one newly qualified teacher told the ASTI annual conference in 2011, "As graduate teachers struggle to become an active part of the school community through part-time work, it has become apparent that our best chance of finding full-time work is to find it abroad - emigration is the new permanency".

The 2009 OECD TALIS Report stated that **less than three-quarters of second-level teachers at Junior Cycle level are in permanent employment,** compared to a TALIS country average of 85%. Contractual status is closely related to teachers' age with **less than one quarter of teachers under 30 in permanent posts** compared to 76% for those over 30.

Cuts in salaries for new entrants to teaching have been devastating. Young professionals who are dedicated to teaching need to be able to make a basic living from it. Not only are **new teachers receiving less pay for the same work,** but the majority of them are not on full time hours so are only receiving a fraction of the new reduced salary. The employment conditions of new entrants to teaching can only be described as increasingly precarious.

Cuts to the pupil teacher ratio and to specialist teaching resources in recent years have exacerbated the conditions facing new and young teachers. Second-level schools have **lost approximately 2,000 teaching posts since 2009.** This is despite the growth in the second-level school going population during this time. Many schools have had to drop key subjects or sacrifice the quality of classroom learning by placing students in larger classes and/ or teaching more than one syllabus during a class period.

What can be done?
In 2011 the Minister for Education and Skills appointed an International Review Panel on the Structure of Initial Teacher Education Provision in Ireland. The Panel reported in July 2012. These international experts noted the "high calibre of entrants to Irish initial teacher education" and concluded that "the academic standard of applicants is amongst the highest, if not the highest, in the world".

They expressed surprise that the **issue of new teacher supply and demand had not been addressed in Ireland** as it has been in other countries and recommended that Ireland put in place appropriate databases and forecasting mechanisms in order to ensure the correct balance between the demand and supply of teachers. The ASTI believes that such action would help to ensure that those who enter teaching can at least have an expectation that they can make it their career.

The ASTI has presented plans to the Department of Education and Skills for a panel entry system to second-level teaching. Such a panel – which already exists at primary level – would mean that temporary teachers, many of whom move from school to school during the early years of their careers, could build up an entitlement to permanency based on teaching service. We will continue to pursue this matter in the current school year.

The ASTI will also continue to campaign for much needed staffing resources in second-level schools. All schools and teachers are doing much more with fewer resources. There is no room for further cuts. Students need their teachers.

The ASTI believes that **reasonable job security** and the **chance to earn a living are essential** if we are to continue to attract and retain quality teachers into the profession. This issue is central to protecting the quality and integrity of our young people's education.

Attendees at the ASTI seminar for newly qualified teachers

EDUCATION IN THE MEDIA

Quinn orders report on mistakes in exam papers

June 12, 2013

Education Minister Ruairi Quinn has ordered a report from the State Examinations Commission on mistakes in maths and other exams over the last week.

His request comes as the SEC apologised for the distress and confusion caused to students when it admitted there were three other errors in maths papers, in addition to one in Monday's higher-level Leaving Certificate exam.

It has now emerged that:

*There was a typographical error in a functions and graphs question in Friday afternoon's foundation-level Leaving Certificate paper 1, sat by around 2,400 students. It was detected after the paper was printed but the SEC decided not to read a correction to students as it might have caused more confusion than assistance;

*A calculus question on Friday's Leaving Certificate ordinary-level paper 1, for 1,300 students in 23 schools piloting the Project Maths course, asked candidates to complete tasks no longer on the syllabus for them;

*In Friday's Irish-language Junior Certificate higher-level maths paper 1, the phrase 'even number' was incorrectly translated as 'whole number' for around 1,500 students.

www.irishexaminer.com/ireland/quinn-orders-report-on-mistakes-in-exam-papers-233877.html

---

Primary teachers vote to accept Haddington Road deal

June 17, 2013

INTO executive had urged acceptance of deal

Primary school teachers voted yesterday to accept the proposed new Haddington Road agreement on reducing the State's pay and pensions bill.

In a ballot, members of the Irish National Teachers' Organisation (INTO) voted in favour of the deal by 63 per cent to 37 per cent.

The executive of the INTO had urged members to accept the Haddington Road proposals.

The proposed restoration of supervision and substitution allowances was an important factor in the Irish National Teacher's Organisation accepting the new Haddington Road agreement, the trade union's general secretary has said.

Speaking to RTÉ this morning Sheila Nunn said the allowances would be restored in the 2016-2017 and 2017-2018 school years.

"I think teachers are comforted by the fact that while the money is being taken from them now, there is a clear restoration in the proposals that they will see that money coming back to their salary scales," she said.

The decision by national teachers to accept the new proposals represents a major boost for the Government in its plans to reduce the public service pay bill by €300 million this year and €1 billion over three years as part of an agreement with unions.

Ms Nunan said it was clear that teachers viewed the Haddington Road proposals as better than the government's alternative proposals.

"Teachers have not so much backed the Haddington Road proposals as rejected the government's alternative," she said.

Under the three-year Haddington Road proposals, which would come into force in July, teachers would cease to be paid the current supervision and substitution allowance.

However, salary increases of €796 would be applied to incremental scale points in the 2016-17 and 2017-18 school years (total increase of € 1,592) in compensation for the loss of the supervision allowance.

Teachers earning less than € 35,000 would face one three-month increment freeze during the course of the agreement.

Teachers earning between € 35,000 and € 65,000 would have two increment freezes of three months each during the course of the agreement.

EDUCATION IN THE MEDIA

Teachers earning over € 65,000, along with other higher-paid public service staff, would face pay cuts. The reductions for teachers would run at between 5.5 per cent and 6 per cent.

However as part of the changes introduced under the Haddington road proposals, there is now a provision to restore original salary levels in two equal phases – on April 1st, 2017 and January 1st, 2018.

The Government has warned that it will impose cuts unilaterally on public service groups that do not accept the Haddington Road proposals.

Under legislation introduced last month, the Government can cut salaries for those earning more than €65,000 and suspend the payment of increments.

The legislation also contains measures allowing Ministers to reduce non-core remuneration or increase the working time of public servants.

The executives of two other teaching unions, the Association of Secondary Teachers Ireland (ASTI) and the Teachers' Union of Ireland (TUI) have effectively rejected the Haddington road proposals and, to date, have announced no plans to ballot members on its provisions.

www.irishtimes.com/news/primary-teachers-vote-to-accept-haddington-road-deal-1.1431747

TUI and ASTI now favour Haddington Road ballot

Saturday, June 22, 2013

The leaders of two teacher unions have reversed views that their 30,000 members should not be balloted on the Haddington Rd deal.

But the decision of the Association of Secondary Teachers Ireland (ASTI) standing committee needs the backing of its larger 180-member central executive council, which will not meet until August, to decide if the union's 17,000 members will be given a vote on the deal. The ASTI standing committee and the Teachers' Union of Ireland (TUI) executive said a month ago that the Haddington Rd proposals from the Labour Relations Commission were not different enough from the Croke Park II deal already rejected by both unions, to allow fresh voting.

But the mood was different when the two union leaderships met together yesterday after a week when Siptu and the Irish National Teachers' Organisation announced votes in favour of the deal. The acceptance of the deal by the Garda Representative Association and Psychiatric Nurses Association was also announced yesterday.

The ASTI and TUI also considered legal advice on the law, that would see public servants whose unions did not sign up to Haddington Rd lose out on restoration of pay cuts to those earning over €65,000 and on the lifting of freezes on salary increments.

The TUI ballot is not likely until late August at the earliest, leaving uncertainty over whether members will do supervision and substitution work in September.

www.irishexaminer.com/ireland/teacher-unions-now-favour-haddington-rd-ballot-234813.html

Contradictory policy messages about student welfare and support

Bernie Judge *Education/Research Officer with the Teachers' Union of Ireland (TUI)*

Recently published government policy documents are contradicted by policy decisions

January 2013 brought the publication of two significant policy documents by the Department of Education and Skills and Department of Health, both of which seek to increase the level of support available for young people.

Well Being in Post-Primary Schools: Guidelines for Mental Health Promotion and Suicide Prevention is a response to strong evidence of growing incidences of poor mental health and self-harm among young people and an increase in youth suicide.

In Ireland the cost of poor mental health was estimated to be 2% of GNP (€3bn) in 2006. An investigation by Headstrong (National Centre for Youth Mental Health) found that every town and community has a small number of young people living on the edge and many young people are unable to cope with the problems they face (2009).

International research shows that mental health promotion is most effective when it takes place early in life and that school is a favourable location to start support programmes and initiatives. Therefore, guidelines to support practice in schools are welcome. Correctly, the good work already being done in schools (SPHE, Guidance, Pastoral Care, other initiatives) is highlighted. However, the guidelines seek to bring greater coherence to current practices and emphasise a stronger focus on a whole-school approach and co-ordinated links with out-of-school services (health, youth, community).

The Action Plan on Bullying

The Action Plan on Bullying is also a comprehensive policy document. It lays the foundation for training for parents and boards of managements, the identification and provision of appropriate professional development for teachers, a public awareness campaign, a national anti-bullying website and the review of anti-bullying procedures for primary and post-primary schools.

Bullying is a social phenomenon and a multi-faceted approach, involving local communities, the family, social and health services and schools, is necessary. Explicit acknowledgement that schools already have anti-bullying measures in place and that they can only shoulder some of the responsibility for taking actions that prevent or counteract bullying is, therefore, welcome. However, as can be expected, school is seen as a place that has a strong influence on students' attitudes and behaviour.

In this context, efforts to increase capacity in schools, families and society to avert or address bullying merit serious consideration. Immediate development of new anti-bullying procedures for schools was given high priority and the Department of Education and Skills invited the education partners to participate in a working group to prepare new procedures for consultation and for implementation in the academic year 2013-2014.

Contradictory policy

The publication of these two policy documents can be taken as a demonstration of a laudable and welcome government commitment to the welfare of students and young people. Such effort would, however, be more impressive and instil greater confidence in teachers and principals if it did not lie alongside contradictory policy decisions; decisions that have seen schools lose teachers, guidance and counselling support and middle management posts on an on-going basis since 2008.

Teachers and principals live with the consequences of poorly, thought out and disconnected policy decisions each day and it is difficult to imagine how the coherent approach advocated will emerge. They understand the negative impact the education cutbacks have had on the state of 'health' of their school. The critical point is that the reduction in teacher numbers and management posts and diminished access to the expertise of guidance counsellors restricts how schools can support young people in developing the personal attitudes, skills and competences to cope with day-to-day adolescence life and prepare for adulthood.

Impact of budget cuts

A TUI study (2012), conducted by an independent company Behaviour and Attitudes gathered extensive data on the impact of the budget cuts on schools and students. In a sample of 88 schools close to a quarter (22%) reported that the level of pastoral care had been reduced by September 2012 and 19% reported reductions in guidance provision.

Following the decision to withdraw provision for ex-quota posts many more schools reported expected reductions in these critical areas from September 2012 - 63% reported an expected reduction in guidance provision and 50% reported an expected reduction in pastoral care services.

Later detail provided by schools confirmed that this drastic reduction in these essential services has become a reality. The allocation of a year head (from the reduced pool of senior posts) to each year group, seen by many as the key to strong pastoral care systems, is now a luxury in most schools. 70% of all respondents in the study (283) ranked the resulting negative impact on support and welfare services to students as high but management felt they had little choice.

Percentage schools reporting a reduction in pastoral care and guidance and counselling support (Source: Internal TUI Study, 2012)

A recent small, localised study across 12 schools on the east coast paints the reality that arises from the removal of ex-quota provision for guidance. By September 2013 half of the schools involved had reduced discrete provision for guidance and counselling by over 50% and one third had reduced it by over 60% (the highest reduction was 85%).

Just one quarter of the schools surveyed had retained discrete provision for guidance at over 80% of the original allocation. At the time of the study one school indicated it no longer had a guidance counsellor. Feedback also flagged that some guidance provision was now general in nature and delivered by non-specialist teachers or guest speakers.

Additional data and commentary from personnel in these schools showed that within the discrete time allocated to guidance work, many guidance counsellors are now expected to concentrate on delivering guidance to whole class groups.

These trends have also been identified by a recent independent national study (LifeCare Psychological Services) in 240 second level schools which found that the amount of time guidance counsellors are spending on timetabled class room activity has increased by 19.8% which can include curriculum guidance, subject teaching, SPHE and other activities.

Both studies emphasised the provision for one-to-one support sessions as the biggest casualty of the removal of ex-quota guidance posts. The LifeCare Psychological Services study found a 51.4% reduction in the time available for one-to-one student counselling with guidance counsellors struggling to fit this in around timetabled and other commitments.

The highly specialised expertise of the guidance counsellor and the 'necessary confidential space' are, therefore, no longer readily available to students who need individualised, high support to deal with personal issues and/or career advice. Individual sessions are by necessity restricted, often reserved for the extreme case that presents after a student has already endured significant personal distress or trauma.

Notably, some guidance counsellors are not facilitated in attending their personal supervision sessions; an essential to ensure best practice. In addition, the guidance counsellor can no longer assign time to core planning or co-ordination activities that support other staff with less specialist expertise in working with students.

These trends clearly conflict with the whole-school strategy advocated. Both sets of guidelines/procedures recognise that someone has to have core responsibility and a small number of staff should have lead roles in order that effective responses are planned, co-ordinated and delivered. Critically, there is repeated reference to guidance, counselling, pastoral care services and care teams as core supports in identifying needs, planning, intervening, monitoring and review.

Diminished school capacity
Yet school capacity in all these areas has diminished, challenging even the most imaginative principals and teachers in terms of how they will prioritise the implementation of any new guidelines and procedures. What seems to have escaped the policy makers is that guidance counsellors have additional professional expertise that is critical to the development and continuity of strong care and support systems in schools. If, as has been reported, they are restricted in the time available or in how they use their time they will not be able to deploy this expertise in a manner that will best suit the needs of the whole-school community and individual students.

While the procedures and guidelines to address bullying are still under review (at the time this article was published), the guidelines for mental health promotion and suicide prevention are agreed and clearly articulate a continuum of support with three levels:

- 'Support for All' - universal support for all students
- 'Support for Some' - targeted support for the mild or transient needs of some
- 'Support for a Few'- intensive, individualised support for more complex and/or enduring needs.

It is difficult to see any compatibility between government guidelines that clearly expect more time and attention to be given to student welfare and the plight of schools in a resource stripped environment with many competing priorities. In such an environment it is not surprising that schools are expressing considerable concern that:
- most students will not receive the general support they deserve;
- the short-term targeted support required by some will be inadequate and restricted;
- those that need intensive interventions will be short changed by the system as too little support will come too late.

Failure in this regard will have negative consequences for the current generation of young people which, as identified in national and international reports, will simply cost the state more in the long term.

EDUCATION IN THE MEDIA

Anger as 1,049 retired teachers used for exams

July 04, 2013

A THOUSAND retired teachers supervised this summer's State exams, prompting criticism of schools for not hiring more new graduates.

A call has been made to use "more forceful" methods to ensure that newly qualified teachers are taken on, including reducing the autonomy enjoyed by schools. "Unfortunately, we saw 1,049 retired teachers re-employed to supervise this year's Leaving and Junior Cert exams, with only 250 unemployed teachers hired," Labour Senator Mary Moran said.

She called on Education Minister Ruairi Quinn to put more pressure on schools to hire newly graduated and qualified teachers instead of retired teachers.

While the figure of 1,049 is down from the 2012 number of 1,311, the "margin has not closed enough", Ms Moran said. She added: "Minister Quinn, myself and many others would like to see across the board preference given to newly qualified teachers.

URGED
"In fact, the minister has publicly urged schools to give preference to newly qualified graduates.

"While I welcome this move, I would also like to see a more forceful and deliberate means of ensuring that this is the case."

The Association of Secondary Teachers Ireland (ASTI) pointed out that it is the State Examination Commission (SEC) which hires teachers for the Leaving and Junior Cert exams.

An ASTI spokeswoman told the Herald: "I know the figures are coming down. We would welcome that." She added that ASTI had also lobbied very strongly for the Department of Education to introduce guidelines about the hiring of new recruits, which were brought in two years ago.

"We would have lobbied very, very strongly to get something like that in place. If and when it (retired teachers are hired) occurs, we would be concerned that procedures are not being followed," she added.

Senator Moran said a total of 3,365 teachers graduated last year. "We need to give these teachers and the 3,000 more teachers who'll graduate this year hope for job prospects if we want to keep them in the country.

"Re-employing retired teachers is counterproductive in keeping these teachers on our shores," she added. It emerged earlier this year that retired teachers were being employed on long-term contracts in primary schools, while unemployed graduates were struggling to find work.

Promised legislation designed to ensure that unemployed teachers get priority had still not been implemented.

SUBSTITUTES
Some 22 out of 104 retired primary teachers employed in schools last December were on long-term contracts. Department of Education figures from February showed 82 retired teachers were employed as short-term substitutes in primary schools that month.

Principals argue that, when staff members become ill, they take on whoever is available.

comurphy@herald.ie
www.herald.ie/news/anger-as-1049-retired-teachers-used-for-exams-29395498.html

A 2020 Vision for Education

Jim Moore *Former President of the National Parents' Council Post Primary*

Parents of children attending post primary schools and colleges have a responsibility to help shape the future of education

The National Organisation for parents, NPCpp, consistently works to address this issue. Led by NPCpp, the Post Primary Education Forum (PPEF) was founded in 2007 in order to provide a coherent voice on second-level education in Ireland.

'2020 Vision' launched
More recently on April 23rd last the Post-Primary Education Forum (PPEF) – a coalition of parents, teachers and school leaders and managers – launched "A 2020 Vision for Education". The document sets out an ambitious, yet practical, plan for enhancing second-level education in Ireland.

The PPEF recognises that in these difficult times, it is more vital than ever before that parents, teachers and schools adopt a coherent voice in relation to how education should be improved and developed; a shared vision of where we want to go and how we want to get there.

The members of the forum are the National Parents Council Post-Primary, the teacher unions, and the school leaders and management bodies. As education practitioners and end users, we share a common belief that those most closely involved in the second-level system on a daily basis are best placed to formulate an ambitious, yet feasible, vision which has the educational outcomes and experiences of all students at heart.

Recommendations
- **Establishment of learners charter**
  As a parent, I am very happy to see a central focus on the needs of second-level students in the document and in its recommendations. The first recommendation calls for a Learners' Charter to be established, the case for which is both evident and urgent. This Charter would set out minimum rights for students in relation to such areas as curriculum, student voice and welfare, teaching and learning, and resources. It is vital that students and parents have clarity on what they can expect from their experiences of the second-level education system.

- **Parental engagement**
  The report emphasises the need to increase parents' participation in second-level education. This includes giving parents a firm and consistent role in education policy development at national level as well as adequate opportunities to become involved in on the ground in second-level school communities. Research affirms that parental engagement at second level can have positive outcomes for the parents, their children, the school community, and the wider community. Schools today are much more open places for parents than in the past. Many schools are innovative and progressive in their work to ensure parents feel welcomed and are encouraged to participate in the school community. We must build upon these achievements.

- **Investment in education**
  Among the key recommendations in the report is a call for a commitment to increase investment in education in this country to 7.5% of GDP and to maintain investment at that level as a minimum. Other recommendations cover such areas as inclusivity, ICT delivery, special educational needs and the status of teaching.

- **Green paper on education**
  We are also calling for a Green paper on Education to chart the direction Irish second-level education will take over the next ten to fifteen years. It is not enough for the Government to look only to itself in order to produce such a Green Paper. It must precede such an initiative with widespread consultation with those most directly involved in the delivery of that education: parents, teachers, students and school management - in other words, consultation with those of us who make up the PPEF, each of whom is committed to genuine dialogue with the Department of Education and Skills in order to improve the education service for all. If the Minister grasps the opportunity to cement this constructive partnership approach, it will bring consensus on workable strategies and innovations, it will strengthen mutual respect and trust between all the education partners, and, ultimately, it will have benefits for all of society.

Frontline participants must be heard
We believe "A 2020 Vision for Education" articulates a balanced approach to the development of education, one that is based on the daily realities of students, teachers and schools. The vision we articulate is important in that it gives voice to the concerns of those operating at the frontline in Irish second-level schools. National policymakers in education have much to add to the debate on improving education, but tend to take a macro perspective attuned to realities other than those of educational practitioners and their students. Too much emphasis on the macro perspectives of policy can put the quality of learning environments to the side-line of policy-makers' vision.
It is important that the education debate in Ireland does not become the exclusive property of business interests and of economists. Frontline participants in education must be included to ensure students and their experiences remain at the heart of the discussion about educational experience.

Download "A 2020 Vision for Education" at www.npcpp.ie

Post Primary Education Forum 2012
L to R: Mr Michael Moriarty (ETBI), Mr Clive Byrne (NAPD), Mr Diarmuid de Paor (ASTI), Mr Ciarán Flynn (ACCS), Mr Paul Beddy (NPCpp), Ms Deirdre Keogh (ETBI), Mr Noel Merrick (JMB), Mr Michael Redmond (JMB), Mr Declan Glynn (TUI), Mr Don Ryan (TUI), Mr Jim Moore (NPCpp)

Some flourish but some don't

Bernadette O'Sullivan *teaches on NUIG's MA in Journalism and on the BA Connect with Journalism*

Is the dominant culture of education at odds with the fundamental principles of human flourishing?

Ninety gorgeous young women in high heels and short frocks surround Fr. Diarmuid Hogan. No, this is not a Fr. Ted moment. A priest has not lost his way and ambled into the Ladies section of a department store.

"As a man of six foot two," Fr. Diarmuid tells the assembled pupils, teachers and parents at the Graduation Ceremony in Salerno Secondary School in Galway, "I am not intimidated by the six inch heels."

School graduands in every county in Ireland have assembled in similar circumstances in the weeks preceding the Leaving Cert to mark the end of their school days.

Salerno's head girl, a future Mary Robinson or Mary McAleese perhaps, who already sounds like she could run the Department of Education (watch out Minister), if not the country, is adamant: "We are more than points on a piece of paper", she announces to the 450 assembled guests. "These points will not define us."

Fr. Diarmuid, who is Chaplain to thousands of students at NUI Galway, quickly picks up the young woman's point that students will forget much of what they have been taught over their five years at secondary school.

"They may not remember what their teachers have taught them," says Fr. Diarmuid, "but they will remember how their teachers made them feel."

And if the hugging and kissing of teachers and school girls - many in tears - is anything to go by, the "mentors" in this school, like many of their colleagues in schools across the country, have made thousands of pupils feel valued, happy and confident to face the next phase of their young lives.

But sadly this is not the experience of many other youngsters who, year after year, can't engage with the "points system", who don't or can't or won't even stay in school long enough for the leave-taking ceremony. Many of those who stay are completely disengaged from the culture of what some would argue is a one-dimensional version of academic success that dominates in countries like Ireland, the UK and the US.

According to world-renowned educationalist, Sir Ken Robinson, "there are three principles on which human life depends to flourish – diversity, curiosity and creativity".

Sir Ken Robinson

"They are contradicted," he says, "by the culture of education under which most teachers have to labour and most students have to endure."

"Human beings are naturally different and diverse," he told the audience in his recent lecture for Ted.com, 'How to escape Education's Death Valley'. He argues that education is predominantly based on conformity not on diversity as a fundamental first principle for learning to flourish.

"What schools are encouraged to do is to find out what students can do under a very narrow spectrum of achievement," he says. He compares some of the curriculum to "low grade clerical work", explaining that "Kids prosper best with a broad curriculum that celebrates their various talents not just a small range of them." "A real education has to give equal weight to the arts, the humanities [and] to physical education," he adds.

Children's rights guru and Chief Executive Officer with the children's charity Barnardos, Mr. Fergus Finlay, concurs:

Mr. Fergus Finlay

"The school system is structured to oblige children to fit in rows and take instruction from teachers in rigid structures, which are heavily unionised and with a rigid curriculum. From an early age children are pointing in one direction - the direction of points. [There can be] no curiosity or creativity."

Yet according to Professor Robinson: "Curiosity is the engine of achievement." We stifle this second principle that allows human life and learning to flourish at our peril. The dominant culture in education as we know it in countries like Ireland, the UK and the USA is focused, Professor Robinson argues, not on "teaching and learning, but testing". His argument is that teaching is a "creative profession".

"Teaching properly conceived is not a delivery system," he says. "[It is] not there just to pass on received information. Great teachers do that. But what great teachers also do is mentor, stimulate, provoke, engage."

In place of this vital principle of curiosity, says Robinson, we have "a culture of compliance". Our children and teachers are "encouraged to follow routine algorithms rather than to excite that power of imagination and curiosity". Or, as one 17 year-old Galway Leaving Cert student named Catherine puts it, "there has to be a difference between learning and learning off".

If Robinson is right about over-compliant learning, is it arguable that the most compliant learners are those who succeed to University where third level educators often find themselves trying to reignite students' individual creativity and curiosity? Could this explain why some third level first years struggle to engage in self-motivated and self-directed learning, when the safety net of rote learning is removed?

While Professor Robinson acknowledges the need for standardized testing, he says it should not dominate education but rather be something which is "diagnostic". It should support - not obstruct - learning and progress. The Salerno graduands, in their beautiful array of frocks, already instinctively understand creativity and individuality as they sing out their radiant hearts in the Cyndi Lauper classic "True Colours".

These teens don't need Professor Robinson to spell out the importance of the third principle necessary for humans to flourish - creativity. "It's the common currency of being a human being," he insists. "It's why human culture is so interesting and diverse and dynamic... We all create ourselves through this restless process of imagining alternatives and possibilities... One of the roles of education is to awaken and develop these powers of creativity, and what we have instead is standardization."

From the very start the education system could empower children and teenagers to colour themselves in, within a flexible education structure which values the arts, the humanities and physical expression through voice, dance and sport, as well as emotional intelligence through the imparting of real life skills, along with the traditional subjects, which not every child can engage with for a multiplicity of individual reasons. Should we be allowing young people have a broader range of choice at senior cycle – giving them the freedom to choose subjects they are interested in and are good at, from a much broader spectrum, instead of forcing them to rote learn information they are likely to forget the moment the exam paper is complete?

This conformity towards standardized testing as a one directional goal in education is a barrier to the richness of real learning for many young people.

"Barriers," says Mr. Finlay, "come from attitudes, structures, and people." He cites Austria where children with special education needs go into mainstream and if more than four in the class have special needs another teacher is provided. Special needs are classroom based, not children based, Finlay explains.

Robinson too looks to our more progressive European neighbours as an example of best practice. Finnish schools are top in science, maths and reading and they include arts and humanities, he explains.

What all the high performing systems in the world do, Robinson explains, is "individualize teaching and learning. They recognize that it's students who are learning and the system has to engage them, their curiosity, their individuality and their creativity."

Robinson cites "alternative education programmes" in Los Angeles designed to get children back into education, which succeed outside the normal structures. They are very personalized, have strong support for the teachers, close links with the community and a broad and diverse curriculum.

Similar work is being done by the Office of the Ombudsman for Children (OCO) here in Ireland. Though not purporting to be an expert on education in Ireland, the Children's Ombudsman Ms Emily Logan points out how teaching and learning that are tailored to the particular needs of youngsters have huge positive influence in their lives.

Ms Emily Logan

"The important role individual teachers can play in lives of children has also been borne out in the special projects we have conducted, including the Separated Children project where we worked directly with children who are outside their country of origin and separated from both parents, or guardian," she explains. "Through our discussions with the young people it became obvious that they felt that having supportive and encouraging teachers really made a difference to their day to day lives."

Ms. Logan's office has engaged directly with hundreds of schools across the country and heard from thousands of children, parents and professionals working in the education system. "Through this work", she explains, "we understand that schools occupy a vital place in the lives of children, their families and communities."

Like Professor Robinson, Ms. Logan highlights the dividends of personalized learning for young people in the education community who don't fit snugly into the dominant culture of school. "The young people who took part in OCO's project on St Patrick's Institution also spoke highly of the teaching staff, praising their flexible and supportive approach, their teaching skill and their respectful attitudes towards the young people themselves," she explains.

"It was apparent from the way the young people spoke about the educational opportunities available to them in St Pat's that their decisions about which classes to attend and persevere with are informed not only by their interests, but also by the attitudes and skills of individual teachers."

Professor Robinson agrees: "There is no system in the world or any school in the country that is better than its teachers."

www.ted.com/talks/ken_robinson_how_to_escape_education_s_death_valley.html

WHO'S WHO

The WHO'S WHO Profile introduces people who are making an important contribution to education in Ireland today.

Meet
Joan Crowley O'Sullivan

POSITION: National Director, Professional Development Service for Teachers (PDST)

Where did you grow up?
Tralee, Co Kerry.

What is your earliest childhood memory?
Going on holidays to Ballyheigue and long got summers.

Where did you go to school/college?
I attended the Presentation Primary and Post-Primary Schools in Tralee. My college days were in Carysfort College, Dublin and in the University of Limerick.

To what extent did your education shape who you are today?
The Presentation sisters were an enormous influence in that they provided their students with a variety of wide-ranging experiences in order to assist students become the best that they could be-whatever that would eventually be. Study, of course, was an important part of school life. I remember as students we were brought to the Young Scientist Exhibition every year, to the Christmas pantomimes in Dublin, on school tours abroad, to debating and musical competitions, drama productions, feiseanna, basketball, tennis, camogie and all sports.

They looked for every opportunity that would contribute to our development. We even had an elected Students' Council. In the early seventies these were considered very progressive. Also, we had great fun -a very important ingredient. They prepared us for living in the world and were very enlightened as to how their students could contribute to society. Nothing was a barrier and they certainly encouraged us to pursue our dreams.

What attracted you to work in education?
Both my parents were post-primary teachers so education was part and parcel of my life growing up. I was attracted by the opportunity teaching presented in influencing and impacting on a student's development - for the good. Teaching provides you with a great opportunity to make a difference. My parents and my own teachers at primary and post-primary were very significant role models. They really enjoyed their teaching and conveyed that at home and as a student in the classroom.

What are the main responsibilities of your job?
The main responsibility is to lead, manage and develop the work of the Professional Development Service for Teachers (PDST) with a team of teachers who are seconded out from schools to provide high-quality professional development and support for teachers and schools to empower them to provide the best education for all their pupils

What does a typical working week involve?
It varies a lot from week to week. PDST is one of a number of support services of the Teacher Education Section (TES), Department of Education and Skills, Athlone. TES has responsibilities from

initial teacher education to induction and TES promotes the quality of teaching and learning through the provision of quality teacher training programmes, CPD and support for principals and teachers.

My working week can include liaising and meeting with TES, working in the PDST Head Office in Dublin, meeting with the various PDST teams, meeting with groups of teachers and visiting schools.

What do you enjoy most about your work?
The variety is wonderful and I never get bored! I take great satisfaction from meeting with teachers, examining the opportunities of developing creative ways to support them in order to enhance learning and teaching for their students. Having an opportunity to contribute - and hopefully make a difference - is very rewarding.

What do you enjoy least about your work?
Paperwork - but it has to be done! Recording and documenting are a very important and necessary part of life. They serve as a means of recording 'the story' of what we do, how we do it, why we do it and how we can learn from what we have done.

What do you do to relax?
My friends tell me 'talking'! Whilst I enjoy conversations I love reading, the beach, travel, and theatre. Kerry football is a first of course, ó dhúchas, but living in Limerick I have to support hurling, football and Munster rugby.

Have you a message for teachers?
It is important to remember and revisit the initial spark that set you on the road to becoming a teacher. Sometimes as teachers we don't get the time to reflect on why we entered the profession. I would also like to let teachers know that with an ever-changing environment PDST is there to support you in your work with students.

Have you a message for students?
If you need help, advice or support in school ask your teacher who may be able to help or find you some support. 'Asking' is often the most difficult first step! Don't hesitate!

What plans have you for the future?
Continue to do the best that I can for teachers and their students.

Join us in the telling of the story of Irish education

clearly   year on year

concisely   as it happens

impartially   as it is

Online: www.educationmatters.ie
Telephone: 091 637951
Text: 086 0809969
Email: info@educationmatters.ie

Education Matters Yearbook is supported by

NUI Galway
OE Gaillimh

Chapter 4
Third Level

Contents

		Page
1.	**Restructuring Higher Education** Tom Boland	146
2.	**Finding a fair, efficent entry system** Prof James J Browne	152
3.	**Equality of access is impeded by our social structures** Cliona Hannon	156
4.	**Quality and Qualifications Ireland (QQI)** Dr. Padraig Walsh	160
5.	**Institutes of Technology: merging and upgrading** Denis Cummins	164
6.	**Could Private Colleges become Private Universities?** Diarmuid Hegarty	168
7.	**Breaking of an agreement** Dr Rose Malone	172
8.	**Exporting Newman and Importing Confucius** Prof Liming Wang	176
9.	**University Ranking – Looking past the shop window** Trevor Holmes	180
10.	**CPD in Higher Education: emphasising learning to teach** Iain MacLaren	182
11.	**Professional Well-Being in the University Sector** Mike Jennings	185
12.	**Preparing Teachers for Ireland's future** Dr Mary Fleming and Dr Manuela Heinz	188
13.	**SUSI's difficult first year – can she recover?** Cat O'Driscoll	192
14.	**How can we best help students to help themselves?** Dr Claire Laudet and Amanda Piesse	194
15.	**Addressing the mental health needs of third level students** John Broderick	196
16.	**Whos' Who** Professor Mary O'Sullivan	198

Introducing the Third Level Chapter

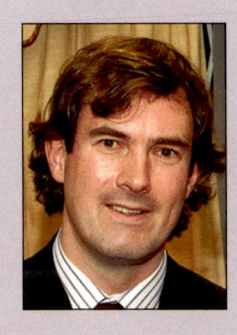

by Tony Hall, *Editor*

2013 has marked a very significant year for third-level. In the opening article of this chapter on higher education in Ireland, Tom Boland, Chief Executive of the Higher Education Authority (HEA) sets out the vision and criteria for the future configuration and design of Irish higher education.

In his article, President of NUI Galway, Professor Jim Browne considers the salient issue in Irish education of the reform of the points system, and student entry to third-level. He notes that balance is an essential consideration, in offering common and specialist programmes at third-level, especially considering the contemporary and future importance of research-led teaching, universities' respective, distinctive profile in particular areas of expertise, and the need to offer students choice. Dr. Padraig Walsh, Chief Executive of Quality and Qualifications Ireland (QQI) outlines the role and vision of the QQI as the single agency for quality in the tertiary education and training sector in Ireland. His article discusses how the new agency aims to support and oversee a system of quality-assured qualifications for learners, where they can flexibly and seamlessly transfer and progress through the Irish National Framework of Qualifications (NFQ).

In his article, Dr. Denis Cummins, President of Dundalk IT and Chairman of Institute of Technology Ireland (IoTI) considers strategic developments taking place in the institute of technology sector.

As throughout the Education Matters Yearbook 2013, relevant news and media items, pertaining to the story of Irish higher education in 2013, are interleaved with the key articles. These also include, amongst others, working conditions for, and the professional well-being of teachers and researchers at third-level in 2013; university rankings; continuing professional development and the new emphasis on learning to teach at third-level; and the changing landscape of initial teacher education in Ireland. There is also a review of the first year of the new Student Universal Support Ireland (SUSI) by Cat O'Driscoll, Vice President for Academic Affairs & Quality Assurance, Union of Students in Ireland; and two articles on students' well-being, and how students might be best supported in their transition to, and through higher education.

The 'Who's Who' profile in Irish education is: Professor Mary O'Sullivan, Dean of the Faculty of Education and Health Sciences, University of Limerick and Founder/Co-Director of the Physical Education, Physical Activity and Youth Sport (PEPAYS) Research Centre at UL.

Third Level

Restructuring Higher Education

Tom Boland
Chief Executive Higher Education Authority (HEA)

Irish higher education is undergoing tremendous change.

Much of the change is driven by external constraints and particularly the difficulties in the public finances.

The IPA in their review of public service reform this year noted that the HE sector has seen a 14.9% increase in student numbers since 2008-09 while facing a fall in staff numbers of 7.3% over the same period. At the same time international higher education continues to develop and progress and all our institutions must continue to improve performance so as to compete in the increasingly intense globalized higher education system.

Many of these forces for change were identified in the National Strategy for Higher Education at its publication in 2011 – they have only increased in magnitude since then. But that strategy also recommended a number of changes to our system to better enable our HE system to manage such change.

Key amongst those has been **reorganizing the configuration of higher education**. Accordingly, in February 2012, the HEA issued a consultation document to the sector setting out its vision for the future HE system and requesting institutions to make submissions as to their particular role within this overall system. The intention was to both set a national direction, while also allowing institutions to set out their views as to where they would best fit within the system of higher education.

The HEA also provided the **criteria and process for designation of Technological Universities.** This was a further major recommendation of the National Strategy. The strategy recognized that some institutes of technology had made very significant progress in terms of their teaching and research and that a development path should be in place to allow them to be considered for designation as technological university.

The process and criteria laid out provide for extensive scrutiny, both from a national and an international perspective, of the strength of the case for designation. They also confirm that where any merged institutes are designated as technological universities, they will continue the underlying mission of **focus on engagement with enterprise, and providing graduates for the labour force.**

During the course of 2012-13, the HEA engaged with institutions – both through their written submissions and also through dedicated meetings with institutions - on their views on the future configuration, and also commissioned external advice to help inform such final configuration. Key amongst this was a long term study by the ESRI of the future demand for higher education. That study confirmed the **need for significant increases in graduate outputs** (of the order of 25% over the next 15 years) to meet the future skills needs of the economy.

The HEA has recently presented a set of policy advice to the Minister on foot of this process. The Minister has now formally responded to this advice and set out major decisions in respect of configuration. Some of the major highlights are as follows.

Institute of technology sector

3 groups of institutes have been approved to move to the next phase of planning for possible designation as Technological Universities. These are: DIT, IT Blanchardstown and IT Tallaght; WIT and IT Carlow; Cork IT and IT Tralee.

The Connacht Ulster alliance of GMIT, IT Sligo and Letterkenny IT should continue and deepen its linkages to facilitate moving towards a full merger in the medium term.

University sector

A range of strategic alliances are proposed, including some mergers with teacher education institutions.

Other institutions funded by the DES

Funding for such institutions will transfer from the DES to the HEA following necessary legislative change.

Regional clusters

Regional clusters will be formed from among the institutions covering the South, Mid West, West and Dublin/Leinster cluster with two pillars. Each university and institute will be part of a regional cluster. The clusters will have considerable autonomy in terms of their governance and operation, but they will have as first priorities

- Shared coordinated academic planning
- Regionally coordinated approach to transfer and progression pathways for students between higher education institutions.

Thematic reviews

Finally, the Minister also requested the HEA to process with thematic reviews in the areas of engineering and nursing education in association with the Department of Education and Skills.

Next steps – strategic dialogue

The landscape process is itself only one part of the ongoing reform within higher education. The national strategy had also recommended a new funding and governance arrangement within the system of higher education. A new strategic funding element is being introduced that seeks to allocate funding not just on the basis of student numbers and the subjects being studied, but also on the strategic intent of institutions, how well they are aligned with national goals, and how successful institutions are in delivering against their strategies.

The Minister in his response to the HEA has set out the national priorities which he expects the HE system to address. The HEA expects to commence the process of strategic dialogue in the summer of 2013 and to develop the process over the coming years.

HEA event where Lord David Puttnam, Chancellor of the Open University delivered the 5th Annual Erasmus Lecture at George's Hall, Dublin Castle on 31 May 2012.

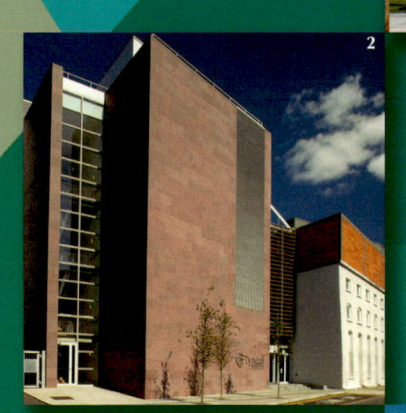

1. National University of Ireland
   49 Merrion Square, Dublin 2
2. Tyndall National Institute, UCC
3. The Engineering Building, NUI Galway
4. UCD Veterinary Science Building and Hospital
5. York House, RCSI
6. Biosciences and Electronic Engineering Building, NUI Maynooth

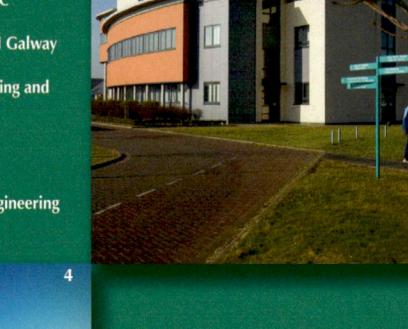

Ollscoil na hÉireann
National University of Ireland

The National University of Ireland – Ireland's federal university

The National University of Ireland (NUI) is a federal university with campuses spread across Ireland and with over 250,000 graduates across the world. There are four constituent universities and a number of other associated colleges in the federation, making NUI the largest element of the Irish university sector. With their common history and traditions, the NUI universities and colleges contribute to social, cultural and economic advancement and share the following values:

- offering intellectually rigorous undergraduate and postgraduate programmes
- providing a lively, stimulating, diverse campus environment
- welcoming international students
- nurturing talent, creativity and innovation
- generating new knowledge through intensive research
- sharing knowledge in partnership with industry, business and the community
- extending global reach through transnational partnerships
- creating opportunities for lifelong learning
- promoting civic engagement
- transmitting culture to new generations.

University College Cork
Tel: (353 21) 490 3000
www.ucc.ie

University College Dublin
Tel: (353 1) 716 7777
www.ucd.ie

National University of Ireland, Galway
Tel: (353 91) 524411
www.nuigalway.ie

National University of Ireland, Maynooth
Tel: (353 1) 628 5222
www.nuim.ie

Royal College of Surgeons in Ireland
Tel: (353 1) 478 0200
www.rcsi.ie

Shannon College of Hotel Management
Tel: (353 61) 712213
www.shannoncollege.com

National University of Ireland 49 Merrion Square, Dublin 2
Telephone: (353 1) 439 2424 Fax: (353 1) 439 2466 Email: registrar@nui.ie
Website: www.nui.ie

EDUCATION IN THE MEDIA

Universities confer degree on Feeney

September 06, 2012

The Universities of Ireland, North and South, have conferred an honorary degree on the philanthropist Chuck Feeney in Dublin Castle this afternoon.

Former president Dr Mary Robinson, chancellor of the University of Dublin, said Mr Feeney had used his wealth to help people anonymously. "The beneficial effects of Mr Feeney's dedication to the achievements of our community are incredible," she said.

She said Mr Feeney's Atlantic Philanthropies had made extraordinary investments both within and outside the walls of educational institutions, "and nowhere more so than on the island of Ireland". She also noted Mr Feeney's commitment had helped break down social barriers in Northern Ireland.

Mr Feeney responded with modesty: "I feel embarrassed as really I should be from all this attention but I want to say that I genuinely and sincerely appreciate your kind words" he said.

... NUI chancellor **Maurice Manning** described the event as a unique and historic occasion because it was the first time every university in Ireland had come together to honour "a very special person".

www.irishtimes.com/news/universities-confer-degree-on-feeney-1.735063

Trinity merger with UCD not 'desirable', says Minister

September 26, 2012

MINISTER FOR Education Ruairí Quinn and three university presidents last night moved to distance themselves from a controversial report recommending a merger of University College Dublin with Trinity College Dublin, and other radical changes. Mr Quinn said such a merger was "neither feasible nor desirable", while key elements of the report "would not be acceptable to Government".

The report from an international panel chaired by Prof Frans Van Vught of the European Commission proposes that the State's more than 20 higher education colleges be consolidated into six.

In a statement, the Department of Education said Mr Quinn "has concerns about some of the recommendations in the report which were not in accord with stated Government policies, such as the suggested merger of Trinity College and UCD".

The department and the HEA are in the process of implementing the 20-year National Strategy for Higher Education – Hunt Report – which proposes more modest changes.

In a joint email yesterday, NUI Maynooth president Dr Philip Nolan and Dublin City University president Brian

L to R: An Taoiseach Enda Kenny, Chuck Feeney and former Chancellor of University of Limerick, Peter Malone at the conferring of an honorary degree on the philanthropist Chuck Feeney in Dublin Castle

Third Level

EDUCATION IN THE MEDIA

MacCraith moved to reassure staff that "no merger of DCU with NUI Maynooth is envisaged, nor would it be supported by either of the presidents of the two institutions"

TCD provost Dr Paddy Prendergast said a UCD-TCD merger "does not accord with Government policy, nor does it represent the views of the HEA [Higher Education Authority]". He also confirmed that no merger discussions had taken place with UCD.

It's important to note how the modus operandi of the Van Vught team - leading world authorities on higher education - was so different from traditional expert groups on education and much else. Normally, these tend to be comprised of stakeholders or vested interests from the particular sector under scrutiny.

www.irishtimes.com/newspaper/opinion/2012/0926/1224324426137.html

---

Third-level extravagance

September 29 2012

The payment of unauthorised allowances of €7.5m to senior academics, raises serious questions about the manner in which our universities and other third-level institutions are run.

Between June 2005 and February 2011, 223 academics were paid a total of €7.5m in allowances which had not been authorised by the Higher Education Authority. Yet at the same time they were shovelling out public money in unauthorised allowances, the presidents of our universities were queuing up to tell us how strapped for cash their colleges were.

The payment of the unauthorised allowances has been justified by UCD president Hugh Brady on the grounds that they were "the international norm" and that they were necessary to "persuade" staff to take on leadership and management roles.

Irish academic salaries are more than 30pc higher than those in the UK. The notion that legally banning these unauthorised allowances, as Education Minister Ruairi Quinn is now planning to do, will choke off the flood of suitable applicants for these very well-paid and pensionable jobs is simply absurd.

Mr Quinn should ignore the academics and ban these unauthorised payments without any further delay.

www.independent.ie/opinion/editorial/thirdlevel-extravagance-28815604.html

---

DCU awards most top degrees

October 23, 2012

Students from Dublin City University are more likely to graduate with a first-class honours degree, while over half of Trinity College graduates since 2005 have left college with a 2.1.

An Irish Times survey of graduating grades handed out by Irish universities since 2005 has found that the proportions of first-class honours degrees, 2.1s and other grades can vary quite considerably from institution to institution.

DCU, for example, has awarded the highest proportion of first-class honours degrees, with an average of 19 per cent managing to score top marks over the seven years surveyed. An average of 16 per cent of students graduated with first-class honours from Irish universities over the same period.

NUI Galway and the University of Limerick awarded the lowest proportion of firsts over that time with 14 per cent of students making that grade.

The proportions of students graduating with upper second-class honours (2.1) degrees are much more variable. An average of 56 per cent of TCD graduates left college with a 2.1, while 51 per cent of UCC's graduates achieved the same feat over the time period.

UL awarded the lowest proportion of 2.1s over that time – 36 per cent of UL graduates were awarded a 2.1 – a full 20 percentage points lower than TCD's average. The national average was 47 per cent.

Some 49 per cent of graduates from UCD, Ireland's largest university, left college with a 2.1 and DCU awarded a similar proportion of 2.1s over the seven years surveyed. NUI Maynooth was only slightly below the national average at 46 per cent, while 43 per cent of NUI Galway's graduates left with a 2.1 degree.

www.irishtimes.com/newspaper/ireland/2012/1023/1224325578074.html

Finding a fair, efficent entry system

Professor Jim Browne *President, NUI Galway*

In my view, the existing CAO points system scores highly on several criteria

There has been much discussion about the mechanisms for allocating scarce University places in general, and the so called 'points race' in particular.

Some reforms have been undertaken, the most significant being the use of the HPAT examination to help determine entry into medical courses. This year the Irish Universities Association, following on from a request from the Minister for Education and Skills, developed some ideas on how the system might be reformed. The Minister had expressed concern that the 'benefits of any broader senior and junior cycle reforms might be undermined by the demands and pressures of competitive entry requirements for higher education, which can heavily influence teaching approaches, learning behaviours and subject choices form the Leaving Certificate examination'.

Of course the first point which has to be made in any discussion on University entry is that any system of allocating University places will have to deal with the reality that there are programmes where demand greatly outstrips supply and no allocation system, short of demand determining supply or 'free entry', can overcome that reality. For those high demand programmes, entry will remain competitive, in some cases very competitive, no matter what allocation system is put in place. The expected outcome of any reform then is unlikely to have significant impact on the level of competition; however it might help promote more rational subject selection, better teaching and learning approaches and ultimately better learning outcomes for students.

The university Presidents recognise that the structure and content of the second level curriculum, the methods of assessment and the transition to third level are all interconnected. All of the available evidence suggests that entry to University influences subject choice and indeed learning and teaching behaviours at second level. Can we reform the CAO points system to drive different and perhaps more appropriate learning behaviours at second level? Could we for example develop an entry system which would reward creativity rather than mere rote learning?

What is clear is that there are a number of principles which are the foundation of any good entry system. The system must reward student effort and achievement. It must be understandable, transparent, and maintain a high level of public trust. It must promote equity of access and be as efficient and cost effective as possible. In my view the existing CAO points system scores highly on all of these criteria. Where it is perhaps less successful is in promoting positive educational outcomes – arguably it promotes rote learning – and it may distort subject choice, in that some students select subjects on the basis of their perceived potential points value. Having said that, it has to be recognised that Leaving Certificate outcomes are a reliable indicator of University performance.

Taking this perspective the University Presidents brought forward some very specific proposals for reform. These include
- a proposal to reduce the Leaving Certificate grading scale from a 14 to an 8 point scale,
- a move towards more common entry programmes,
- the possibility of incentivising strategically important subjects.

Number of points
Reducing the number of points on the grade scale provides for less granularity in marking which is likely to positively impact assessment and therefore teaching and learning. It is likely to lead to more applicants having similar scores and therefore increased use of random selection to allocate places in some programmes. The use of a bonus scheme for Honours Mathematics is seen to have attracted more students to this traditionally less popular programme.

Common entry programmes
Perhaps the most controversial proposal emerging from the universities is that which advocates a shorter menu of programmes for prospective students, through the increased use of common entry programmes for potential university students. Over the years the number of options available has increased significantly, although it is the case that the number of programmes available in most of the Universities is not high by international standards.

However concern is frequently expressed that the number of programme offerings causes confusion to students and sometimes results in very competitive entry and associated high points because the number of available places is small. There is also the suggestion that narrowly defined specialist entry programmes promote too early specialisation on the part of students. Common entry programmes, on the other hand, allow students to postpone their choices of specialist courses until later in their University life, and therefore presumably make better-informed decisions. The proposal is that students might be encouraged to enter generic or common programmes and then make their specialist choices at the end of first year. For example engineering students might be all entered into a common first year programme and then elect to embark on a specialist programme in say mechanical, electronic or biomedical engineering as they enter second year.

The NUI Galway experience
At NUI Galway we have had some interesting experience in this regard. For many years now we have offered a combination of 'common' and 'specialist' entry into our major areas, including Arts, Science, Business and Engineering. The experience is interesting; we find that there is a demand for both. There are students who are clear that they wish to commit to say biomedical engineering from the very beginning: others prefer to postpone the decision as to their specific field of engineering study until later.

But interestingly, when those who opted for the common stream come to make a decision as to their specialist programme at the end of first year, the pattern of enrolment is not different to what was evident among those who selected specialist courses at the point of entry to University – the same percentages chose biomedical, civil, mechanical, etc. That is not to say of course that individual students did not

Students at the Quadrangle in NUI Galway

change their minds during the year in University. There is a similar pattern in Arts, Science and Business where again subjects and programmes which were in very high demand at entry remain in high demand at the end of first year when students come to make choices. Effectively the competition for scare places now takes place at the end of first year rather than at the entry point to the University. Arguably the student options are now more limited given that he or she is now limited to a single institution.

A further point which should be borne in mind is that the Higher Education Authority has in recent years **encouraged the universities to develop distinctive missions and strategies to differentiate themselves.** Through major research infrastructural investment programmes the universities have succeeded to some extent in doing this. The result is that individual universities have now developed specialist facilities and expertise in particular areas. Given that research-led teaching is the hallmark of a University education it would be short-sighted of the universities not to continue to offer a small number of specialist undergraduate programmes to allow students to benefit from this expertise. Thus for example NUI Galway will continue to offer specialist programmes in our particular areas of strength including Marine Science, Biomedical Science, Theatre and Drama Studies, Human Rights etc. Such programmes are of interest to a growing cohort of students nationally and it will be important to ensure that that cohort continue to have the choice to pursue fields of interest that they are committed to.

Getting the balance right
At the end of the day the debate between the merits of common and specialist entry programmes, as with many aspects of life, comes down to a question of achieving the right balance. Common and specialist programmes are perhaps serving 'different markets'. There are many pre University students who prefer to defer decision-making and who will benefit from the common entry mode. Others are clearer in their preferences and they too should be accommodated with specialist entry routes.

EDUCATION IN THE MEDIA

Universities Bill will stifle the innovation we need

Brian Lucey, Professor of Finance, TCD

November 20, 2012

The Universities (Amendment) Bill 2012 is shutting the stable door after the horse has bolted. The core issue driving these radical proposals is the payment, by colleges, of unauthorised allowances to some senior staff.

The Bill is a knee-jerk reaction by regulators who have failed to keep time with the pace of change in modern tertiary education, with changing educational markets or with the balance of accountability and flexibility needed to confront national and international challenges.

Slapping down bolshy universities may have populist appeal, but we should beware of Greeks bearing gifts. In that regard the proposals are a transparent attempt by the Civil Service to take control of the sector by plugging university policy into a centralised and dirigiste Civil Service model and to neuter both governing authorities and the Higher Education Authority.

In reacting to them we need to decide what we want academia to provide for the State and how universities can best serve the common good. As in all things, proportionality is also worth striving for.

The main provisions of the heads of Bill are to issue directions to a university if there is concern about "a policy decision made by the Government or the Minister in so far as it relates to the remuneration or numbers of public servants employed in that university, or a collective agreement entered into by the Government or the Minister".

There is also provision for the Minister to send in the troops in the form of an "investigator" to inquire into any of these matters, regardless of whether any cause for concern has been established. This can lead to a transfer of functions away from the universities to the Minister or, even more worryingly, to the Civil Service bureaucracy on Marlborough Street or its agents.

Part of what drives this desire for control is the thinly disguised belief that universities are really secondary schools for young adults, that academics are lazy charlatans, that most research is self-indulgent faffing about and that the facilities lie idle for most of the year.

EDUCATION IN THE MEDIA

None of these accusations survives the barest scrutiny, and the 2010 Comptroller and Auditor General report on Irish universities states that the sector provides good value for money under difficult conditions. That value for money is seen in the education provided to record numbers of students with reduced funding and the growing contribution to knowledge and creativity.

Perversely, these achievements are regularly praised by Government while, at the same time, the fabric of the proposed legislation seeks to undermine them.

In this respect the Government needs to try to be more aware of the delicate balance needed to manage intellectual organisations. Universities are about human capital and knowledge creation, similar to the goals of Apple and Google. In great part their capital walks out of the door every evening. Few people would think it a good idea to impose the management structures of 1920s Ford on Apple, but the Government is proposing such a course of action with its universities.

Organisations are different, and blindly applying a Civil Service approach to running universities will undermine tenure (making academics more vulnerable than civil servants), change the character of academic freedom (that is, make academics think twice about attacking Government policies with awkward evidence) and make Ireland less attractive to international talent, something we need now more than ever.

A win-win is needed: universities need to be freed to do their job and increase student numbers and experience success and failure. That means we need to have an adult conversation about fees. Fees need to be supported by either a graduate tax or a properly functioning loan market.

In the interim, challenge university managers to lead their institutions. Give them the monies that the State deems an appropriate amount to subsidise research and education for the common good; then let them get on with their business.

Ireland will need smart people and nimble institutions to survive. The University (Amendment) Bill stifles both.

First published in the Irish Times, November 20, 2012

www.irishtimes.com/news/education/universities-bill-will-stifle-the-innovation-we-need-1.554599

No extra cash for colleges without reform, says Quinn

November 22, 2012.

EDUCATION Minister Ruairi Quinn will tell third-level college heads today they must get their houses in order before receiving any extra money to deal with expanding student numbers.

The minister will outline the reforms he wants in higher education at a meeting with the heads of universities, institutes of technology and other colleges.

His key message will be the need to ensure that the system is delivering value for money, before extra funding is considered.

Mr Quinn wants to see a range of changes including college mergers, greater collaboration and an end to unnecessary duplication of courses. There are, for instance, 30 schools of engineering, many offering similar programmes.

The minister is setting out his stall against the backdrop of significant challenges facing the higher education system.

Third-level colleges are feeling a double pinch, with cuts in state funding putting a squeeze on finances at the time that student numbers are growing.

Experts say the higher education system, which currently costs about €1.3bn a year, will need an extra €500m a year, within about five years.

The big decision that will eventually have to be taken is whether that extra funding should come from the State or by asking students to pay more.

Mr Quinn has no plans to ask students for more, beyond his proposals to raise the Student Contribution Charge – currently €2,250 – to €3,000 by 2015.

But the economic think-tank the ESRI has fuelled the debate with a new report saying the time had come to consider a state-backed student loan scheme, which would see graduates repaying the cost of their degree once their salaries hit a certain level.

www.independent.ie/lifestyle/education/no-extra-cash-for-colleges-without-reform-says-quinn-28904295.html

Equality of access to third level is impeded by our social structures

Cliona Hannon *Director of Trinity Access Programmes (TAP)*

All students with ability and motivation should be able to progress to third level

The recent film 'Lincoln' tells a tremendous story about how Abraham Lincoln built support for the 13th amendment to the constitution, to abolish slavery. It is 150 years since his Gettysburg address in which the rallying call was that "government of the people, by the people, for the people, shall not perish from the earth."

Last year, the OECD published a report titled 'Divided we stand', demonstrating the scale of the widening gap between the well off and those on low incomes across the developed countries. Joseph Stiglitz, former World Bank economist, paraphrases Lincoln when he characterises the ways thing are in 2013 as 'Of the 1%, by the 1%, for the 1%. Countries with greater inequality also have less equality of opportunity – what is called the Great Gatsby curve – so this gap persists.

One of the most effective ways in which to create opportunity and provide greater individual freedom of choice is through education. In Ireland, many people believe we have a fair and meritocratic education system. There is free secondary education, the entry system to higher education is based on an objective points score achieved in open competition with all others. But let us briefly take a look at two exemplar students – using the Great Gatsby theme – Daisy from Dundrum and Jay from Ballyfermot.

Jay has a 10% chance of progressing to higher education and many of his class were early school-leavers. He works part-time and he is hoping to progress to higher education and become a teacher. Few of his classmates are aiming for university and, as no-one in his family has attended third level, he is worried it will cost his mother a lot and that he won't 'belong'. He is also worried he won't get the Leaving Certificate points he needs for entry to higher education, as there have been quite a few changes in his teachers over the Leaving Certificate cycle. Jay needs to achieve more than 470 Leaving Certificate points to get a place on a teaching course.

Daisy, on the other hand, is confident she is on target to study Law at university as her hard work and extra tuition have helped to raise her grades from a high B to an A. Nine out of ten students in Daisy's area progress to higher education. Daisy has been working through university prospectuses with her parents and guidance counsellor since first year. Daisy had a fantastic Transition Year during which she used the time to get some direct experience in different legal environments, thanks to a range of family members who work in law firms. This has confirmed her university ambitions.

Evidence shows that if they do both get to College, the chances of Daisy graduating are higher than Jay, even if he does better than she does in the Leaving Certificate. There is a 90 point attainment gap between these two students in the Leaving Certificate exam. Throughout school, college and at graduation, Daisy and Jay will have very different support and professional networks available to them.

Higher education is both a private and a public good. It benefits the individual but also wider society. It is easy in today's highly competitive, globalised market, to focus only on the potential vocational, professional or business-related merits of educational activities. However, research has demonstrated the fundamental importance of developing 'social capital' within our communities and organisations so that we maintain the kind of 'high trust' environment that is conducive to both social and economic development. The value of higher education within Irish society has intensified because, as the Provost of Trinity College Dr Patrick Prendergast said, "A society that lives by its wits…and not through low labour rates or the exploitation of natural resources, needs to have people educated to the highest international levels if it is to create employment in a global economy."

Creating a more diverse university campus means a diversity of perspectives and experiences, which are crucial because this enables us to think creatively, build our knowledge about the world and imagine different futures.

Although there has been progress by higher education institutions in widening access to higher education, there remain considerable obstacles for students from socio-economically disadvantaged backgrounds. The HEA's 2013 national higher education admissions targets for under-represented groups will not be met. Significant efforts by HEIs in outreach and alternative admissions routes (such as the DARE/HEAR schemes and FETAC progression) still deliver only a few thousand additional target students into the higher education system each year.

In Trinity, for example, where we celebrate 20 years of the Trinity Access Programmes this year, only 5% of the student cohort enters first year from socio-economically disadvantaged backgrounds. The 1,300 students who have successfully progressed to the College since 2003 have performed very well and clearly demonstrated their potential academically, socially and in the labour market. Their outstanding success demonstrates that these low figures, and indeed continuing flat progression rates from many DEIS schools, represent a persistent waste of human potential.

This situation is not caused, nor can it be fixed, by HEIs or DEIS schools in isolation.

Rather, it relates to broader issues about how our society is structured and which social groups have access to and control over resources. It is not possible to effect anything more than change at the margins within present structures. This does not, however, mean that there is no point in attempting progress at all. Indeed, it makes it all the more imperative to continue these small scale 'reform' efforts, in the hope that a critical mass of disruptive innovations over time will create a 'tipping point' where the real questions about persistent inequalities are more openly named and challenged.

Despite this picture, it is an exciting time to be involved in education in Ireland. Over the past two years there have been a number of encouraging developments, including significant efforts to reform the second level Junior Cycle and admissions to higher education. Increasingly, connections between the quality of the second level environment, access to higher education and the ability to critically engage with the higher education teaching and learning environment are being more explicitly explored.

TAP undergraduate students – amazing ambassadors

It is important that all students with ability and motivation can aim to progress to third level.

However, it is essential that the quality of their teaching and learning environment at second and third level reflects what is required of a developed, democratic, highly skilled nation – namely, critical engagement with content, the opportunity to engage meaningfully with that content and to learn through the joint facilitation of teacher and technology.

The notion of upward social mobility through hard work was captured in James Truslow Adams' definition of the American dream: "life should be better and richer and fuller for everyone, with opportunity for each according to ability or achievement regardless of social class or circumstances of birth."

The continued, ambitious pursuit of a reform agenda that links quality of education to access and progression is crucial to realising that dream. 'Access' to higher education is not simply about creating routes of progression but also people's capacity to contribute as active, engaged citizens to the re-construction of a more ethical, values-based republic. Neither is 'access' about moulding the individual to the institutional culture: the higher education institution must also be prepared to shift its norms. It is not about continuing to work with existing, flawed systems that do not fully develop or prepare all students with potential.

Rather, it is about re-thinking who learns, how they learn and how this educational currency is used to gain access to higher education. It is about being prepared to critique and fundamentally change these practices, and model what is expected within a truly knowledge-based economy, by being innovative, entrepreneurial and embracing evidence-based, timely transformations.

This is a time for radical change, in how we engage all sectors of society fully in the educational process, in how we teach and how we learn, and how best we enable transformation of existing processes through collaboration and technological advances.

EDUCATION IN THE MEDIA

Budget 2013 Education: 6,000 to lose up to €1,500

December 06, 2012

More than 6,000 students will lose up to €1,510 each in grant aid next year as income levels for grants are reduced. About 5,300 grant recipients are expected to lose amounts ranging from €300 upward, depending on the level of support they would have qualified for this year and how far they live from college. A further 863 who do not get a grant will only have half the €2,500 student contribution paid for them, while over 200 are expected to have to pay the full fee instead of just half from next year.

The losses are the result of a 3% cut to the family incomes below which grants are payable. It will see the threshold for the maximum standard rate of grant reduce from €41,110 to €39,875.

An estimated 1,547 of those getting the full grant are liable to lose either €610 or €1,510, depending on distance between home and college, by falling into the 50% grant category. Another 1,200 who would previously qualify for a 25% grant will get none, although they will still be exempted from the €2,500 fees, which are increasing from €250 as expected.

Mr Quinn has not cut the actual grant rates and is leaving income thresholds for the special rate payable to students from lowest-income families unchanged. He said it was regrettable that about 8% of the 80,000 college students getting a grant would be affected, but income limits had not changed for three years even though average wages fell almost 8%.

The €250 increase to the student contribution is to be followed by similar rises over the following three years. This is despite the recent ESRI recommendation to introduce a loan scheme, under which students would begin paying back their college tuition costs once they reach a certain level of earnings after graduation. Mr Quinn repeated that he wanted to see colleges address duplication of courses and other inefficiencies before looking at how to get extra funding into the system.

In addition to a 2% cut in funding for third level, he is also imposing a €25m cut from their budgets, following revelations by the Comptroller and Auditor General of large cash reserves held by many colleges.

www.irishexaminer.com/budget/news/budget-2013-education-6000-to-lose-up-to-1500-as-income-levels-for-grants-reduced-216150.html

EDUCATION IN THE MEDIA

Tralee charity opens branch for students as demand rises 40%

December 10, 2012

A St Vincent de Paul Society in a provincial town has witnessed a 40% rise in demand for its service.

The society in Tralee has also been forced to open a new branch to assist hard-pressed institute of technology students living in Kerry's county town. The assistance is being provided in conjunction with student support groups.

IT Tralee students union president Niall Harty said many students were suffering poverty because of Government cuts and are facing electricity cut-offs because they can't pay their bills.

He said it was vital for the Government to continue paying the students' assistance fund, but there was no provision for continuing the fund after 2013.

Christy Lynch, of Tralee's St Vincent de Paul, said some students were finding life very difficult, because they had lost so much financial support.

"We've found situations where students can't pay the rent, or feed themselves, and neither can their parents afford to help them," he said.

www.irishexaminer.com/ireland/tralee-charity-opens-branch-for-students-as-demand-rises-40-216527.html

Almost half of college students felt suicidal

December 10, 2012

Almost half of college students have thought life was not worth living but most who are having serious problems do not seek help, research on young people's mental health shows.

Students who have problems with drinking and those who are bisexual or unsure about their sexual orientation were found to be more likely than others to have severe distress or suffer from depression and anxiety.

Of 8,000 third-level students aged 17 to 25:
43% have at some point thought their life was not worth living;
- 21% reported deliberately hurting themselves, without wanting to take their own life;
- 7% have tried to take their own life.

But the study by the School of Psychology at University College Dublin for Headstrong — the young people's mental health organisation — found major knock-on effects of bullying that happened before students even started college.

Those who have been bullied were twice as likely as others to self-harm or attempt suicide, but lead researcher Dr Barbara Dooley said this relates to bullying at any stage of their lives.

"For only 9% of those who were bullied, it had been in the last year. It's more likely to have happened when they were in second-level.

"It shows how bullying at any point can have long-term effects on mental health of young people," said Dr Dooley who is also Headstrong's research director.

… College itself is the biggest cause of stress, followed by money and work, but only 62% said they would talk to someone if they had a problem and young men are less likely to do so. Rates of suicidal thoughts, self-harm, and suicide attempts were highest among young people who did not seek help or talk about their problems.

www.irishexaminer.com/ireland/almost-half-of-college-students-felt-suicidal-216533.html

Quality and Qualifications Ireland (QQI)

Dr. Padraig Walsh *Chief Executive of Quality and Qualifications Ireland (QQI).*

A single agency for quality in the tertiary education and training sector in Ireland

In November 2012, the Minister for Education and Skills commenced the Quality Assurance and Qualifications (Education and Training) Act that established Quality and Qualifications Ireland (QQI) and fulfilled a promise given by the previous Government to establish a single agency with responsibility for quality assurance and qualifications of further and higher education and training in Ireland.

QQI replaced four bodies that had previously dealt separately with the different sectors of further and higher education: the Further Education and Training Awards Council, the Higher Education and Training Awards Council, the National Qualifications Authority of Ireland and the Irish Universities Quality Board.

The Act consolidated many of the functions of the legacy agencies but also assigned QQI with some new and important functions, in terms of the provision of information to Irish and international students. Part of the Government's strategy for international education is to introduce an International Education Mark to support this important export market. The benefits of the Internet age come with unfortunate downsides. It has become much easier to establish so-called degree mills alongside accreditation mills that purport to offer quality-assured qualifications but in many cases only relieve students of large sums of money for what are essentially worthless credentials.

Under the Act, QQI has been charged with the development of a statutory code of practice for international learners who come to Ireland to study and QQI will be able to award the International Education Mark (IEM) for higher education institutions and English language training schools who have been evaluated and found to be in compliance with the code of practice. The IEM is intended to protect international students from rogue providers offering bogus or worthless qualifications and it is anticipated that the criterion for issuing visas to students wishing to study in Ireland will include the requirement for the receiving institution to have been awarded the IEM.

Another new aspect of the legislation is for QQI to maintain a database of programmes and awards that are recognised though the NFQ (National Framework of Qualifications) and also a register of providers of education and training. The database and register will contain information such as programme level and award type (major, minor, special purpose etc.) and also whether a provider has, for instance, the IEM.

QQI is also the national recognition and information centre (NARIC). This means that QQI facilitates graduates that have come to Ireland in having their overseas qualifications recognised here for the purposes of employment or to further their education. We are all also only too well aware of the necessity for many recent Irish graduates, and those who have fallen victim to unemployment during the current economic downturn, to emigrate in search of employment opportunities. QQI continues to provide an important service in terms of assisting Irish graduates and overseas employers with the evaluation of Irish qualifications for the purposes of employment or access to further education opportunities overseas.

The information explosion of the past 25 years has meant that we are now used to being able to access a multitude of information sources on goods and services such as Tripadvisor and Which magazine. People have become more familiar with the many international ranking tables, for the World's premier universities.

Universities in Ireland have been conducting self-evaluations and external peer review reports of academic departments and student support services since the mid-1990s. The higher education legacy bodies that came together to form QQI have, since 2005, been publishing external evaluations of all of Ireland's higher education and training institutions, both public and private.

QQI will continue this process upon its establishment and one of the challenges it has is to ensure that these reports contain information that is helpful and understandable to the informed lay reader (including prospective students, their parents and potential employers) as well as to quality assurance and education professionals. While the reports arising from QQI evaluations of higher education institutions will never be the primary source of information for prospective students choosing a course or a college, QQI intends that they should make up some of the information set needed to make an informed choice.

The 2012 Act also increases QQI's role in ensuring that learners can gain access to, transfer within and progress through the different parts of the Irish National Framework of Qualifications (NFQ). The 10 levels of the NFQ are based on standards of knowledge, skills and competence to be acquired by learners prior to graduation.

Since the development of the National Framework of Qualifications (NFQ) in 2003, there has also been a steady increase in the number of candidates with FETAC (now awarded by QQI) qualifications eligible to apply to Higher Education through the Central Applications Office (CAO), alongside the more traditional applications on the basis of the established Leaving Certificate and UK A-level qualifications. For the cohort intending to apply through the CAO to higher education institutions in 2013, close to 15,000 have indicated that they will do so with FETAC qualifications at Level 6 in the NFQ.

There are many significant changes taking place in our post-primary, further and higher education sectors and QQI is centrally involved in many of

NATIONAL FRAMEWORK OF QUALIFICATIONS

these developments. The changes taking place in further education and training includes the dissolution of FAS and the movement of some of its former activities into the Department of Social Protection, the establishment of SOLAS, which will be responsible for the funding of training and the amalgamation of 33 Regional Vocational Education Committees and the 16 former FAS training centres into 16 local Education and Training Boards (ETBs) in 2013.

Just as the awards arising from education and training activities of the VECs and FAS were made by the former Further Education and Training Awards Council, QQI will continue to quality assure and certify the awards of the ETBs when they are established.

The NFQ is now a decade in existence and QQI has the role of 'custodian' of the Framework. QQI has a central role in developing the standards on which the NFQ awards are based and in ensuring that the awards that gain access to the framework continue to have relevance. This includes all the mechanisms for awards being included in the NFQ such as:

- direct awarding by QQI (the programmes of FAS, the VECs, public and private further education colleges and private higher education colleges);
- the awards of the Institutes of Technology (under delegated authority from QQI);
- the awards of the universities and the Dublin Institute of Technology and awards that have been aligned by QQI (such as those from City and Guilds and other UK awarding bodies).

What difference will QQI make to learners?
QQI's function is to oversee a coherent system of quality-assured qualifications for the benefit of learners. We hope, through our work (largely mediated through the providers of education and training) that learners will have a smoother path through the qualifications system and that they will have access to useful information about the opportunities for education and training that are available to them, including the quality of the programmes that they sign up for.

EDUCATION IN THE MEDIA

International third-level students worth €900m to economy

Friday, December 28, 2012

'Education in Ireland', an umbrella brand for the promotion of Irish higher education, is working overseas to recruit more foreign students to Ireland. The revenues generated by such students can help to plug funding shortfalls in the sector, writes John Daly

Irish universities and third-level institutions are discovering that the revenue from foreign students coming to Ireland for their degrees is helping to plug the financial gaps resulting from the recent funding cuts.

As many as 32,000 international students are currently undertaking third-level courses in Ireland, with the combined estimated revenue worth €900m to the Irish economy.

International students in third-level colleges grew by 2% in 2012, while universities saw an 8% increase.

Education in Ireland — an umbrella brand for the promotion of Irish higher education — is managed by Enterprise Ireland with the support of the Department of Education.

It has targeted potential markets in India, China, north America, the Middle East, and Malaysia.

The brand has appointed leading Irish cricketer Kevin O'Brien to help promote Ireland as a destination for Indian students — a key growth market for Education in Ireland.

More than 150,000 Indian students travel overseas each year to take up full-time taught postgraduate programmes, with about 1,000 Indian students studying here.

Mr O'Brien is well regarded in India following his success at Bangalore in 2011, where he set the world record for the fastest century ever scored at a World Cup.

"Ireland's worldwide reputation for high quality education is built on the solid foundation of commitment to excellence," he said.

Mr O'Brien will work closely with Education in Ireland to promote Ireland as a destination of world class education through one-to-one meetings with students at education fairs and participation at Trusted Agents' Workshops.

Third Level

EDUCATION IN THE MEDIA

Marina Donohoe, head of education at Enterprise Ireland, said the nature of Ireland's knowledge intensive export economy makes a perfect fit for Indian students seeking to gain internationally recognised qualifications in dynamic growth sectors, including ICT and life sciences.

"Indian students can make a significant contribution to the intellectual and cultural wealth of campus life, while benefiting from a world-class education in an English-speaking country renowned for its friendliness and safety," said Ms Donohoe.

"Ireland's high-calibre educational institutions are keen to encourage more bright young Indian students to study here."

While an Education Ireland report showed that enrolling an international student in Ireland generates, on average, over €16,000 a year in fees and living expenses, recent research by the Ahain Group shows the greater potential benefits that could accrue to higher education from deployment of appropriate social business strategies.

Citing strategies which have proven to be very successful for international student recruitment by a number of north American colleges, it offered recommendations on how deployment of similar strategies could benefit the Irish higher education sector.

Managing partner at the Ahain Group, John Twohig, said that the report highlights the speed at which change is taking place in the international student recruitment sector, due to use of cleverly deployed social campaigns on social media platforms such as Facebook and YouTube.

"Traditional recruitment methods are already out-dated, being replaced by the social business model which offers low cost, high value targeted methods of attracting international students," said Mr Twohig.

Increasing the number of international students would also lead to job creation, both inside and outside the higher education sector, as they contribute additional fees and living expenses while studying.

"The fact is that the institutions are suffering large cuts in their budgets from Government so increasing international student recruitment would bring much needed revenues to assist in protecting the quality of education given by our institutions," said Mr Twohig.

Local benefit
The significant economic benefits international students can bring to a particular region are underlined by figures focused on the University of Limerick.

International students attending the university in a given academic year are worth €15m to the mid-west region, with 2,200 overseas students currently enrolled there — the largest number in the university's 40-year history.

The €15m figure is based on student spending estimates of between €7,000 and €12,000 in one year, but does not include tuition fees.

"The benefit is spread across the mid-west, with many international students visiting attractions in Kerry, Clare, Cork, and Galway at the weekends," according to Josephine Page, of the UL International Education Division.

"In addition, many students have parents and friends who will come and visit, so the real value of such students visiting may be as high as €20m," Ms Page added.

www.irishexaminer.com/business/features/international-third-level-students-worth-900m-to-economy-218014.html

Picture: wwwthepienews.com

Irish cricketer Kevin O'Brien and Marina Donohoe, head of education at Enterprise Ireland.

Institutes of Technology: Mergers and University Status

Denis Cummins *President of Dundalk IT and Chairman of Institutes of Technology Ireland (IoTI).*

Institutes of technology believe that they are already universities in all but name

On May 30, 2013, the Government finally published the Report to the Minister for Education and Skills on system reconfiguration, inter-institutional collaboration and system governance in the Irish Higher Education System.

The report had been prepared by the Higher Education Authority and was, in fact, the latest in a series of four reports that had been prepared on this subject in just over two years.

The 'future landscape' of higher education described in these reports had already been set out to the extent that there were no new surprises in this latest one.

The report recommended clusters, mergers and strategic alliances but by far the greatest impacts of change will be felt in the Institute of Technology (IoT) sector.

The key recommendation is the possibility of institutes coming together on a regional basis first to merge and then to attain technological university (TU) status.

Technological University status will only be conferred when exacting criteria - such as the proportion of staff with PhDs reaching 45% - have been met. Already a number of potential new technological universities have been signaled:

South East TU (WIT - ITC);
Munster TU (CIT - IT Tralee);
Dublin TU (DIT – ITB - ITT);
The Connaught Ulster Alliance (LyIT – ITS - GMIT) is also likely to seek TU status.

While the majority of IoTs are intent on becoming technological universities, a number of others are concentrating on enhanced relationships with neighbouring universities, e.g. DkIT with DCU, DLIADT with UCD, LIT with UL and AIT with NUIM.

The institutes feel this new status is no more than they deserve as they have had a transformative impact on the regions they serve. They have improved the quality of life of their graduates but this will also impact future generations since almost all who get a higher education ensure that their children achieve this too.

A recent independent study undertaken by BiGGAR Economics on the socio-economic impact of Dundalk Institute of Technology shows that, for each €1.00 of exchequer spend at the Institute, the return on that investment is €7.50.

The biggest overall impact that it has had is on improving workforce productivity in the region it serves. There can therefore be no doubting the contribution to economic and social development that IoTs have made.

Institutes of Technology also believe that they are already universities in all but name having a comprehensive range of undergraduate programmes, an active research programme including the ability to award PhDs, and regionally focused enterprise support programmes.

Despite this, concern about 'mission drift' is a recurring theme from policy makers and in media commentary. The concern here is twofold:

1. to ensure that IoTs remain firmly embedded at levels six and seven on the national framework;
2. that IoTs refrain from offering 'non-traditional' areas such as humanities.

I reject both: the former on the basis that entry level to most careers in our knowledge-intensive society is moving to a minimum level eight; the latter because the Institutes have approached disciplines such as humanities in innovative ways using their acknowledged strengths in the application of technology to these disciplines.

Rather than accusing the institutes of mission drift, they should be acknowledged for their responsiveness and for remaining relevant. In addition, their researchers compete successfully on both national and international platforms for funding and their outputs in defined areas of national strategic relevance are significant.

We look forward to the emergence of the technological university sector as one that will bring forward into it elements of the mission of institutes of technology that differentiate it from traditional universities, such as comprehensive provision at all levels 6-10 and focused research and enterprise supports that meet regional and national needs.

EDUCATION IN THE MEDIA

Trinity offers students new alternative to points race

January 14, 2013

TRINITY College Dublin (TCD) is launching a radical alternative to sole reliance on CAO points for entry for certain college courses, starting in 2014.

Under the ground-breaking initiative, a student's general performance at school and other personal information will be used to decide who gets a place.
TCD will test the alternative entry route by offering a limited number of places in three courses in September 2014 and September 2015.

Ten of 90 first-year places in law, 10 of 40 places in history and five of 15 places in ancient and medieval history and culture are being reserved for the new admissions route.

The scheme will run for at least two years and will act as a feasibility study for other universities as part of the wider review of the points system.

... The courses involved in the TCD scheme generally require more than 500 points, but using the alternative route, school-leavers could achieve a place, perhaps with up to 100 points less than the CAO cut-off.

TCD dean of undergraduate students Dr Patrick Geoghegan said it was about trying to match the right person with the right course.

As well as their Leaving Cert results, students will be assessed in two other ways – a Relative Performance Rank (RPR) and a personal information statement.
The RPR will compare the CAO rank of the applicant with others from their school and could help a student with ability, who, as a consequence of some disadvantage, fell short of cut-off points required, to gain entry.

The personal statement will cover matters such as why a student is interested in a particular course and details of any special circumstances, ranging from illness to sporting achievements, as well as a short essay giving students an opportunity to express themselves freely.

... The initiative was endorsed by the dean of admissions at Harvard University, William R Fitzsimons, who advised Trinity on the matter and is in Dublin today for its official launch.

www.independent.ie/lifestyle/education/trinity-offers-students-new-alternative-to-points-race-28958214.html

EDUCATION IN THE MEDIA

Universities propose regional clusters

January 11, 2013

The higher education system should be reconfigured into five regional clusters, according to new proposals from the university presidents.

But the presidents rule out any forced mergers of colleges. They stress colleges should continue to be "autonomous institutions operating through their established management structures".

The proposals by the Irish Universities Association, the umbrella body for the universities, come in response to pressure from Minister for Education Ruairí Quinn for some rationalisation among the seven universities, 14 institutes of technology and more than 20 other colleges that make up the higher education system.

The proposals are framed as part of the process to build a new "landscape" for higher education in Ireland. The Higher Education Authority will publish its own "draft configuration" of the system shortly.

The proposals from the presidents are unlikely to win favour among some institutes of technology who are seeking reconfiguration as a technological university. University presidents oppose the establishment of a technological university.

The presidents see a regional cluster as a group of colleges "collaborating and co-ordinating activities across a broad range of areas within a defined region". Clusters, they say, would be based on a formal written agreement among the members on core operating principles.

Making the case for the new clusters, the presidents say the goals would need:
- To enhance the student experience and optimise the efficiency and effectiveness of educational provision within the cluster by facilitating joint planning of educational provision and effective inter-institutional collaboration;
- To promote collaboration and to ensure critical mass in research and more effective knowledge transfer and commercialisation;
- To engage more coherently and systematically with stakeholders.
- The clusters, the presidents say, should have a formal governance structure comprising the relevant senior officers of the member institutions together with the "rules of engagement" which comply with individual institutional governance and autonomy.

The five regional clusters proposed by the university presidents are:

North/West
NUI Galway; Galway-Mayo IT; Sligo IT; Letterkenny IT; St Angela's College; Shannon College of Hotel Management.

Mid-West
University of Limerick; Limerick Institute of Technology; IT Tralee; Mary Immaculate College of Education; St Patrick's College Thurles.

South
University College Cork; Cork Institute of Technology; Waterford Institute of Technology; Carlow Institute of Technology. Dublin /North East/ Midlands

Dublin /North East/ Midlands
NUI Maynooth; Dublin City University; Royal College of Surgeons; Athlone IT; Dundalk IT; National College of Ireland; St Patrick's College of Education; All Hallows College; Mater Dei Institute; Church of Ireland College of Education and Froebel College of Education.

Dublin
Trinity College; UCD; Royal Irish Academy of Music; Marino Institute of Education; National College of Art and Design; Institute of Art, Design and Technology Dún Laoghaire; Institute of Public Administration; Institute of Bankers.

www.irishtimes.com/news/universities-propose-regional-cluster-plan-1.956585

Colleges to merge in biggest third-level shake-up

January 16, 2013

The number of publicly-funded third-level colleges in Ireland is to be cut from 39 to 15 in the biggest ever shake-up of higher education.

EDUCATION IN THE MEDIA

The Higher Education Authority (HEA) has proposed a radically altered third-level landscape aimed at improving quality, meeting demand and getting better value for money.

Colleges will have to merge or get involved in closer collaborations, either on a regional level or on the basis of specialism.

Initially, the HEA envisages a reduction to 24 colleges, but ultimately it wants just 15, which, in turn, would be part of five regional clusters.

The HEA board yesterday agreed the proposals and its senior officials will now consult with colleges before a recommendation is presented to Education Minister Ruairi Quinn in March.

While some dialogue will take place, colleges have little scope to opt out of the final arrangement, as future funding will depend on being part of the required change.

There are no plans to merge universities, but the HEA said "significant consolidation" was envisaged among institutes of technology.

A number of formal alliances have already emerged in this sector and some of these partnerships have made submissions to be promoted to the proposed new Technological University status. In other cases, it suggests that institutes of technology, or other small colleges, come in under the wing of a university in the region.

The HEA finalised its plans after first asking the colleges to come up with ideas about how they could contribute to a reform of the sector.

At a meeting last November, Mr Quinn made clear that some submissions were based on "wishful thinking" and had fallen short of what was required in the national interest.

The HEA said a key objective of the reconfiguration was to protect the distinctive roles and mission of universities and technological institutes, while delivering the quality outcomes in teaching, research and engagement for students and stakeholders.

A particular focus of regional collaboration will be joint academic planning, that would, for instance, lead to the elimination of wasteful duplication of courses.

The 39 colleges currently receive over €1bn a year and have 170,000 students enrolled but student numbers are set to rise dramatically in coming years.

The 39 include the teacher-training colleges and work is already under way on reducing their number from 19 to six through a series of mergers with universities, including an Institute of Education involving both UCD and TCD.

A review of the provision of creative arts programmes at third-level in the Dublin area is also due to finish soon and will feed into the reconfiguration process. Unnecessary duplication of courses in engineering, business and law in both the universities and institutes of technology (ITs) is costing the State millions every year.

Although not covered by yesterday's document, down the line, reform of the third-level sector will also include issues such as staffing, the length of the academic year and the thorny issue of funding and whether students should contribute more.

www.independent.ie/lifestyle/education/latest-news/colleges-to-merge-in-biggest-thirdlevel-shakeup-3354720.html

---

Unions warn college merger plan will hurt staff and students

January 17, 2013

The Higher Education Authority (HEA) is finalising a report aimed at reducing the number of publicly funded colleges from 39 to 15.

It will involve mergers particularly in the institutes of technology (IT) sector, and greater collaboration generally between colleges.

The Teachers Union of Ireland (TUI) represents about 4,000 lecturers in institutes of technology.

Deputy general secretary Annette Dolan said there was an unfair targeting of that IT sector, while universities escaped unscathed.

And the Irish Federation of University Lecturers (IFUT) asked about the impact on students who, as a consequence of mergers and some closures, would inevitably be forced to travel greater distances to study and pay for accommodation.

http://www.independent.ie/irish-news/unions-warn-college-merger-plan-will-hurt-staff-and-students-28959580.html

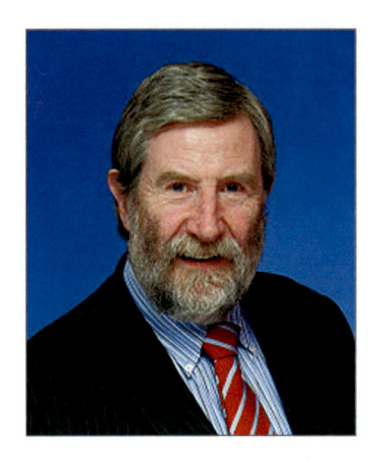

Could Private Colleges in Ireland become Private Universities?

Diarmuid Hegarty *President of Griffith College and Chairman of the Irish Higher Education Quality Network (IHEQN)*

"Private higher education colleges have emerged to fill a void."

Many changes have occurred in recent years in the higher education sector, particularly as regards participation of private institutions. Forty years ago, in 1973 when Griffith College was established, who would have thought of students getting their degree from a private third level institution? Today who would think it possible to get a university degree from a private university?

In the last twenty years many private institutions have been established and the major ones now members of the Higher Education Colleges Association (HECA), the umbrella body established just over 20 years ago. These institutions now cater for over 20,000 students and provide more than 100 courses at Bachelors, Masters, and post-degree professional level.

The academic courses are listed on the CAO, and HECA is recognised by the Department of Education & Skills (DES). For eleven years, from 2001 to 2012, the private colleges were represented on the Higher Education and Training Awards Council by Diarmuid Hegarty, President of Griffith College and author of this article. Full-time students participate in the ERASMUS programme and HECA has nominated staff of its member colleges to act as Bologna Promoters supporting the Bologna process.

In addition, HECA has nominated two representatives to sit on the Irish Higher Education Quality Network (IHEQN) which is a representative body of the universities, the Institutes of Technology, the private providers, Qualifications and Quality Assurance Ireland (QQI), the Higher Education Authority (HEA), and DES. The current Chairman of IHEQN is Diarmuid Hegarty. HECA members have also served as committee members on various academic boards of HETAC.

A new departure is the provision, in the Qualifications (Education and Training) Act 2012, for delegation of authority to make awards to private institutions. At present this right is only enjoyed by Institutes of Technology. Once the Minister for Education has determined the eligibility conditions, private colleges meeting them will be able to apply for delegation of authority to make awards which will mean that the name of the institution (rather than HETAC or QQI) will appear as the awarding institution on degree parchments.

On the funding side, the private colleges have been awarded substantial contracts by the HEA to educate students under the Springboard, ICT and FÁS Momentum labour market activation initiatives. The HEA policy in this regard was clearly enunciated by its chairman John Hennessy in April 2012 who said: "The continuing demand for higher education can no longer be fully met by the publicly funded institutions". He noted: "The private colleges are often in a better position to deliver better programmes."

In this respect, Ireland is following other countries and particularly the Scandinavian countries which have been very successful in recent decades in stimulating efficiencies in their public sector institutions by creating competition between public and private sectors.

In **Norway**, students are funded by way of loans by the national student loan body Lanekassen to attend courses in both public and private sector institutions inside and outside Norway. In the event of the student being successful in examinations on their first attempt, 25% of the loan is converted into a grant which is a great incentive to study.

In **Sweden**, private companies compete for public contracts with government bodies, and learners are permitted to shop around for best value and apply their funding accordingly.

Denmark goes one step further in optimising student choice. In addition to using public funding in private schools, they are also allowed to make up any excess cost of their chosen course from their own funds stimulating competition, not just on cost but also on reputation and quality.

The recent success of the Scandinavian countries has demonstrated the benefits of a higher education policy which is not a captive of ideology. Irish learners, particularly lifelong learners, would really benefit from breaking the chains of this captivity.

In the UK the Department for Business, Innovation & Skills is also working towards making the higher education system more efficient, diverse, financially sustainable and consumer focussed and to ensure higher education institutions provide innovative, high quality learning by asking learners to become the paymasters and by reviewing the way alternative providers can access funding. The Minister David Willetts proposes allocating 20,000 state-funded places to private colleges charging less than £7,500 per annum and extending the University title to private colleges with 1,000 or more full-time equivalent students on degree programmes.

It is also fair to say that private colleges have adapted more quickly than the universities in developing online courses to suit students working at their own pace at home. Again, public sector institutions are constrained by ideological and employment restrictions which came to light in the debate on online teacher training subsequently proven viable by Hibernia College. The result is that Ireland's public sector institutions are losing out on the funding opportunity of developing markets for online degree courses from Iceland to India.

Perhaps the best testament to the above comes from a great champion of the public sector Ed Walsh, the founding president of the University of Limerick, who stated in a Sunday Business Post article on 14th of April this year:

"Private higher education colleges have emerged to fill a void. They have developed niches of excellence and, in certain areas, already outflank the publicly-subsidised colleges and universities. …One should hardly be surprised that the private colleges have the potential to excel, given the fact that, of the ten best universities in the world, six are private and operate as no-nonsense corporations."

But what of the prospect of a private university? The recent long overdue government decision to give Institutes of Technology the title of University of Technology moves us one step closer. It is worth noting that the recent Technological Universities Quality Framework document, produced by Institutes of Technology Ireland (IOTI), focuses on principles of quality rather than on funding or ownership status.

If quality considerations alone figure in the decision as to eligibility for the title University of Technology, there is no reason why the learners of Griffith College should not have their degree from a private university. All that is required is that ideology should release its captive to share with all learners the full fruition of its energies.

EDUCATION IN THE MEDIA

College backs down in redundancy dispute

January 23, 2013

Year-long industrial dispute approaches resolution as Trinity agrees to re-hire staff.

Move comes after intervention of Department of Education and threat of action by union; IFUT: issue not closed until three workers have "acceptable" deals.

College authorities have backed down in the long-running industrial dispute over staff redundancies in Trinity and begun re-hiring the staff laid off in late 2011 and early 2012. The move comes as a resolution to a nine-month stalemate following a Labour Court recommendation in April 2012 which supported their reinstatement.

Trinity had previously argued that the recommendation was not binding and that, despite entering the Labour Court process in "good faith", they were "unable to implement the recommendation on reinstatement due to the precedent it would set and the risk of ensuing unsustainable costs". However, in a statement to Trinity News on Monday, Trinity confirmed that it "accepted" that the recommendation was "binding".

The Irish Federation of University Lecturers (IFUT), which represented the staff, had successfully argued in the Labour Court that their contracts of indefinite duration (CIDs) were permanent and that they could therefore not be made redundant under the Croke Park Agreement. In September, the Department of Education strongly backed the union's position, warning Trinity that the recommendation was "both final and binding" and to implement the Labour Court's recommendation "immediately" or face "consequences"...

Mike Jennings Secretary General, The Irish Federation of University Lecturers (IFUT)

trinitynews.ie/college-backs-down-in-redundancy-dispute/

Farmers and self-employed face clampdown over student grants

February 04, 2013

Farmers and self-employed business people face a five-year trawl through their accounts and assets in a clampdown on student grants.

The Government is planning to tighten up the rules on means testing to ensure clever accounting can't be used to "hide their assets".

Education Minister Ruairi Quinn's inclusion of farmland in means test changes comes despite vehement opposition from Fine Gael.

At the moment, the student grant is only assessed on the income of the parents in the year running up to when they apply for a college place and doesn't include assets owned.

For years, this has led to the perception of hard-pressed PAYE workers marginally failing to meet the income criteria and being refused the grant, while the children of many asset-rich businessmen and farmers get the full allowance.

But Mr Quinn plans to change the system to include a capital asset test, as he believes farmers and self-employed business people can manipulate their income to get grants.

Under the new system, assets such as farms, shops and businesses worth over €750,000 will be included in the means tests.

... The inclusion of assets in means testing was included in Budget 2013, so the change is coming...

www.independent.ie/irish-news/farmers-and-selfemployed-face-clampdown-over-student-grants-29047710.html

Third Level

EDUCATION IN THE MEDIA

Education must focus on needs of employers, says Ruairí Quinn

February 16, 2013

Education across the EU needed to be more in tune with the needs of employers, EU education ministers agreed yesterday.

Minister for Education Ruairí Quinn, who chaired a meeting of ministers, said education had a vital role in tackling the Europe-wide issue of youth unemployment. "The current youth unemployment rate is close to 23 per cent across the European Union, yet at the same time there are more than two million employment vacancies that cannot be filled," he said.

Noting that Ireland's "core aim" during its presidency of the European Council was to seek ways of supporting sustainable jobs and growth in Europe, he said education was no different.

"With unemployment, particularly youth unemployment at painful levels across Europe, the key role education and training should play in tackling and resolving this crisis is obvious.

"Education ministers from across Europe's 27 member states yesterday adopted conclusions on an education strategy, "Rethinking Education", which aims to modernise the education system for the labour market. In particular, it calls for a benchmark on foreign language learning, and a development of IT and entrepreneurial skills.

Proposals to improve apprenticeships available in Europe, including the sharing of successful apprenticeship models between member states, were also discussed at yesterday's meeting.

Mr Quinn also emphasised the need for European workers to upskill in specific areas.

Erasmus for All
Ireland's key challenge during its presidency in the education portfolio will be gaining European Parliament support for the European Commission's "Erasmus for All" programme. This will replace the seven existing EU and international schemes for education, training, youth and sport.

According to the European commissioner for education, Androulla Vassiliou, this will allow a greater flexibility in transferring money...

She also welcomed last week's agreement on the seven-year EU budget, noting the programme obtained a 40-50 per cent increase in funding...

www.irishtimes.com/news/education-must-focus-on-needs-of-employers-says-ruair%C3%AD-quinn-1.1252532

Third university hires debt-collection agency

February 14, 2013

A third Irish university is using debt-collection agencies to recoup outstanding student fees.

Dublin City University (DCU) has hired debt collectors to track down students who have not paid their full student contribution fees. This follows decisions by UCD and the University of Limerick to use similar methods.

DCU did not clarify if debt collectors are targeting currently enrolled students or former students or both. And the university has not ruled out bringing students to court to get them to clear their bills if the debt collectors have no success.

Third-level students are currently paying annual contribution fees of €2,250 to their colleges and institutes of technology. The payment covers the cost of student services and examinations.

... A DCU spokesperson said they use "a third party independent agency where necessary to follow up on outstanding amounts owing to the university".

"The third party agency operates under procedures and protocols agreed with the university.

"Prior to sending any outstanding amounts to the third party the university goes through a significant process of engagement with the students."

www.independent.ie/irish-news/third-university-hires-debtcollection-agency-29068741.html

Negotiating and re-negotiating the breaking of an agreement

Dr Rose Malone *President of the Irish Federation of University Teachers (IFUT)*

"We used to *be* the university, now we *work for* the university."

The austerity years following from the most recent worldwide recession and depression have been challenging for almost everyone in Ireland. In the university sector they have contributed to a fundamental shift in self-perception of workers and a fundamental shift in the relationships between them and university management. Indeed, use of terms like "workers" and "management" would, until recently, have been anathema to many academics. As one lecturer put it, "We used to be the university, now we work for the university".

Austerity is not, of course, the only driving factor in this process. Increasing corporatisation of the universities has led to the development of a new language of performance management, development systems and workload models, and foundational concepts such as tenure and even academic freedom are increasingly under threat. Up to relatively recently, the language of industrial relations would not have been the language used to highlight the significant developments of the university year. Academics must now, however, develop a new identity as public servants at a time when the concept of public service is itself under threat. This paper, then, outlines the process of negotiating the latest public service agreement in the context of a shifting conceptual landscape for academia and the public service.

IFUT is the smallest of the Irish education unions with just 2,500 members. It is, however, one of the most diverse. The majority of members are lecturers whose work combines teaching at undergraduate and post-graduate levels, with research and administrative duties. IFUT membership also encompasses researchers, librarians and senior administrators. As well as diversity in the type of work carried out by members, IFUT membership also includes a wide diversity of grades, from college presidents to hourly paid lecturers and researchers on short-term contracts. A growing part of the work of IFUT relates to the vindication of the rights of members to whom the Fixed Term Workers' Act (2003) applies.

IFUT entered into the Public Service Agreement which became known as "The Croke Park Agreement" (more accurately, Public Service Agreement 2010-2014) with considerable reluctance. The determining factors in its eventual acceptance were a promise of freedom from pay cuts and protection from compulsory redundancy. The most difficult section for IFUT members was a clause referring to the possible re-negotiation of contracts of employment. The positive aspects were, however, just sufficient to ensure the acceptance of the proposals after a second ballot.

The entire public sector was shocked when Minister Brendan Howlin began to speak of the necessity of asking for yet more sacrifices and initiated the talks which became known as "Croke Park 2" (even though they were not held in Croke Park or its environs). IFUT entered these talks with great misgivings as members felt a deep sense of betrayal at the unilateral breach of an agreement which still had more than a year to run. When the draconian proposals emerged from the talks, it took very little time for the Executive Committee to recommend, unanimously, that members reject them, which they did by a margin of 3:1. Members braced themselves for a campaign of resistance to pay cuts, loss of increments and less flexible working arrangements.

The invitation to enter a new round of talks came to the education unions rather later than it did to the remainder of the public sector. By this time, INTO, ASTI and TUI had all rejected "Croke Park 2" out of hand and the latter two unions had balloted for industrial action "up to and including strike". IFUT had decided at its Annual Delegate Conference not to re-enter talks on "Croke Park 2" without a decision of a Special Delegate Conference.

By the time the invitation to enter talks was issued, proposals to include restoration of the original pay scales had emerged, together with proposals to delay rather than abandon payment of increments. This was sufficient to allow the Executive Committee to decide to re-enter talks, without preconditions, on a new set of proposals which became known as the "Haddington Road Agreement".

The Haddington Road talks were held on a sectoral basis and this represented a departure from previous patterns of public service pay talks. While proposals on overall pay scales, increments and flexitime were made on a collective basis, each sector within the public service (health, education, defence, etc.) was involved in separate talks on specific issues. The education talks were concentrated into one 12-hour period, finishing at 5am. The practice of all-night talks appears to have become embedded in the process of negotiation in the public service.

A brief summary of some of the main points of the Haddington Road proposals as they apply across the public service is as follows

- For those on salaries of 65,000 and above, pay cuts, ranging from 5.5% at the lower end to 10% for those on more than 185,000, will apply. This reduction in pay is to be restored for those on up to approximately 100,000 "within a maximum of 18 months of the end of this 3 year agreement"
- For those to whom increments are due to be paid, an increment freeze will be applied after the payment of the next increment. The length of the freeze will vary depending on the level of pay, i.e. for those on salaries below 35,000 a 3-month freeze will apply so that increments will be paid after 15 rather than 12 months; for those on 65,000 and above, two 6 month freezes will apply during the agreement.
- Public service pensions will be aligned with the payment reductions, so that the measures will apply to those on pensions of 32,500 or greater
- The current flexitime arrangements will continue to apply for certain grades, except that from 1 July 2014, the maximum of flexi leave allowed in any flexi period is one day.

In the university sector a number of additional provisions are proposed:

- An Expert Group is to be set up to consider and report on the level of fixed-term and part-time employment in lecturing. As a priority, the group is to report on the reduction of the qualification time for the awarding of Contract of Indefinite Duration (CID) from four years to three
- Academic staff are to work an extra 78 hours per annum
- The examination marking fee is to be reduced to 75% of current rates.

These proposals represent a slight (or, in some cases, non-existent) improvement over the rejected proposals of Croke Park 2. The promise of restoration of pay scales is hedged around with provisos and the setting aside of Croke Park 1 remains as a deep wound to the trust of members in any future promises.

A major difficulty for IFUT inheres in the diversity of membership, described above. The proposals demand sacrifices of all members, but the improvements on "Croke Park 2" (if any) are not evenly spread. There are no improvements for senior staff, above the cut off for restoration of pay scales. The benefits are greatest for those at the lower end of incremental scales and for those to whom flexitime arrangements apply.

It is a matter of great concern to IFUT that the growing casualization in universities is not comprehensively addressed. The promise of an Expert Group is limited by reference to "lecturers", leading us to fear that the situation of researchers will not be addressed. The requirement to work an extra 78 hours per annum is deeply insulting to members who have seen their average weekly hours increase to almost 60 as a result of modularisation.

A key factor that sets the Haddington Road proposals apart from all previous pay negotiations in the public sector is the manner in which the agreement is to be implemented. Instead of a collective vote of unions affiliated to ICTU, each union accepting the proposals is required to register a collective agreement with the Labour Court. Those who do not do so will have the full rigour of the legislation known as FEMPI (2013) (Financial Emergency Measures in the Public Interest) applied to them. This means that the pay cuts and any other measure deemed necessary will be applied by ministerial order. This represents a major departure from previous industrial relations practice and may have lasting repercussions for the trade union movement as a whole.

At time of writing, IFUT, following a Consultative Conference of members, is considering the arrangements for balloting on these proposals. Whatever the outcome of this process, it is clear that turbulent times lie ahead. As a small union, with a diverse membership in a sector buffeted by recession, IFUT is facing the challenge of steering through turbulent times for the benefit of its members and of the university.

EDUCATION IN THE MEDIA

USI President welcomes affiliation changes

March 05, 2013

There were big changes in USI over the past week, with UCD dropping out and DCU rejoining.

Due to a series of referendums held by University College Dublin (UCD), NUI Maynooth (NUIM) and Dublin City University (DCU) recently, there have been several reforms in affiliation with the Union of Students in Ireland (USI), which represents the Irish student body. While DCU voted to re-affiliate with USI after a decade, and Maynooth's referendum resulted in huge support of USI affiliation, UCD has decided to end the affiliation between the college and USI.

USI President, John Logue, declared: "The unique circumstances in UCD, with their Students' Union in financial difficulty, resulted in a vote to leave USI to focus on local issues. I have no doubt we will work with UCD again in the future and, with the return of DCU and a reaffirmation of Maynooth students' support, USI can only go from strength to strength."

According to the UCD Students' Union, 62% of their 2,276 students voted to leave USI. UCD Students' Union President, Rachel Breslin, had previously indicated that a deal had been made to ensure the university would reform USI if it continued to be affiliated. Suggestions for improvement had included the introduction of direct elections for the USI Presidency and a review of the fee structure for affiliation…

www.sin.ie/2013/03/05/usi-president-welcomes-affiliation-changes/

Newly elected President of the USI (Union of Students in Ireland) Joe O'Connor GMIT at The Congress 2013. Picture: Andrew Downes.

Third Level

EDUCATION IN THE MEDIA

More Irish 30-somethings have degrees than anywhere in EU

April 18, 2013

Ireland is the graduate capital of Europe, with a bigger share of 30-somethings holding a degree than anywhere else in the EU. Over half of Irish 30- to 34-year-olds now have a third-level qualification, the only EU country to pass the 50pc mark.

Among women, the figure is even higher, with 58pc of Irish females in that age bracket having completed third-level education, compared with 44pc of males. New figures from Eurostat track how Ireland's impressive graduate output over the past decade has put it to the top of the leaderboard.

The continuing rise in Ireland's graduation rate has seen it come from behind to pass out countries such as Finland, which have highly rated education systems.

In 2002, when 32pc of Irish 30- to 34-year-olds had a degree, the comparable figure in Finland was 41pc, but in 2012, Finland's 46pc was trailing behind Ireland's 51pc.

Meanwhile, a detailed analysis of this year's CAO applications confirms the shifting trends in the areas of study being undertaken at third-level, as school-leavers and other college hopefuls follow the promise of jobs in hi-tech sectors.

There has been a significant increase in applications to study science, technology and engineering over the past five years, according to the analysis by the Higher Education Authority (HEA).

Technology now accounts for 21pc of all Level 8 (honours degree) courses and within that category, computing has seen a 51pc rise in first-preference applications since 2009.

www.independent.ie/lifestyle/education/more-irish-30somethings-have-degrees-than-anywhere-in-eu-29204701.html

First MOOC on theme of Irish identity

April 20, 2013

A free MOOC, presenting a broad overview of Ireland to prospective visitors, is being designed by Hibernia College in association with The Gathering.

The new MOOC (Massive Open Online Course), Exploring Irish Identity, was launched by Jimmy Deenihan TD, Minister for Arts, Heritage and the Gaeltacht, on April 10.

Free of charge and starting on 27 May 2013, the MOOC will have a potential audience of 70 million people around the globe who claim ancestral links to the island of Ireland.

The MOOC will explore Irish history, literature and poetry, theatre and film, language, art, sport and landscape in a series of eight two hour presentations to achieve a braod overview of how history, geography and culture have interacted to create divergent, and sometimes contradictory, ideas of what it means to be Irish.

President of Hibernia College Dr Sean Rowland said: "MOOCs have grown enormously in popularity and scope over the last 18 months. They are now offered by many acclaimed international educational institutions. Up to now, there is not a single programme related to Irish identity on any of the MOOC platforms. Hibernia College is delighted to address this."

Pictured at the launch of the first ever MOOC on Irish Identity (l to r): Professor Tom Mitchell Former Provost of Trinity College, Jimmy Deenihan TD Minister for Arts Heritage and the Gaeltacht, Sara McDonnell Executive Vice-President Hibernia College, Jim Miley The Gathering.

Exporting Newman and Importing Confucius: The Idea of a University

Professor Liming Wang *Director of the Confucius Institute at University College Dublin*

If Newman and Confucius had a conversation today, what might they say?

Newman wanted UCD to provide "an education which gives a man a clear, conscious view of his own opinions and judgements, a truth in developing them, an eloquence in expressing them, and a force in urging them".

The Idea of a University, originally delivered by the great educationalist and founder of University College Dublin (UCD) John Henry Newman in 1852, and published in 1873, is today a world classic. Although translated into Chinese in 1996, this work on his philosophy of education has still not had the influence on the Chinese education system that could be expected.

The values of questioning, challenging and coming up with creative solutions, which are at heart of Irish education, are in short supply in the current Chinese school system.

Chinese middle school students have grown up in a society where they are taught in class from a young age to respect the way things are – but this needs to be changed. We can accomplish this change through the building of new world-class cooperative education institutions such as the Beijing-Dublin International College (officially opened by Minister Ruairi Quinn in Beijing on March 15, 2013). UCD has also been in discussion with China Agricultural University to establish a new international university (UCD Yantai) in the beautiful coastal city of Yantai, China. At least 5,000 Chinese students are currently studying in Irish universities like these in China, and it is through these institutions that we can introduce a new conceptual framework for modules and courses imbued with the aforementioned Irish values.

This is part of UCD's vision - to create world-class partner universities around the world which have a unique attraction. This uniqueness is manifested in the concept of 3 As and 3 Cs, which, to the best of my knowledge, have been combined here for the first time.

The three As

The 3 As have sprung from my experience working in a high tech society like Ireland where a bewildering array of information is readily available on your iPhone, tablet or laptop at the click of a mouse or the swipe of a hand. This information explosion in our new digital world, especially in the IT and ICT sectors, is influencing education systems. Now the emphasis is not on how much knowledge you can absorb but rather how you develop your skills to best utilise said knowledge. And so we need to teach these young learners the 3 As: Analyse; Assess; Apply. These skills are even more relevant for Chinese learners who have to compete in an international marketplace where these proficiencies are generally more prevalent, and thus pose a significant challenge for young Chinese professionals.

The three Cs

The 3 Cs have their roots in my reflection of the traditional Chinese values stemming from Confucianism, which promote a non-confrontational approach to situations and senior figures, a deep rooted respect for authority and an automatic acceptance of conventional thinking. In the appropriate circumstances the importance of these values cannot be denied, but on the international stage a more proactive challenging approach is needed. Hence the 3 Cs: Critical; Creative; Challenging. If Chinese students can grasp these new modes of thinking they can not only start to think outside the box, but question what the box is, who made it and why.

Working through these concepts led me to examine the differences between the eastern and western education systems. I was able to do this from my own experience and also through the differences in my son's schooling here in Ireland compared to what he had experienced back home in Beijing.

When my son first went to school here, he came home after the first day and was really excited to tell me how it went – and the biggest news he had was that he and his classmates were allowed to go to the toilet during class time. This is absolutely not possible in Beijing, or anywhere in China. This is a very simple example, and may seem strange to Irish and western readers. But it does hint at respect for basic human rights, and the general freedom enjoyed here. Another example is that practical skills are encouraged and trained, and this is even evident from an early stage when kids are given the opportunity to do various projects in class and in their own time as homework, again absent from Chinese schooling.

The three Hs
This has now led me to follow up with another trinity of concepts, the 3 Hs, from traditional Chinese values.

Holistic
Chinese are better at seeing the big picture, taking the holistic view. Going back in history, we can see that early Chinese astrologists believed that there was an inclusiveness about the galaxy, and that continues to this day. The same is true about Chinese medicine. In traditional Chinese medicine, the entire body and its different functions are linked and interfering with one element will influence many others. This is one of the core teachings of acupuncture, where a specific point in, say, the sole of your foot can be stimulated to help heal another area, for example the lungs. We often feel that in the west it is all about the details and quick solutions, sometimes without considering the bigger picture or the project as a whole.

Harmonious
The concept of 'he' comes from the home, the clan system, and this has developed over time into today's society. This can also be traced back to Confucianism. The general concept in Chinese society is to work for the collective – for other students, the school, the family, the workplace, society and so on. In the west, kids are encouraged from a young age to be individuals and develop the ability to be independent in many disciplines. In China, however, you should compromise yourself for the larger unit.

Hierarchical
Confucius was mainly interested in how to bring about societal order and harmony. He believed that mankind would be in harmony with the universe if everyone understood their rank in society and were taught the proper behaviours of their rank. Confucius devised a system of interdependent relationships - a structure in which the lower level gives obedience to the higher (extending from the family level to the national). Though modern China has moved past these narrowly defined roles, the Chinese today are still used to thinking in terms of hierarchy. They tend to respect hierarchy and differences in status much more than westerners.

I often wonder if Newman and Confucius had a conversation today, what would be the result? One thing can be certain: it would be quite unique and the concepts they would produce would be truly innovative, as we must be now.

There should be options and open classes for innovation available to all students, regardless of their major. Only then can you say you are really being unique and encouraging innovation. We could unite what's best in the above teachings from east and west and bring about recognition and understanding of those differences. This would enable the students of today to paint with a full palette and create innovative masterpieces for tomorrow.

EDUCATION IN THE MEDIA

RIA chief highlights longer-term goals of education

June 01, 2013

The short-term needs of the economy should not detract from the long-term goal of creating an "intellectually stimulating" third-level education system, the president of the Royal Irish Academy (RIA) has said.

Luke Drury was speaking at the admission of 20 members to the academic institution, including Chief Justice Susan Denham and former Northern police ombudsman Nuala O'Loan, both in the humanities.

On the restructuring of the third-level system announced this week, Prof Drury said he was "broadly encouraged" by the proposals.

"Looking to the students of tomorrow, who will sit their first Leaving Certificate paper in five days' time, we must surely wish for them a future as engaged citizens in a smart society and not just alienated workers in a smart economy. As the Minister has outlined, this can only be achieved if we have equitable access to an intellectually stimulating third-level system.

"Even if the immediate priority has to be the rebuilding of the economy, our long-term aim should be to make Ireland one of the most culturally rich and intellectually stimulating places in the world, an island of creative ideas capable of attracting the brightest and most interesting minds from around the world."

The new members in the sciences are: Mark Crowe (UCD), Kevin Devine (TCD), Alan Dobson (UCC), Pat Guiry (UCD), Christopher Hardacre (QUB), Gerard Kiely (UCC), Christine Maggs (QUB), Alan Smeaton (DCU) and Cormac Taylor (UCD).

Other new members in the humanities and social sciences are: David Farrell (UCD), Michael Gallagher (TCD), Peter Gray (QUB), Tomás Ó Carragáin (UCC), Terence O'Reilly (UCC), Rosalind Pritchard (UU), Peter Simons (TCD) and Sally Wheeler (QUB).

Two honorary members were admitted: David Dumville, history professor at the University of Aberdeen; and William Hayes, former pro-vice chancellor of the University of Oxford.

www.irishtimes.com/news/ria-chief-highlights-longer-term-goals-of-education-1.1413669

Irish universities 'intimately engaged' with non-democratic regimes

June 11, 2013

Former RCSI Bahraini chief Prof Tom Collins says other colleges need to face up to their ethical responsibilities. Irish third-level institutions are "intimately engaged with regimes that have human rights' questions to answer", the former head of the Bahrain campus of the Royal College of Surgeons in Ireland (RCSI) has said.

Addressing a conference on ethics in education, Prof Tom Collins said that, while the RCSI has been the focus of much public scrutiny, other universities had questions to answer about their relationship with non-democratic countries.

He noted that in 2009 China and Malaysia, two countries which were criticised in various Amnesty International reports, provided 31 per cent of non-EU students to Irish third-level institutions. This was worth €61 million to the sector, and was much sought-after funding as it was one of the few income streams universities had discretion over.

"The NUI [National University of Ireland] is silent on that issue and I don't think it can be silent," he said.

Academic freedom
A drift towards commercialisation at third-level was putting academic freedom at risk, he added.

"It can be difficult to reconcile being a critic with being an enterprise. It's difficult to envisage a Chelsea footballer wondering about Roman Abramovich's human rights' record," he said.

Prof Collins, who resigned his post in Bahrain earlier this year over the cancellation of a conference on medical ethics, reiterated his support for the RCSI to remain in the country.

Professor Tom Collins

Little impact
"Withdrawing would have little impact on anyone other than the college, its students

EDUCATION IN THE MEDIA

and staff," he said. Ireland had "moral authority but no muscle" to bring about change in the region but it could build alliances.

"The only way now is for western institutions to coalesce around a shared commitment to democracy." Among those attending the Royal Irish Academy conference 'Values in University Education: from Academic Freedom to Impact' was President Michael D Higgins, who shared some concern about the direction Irish universities were taking.

Referring to a "flaw" in the system, the President said:

"Rather like the siege of Troy if you let the Trojan horse of the business model come in and if it, in fact, stifles creativity in relation to the management of staff in creative settings you are already really defending your city after you have lost it."

As a former minister, he had encountered people both at a senior level in government and in the university sector becoming "seduced" at times by "the magic in the business model," he added.

"Then, as the magic of the business model turns to ashes all around them everybody foosters and flusters and suggest perhaps out there, in the ether, is a technology that will save us all. I actually think we need more philosophy."

Earlier, Trinity College Dublin's provost, Prof Patrick Prendergast, said universities were "up against a very sophisticated Government" in terms of communications, and they needed to convince the public of the value of academic freedom.

"Government control of universities, though it might seem like the right thing to do, is self-defeating," he said.

Contrary to some perceptions, Thomas Estermann of the European University Association told the seminar Ireland ranked sixth-highest in Europe for organisational autonomy and highest for academic authority. However, he said this ranking may have slipped somewhat with the introduction of the Universities (Amendment) Bill 2012.

www.irishtimes.com/news/education/irish-universities-intimately-engaged-with-non-democratic-regimes-1.1423820

EU group wants teacher training for lecturers

23 June 2013

University lecturers should be required to take teacher training classes, according to an EU commission on higher education led by the former president of Ireland Mary McAleese.

The call for mandatory teaching certificates is one of 16 recommendations made by an EU high-level group set up last year to examine the modernisation of higher education.

Other recommendations in the group's "report to the European Commission on improving the quality of teaching and learning in Europe's higher education institutions", published on 18 June, include putting more focus on helping students to develop entrepreneurial and innovative skills and the creation of a European Academy of Teaching and Learning.

The report's publication follows almost a year of consultation with universities across Europe, while evidence panels were held in Brussels and Rome. "Higher education teaching staff have to be given the training and support they need to do an excellent job," said Professor McAleese, a former pro vice-chancellor at Queen's University Belfast.

"Our report shows how this can be done," she added. The report also recommends that higher education institutions and national policy makers, in partnership with students, should establish counselling, guidance, mentoring and tracking systems to support students into higher education and and beyond.

Lesley Wilson, secretary general of the European University Association, which represents higher education institutions in 47 countries, welcomed the report's findings.

"It draws attention to issues that are crucial for Europe's universities, their staff and students, and echoes many of the issues related to teaching and learning that have or are currently being addressed by EUA through its different activities," she said.

The EU group will now begin work on a new report assessing the impact of new methods of delivering quality higher education, such as massive open online courses (Moocs), which is due to be published in June 2014.

www.timeshighereducation.co.uk/news/eu-group-wants-teacher-training-for-lecturers/2005014.article

University Ranking – Looking past the shop window

Trevor Holmes *Vice President for External Relations, University College Cork (UCC)*

We ignore at our peril the slippage of Irish higher education in international rankings

The time has come for a national debate amongst all stakeholders on the growing influence of university ranking on higher education. The slippage of Irish universities in certain ranking systems is a complex and concerning development impacting on our ability to compete internationally. While all Irish universities have a regional catchment area, the data supports the fact that, collectively, we ignore at our peril the standing and performance of Irish higher education internationally. A significant change in thinking is required if we as a nation are to thrive on what is now a global playing field.

The decline in funding of Irish universities over several years, compounded by a less than subtle mandate to reduce staff numbers, has had a major impact on staff-student ratios, a key indicator used by international ranking systems. All Irish universities are to be commended for their fortitude in facing these difficult circumstances - TCD, UCD and UCC all ranked within the top 200 universities globally according to QS 2012.

All Irish universities have suffered unduly in the most recent Times Higher Education Supplement (THES) Rankings – the national economic difficulties and the subsequent damage to Ireland's international image and reputation have all impacted negatively. Yet that is not the full story: in the most recent QS subject scores, all Irish universities performed well on a worldwide ranking by subject, gracing the top 50, top 100 and top 200. This speaks volumes for the on-going work in all these institutions and we need to credit the dedication of our academic communities for that.

The notion of 'scale' continually resurfaces as a national solution to future thriving in these rankings. Quality propels a university through any rankings system and ultimately ensures its success in far broader domains, whether it has 2,000 students or 20,000 students. Some commentators suggest our best hope lies in consolidation and ensuring at least one 'university of scale' resides within the top tier ranking systems. That is a flawed approach, which certain Asian countries appear to be following, positioning a single university as favourably as possible through resource concentration. This 'eggs in one basket' outlook is misguided and does a disservice to higher educations' many stakeholders. The fundamental point constantly overlooked in this discussion is that scale simply does not equate to quality. Caltech - the California Institute of Technology - is the quintessential case in point.

Ranking systems vary in focus, but those who do not rely on a subjective opinion element could be said to have greater validity. Irish universities can struggle in competing systems that rely heavily on a reputation element - for reasons already outlined we cannot compete with some global heavy hitters. Rankings systems, while imperfect, do matter to the outside world. It is vital however to acknowledge their shortcomings and to balance subjective reputational measures with other objective hard data. The Leiden rankings reflect such an approach to research-intensive universities, which this year highlighted UCC's commendable performance in terms of scientific impact and collaborations.

The reality is simply that these ranking systems are an important global shop window and the demand for such insights is only increasing. Cognisant of all the challenges, at UCC we are always interested in supporting innovation. The European Commission's 'U-Multirank' is a good case in point. UCC is partaking in the pilot of this multi-dimensional ranking system, which will allow a more nuanced output by considering research, teaching, international orientation, knowledge transfer, and regional engagement and growth. UCC, as the comprehensive university of the south of Ireland, welcomes this more inclusive methodology as it better represents the broad dimensions of the student experience and what a university education actually stands for.

As the leading Irish university with our international student cohort, according to the International Student Barometer, we also feel strongly that the voice of all students should be heard in ranking systems. It is only now with the advent of U-Multirank that the student voice will actually be properly considered - a point we have continually made to some of the larger rankings systems.

Finally, a number of simple asks, perhaps for the HEA and the whole sector to consider:

Proactively harness the student voice in a consistent way across the universities, through a national student survey. Allow this to become the official voice of student experience into ranking systems.

Collectively support actions that genuinely reflect differentiators of mission across the seven universities, perhaps differentiators in subject areas, so that we can all compete in a collaborative fashion internationally, showcasing Irish higher education and our individual institutions at our very best.

Recognise the considerable effort required by each institution to complete each ranking submission. A mechanism to facilitate the HEA's formal role in collecting institutional data as the national feeder into each submission would do more than eliminate the resource drain such duplication entails. It would also introduce a far greater quality vetting of the actual data, trumping the current process whereby a ranking system provider has no robust way of truly verifying data submitted.

In conclusion, in times of national difficulty, it is important that each part of the system operates together for the benefit of the whole. As stated at the outset, the time is right for a robust national debate among all the key stakeholders on this sensitive topic. It is critical to our national strategic ambition that the future standing and value of Irish higher education is not undermined or negatively impacted through the influential of the myriad of international league tables.

CPD in Higher Education: the new emphasis on learning to teach

Dr Iain MacLaren *Director of the Centre for Excellence in Learning & Teaching (CELT) at NUI Galway*

The era of the amateur scholar is now well behind us

It is only in recent years that the notion that teaching at university level requires professional training. For many outwith the sector, that often comes as a surprise, even though those within clearly understand that the emphasis has long been on establishing your reputation and professional standing through research output. To be recognized within your disciplinary community requires more than just the ability to talk about your subject, you need to prove that you can 'walk the walk' by actually contributing to the pool of knowledge in that subject, by pushing its boundaries (however slightly) and that requires you to focus much of your time, energy and enthusiasm on research. Indeed, within the university sector in particular, promotion has largely only been possible through research productivity. In theory, teaching has equal weighting in many promotion schemes, but in practice, particularly given that research is easier to measure than teaching skill and impact, most staff would concur that there has historically been an inherent bias in the system.

Things are changing, however, and now most institutions, whether universities or IoTs, have some form of training provision in the area of teaching and learning. Some have formal professional, postgraduate level qualifications ranging from Certificate to Masters level and encompassing topics such as teaching large classes, technology enhanced teaching, postgraduate supervision, course design and assessment methods. Across the IoT sector there has also been modular provision via the LIN (Learning Innovation Network) project, enabling participants to pick up credits for modules offered from partner institutions. This flexible delivery approach, building on ideas of credit transfer and accumulation, is likely to continue to grow in future years as it permits training and professional development to be scheduled at times and at a pace which respects the already heavy workload of many in the sector.

Whilst some countries (such as the UK) have programmes specifically targeted to new lecturing staff, many of the offerings in Ireland actually appeal to both new and well-established lecturers and having a mix within any given cohort adds a richness to the experience. However, there is an increasing move towards focusing on new starts and whilst this is important we mustn't be tempted to neglect those who may welcome an opportunity to refresh their approaches and perhaps even 'unlearn' some habits! So any effective framework requires not just initial training, but also a longer term - indeed career-long - provision of continuing professional development (CPD). Interlinking with other aspects of contemporary academic practice (such as research supervision, departmental management, grant preparation, external examining, etc) will also bolster such programmes.

It is interesting to note, then, that the recent report to the European Commission by the High Level Group (chaired by former Irish President,

Mary McAleese) on the Modernisation of Higher Education has focused on teaching and learning. Their first publication (June 2013) is titled "Improving the quality of teaching and learning in Europe's higher education institutions" and makes a number of strong recommendations, including:

"All staff teaching in higher education institutions in 2020 should have received certified pedagogical training. Continuous professional education as teachers should become a requirement for teachers in the higher education sector."

Such is a major commitment given the numbers of staff and the timeframe and it remains to be seen how such is interpreted and implemented in each member country. The group also realizes that high quality teaching needs to be factored into career progression and another of their recommendations is,

"Academic staff entrance, progression and promotion decisions should take account of an assessment of teaching performance alongside other factors."

The guiding principles that they have based their work on include "that teaching and learning are fundamental core missions of our universities" and colleges and that "academic staff are employed not just to teach, but to teach well, to a high professional standard."

Within Ireland, the Minister for Education & Skills announced in November 2012 the establishment of a new National Forum for the Enhancement of Teaching & Learning (in Higher Education) and this organization is now up and running, comprised of representatives from across the sector. The Forum is currently defining its operational work-plan and outlining its targets for the next two years, but this gives a significant strategic focus for the issue of CPD, particularly with regards the teaching dimension and it is expected that it will also bring a coherence to activities and more widespread sharing of practice and collaborative initiatives.

The Forum is also establishing international links and will learn from proven best practice elsewhere. One area of interest is that of a Professional Standards Framework, such as has been drafted in the UK by its Higher Education Academy. This describes the skills, knowledge and attributes that are appropriate for members of academic staff and emphasizes the importance of CPD and reflective practice. But CPD is not restricted just to teaching. There are a number of initiatives being developed in the sector that target research skills, managing research groups, academic integrity, ethics, and writing successful funding applications.

All of these indicate how the era of the amateur scholar is now well behind us and that continuing to reflect on our own skills and experience, alongside a willingness to try new approaches, improve our confidence and be imaginative about how we conduct our work in the contemporary, globalized environment of higher education are hallmarks of the modern academic.

The CELT Conference team: Margaret Forde, Mary Bernard, Dr Sharon Flynn, Bernadette Henchy, Dr Michelle Tooher (conference organiser), Blaneth McSharry, Dr Kelly Coate & Dr Iain MacLaren. The conference, "Thinking Differently: New Curricula, New Skills in Higher Education" was held in NUI Galway in June.

Mary Immaculate College
Coláiste Mhuire gan Smál — OLLSCOIL LUIMNIGH UNIVERSITY OF LIMERICK

making a difference

www.mic.ul.ie

The College promotes excellence in teaching, learning and research through taught programmes and research degrees. It serves the needs of a growing and diverse student population of over 3000 students. Undergraduate programmes at B.Ed. and B.A. level and a range of postgraduate programmes in Arts/Humanities and Education at Diploma, Masters and Doctorate level are offered at the College.

Undergraduate Degree Programmes:

BA in Liberal Arts: (MI004)
This four-year honours degree programme offers a wide range of Arts subjects (English, French Studies, Gaeilge, Geography, German Studies, History, Léann Dúchais, Mathematics, Media and Communication Studies, Music, Philosophy, Psychology, Theology and Religious Studies).

BA in Early Childhood Care and Education: (MI007)
This four-year honours degree programme is designed to provide an exciting and challenging programme for those interested in working with young children in a range of educational settings.

B.ED: (MI005 and MI006)
This four-year honours degree programme is a recognised qualification for primary teaching. The course comprises theoretical education, pedagogy of curricular areas, and teaching practice in primary schools.

B.ED in Education and Psychology: (MI008)
This four-year honours degree programme is a joint degree in Primary Teaching and Psychology (B.Ed.). Graduates of this programme will be eligible to practise as primary school teachers and also have the option of pursuing postgraduate studies in Psychology. The course would be particularly suitable for, though not confined to, students who wish to specialise subsequently in the field of Educational Psychology.

Postgraduate Programmes:

Mary Immaculate College also offers a wide range of postgraduate qualifications up to and including Masters and Doctoral degrees in Arts and Education.

Further Information
Mary Immaculate College, South Circular Road, Limerick.
T: (353) 061 204929 | E: admissions@mic.ul.ie | W: www.mic.ul.ie

Professional Well-Being in the University Sector

Mike Jennings *General Secretary of the Irish Federation of University Teachers (IFUT)*

All is not well in the Irish university sector

As a child I recall being teased by my father. He would ask "do you know the story about the three wells?" and when we said no he'd reply "well, well, well".

I'm not sure there are three but there are certainly two valid interpretations of the phrase "Professional Well-Being in the University Sector". The first refers to how "well" is the profession of academics (i.e. the occupation of those who were traditionally thought to make up the university community). The other interpretation refers to the wellness or otherwise of those who are professionals in universities. Regrettably, neither the professionals (academics) nor the profession (the academy) is in a well state and the prognosis is even less good.

Ironically, the current condition of university professionals is rendered even less well/ more unwell by the contrast between their "actually existing situation" and the public perception/ folk memory of their lot.

It is bad enough that one works an average of 50 hours per week (see box below) but it is even worse when you are constantly portrayed as having one of the handiest, cushiest jobs in the world. The combination of being overworked and undervalued is indeed a lethal one.

There is an enormous amount of literature dealing with the topic of professional/employee well-being. Indeed, if you google the phrase "professional well-being in universities" you will be offered access to an astonishing 193 million references. A constantly recurring theme in discussion on well-being is the issue of stress.

It is a truth universally acknowledged that one of the most potent generators of stress is powerlessness or lack of control over one's own work. No wonder then that stress levels among academics are at an all-time high and are still rising. Ask any scholar to name the top three worst developments in his/ her working life during the course of his/her career and the chances are that phrases such as "managerialism", "corporatism", "micro-management" and "administrative overload" will tumble out over and over again in response.

Despite the fact that academics are employed in the first place precisely because they have demonstrated that they are experts in their field, it is quite remarkable, and remarkably frustrating, to note that they are given less and less freedom and scope to set their own goals and map-out their own priorities and ambitions. There is probably not an academic left on the planet who cannot give personal testimony to the encroachment of administrators and administrative tasks into their daily working life.

There is a veritable culture of compulsive obsessive behaviour in university management today. Where once creativity was king, now metrification and measurement are the new most valued orders of the day. Once it was originality and daring to innovate; now it is the ability to record, to count, to enumerate. More time is spent, and demanded, in form-filling than in thinking.

So, if the professionals are not well, how fares the profession? Again, the report card is of the dispiriting "could do better" variety.

Most people accept that the modern concept of a university can trace its lineage back over six hundred years. In all that time two characteristics were seen as fundamental 'sine qua nons' if an institution was to be worthy of the "u" name - Academic Freedom and Institutional Autonomy. Well, in recent decades things have really changed and not for the better.

A Danish academic friend of mine is fond of stating "yes, by all means change, remodel and dilute all of our essential characteristics but, please, do not call the product a university".

In Ireland university autonomy is a complete fiction. It does not exist. In the relatively short period since the 1997 Universities Act was made law we have seen more (and an increasingly centralised) control being exerted not only over total finance packages and budgets but also now over individual appointments, salary levels, increments, staffing numbers and ratios. Universities, and more precisely the academics within them, used to decide what to research and what to teach. Now such decisions are taken by all-powerful external funders who have no accountability and whose ultimate goal is not the discovery of new knowledge but the pursuit of opportunities for profit.

The idea that we should "let the lamp of knowledge lead where e'er it shines" now seems quaint and anachronistic. Now courses of study must be "market driven" and "linked to the demands of the economy" (note not the well-being of society, rather the more bossy 'demands' of a soulless economy).

Academic Freedom is misrepresented as reckless individualism or selfishness and derided. This methodology is depressingly familiar and has a demonstrable success rate. If you want to kill something off you distort its meaning and thus subvert its reality and virtue.

But what will be our fate when the mockingbird of Academic Freedom is finally killed off? What will replace free thinking inquiry? When all we are left with are analyses of short-term problems, who will equip us to confront the problems which we do not yet even see?

"Well, indeed", as my father might say, "well indeed, who?"

The Academy is not well. The institutions with the title "university" are not well and the community of scholars who were once presumed to constitute those institutions bearing that title are not well. Inevitably therefore, our society is less well than it deserves to be. It seems there are three "wells" after all, all of them unwell.

My father would be tickled by the idea of three important "wells" being all "unwell". The rest of us should be less amused and less complacent.

> "I believe that the community's duty to education is, therefore, its paramount moral duty. By law and punishment, by social agitation and discussion, society can regulate and form itself in a more or less haphazard and chance way. But through education society can formulate its own purposes, can organize its own means and resources, and thus shape itself with definiteness and economy in the direction in which it wishes to move."
>
> John Dewey

Time for change?
Time to teach!

Now Enrolling

NOW ENROLLING

Hibernia College is now enrolling for its primary and post primary teacher education programmes. Both are academically accredited by HETAC and professionally accredited by the Teaching Council. Because the programmes are delivered through a blend of online and onsite tuition, they are ideal for anyone who wishes to structure their study around personal and work commitments.

HIGHER DIPLOMA IN ARTS IN PRIMARY EDUCATION

Established in 2003, graduates from this programme now work as primary school teachers and principals around the country. The programme currently includes three blocks of school experience and teaching practice, three weeks in the Gaeltacht and onsite workshops at weekends.

PROFESSIONAL DIPLOMA IN EDUCATION (PDE)

Based on our highly successful Primary Education programme, this programme was established to encourage a broader range of people to consider post primary school teaching as a career. The programme currently includes three blocks of school experience and professional practice and onsite workshops at weekends.

KEY FACTS
- Professional accreditation: The Teaching Council
- Academic accreditation: HETAC (Level 8)
- Intakes: Spring and autumn
- Duration: 2 years
- Delivered online and onsite at regional centres throughout Ireland

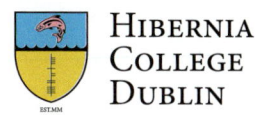

HIBERNIA COLLEGE DUBLIN

hiberniacollege.com

Live. Learn.

Preparing Teachers for Ireland's future

Dr Mary Fleming *Head of School of Education, NUI Galway*
Dr Manuela Heinz *Director of Teaching Practice, School of Education, NUI Galway*

New policies, practices and challenges for initial teacher education at post primary

Changes at teacher education policy level
Since the establishment of the Teaching Council in 2006, teacher education in Ireland has undergone major policy changes. The publication of the Continuum of Teacher Education in 2011 with its emphasis on cohesion and connection in teacher education policy and practice across all phases of the teaching career provides the framework for significant changes, including the reconceptualization of both concurrent and sequential Initial Teacher Education (ITE) programmes

The Criteria and Guidelines for Providers of Initial Teacher Education (Teaching Council, 2011) emphasize the expectation that graduate teachers have the competence to engage professionally as lifelong learners throughout their career. To support this development initial teacher education programmes need to be integrative in design and delivery. Linking theory and practice of learning and teaching through reflective and systematic inquiry will therefore be central to future ITE programmes aiming to develop students' core skills in reflective practice and research/enquiry-based learning. An increased emphasis on literacy, numeracy and inclusion is also evident.

School Placement
Integral to all ITE programmes and central to student teacher development must be the School Placement element of the programmes. What is envisaged is the development of new and innovative school placement models based on a partnership approach between HEIs and schools. Structured in-house support by experienced teachers who take on greater responsibility for student teacher development together with extended periods of school placement in two different placement schools are important features of the new models of school placement.

Programme Duration
To facilitate the envisaged innovative reconceptualization, the duration of most current ITE programmes will be extended with the new minimum duration of 4 years for undergraduate concurrent programmes (starting in September 2013) and 2 years for postgraduate consecutive programmes (starting in September 2014). This will signal the final extinction of the 'H Dip' despite being replaced, in recent years, by the Postgraduate Diploma in Education followed by the Professional Diploma in Education as many of the new postgraduate programmes for post-primary teaching have been redesigned as level 9 programmes with a new title of Professional Master of Education / Máistir Gairmiúil san Oideachas.

New Structure for Initial Teacher Education Provision in Ireland
In April 2012, the Minister for Education and Skills announced a major review of publicly provided teacher education in Ireland aimed at identifying a new structure for ITE so as to strengthen and deepen the quality of provision. The international panel of reviewers recommended that teacher education provision

in Ireland should be consolidated according to the following configuration:

6.1 Dublin City University - St. Patrick's College Drumcondra - Mater Dei Institute of Education
6.2 Trinity College Dublin - Marino Institute of Education - University College Dublin – National College of Art and Design
6.3 National University of Ireland Maynooth - Froebel College
6.4 University of Limerick - Mary Immaculate College - Limerick Institute of Technology
6.5 University College Cork - Cork Institute of Technology
6.6 National University of Ireland Galway - St. Angela's College Sligo

Considering that the current provision of ITE in Ireland encompasses 19 state-funded providers (plus three non-funded providers – Hibernia College and two Montessori colleges) offering 40 ITE programmes for primary and post-primary level, the restructuring of publicly funded ITE provision into 6 larger, university-based centers marks a significant change in the ITE landscape.

Teachers as lifelong learners and the centrality of school-university partnership

The new policy on the continuum of teacher education sends a strong message to beginning and experienced teachers as well as teacher educators and school leaders. It recognizes that ITE cannot provide teachers with all the knowledge and skills needed for a demanding career spanning up to a number of decades and situated in increasingly complex social and educational settings. Many of our mature student teachers comment on the drastic changes they are faced with in schools year after year. They are surprised, even taken aback, by the changed dynamics in the classrooms, diversity of students' cultural backgrounds, new educational technologies, changed social relationships in families, school communities and online settings. Teacher educators and policy makers are aware that in these times of fast social and policy change, ITE ought to focus on providing teachers with a set of high-level beginning competencies and ample opportunities to enquire into, question, and improve their own practice.

At NUI Galway we are looking forward to the opportunities related to engaging our student teachers in collaborative action research projects during the 2nd year of their postgraduate studies. We envisage that graduates of our newly reconceptualized Professional Master of Education / Máistir Gairmiúil san Oideachas programmes will have developed a critical awareness and understanding of the unique dynamics of learning and teaching in school environments as well as proficiency with research-based teaching and enquiry-based practice. Systematic and collaborative enquiry into teaching practice and learning in schools is, of course, of great interest to and also dependent on the support of school leaders and practicing teachers. A research-based approach to teacher education throughout the continuum will require close collaboration of all involved.

Over the next year it will be one of our central aims to work together with principals and experienced teachers in our partner schools to build a platform for practitioner research where teachers and education lecturers at all stages of their career can interact and collaborate through co-enquiry into their professional practice with the shared goal of enhancing learning and teaching in schools and in teacher education. We strongly believe that the creation of a platform for practitioner research will make an important contribution to the professionalization of teachers and teacher educators, who can, together, affect education practice and policy at local and national level through collaborative inquiry, knowledge creation and advocacy. The springboard for this initiative will be our partner school network which we launched in September 2011. Over the past 2 years we have been fortunate to work closely with 26 schools and many committed and highly experienced teachers to build more integrated ITE programmes and enhanced in-school support for our student teachers.

Throughout the past two years we held a series of seminar days and meetings with practice educators (experienced teachers who support student teachers' development in our partner schools) in the Galway Education Centre, NUI Galway, and post-primary schools. During these collaborative seminars we shared our experiences, expectations and problems and discussed issues related to teacher development, mentoring, ITE and teaching and learning more generally. The support and enthusiasm of the teachers involved has been truly inspiring and one of the central findings of our first review of this initiative has been the immense benefit gained by all involved from closer collaboration between school-based practice educators and university school placement tutors.

Based on our experience we wholeheartedly agree with the Teaching Council's aspiration that HEIs and schools develop new and innovative school placement models based on a partnership approach. In our view collaborative partnership is the way forward.

Conclusion
Recent ITE policy changes led by the Teaching Council and recommendations forwarded by the ITE review panel mark the beginning of a major cultural shift in teacher education in Ireland whereby the preparation of teachers for the future is now seen to require much more interaction and close collaboration between a wide range of stakeholders and experts. Teacher educators will play a vital role bringing this vision to fruition. Our challenge for the year ahead is to further develop and grow our collaborative partnership network both in the school settings and in the university and to reflect deeply and holistically on our experiences and those of our partners. We join Feldman in supporting Vera John Steiner's belief that 'together we create our future' (Higgins et al., 2012, Feldman, 2006, xiii).

References
Feldman, D.H., (2000). Foreword. In Steiner. J. V., Creative collaboration USA: Oxford University Press.
Higgins, A., Heinz, M., McCauley, V. and Fleming, M. (2012). Creating the future of teacher education together: The role of emotionality in university-school partnership. Procedia-Social and Behavioral Journal. Available at www.sciencedirect.com. ISSN: 1877-0428.

EDUCATION IN THE MEDIA

Thousands of teachers hit in pocket as increment freeze begins

June 29, 2013

Thousands of second-level teachers and university lecturers face losing their increments from next week because they haven't accepted the Haddington Road deal.

The harsh reality is brought home in circulars issued by the Department of Education in recent days. Incremental progression will be suspended for three years with effect from July 1 for those who have not signed up to Haddington Road, the department has advised.

This is provided for in the legislation that the Government pushed through to ensure they could impose pay cuts in the absence of agreement on a deal.
About 20,000 second-level teachers as well as university lectures are eligible for an annual increase, payable on the anniversary of their appointment.

Because of the academic year, it is likely that most increments would have been due in September and October.

Unions that have accepted Haddington Road are subject to less severe arrangements in relation to increments and the squeeze varies according to salary level.
Staff on salaries under €35,000 are facing one three-month increment freeze, those on between €35,000 and €65,000 will suffer two three-month increment freezes and those on €65,000 or more will have two six-month freezes.

Unlike second-level teachers and university lecturers, primary teachers, members of the Irish National Teachers Organisation (INTO), have voted on, and accepted Haddington Road.

Second-level teachers were left exposed to the rigours of the legislation when they decided not to ballot on the deal.

The Association of Secondary Teachers Ireland (ASTI) and the Teachers Union of Ireland (TUI) initially said they did not accept the Haddington Road proposals as a final offer. However, last week the leaderships of the two unions decided to go ahead with ballots, but because of the school holidays, they cannot take place until September.

Members of both unions had previously endorsed industrial action in the event of imposed cuts, but that threat has been lifted with the belated decision to ballot.

ww.independent.ie/lifestyle/education/thousands-of-teachers-hit-in-pocket-as-increment-freeze-begins-29381968.html

School of Education

NUI Galway
OÉ Gaillimh

NUI Galway has been involved in **Initial Teacher Education (ITE)** provision - in the area of Post-Primary Teacher Education - since 1915. The School of Education, NUI Galway offers a range of initial teacher education programmes for pre-service, post-primary teachers, and continuing professional development and educational research programmes for teachers and educators across sectors: primary, secondary and tertiary.

At graduate level, in consecutive, initial teacher education for the post-primary sector, the School provides the:

- **Professional Diploma in Education (PDE)**
- **Dioplóma Gairmiúil san Oideachas (DGO)**, for education through the medium of Irish.

In collaboration with the School of Mathematics, Statistics and Applied Mathematics (NUIG), the School of Education offers a concurrent, undergraduate teacher education degree:

- **B.A. Mathematics and Education**, which qualifies graduates to teach Mathematics and Applied Mathematics to honours Leaving Certificate level in post-primary schools.

For the continuing professional development of experienced, practising educators, the School of Education offers:

- **Postgraduate Diploma in Special Educational Needs** (supported by the Department of Education and Skills),
- **Master of Education**, which combines coursework with thesis research.

The School of Education facilitates several modes of research study at **Master (MLitt)** and **PhD** levels; there are full-time and part-time options available for both. The School's areas of research interest and expertise include

1. Initial and professional teacher education
2. Educational leadership
3. Socio-cultural issues in education
4. Civic engagement and community engaged research
5. Science, Technology and Mathematics Education (STEM)

ICT and the **creative and innovative use of educational technology** underpin the School of Education's research and teaching programmes, and the School has developed partnerships with a number of leading ICT providers. An example of technology innovation within the School of Education is the **Science Education Resource (SER)** where, supported by School of Education staff, DGO and PDE students have developed a series of iBooks, in both **English** and **as Gaeilge**. Available to download from **Apple's iBook Store** under the search term, 'Science Hooks', these interactive, bilingual resources cover key concepts and topics in Junior Cycle **Physics**, **Chemistry** and **Biology**.

For Further Information on the School of Education, NUIG Contact:
Dr Mary Fleming
Head of the School of Education
School of Education, NUI Galway   Phone: 353-91-494071   Email: mary.fleming@nuigalway.ie

SUSI's difficult first year – can she recover?

Cat O'Driscoll *Vice President for Academic Affairs & Quality Assurance, Union of Students in Ireland (USI)*

'SUSI has a long way to go to build up the trust of students and their families'

The call for a centralised Grant Awarding Authority had come from a number of sectors, including the students. Significant diversity in the assessment and processing of applications across Ireland was creating inequality and the great potential savings in time and costs made it a no-brainer. The Student Support Bill was enacted, the tender was awarded and Student Universal Support Ireland (SUSI) was set up under the management of City of Dublin VEC.

Everything looked good: excellent branding, online application forms, a support desk available by phone and email and a helpful video. Grant applications had moved into the 21st century. What could possibly go wrong? Every July, USI holds Students' Union Training for the new SU officers in Ireland. As many students will approach their SU with grant queries and issues, the newborn SUSI delivered a presentation in July 2012 to explain the entire application process. A communication structure was agreed between SUSI and USI in the form of a small forum to address any issues that might crop up. Here at USI we felt prepared – but we were far from it.

The first issues arose in August 2012 when over 60,000 students were filling in the online application before the August 31st closing date. Applications forms were crashing on certain browsers; confusion arose around dependency on parents; the support desk became very busy and did not have the answers for all the questions being asked. The primary concern was the lack of clarity over how long it would take for grants to be paid out. There was no tracking system, no guide to the number of processing stages to come, and too often no answer to emails.

The closing date passed and documentation packs were sent out to students. Depending on the information given on the application form, each student received a list of documentation to be provided. Though the system seemed clear and simple, this is where the serious problems began. Documents packs didn't arrive or arrived without the pre-addressed envelope. Confusion arose around the forms and statements needed, with many students sending in partially completed packs. This was further exacerbated by incorrect advice from the helpdesk - when students finally managed to get through.

From mid-September Students' Unions were inundated with complaints and concerns over 'lost' document packs and calls for the Data Protection Commission to be involved. A number of factors were causing these concerns. When a student returned the document pack containing photocopies of important personal files including birth certs, P21 statements, social welfare forms and in some cases very private information on legal separations and divorce, these were scanned onto the SUSI system. In the scanning process a large number of forms were mistakenly scanned onto a different application, leading to students receiving multiple reminders to submit packs already sent in. Automatic reminders did not take into account the significant time delay which had built up, so as students phoned the help desk to explain that they had already sent in their pack but had received a reminder, the operator pulled up their application to find that there were no scanned documents attached. Panic ensued.

As we came into October the help desk phones were receiving thousands of calls and unable to answer thousands more. Students were being denied access to libraries and college email accounts due to outstanding fees, landlords were looking for rent payments and there was no clear indication as to when grant payments would be issued. The Higher Education Authority stepped in to ensure colleges allowed students full access to facilities as they awaited grant approval. As approval and refusal letters began to issue, more problems arose. Students in receipt of the Back to Education Allowance since 2009, and entitled to maintenance payments, were being refused, students studying in Northern Ireland were being refused and postgraduate students were being given very unclear information about their entitlements.

The SUSI forum met to discuss the issues and propose solutions. USI rolled out an information campaign with SUSI in a hope to reduce the pressure on the support desk and encourage students to supply documentation.

In November, the call from USI and Public Representatives for SUSI to receive more staff and resources was answered by the Department of Education, with An Taoiseach Enda Kenny promising students all grants would be finalised before December 31st and Minister Quinn formally apologising in the Dáil.

As Christmas drew near, the delays continued with dangerous consequences. Students were going without food and heat, the Student Assistance Fund and St Vincent De Paul emergency funds had been disbursed. Some students were dropping out whilst others were taking drastic action to stay in college, approaching money lenders, defaulting on loans and borrowing from their already cash-strapped families. Only half of the 66k applications had been processed, the helpdesk was still under severe pressure and Students' Unions began to set up food boxes and emergency funds with their tight budgets.

After Christmas the delays continued at alarming levels. A review was called for as SUSI began to prepare for year two, linking up with CAO ahead of its February 1st deadline. The SUSI forum met to establish mechanisms for dealing with emergency cases as students were served eviction notices from landlords and were denied exam results from colleges. The review was commissioned by the City of Dublin VEC to be conducted by Accenture.

As Easter drew near, the majority of payments had been issued, with for the most part only difficult and complex applications outstanding. The review conducted by Accenture consulted the many stakeholders and examined the inner structures of SUSI. Plans for year two aimed to reduce the major problem areas from year one with agreements between bodies including Revenue, Social Protection and CAO to share information, massively reducing the need for documentation. The Review picked up on everything with no big surprises. SUSI implemented many of the recommendations rapidly and launched a centralised website susi.ie in June.

Though the issues from year one appear to have been corrected, SUSI has a long way to go to build up the trust of students and their families. No one can afford a repeat of this year's crisis.

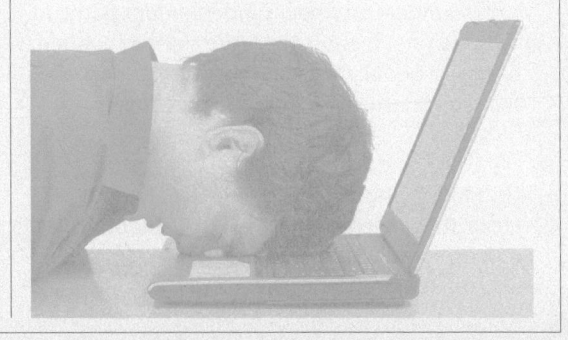

How can we best help students to help themselves?

Dr Claire Laudet *Senior Tutor TCD*
Dr Amanda Piesse *Dean of Students TCD*

The pressures on students include academic, financial, domestic & social

Talking to colleagues who work on a daily basis with helping students to resolve difficulties, it quickly becomes apparent that the pressures that students face come from a series of sources – academic, financial, domestic and social.

One of our students' union officers observes that the multitasking that comes along with third level education and living independently seems to be ever- increasing.

There's a tighter points races for courses; assessments come in a wide variety of forms; appropriately-priced accommodation is becoming scarcer; fewer part-time jobs are available. Help is at hand in the form of student services and students' unions, but some students find it very difficult to communicate the enormity of these pressures to anyone.

"It's as if their inability to manage all of these things at once is somehow a failure on their part as they embark on a newly independent path. At the same time though, there are signs of cultural change, especially when talking about and taking responsibility for our own mental health', she says.

Whether it's the counselling service, the health centre, the officers of the students' unions, student-to-student mentoring or peer-assisted learning, the broader the range of supports available the more likely we are to help students to help themselves through the various stages of the third-level experience.

At a time when almost everyone is feeling the cumulative effects of on-going recession, financial pressures are particularly acute. Students from a wider variety of socioeconomic backgrounds and demographics are winning their proper place at third or fourth level and are immediately facing into the student contribution charge, or fees for their Masters or PhD place, before they even begin to think about living expenses, or additional childcare costs, or perhaps putting some care in place for an older person for whom they have responsibility.

Most students underestimate the cost of studying, subsistence and socialising. New students in particular need to be advised early that a grant will only really cover the student contribution and a small part of maintenance, and certainly not the full provision for the academic year.

Students supplementing their incomes with part-time work need to know that up to ten or twelve hours per week of paid work shows benefit both financially and in transferrable skills, twelve to fifteen hours is benefit-neutral to the skillset and over fifteen hours is generally detrimental. Some, though, have little option but to work part time.

We can help by advising about this early on, maybe even as early as Open Day, during orientation and Freshers' week and through budgeting workshops in the early weeks of each semester.

This year, many of the third-level institutions provided for students to pay the student contribution in two tranches. But the difficulties with SUSI left many in financial difficulties that they simply hadn't anticipated. In TCD, requests for financial assistance continued throughout the year, where normally they slow down after January. An increasing number of students from middle-class families are looking for financial assistance, often following loss of income through unemployment.

While the third-level grant scheme and the Student Assistance Fund (co-funded by the EU and the Irish Government, but due to end in 2013, and it's unclear what the new scheme will look like) do help, and third-level institutions often have their own student hardship funds, every student needs some kind of independently-generated income.

Money matters aside, adjusting to different approaches to learning and academic subjects can come as something of a culture shock. Contact hours can be low compared with second level because independent learning element supplementsand complements those hours, and no-one but you is going to monitor your commitment on a daily basis.

These facts may not be immediately apparent. The European Credit Transfer System can work to our benefit here, making it clear in course introduction meetings, handbooks and when setting assignments that 10 credits = 220 to 250 student effort hours and that a 35-40 hour working week is the academics' expectation of students.

It helps too to offer online study aids and workshops as something that all students should engage with, perhaps assigning credits to skills-for-study programmes to facilitate and encourage self-prompted learning.

For students starting third level, the prospect of joining a new community can prompt mixed emotions. Not every moment of every day is going to be easy: orientation programmes and peer support programmes can reassure students that the uncertainties they're experiencing are common enough, and not unique to them.

Being part of a university community doesn't mean that you leave real life behind at the gates. Another colleague observes that as she thought about the students who had been to see her recently about supplemental examinations, she realised that the one thing they had in common was that they had all missed chunks of the year either because of their own or a close relation or dependent's ill health. Broadly speaking, their progress had halted at the stage when they had 'withdrawn' and none of them seemed to have the skills to make up lost ground on their own, let alone re-insert themselves appropriately into the educational process or the university community as social and academic group.

"They did not seem able or willing to use the supports provided (peer learning, friendly and approachable staff member) — or perhaps the supports provided were insensitive to their needs and failed to engage. One student mentioned not going back to a peer group (which she had found very helpful in the first term); when I asked why she didn't pick up where she'd left off, she shrugged. 'I suppose there is the sense of having got off a moving train and not knowing how or when or where or even whether to get back on,' she says.

Perhaps we need to re-examine the ethos of our learning environment; is it fundamentally competitive and exclusive, drawing attention to what learners do not know and cannot do, rather than one which is cooperative, inclusive and encouraging?"

Addressing the mental health needs of third level students

John Broderick *Chair of the Irish Association of University and College Counsellors (IAUCC).*

If young people have one adult they can talk to they will have lower risk factors

What can half a million hours of counselling with nearly 100,000 students over two decades tell us about the mental health of some of Ireland's brightest young people?

For the majority, college life can be an enriching and rewarding experience. But for others, college life can pose several challenges and threats to mental health and well-being as they cope with managing their time, their studies, their health and their finances. Transitioning from dependence to independence and greater personal responsibility can also prove to be demanding with new academic requirements, new freedoms, new relationships and new ways of relating to family and friends.

The third level student population in Ireland is expanding and is becoming increasingly diversified. Over 196,000 full time and part time students enrolled in HEA funded institutions in 2011-12. The number of mature students, international students, students with a disability, and students from lower socio-economic backgrounds has also grown. Yet the provision of counselling services to meet the growing numbers and diverse needs of students has not kept pace.

Several services have seen a reduction in staff in the past four years, as vacated positions remain unfilled. Student enrolments have increased by 16% since 2006-07 while the numbers attending counselling have increased by 33%. The result is that services are seriously overstretched and long waiting lists are now common.

According to data collated by the IAUCC (the representative body for student counsellors), approximately 5% of enrolled students attend counselling each year and avail of an average of 5 sessions. While short term therapy is the norm, several students require more sessions and may require support for the duration of their stay in college.

The majority of students who attend counselling are undergraduates; postgraduates make up approximately 15-20%. Yearly figures also demonstrate that about 63-64% are female. Most students are self referred although other college support services (especially health), academic tutors, and even parents and family are often involved in a student's decision to seek counselling. In the past 6 years, the numbers of students presenting with mental health concerns have steadily increased. Anxiety disorders have increased from 19% to 32%; depression from 9% to 24%; relationship problems from 11% to 24% and academic-related issues from 19% to 29%.

Several services use standardised instruments or symptom checklists of current emotional and psychological functioning as part of initial intake and assessment. Combined results for several reporting institutions reveal that over 80% of intakes score at clinically significant levels. In one institution, a study of approximately 500 students (not attending counselling) revealed a mean baseline index of psychological distress greater than one standard deviation above the test's published norms. By comparison, the mean distress levels reported by students in the week prior to their first meeting with a counsellor were even greater, at two standard deviations above the norm (i.e. at the 96th percentile).

To highlight this growing crisis in student mental health, the IAUCC convened a conference in the Dublin Institute of Technology on December 2012 and brought together over 160 staff and students from third level colleges nationwide, representing counselling, health, psychiatry, disability, chaplaincy, accommodation, peer support, students union, health promotion and academic services.

Delegates were presented with the findings of Headstrong's My World Survey (2012), the first large-scale national study of youth mental health in Ireland. Two senior UCD researchers presented data on 8,053 college students between the ages of 17 and 25, drawn from all Irish Universities, from four Institutes of Technology and from two VEC colleges.

The conference focused on risk and protective factors, help-seeking behaviours and coping strategies employed by students. With regard to mental health, the survey found that 61% of students were engaged in problem drinking (10% of them being alcohol dependent); 43% had felt at some point that life is not worth living; 40% suffered from depression; 38% suffered from anxiety; 21% had engaged in deliberate self-harm; and 7% had attempted suicide. These findings are quite shocking when one considers a typical lecture hall of 100 students - and the detailed exploration of students' experience in a typical Irish university had a profound effect on several academic leaders present.

The research also highlighted that if young people have one **good adult** they can talk to they will have lower risk factors for mental health problems and higher levels of optimism, life-satisfaction and self-esteem. 62% reported that they would talk to someone if they had a problem, with males being less likely to do so than females. The study also found that suicide ideation, self-harm and suicide attempts are higher in young people who do not seek help or talk about their problems. In addition, students who identified their sexual orientation as 'bisexual' or 'unsure' reported higher levels of distress than heterosexual students and much lower levels of protective factors such as social support and self-esteem.

In the UK, a similar crisis in student mental health has been highlighted by the Royal College of Psychiatrist's report into the 'Mental Health of Students in Higher Education' (2011). The report argued that the student population is in some ways more vulnerable than others and that student progress can be easily disrupted by mental disorder and misuse of drugs and alcohol. Of course, underachievement or failure at this stage can have long-term effects on self-esteem and the progress of someone's life.

Outcome measures used by counselling services in IAUCC consistently demonstrate that counselling is effective in significantly reducing levels of depression, anxiety, interpersonal sensitivity and somatic distress in those who attended for 4 to 5 sessions.

Last year the AUCC (the UK's equivalent to Ireland's IAUCC) presented the results of a year-long sector-wide study on the impact of counselling on academic outcomes based on data from over 5,000 students in 65 universities and FE colleges. It found that over 75% of students considered counselling to have helped them stay at university or college, improved their academic achievement, their overall experience in college and helped them develop employability skills. Similar impact studies are currently being conducted by the IAUCC.

WHO'S WHO

The WHO'S WHO Profile introduces people who are making an important contribution to education in Ireland today.

Meet Mary O'Sullivan

POSITION: Dean, Faculty of Education and Health Sciences, University of Limerick; Co-Director of Physical Education, Physical Activity and Youth Sport (PE PAYS) Research Centre

Where did you grow up?
I grew up in Limerick City and attended Presentation National School and St Mary's Secondary School in the city.

What is your earliest childhood memory?
Running on the grass in the People's Park in Limerick City with my younger brother. My Dad would set us to race each other and I loved it as I won! Then my brother got stronger and he began to win and we moved on!

How many siblings have you?
I have three siblings, a sister Carmel and two brothers Terry and Tony.

Where did you go to school/college?
I attended the National College of Physical Education (NCPE) in 1972 to prepare to be a post primary school teacher of History, Physical Education and Geography. Then NCPE became Thomond College of Education in 1975. In 1991 Thomond College became part of the University of Limerick and in 2012-2013 the University of Limerick celebrated 40 years of innovation. I decided after teaching in Co. Cork to enroll for a Masters in Education at the University of Victoria in British Columbia, Canada, and completed my PhD at The Ohio State University in Columbus, Ohio, USA directly after that.

To what extent did your education shape who you are today?
I was always curious and interested in knowing things. My post primary education allowed no access to science subjects of any kind (it was a relatively small all-girls school with limited subject choice) so following Leaving Cert there were few options open to me. I did not feel confident enough or have the financial resources to contemplate attending university which would have required at that time moving away from home. I knew that primary school teaching was not for me and so the creation of the NIHE and the NCPE in Limerick was perfect timing in 1972-1973. I had no science, was not good at languages, loved sport and liked the idea that I could teach so being a Physical Education and Social Studies teacher was for me my best further education option. I did not see myself in the civil service or in the bank!

What attracted you to work in academia?
I did not know what a PhD was when I completed my undergraduate degree. Indeed my view on graduation was that I was now a fully qualified teacher and my higher education was done. However, following years as a teacher, I knew I had lots more to learn and I decided to

take up an offer of a masters degree scholarship I applied for in Canada. While completing the research for that thesis, I met a researcher whose work was aligned with my teacher effectiveness research study and he invited me to take up a Teaching Assistantship and complete my doctoral degree in the USA. So my curiosity about learning and my interest in how teachers learned and taught drew me further into academia and to researching teaching and teacher education issues. I loved the life of teaching prospective teachers who kept me grounded in the realities of school life while also working with doctoral students who kept me intellectually honest.

In what way do you consider yourself well suited to your current position?

I never had the ambition to be a Head of Department or a Dean. But circumstances conspired at different times where I found myself in academic leadership positions and I have over time developed those skills and learned from exemplary leaders I have had the pleasure of working with, and for, along the way. I am passionate about finding ways to support young academics make links with others to further their own ambitions and excellence in teaching and research. While I miss teaching, as a full time administrator I don't miss grading. I do however keep myself intellectually grounded by working with bright and enthusiastic doctoral students. I have had the pleasure of supervising almost 20 PHDs and I love working with them.

What are your research interests?

My research is focused on teaching and learning with specific interest around teacher education and teacher professional development research. I am also interested in how we engage the student voice in curriculum development both in post primary curriculum development and teacher education programmes.

How important is it for academics to publish copiously?

A key value I hold is that you constantly seek to learn about your discipline. You are as a university academic a custodian of your discipline and so academics should be helping to move the discipline forward. Sharing (i.e. publishing) that research is central to my definition of an academic so that you impact on the field, on policy and/or best practice, depending on the nature of the research you conduct. I am not an advocate for publishing for the sake of the number of publications generated. Rather my focus is on publishing in the high prestige journals in my field when I and/or my students have something meaningful to add to the debate, or writing important policy documents that have national importance.

What publications of your own are you most proud of?

Over ten years ago, I was supported by the University of Limerick Foundation to complete a research project while on sabbatical from Ohio State. The purpose of the study was to follow the cohort of teachers who graduated with me twenty years earlier and look at the factors that enhanced and inhibited their effectiveness as teachers of physical education over that 20-year period. During a four month period I interviewed almost half the cohort and found it the most humbling piece of data collection I had ever done while learning about their lives, their achievements, and their regrets as teachers. I got a sense of how the education system treated teachers and how little professional development support they could avail of at that time, yet how resilient they were as teachers. A publication from that work was awarded the best academic research paper some years ago by the Physical Education and Sport Pedagogy Journal. I am proud I could "represent the voices of these teachers" with the narrative of the publication and that it was recognised by my peers.

What are the main responsibilities/ challenges of your job?

The key challenge for me as Dean is to ensure I manage a very challenging budget and align that budget to support the four key priorities of the university's strategic plan (quality of student experience, excellence in research, internationalization of the curriculum and student body, and contribute to the nation and Shannon region). I seek to educate and engage the staff so that we can be smart in how we provide the best quality experiences for our students while enjoying a stimulating and intellectually rich environment for the staff as they develop their research.

What does a typical workday involve for you?
My days are never the same and never boring! They consist of lots and lots of meetings with a diversity of people and groups. I try (but often fail) to allocate a day a week to working on my own research and the writings of my doctoral students. I am usually in to work a little after 8 and leave mostly by six. There are some evenings when I have work engagements and I try to keep the weekend for family and friends.

What do you enjoy most about your work?
Helping to network academics for the purposes of developing their research. Working with my doctoral students and seeing them develop as independent researchers. I like to be in a position where I can influence the alignment of resources with what I and my management team believe are our key priorities in the Faculty of Education and Health Sciences.

What do you enjoy least about your work?
Dealing with difficult people can be draining. Taking the work home (i.e. problems of the day) and dwelling on things is something I don't handle as well as I should.

What would you most like to change?
I would like to not feel pulled in so many directions that I can't do any one thing to the level I would like to.

Are you a workaholic?
If I am honest, probably. But I have slowed down and try to keep weekends more to myself than I did earlier in my career. I don't have children so that has allowed me to spend this time that I would not have been able to do if I had that responsibility.

What do you do to relax?
Love walking on the hills of Clare, Kerry, Cork and Tipperary. There are great loop walks in the Shannon Region and I am working my way through them.

Do you like living in Limerick?
I live in the lovely village of Ballina at the end of Lough Derg where Killaloe, Co Clare, is on one side of the bridge and Ballina, Tipperary, is on the other.

What plans have you for the future?
Return to my professorship and regenerate my research agenda.

Have you a message for academics?
It is a dangerous business telling academics anything. I believe in the concept of every academic being a teacher and researcher but also an academic citizen of their university. I would like more high quality academics to act as academic citizens in support of their institution and in moving that institution to the next level. That is what has driven me to take on the role of Dean and I hope other colleagues will see the value in administrative roles even if only for a period of their academic career. Universities will be better for their quality service.

Have you a message for policy makers?
I would love policy makers to see the value of investing in teachers in terms of supporting local and regional professional development communities of practices where teachers share their expertise and learn from each other. It requires only a modicum of resource for them to meet, try out new ideas in their classrooms, and bring in facilitators to push their thinking and hold them accountable for the goals they set for their own teaching/learning contexts.

Chapter 5
Fourth Level

Contents

	Page
1. **The Irish Research Council - enabling a vibrant research community in Ireland** *Dr Eucharia Meehan*	204
2. **Excellent research that delivers societal and economic impact** *Professor Mark Ferguson*	208
3. **Who's Who** *Professor Barry Smyth*	215

Introducing the Fourth Level Chapter

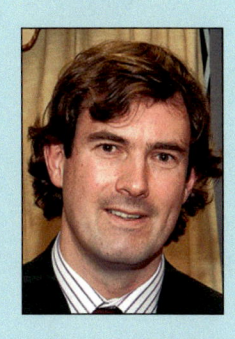

by Tony Hall, *Editor*

On 29th March 2012, Minister for Research and Innovation, Seán Sherlock TD officially launched the new Irish Research Council (IRC), through the merger of the former two councils for research in the humanities and SET (science, engineering and technology), known respectively as IRCHSS and IRCSET.

The opening chapter of the *Education Matters Yearbook* on fourth level is contributed by Dr. Eucharia Meehan, Director of the IRC. In her article, Dr. Meehan outlines the key priorities for the Council, which is responsible for funding research and innovation across all disciplines, and also for fostering and supporting cross-disciplinary and interdisciplinary research. Dr. Meehan also discusses the key strategic relationships between the Irish Research Council and European and international research contexts and funders, in cluding the Euroopean Research Council, Marie Curie and FP7/Horizon 2020. A key area in Irish fourth level education is support for newly graduated PhD researchers, at the crucial, early-career post-doctoral (post-doc) stage. As Dr. Meehan outlines in her article the IRC launched the Cofund initiative ELEVATE, which will enable post-docs to spend time abroad developing further their research, working in collaboration with higher education institutions and researchers internationally. Dr. Meehan concludes her article by outlining the recent exciting and prestigious developments for the IRC and research in Ireland.

Professor Mark Ferguson, CEO of Science Foundation Ireland, discusses how investment in research through the SFI and other agencies is having a significant impact on research capacity throughout the State, outlining key data that include the indicator that Ireland is now ranked in the top 20 countries in scientific global rankings; up considerably from 36th place in 2003. In addition to Ireland's achievements and the strategic challenges ahead, Prof Ferguson furthermore outlines the strategy for taking forward Ireland's scientific research agenda. The SFI Strategy – Agenda 2020 will, it is envisioned, enable researchers and scientists, not only to understand the world but also, potentially, to change it, for the betterment of society and all citizenry.

Salient news and media items pertaining to fourth level are interleaved throughout the chapter on the sector, with the 'Who's Who' for fourth level this year profiling Professor Barry Smyth, Digital Chair of Computer Science at UCD and Direct (interim) of INSIGHT Centre for Data Analytics and Director of CLARITY Centre for Sensor Web Technologies.

Fourth Level

The Irish Research Council - enabling a vibrant research community in Ireland

Dr Eucharia Meehan,
Director, Irish Research Council

In March 2012, a very significant change took place in the Irish higher education and research landscape with the establishment of the Irish Research Council, otherwise known as 'the Council'.

An amalgamation of two former councils, the Irish Research Council for Humanities and Social Sciences (IRCHSS) and the Irish Research Council for Science, Engineering and Technology (IRCSET), the Council was established by the Minister for Research and Innovation, Seán Sherlock TD, to play a distinct funding and policy advisory role in the Irish research landscape.

Supporting excellent research from Arts to Zoology

In continuing the excellent funding work of the former Councils we, the new Council, have been given the role of funding research and the discovery of new ideas and knowledge across all disciplines from Arts to Zoology and furthermore to act as a catalyst to encourage inter-disciplinary research.

Through our programmes we provide opportunities for researchers at different stages of their careers but in particular those at an early stage. We are very much of the view that it is important to enable individuals to become independent researchers and based on the application rate to the Council, many students and post-docs agree with us!

Typically the Council is only in a position to fund 15% of applications after a rigorous international peer review process. Excellence is the criteria for success in applying to the Council and this is a fundamental principle for us as set out in our strategy statement which can be found on our website www.research.ie.

Enhancing long term career prospects and knowledge creation of researchers

The Council of course wants to provide optimum opportunities to those it funds to have successful research careers and to that end we facilitate up to four years of funding for PhD students where it can be shown that the student is getting a quality experience and developing additional knowledge and competencies beyond what is of course the heart of the PhD, the core thesis. Reflecting our ethos, the articulation of the experience that individuals will have in an education context is a strong feature of our application requirements and this is also a unique emphasis nationally.

To provide direct opportunities for those who wish to consider careers outside academia, the Council has been very successful in establishing a number of programmes where there is a partnership with employers – specifically the Enterprise Partnership Scheme which has existed for a number of years and the Employment

Based Programme which was a pilot for us in 2012.

Up to 200 companies have worked with the Council but, since 2012, many other employers are now eligible as partners from within the public, voluntary and NGO sectors. These latter funding programmes underpin a number of key objectives for the Research Prioritization Report. We look forward to continuing to provide innovative and creative opportunities for our researchers through this scheme and in other ways.

A recent example is the innovation within the project scheme(s) where there is an opportunity to develop interdisciplinary proposals across the spectrum, an approach which will help prime the system for developments in the European context under Horizon 2020.

Opportunities for researchers in European programmes and internationally
Of course, enhancing opportunities for our researchers, engagement with European programmes and feeding into the development of programmes in the European context is extremely important. In 2012, we launched a Cofund initiative called ELEVATE which will provide opportunities for postdocs to spend time abroad in any entity performing research whether a company, a higher education institution or another research performer.

Through our functions as the representative body for Ireland across a number of different aspects of FP7 and Horizon 2020 we work tirelessly to ensure that what emerges whether from the European Research Council (ERC), the Marie Curie programme, the Grand Challenges or other aspects of Horizon 2020 serves the needs of the Irish research community. We are the joint national delegates to the ERC, the Marie-Curie programme and represent Ireland on Science for Society and in all humanities and social sciences fora.

A voice for research - a policy advisory role
As mentioned earlier, very significantly the Irish Research Council has been given a completely new role by the Minister as a policy advisory body to him, his Department, the HEA and to national and international entities. At this juncture in the evolution of the Irish research system, this part of our role is particularly important. The Council has 10 members who are active researchers and they are drawn from across the disciplines. Within this Council we have one member from the international community and one from the private sector. Professor Orla Feely is the Chair.

The policy advisory role covers all of research and graduate education and we have been asked by the Minister to pay particular attention to the policy advice for the arts, humanities and social sciences. So that we can give good advice, we are engaging at every opportunity with the research community and then in turn engaging regularly with the Minister and other national stakeholders.

The Future
In our first year we are delighted with the fruits emerging from earlier investments, for example the website for the Down Survey of Ireland (http://downsurvey.tcd.ie). We have also developed a number of strategic partnerships in Ireland where we work with other public bodies and agencies through the project scheme or the employment based scheme.

In the international context we have become the national agent/academic partner for the Lindau Nobel Prizewinners Meeting (http://www.lindau-nobel.org) and we are very proud of the fact that the President of Ireland, Michael D. Higgins, is the Patron of this engagement. We were delighted that 4 of our 5 nominees, selected from our national competitive process, were successful in the incredibly competitive international leg. The representatives of the Irish research system attend the Nobel Prizewinners Meeting with 550 other international researchers and mingle with up to 40 Nobel prizewinners. We look forward to announcing other exciting initiatives and opportunities in the near future but most especially we look forward to engaging with the community so that we can support its endeavours to contribute in a range of ways to our society, the economy and the global knowledge pool.

Check us out on our website www.research.ie.

EDUCATION IN THE MEDIA

2012 RDS/Intel Prize Lecture for Nanoscience

September 17, 2012

Professor Valeria Nicolosi has been awarded the 2012 RDS / Intel Prize Lecture for Nanoscience in recognition of her contribution to the field.

Prof Nicolosi is ERC Research Professor at the School of Physics and Principal Investigator at CRANN, Trinity College Dublin. The Award recognises her world leading research as well as her strong commitment to communicating her research to a diverse audience.

The RDS/ Intel Prize Lecture for Nanoscience was established in recognition of the significant achievements being made by Irish scientists and scientists based in Ireland to the field of nanoscience. Supported by The Irish Times, the award in 2012 is for an early-career stage scientist based in Ireland who has been awarded a PhD degree within the last eight years.

Professor Nicolosi researches novel materials such as graphene and other one-atom materials whose properties make them super strong, lightweight and electrically conductive, and form the basis for new technologies which will enable next generation semiconductor and energy storage devices. Her research has the capacity to impact the development of faster, smaller and lighter mobile electronics devices such as smartphones, tablets and computers.

A gifted and energetic public speaker, Professor Nicolosi routinely makes her research topical and accessible to all audiences and she actively supports the outreach and education programmes within CRANN.

Ms Nicolosi receiving the RDS Intel Prize Lecture for Nanoscience from Mr Leonard Hobbs, Intel Research Ireland and Mr Tony Scott, Chair of the Judging Panel.

Nanoweek Conference to Focus on Commercial Impact of Irish Research

September 17, 2012

The Nanoweek Conference 2012 runs at the Science Gallery in Trinity College Dublin from September 17-21.

Now in its third year, the two-day conference – an initiative of NanoNet Ireland – is this year co-chaired by CRANN, the SFI-funded nanoscience institute. With the overall theme Excellence with Impact, it will focus on the commercial applicability of nanoscience research. High-profile researchers and senior industry figures from multinational and national companies, universities and research institutions will present their experiences of translating University research to industrial impact.

The thematic areas which will be covered are Materials, Medical Devices, Electronic Devices and Sensors. Nanoscience supports these sectors, resulting in €15 billion of exports and up to 120,000 associated jobs nationwide annually.

Minister for Research and Innovation Seán Sherlock said: "Ireland's nanoscience sector supports 120,000 jobs in areas like energy, pharmaceuticals and ICT... It is the Government's intention to continue to prioritise investment in key areas such as nanoscience, and to support an environment of collaboration and flexibility - key to securing the commercialisation of research and the development of new knowledge. This will allow the sector to continue to expand and continue delivering good quality sustainable jobs."

At the Conference, nanoscience researchers will discuss a range of topics including energy storage, advances in diabetes treatment and novel vaccine technologies among others.

Students Gráinne Clarke and Aoibheann Farrelly at the launch of the Magic Materials nanoscience exhibition at the Science Gallery in Trinity College Dublin, a free month long show which explored the peculiar properties of the world's most futuristic and spectacular materials.

EDUCATION IN THE MEDIA

Minister Costello announces education agreement with Brazil

October 11, 2012

Links between Brazilian and Irish institutions have been further expanded by an important new agreement secured.

Minister for Trade and Development Joe Costello has signed a landmark education and research agreement with Brazil during an Enterprise Ireland trade mission to the country. This important new agreement expands further the links between Brazilian and Irish education institutions.

The agreement is part of Brazil's Science Without Borders programme - a Brazilian Government scholarship programme which aims to send 100,000 Brazilian students on undergraduate courses and PhDs courses to study in science, technology, engineering, mathematics and creative industries at top universities around the world. It builds on a previous agreement between Ireland and Brazil announced in June this year for up to 1,500 post-graduate Brazilian students to study in Ireland.

Minister Costello said:
"The agreement marks the start of a new and significant relationship between Brazilian Higher Education Institutes and their Irish counterparts. This is a major boost for the international third level education sector in Ireland."

Marina Donohoe, Head of Education at Enterprise Ireland, added:
"In the context of Ireland's strategy for internationalising Irish higher education, this agreement will help to drive collaboration and growth in research, academic and student exchange between Ireland and Brazil. Ireland's involvement in Science Without Borders at post-graduate and now under-graduate level puts in place the mechanism and funding for an additional 1,400 students per annum."

"There are currently less than 10 institutional links between Brazilian and Irish institutions. Under the *Science Without Borders* scholarship programme, this is expected to rise to over 100 by 2015.

"In terms of economic benefits to the Irish economy, Ireland's inclusion in the Science Without Borders programme has the potential to deliver €15m in fee income, plus an additional €19m in additional spend in the Irish economy."

The agreement was secured in partnership with the Department of Education and Skills with support from Science Foundation Ireland, the Institutes of Technology Ireland, and the Irish Universities Association.

L-R: Mark Ferguson, Director General, Science Foundation Ireland; Glaucius Oliveira, President of CNPq, National Council for Scientific and Technological Development, Brazil; Joe Costello, Minister for Trade and Development; Marina Donohoe, Enterprise Ireland Head of Education; President Michael D. Higgins. Photo: ©Túlio Vidal/Enterprise Ireland

Excellent research that delivers societal and economic impact

Professor Mark Ferguson, CEO, Science Foundation Ireland

We are living in a very exciting time for science as the pace of scientific discovery moves faster than ever before

This is a time of significant political and societal change and market share is won or lost at times of change. The international competition is fierce to attract new industry and to develop new technologies and research breakthroughs that will create economic impact and ultimately the good jobs every country needs. It is in this context that smaller countries like Ireland must compete.

However, the first step in making Ireland competitive in the global marketplace is to acknowledge that Ireland is not simply a scaled down version of much larger countries like the USA or Japan. Small countries like ours have neither the human nor the financial resource to perform all areas of scientific research well, and therefore **we must focus on what we do well.** Ireland has to position itself scientifically both to execute on areas of national importance and to participate widely in a number of important EU research programmes drawing on additional sources of funding to complement SFI funding.

SFI's extended remit
Ireland's scientific research and innovation policies and programmes are planned to both address national priorities including Ireland's unique selling points and to support the broader EU programmes. SFI's remit has been extended to fund applied research in addition to its current remit to fund oriented basic research. We have added a new function to enable SFI to promote and support awareness and understanding of STEM subjects. SFI can also now participate in, and contribute funding to, international research projects which relate to strategic areas of opportunity for Ireland.

These welcome amendments add to a number of important developments in Irish scientific research policy in the past year, including publication of the report of the National Research Prioritisation Strategy Group; a new national framework, guidelines and protocols for IP protection and exploitation, 'Putting Public Research to work for Ireland'; the Governments' Action Plan for Jobs 2013; SFI's new strategic policy 'Agenda 2020'; SFI's Annual Plan 2013; and SFI's achievements summary 'Discovery to Delivery'.

Public investment in research through SFI and other government agencies is making an impact:

- Ireland is now in the top 20 countries in scientific global rankings from a position of 36th in 2003 (Source: Thomson Reuters Essential Scientific Indicators).
- Ireland is third in the world for the quality of its research in Immunology and eighth in the world for the quality of its research in Materials Science.
- SFI supported researchers published over 6,000 papers in 2012 (up 16% on 2011) 1/3 of these are co-authored with internationally based researchers.
- Over the past decade SFI has built a community of approx. 3000 researchers in Ireland's higher education institutes, led by approximately 450 scientists.

- Over 700 companies are taking part in over 1,000 collaborations with SFI research groups, ranging from informal connections to collaborations that involve significant financial sponsorship. The goal of these relationships is to make those companies more competitive via transferring technology and trained people out of the labs and into the companies.
- Irish science has a global reach - SFI researchers engaged in approximately 1,800 academic collaborations spanning 68 countries.
- Last year, Government investment through SFI of approximately €150 million has enabled SFI researchers to leverage a further €170 million.
- Recently we announced the funding of 7 research centres of international scale and excellence with a total funding of approximately €200 million over 5 years from SFI and a further €100 million from industry. This is the largest investment in research projects and the biggest research public private partnership in Irelands' history. We intend to fund an additional 2-3 centres every year and to grow and link the centres using annual funding through Spoke projects.

The SFI Strategy – Agenda 2020

Agenda 2020, SFI's ambitious seven year strategic plan, lays out four key goals, the strategies for achieving them, and the performance indicators that will be used to measure SFI's progress. It begins by considering why governments, and in particular the Irish government, should fund scientific research, and then articulates a vision of a 'preferred future' for Ireland in 2020, in which excellent and impactful scientific research makes a significant contribution to society and national prosperity and in which the population is well educated and comfortable with science and technology both as users and providers.

SFI's four goals are:
1. To be the best science funding agency in the world at creating impact from excellent research and demonstrating clear value for money invested.

2. To be the exemplar in building partnerships that fund excellent science and drive it out into the market and society.

3. To have the most engaged and scientifically informed public

4. To represent the ideal modern public service organisation, staffed in a lean and flexible manner, with efficient and effective management.

In the Agenda 2020 document, each of these objectives is elaborated upon by setting out the reasons why it is important, the actions that will be taken to achieve it and the KPI's that will be used to measure progress. Each year SFI will publish both an audit of progress and an annual plan.

The actions taken include:

- Recruitment initiatives to attract iconic research leaders to Ireland;
- Increased support for early career researchers;
- Support for the development and attraction of European Research Council (ERC) scientists in Ireland;
- Development of significant partnerships with industry, charities and other research funders;
- Development of internationally recognised research centres of scale, excellence and importance to enterprise;
- Investment in research infrastructure;
- Exchange studentships and fellowships with industry;
- Focused international collaboration;
- Development of thematic funding calls;
- Development of 'Ireland as a test bed';

Dr Cora Marrett, Acting Director of the NSF and Prof Mark Ferguson, Director General SFI pictured at the 2nd Annual Global Meeting of the Global Research Council in Berlin, Germany, where an agreement was signed between Science Foundation Ireland (SFI) and the National Science Foundation (NSF) in the United States. The agreement will help to encourage, develop and facilitate research opportunities in the NSFís Graduate Research Fellowship Programme (GRFP) for the best young Irish research talent, under the GROW initiative

- Increased and co-ordinated outreach activities; and
- Development of a lean, flexible, efficient administration.

SFI will fund, within its legal remit, the spectrum of research from curiosity driven, to needs inspired. Eligibility criteria, for example with respect to national priority areas, will be applied intelligently and differentially within each of its programmes.

All proposals will be internationally peer reviewed to determine scientific excellence, using only reviewers drawn from outside Ireland. Only proposals deemed scientifically excellent will be funded. Additionally, all researchers will be asked to explain the potential impact/relevance of their research and this will be internationally assessed, independent of the scientific review by individuals drawn from appropriate backgrounds, e.g. relevant company R&D personnel, technology transfer staff from the world's leading universities, and international investors in early stage companies.

Impact will be widely interpreted, including the supply of trained personnel for industry; potential outcomes of the research project; track record in commercialization, industry interaction or company formation; appropriate company engagement with the proposal; competitive positioning; the reputational benefit for Ireland; societal benefits; and contribution to global challenges. Given Ireland's current important focus on economic recovery, potential economic impacts, both short- and long-term, will be emphasised for at least the next few years.

Innovative Programmes

SFI has also pioneered some innovative programmes aimed at fostering both research excellence and potential economic impact, such as our flexible Partnership Programme and our Hub and Spoke design for our seven research centres of scale. Over €300 million, (€200 million from Government and €100 million from industry), will be invested in these centres over the next five years, which will focus on a broad range of topics including, 'Big Data', ICT, pharmaceutical manufacturing, drug synthesis, connected health, prenatal and neonatal care, photonics, marine renewable energy, nanomaterials and gut-microbiota.

Career Development

SFI has launched career development schemes covering the spectrum of likely employment for its researchers. These include the Industrial Fellowship Scheme, allowing researchers at all stages to spend one year full time in a company anywhere in the world conducting industrial research. The SIRGE scheme allows promising post doctorates to obtain their full independent grant, the CDA (Career Development Award) to allow junior researchers and faculty to develop their research career and the President of Ireland Young Researcher Award (PIYRA) to recognise the most outstanding of the individuals. We also encourage and support applications to the European Research Council (ERC) from researchers within Ireland and ERC applicants to resubmit to the ERC through an Irish Higher Education Institution. In addition successful ERC holders are supported through the ERC Support Programme award. The SFI Research Professorship scheme aims to recruit outstanding candidates to Ireland to lead major research projects in areas of strategic importance.

SFI & Ireland

We want to fund scientific researchers who not only want to understand the world but also want to change it. We want to have an educated and engaged public and to inspire and encourage school children to study STEM (Science, Technology, Engineering and Maths) subjects throughout their education, so that they can subsequently contribute significantly to both society and the economy. We also want to participate fully in relevant international collaborations and programmes, particularly those relating to the EU. We want to fund excellent research that delivers societal and economic impact that this country needs.

SFI looks forward to working with the Higher Education Institutions and all of those involved in the engineering and science eco-system across all sectors in Ireland and internationally to advance science as an important part of our culture and identity.

EDUCATION IN THE MEDIA

Work set to start on €3m research centre in Clonmel

December 10, 2012

Work is to start early next year on a €3m research and development centre in Clonmel.

Contracts have been signed for the project - a collaboration between South Tipperary County Council and Limerick Institute of Technology - which is aimed at boosting new businesses as well as research and development programmes.

It is hoped the 1,400 square-metre facility, to be located just west of Clonmel in the Ballingarrane development campus, will open in the middle of 2014. The development will include research laboratories, conference and meeting rooms, and training rooms.

The contractors are local company Clancy Construction, while the design is by RKD Architects.

"Santa has come early to Clonmel and south Tipperary," was how local county councillor Siobhán Ambrose described the news. "This now means that new and existing indigenous businesses in this area will have an opportunity to avail of these facilities," she said.

"It also means that outside small businesses will have an opportunity to rent out meeting, training or conference rooms should they wish to do so."

"It is hoped that, with the college [Limerick Institute of Technology] next door, this new facility will also support new graduates with specialisation in the sciences area to avail of these facilities," Ms Ambrose said.

www.irishexaminer.com/ireland/work-set-to-start-on-3m-research-centre-in-clonmel-216526.html

SFI Science Summit 2012

November 13, 2012:

The Minister for Research and Innovation, Sean Sherlock delivered the keynote address at the annual SFI Science Summit 2012 which took place over the course of two days in Athlone, Co. Westmeath.

The Minister indicated that implementation of Research Prioritisation represents the central plank of a new national research strategy that will be advanced during 2013.

Attended by over 250 members of Ireland's science and research community, this year's event was titled 'Sharing Science' and focused on science communications, the implementation of research prioritisation, and SFI's new strategic document, Agenda 2020, which was launched at the event by Ministers Sherlock and Bruton.

Minister Sherlock said:
"The Government is committed to ensuring that research and innovation remains centre stage in our economic and jobs strategy, as a means of underpinning economic recovery...

"2013 will be a really important year for the further development of Ireland's research system. We will begin the implementation of research prioritisation in earnest, we will also enact legislation in early 2013 to further extend SFIs remit into the applied research arena, and we shall engage closely with various stakeholders towards developing a new national Science Strategy."

"I call on our scientific community to continue their excellent work and to ensure that we work collectively to ensure that we put our best foot forward for Ireland's economic and societal benefit."

Prof Mark Ferguson, Director General SFI
Baroness Susan Greenfield, University of Oxford
Roger Highfield, Director of External Affairs, Science Museum Group

EDUCATION IN THE MEDIA

€70bn Horizon 2020 programme will boost innovation and jobs across Europe

June 25, 2013

Following lengthy intensive negotiations over the past months, the Irish Presidency has secured political agreement on Horizon 2020, one of its most significant priorities.

Horizon 2020, the EU's €70bn research and innovation programme, will boost jobs and growth across the European Union and in Ireland, according to Minister for Research and Innovation Seán Sherlock who is currently Chair of the Council of EU Research Ministers. He is at present in Brussels for the final formal "trilogue" negotiation between the Council, Commission and Parliament.
Minister Sherlock paid tribute to Commissioner Geoghegan Quinn and her team in DG Research for their "huge personal commitment and creativity in championing, within the Commission, a framework programme for research that will be the engine of the Union's recovery".
The programme consists of three pillars:

1. Excellent Science, which will include funding for the European Research Council, research infrastructures and future and emerging technologies.

2. Industrial Leadership, the truly innovative element of the programme as it contains specific supports for SMEs and for enabling industrial technologies such as nanotechnologies, biotechnologies and ICT.

3. Societal Challenges, which will help ensure that research is directed at areas of most concern to citizens and business-such as health, climate, food, security, energy and transport.

The programme will use a simplified funding model, which means that a greater number of businesses and research providers – small medium and large - can access the programme with less bureaucracy. This in turn means greater diversity in research, greater opportunities for business and greater benefits for the economy at large.

This political agreement now goes to the Committee of Permanent Representatives of Member States for endorsement. The indicative budget of €70 billion is subject to final agreement on the EU's Multi-Financial Framework.

(Cian Connaughton, Department of Jobs, Enterprise and Innovation 0876480809)

Support for high potential start-up companies

Date, 2013

Limerick Institute of Technology (LIT), University of Limerick (UL), Institute of Technology Tralee (ITT) and Enterprise Ireland are collaborating to offer funding and other support to Ireland's most promising entrepreneurs through the New Frontiers programme.

The **New Frontiers** programme – an initiative of Enterprise Ireland - is a tailor made 3-phase schedule designed to support emerging entrepreneurs in their quest to establish themselves as high performance companies. It is intended to facilitate high calibre candidates who possess enthusiasm, confidence and determination and who wish to commit full-time to get a business going.

Budding entrepreneurs are provided with a package of supports including funding of €15,000, free office space, mentoring and workshops to help accelerate their business development. The aim is to equip participants with the skills and contacts they need to start and grow a company.

In Limerick, the programme is being led by Limerick Institute of Technology (LIT). The Institute has been supporting start-ups since 2007 at the Hartnett Enterprise Acceleration Centre, and has helped create almost 100 companies resulting in over 400 jobs. The collaboration with IT Tralee and the University of Limerick will help in widening supports for entrepreneurs in the region.

The New Frontiers programme helped 120 entrepreneurs across Ireland in 2012. Enterprise Ireland has committed to continue support for a further three years.

EDUCATION IN THE MEDIA

Economist to lead landmark EU study

11 JUNE 2013

A leading economist has been awarded €650,000 to fund international research into the global financial crisis.

University of Limerick (UL) lecturer and Irish Independent columnist Dr Stephen Kinsella will lead research aimed at learning from the crisis as well as examining the future growth of the EU.

Dr Kinsella of the Kemmy Business School, University of Limerick (UL), will collaborate with New York-based Nobel Laureate Professor Joseph Stiglitz as part of the research.

Stephen Kinsella

The three-year project will study the evolution of debt and demography in the European periphery and develop new models to understand the European economy.

The €650,000 grant is the largest received at the Business School in four years. Dr Kinsella said: "As a consequence of this funding, UL will become the world's largest centre for stock flow consistent modelling."

www.independent.ie/irish-news/economist-to-lead-landmark-eu-study-29334504.html

---

Tyndall researchers protest against the "pay mess"

June 06, 2013

Up to 100 researchers at the Tyndall National Institute plan to demonstrate this morning at a European Science event being hosted by UCC, in a bid to have their wages brought into line with other staff at the university.

Mike Jennings, General Secretary of the Irish Federation of University Teachers, said the pay of researchers is a third lower than other UCC staff. He said researchers feel they are being discriminated against in terms of pay and conditions, and even the Labour Court has agreed they have a case, but nothing has been done.

Mr Jennings had hoped the issue could be resolved as part of wage negotiations under the Haddington Road agreement. However, attempts to do so were rejected by the Department of Education in spite of intervention by UCC's President, Dr Michael Murphy, who had written last November to the HEA stating that staff in Tyndall 'perform the same functions but receive different rewards', and requesting that 'any disparity could be addressed as soon as possible.'

"The pay rates and conditions have grown completely on an ad hoc basis over the years with no proper planning, no grading structure. It was all done on the basis of short-termism without any coherence and the result is the historical mess of gigantic proportions," Mr Jennings said.

"There is little point in the Government pretending that Ireland can become a hub for research and innovation when research is being treated so shoddily and researchers treated as second-class citizens," he added.

"We are demanding that the Minister and Department of Education address this issue before irreparable damage is done to Ireland's research reputation."

www.irishexaminer.com/breakingnews/ireland/tyndall-researchers-protest-pay-mess-of-gigantical-proportions-596680.html

Tyndall National Institute, Cork

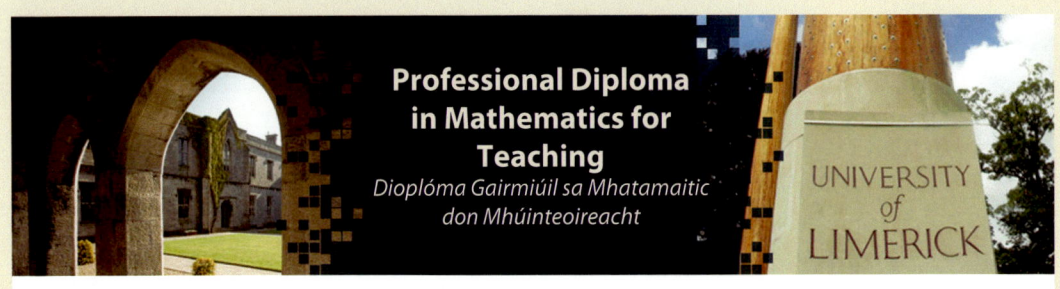

Professional Diploma in Mathematics for Teaching
Dioplóma Gairmiúil sa Mhatamaitic don Mhúinteoireacht

UNIVERSITY of LIMERICK

Introduction

The National Centre for Excellence in Mathematics and Science Teaching and Learning (NCE-MSTL) at the University of Limerick is pleased to invite applications from eligible teachers for this two-year part-time Professional Diploma in Mathematics for Teaching (Level 8)/Dioplóma Gairmiúil sa Mhatamaitic don Mhúinteoireacht. The programme is closely aligned with the needs of out-of-field teachers of mathematics, Project Maths and the requirements of the Teaching Council.

The **Professional Diploma in Mathematics for Teaching (Level 8)/ Dioplóma Gairmiúil sa Mhatamaitic don Mhúinteoireacht** is funded by the Department of Education and Skills as part of the national strategy to support the implementation of Project Maths and improve standards in mathematics education in post-primary schools by upskilling out-of-field teachers of mathematics.

This university accredited professional diploma (Level 8) is delivered nationally in a blended learning mode through local nodes in associate partner institutions located in the regions, in face-to-face and/or on-line modalities.

The Dioplóma Gairmiúil sa Mhatamaitic don Mhúinteoireacht is also offered through the medium of Irish for out-of-field teachers of mathematics in Irish-medium and Gaeltacht schools nationwide.

The programme, designed by University of Limerick and NUI Galway, is jointly accredited by both institutions through their recently established Strategic Alliance.

Aims

The aims of the programme are to ensure that successful candidates:

- acquire the extensive and complex integrated knowledge base including mathematical and pedagogical knowledge that is necessary for effective mathematics teaching at post-primary level with special reference to Project Maths,
- demonstrate an ability to integrate this mathematics knowledge for teaching into professional practice as mathematics teachers,
- develop a high standard of practical competence in mathematics teaching as reflective practitioners during their programme of study.

For Further Information Contact:

Course Director:
Prof (Emeritus) John O'Donoghue
National Centre for Excellence in Mathematics and Science Teaching and Learning (NCE-MSTL)
University of Limerick
Phone: 353-61-234786
Email: John.ODonoghue@ul.ie

http://www.ul.ie/graduateschool/course/mathematics-teaching-level-8-professional-diploma

Registered teachers successfully completing the Diploma will meet the Teaching Council's requirements for Mathematics.

WHO'S WHO

The WHO'S WHO Profile introduces people who are making an important contribution to education in Ireland today.

Meet
Professor Barry Smyth

OCCUPATION: Director (interim) of INSIGHT Centre for Data Analytics; Director of CLARITY Centre for Sensor Web Technologies; Digital Chair of Computer Science at UCD.

Where did you grow up?
Dublin

How many siblings have you?
Three

Where did you go to school/college?
University College Dublin and Trinity College Dublin

To what extent did your education shape who you are today?
Completely - especially my third-level education. I found the Leaving Cert to be far too broad and not deep enough in the subjects that interested me. This all changed at 3rd level and it was transformative.

What attracted you to work in the area of technology?
Since I was a child I was interested in engineering, electronics, and programming. I got my first computer (Sinclair ZX81) when I was 12 and became a computer geek on the spot.

What is CLARITY's main aim?
CLARITY is a partnership between University College Dublin, Dublin City University and Tyndall National Institute, Cork. CLARITY focuses on the Sensor Web, which captures the intersection between two important researches areas - Adaptive Sensing and Information Discovery. CLARITY brings together software and electronic engineers, material scientists and sports scientists to meet joint research objectives.

What areas of IT should Ireland focus on in order to gain competitive advantage?
Right now I am heavily invested in Big Data and Data Analytics so I will say that these are key areas where Ireland can demonstrate genuine impact in a way that can change all of our lives.

What makes you particularly suitable for your current work?
I'm naturally quite analytical and so a good fit with computer science. I also like the collaborative nature of modern research and enjoy the opportunity to build new centres and projects with colleagues.

What are the main responsibilities and challenges of your position?
Right now I have overall responsibility for the new INSIGHT data analytics centre. It's a €70+m research centre that is starting up in July 2013 and I am responsible for all aspects of the centre's operations as its (interim) Director.

What does a typical workday involve for you?
Up at 6am. Email review and responses. Daily planning. Breakfast with the family at 8 and then I DART and cycle into UCD for 9.30. My days vary. I spend about a day a week working with startups in UCD (at the moment HeyStaks). A lot of time is spent working with my direct PhDs and PostDocs on everything from their research progress to paper writing to thesis reviews. I spend a lot of time writing research papers and grant proposals and too much time on administration. I also still teach (a little).

What do you enjoy most about your work?
Everything. Well, except the administration, although in truth that's not so bad - so pretty much everything.

What do you enjoy least about your work?
Very little. Too much admin is a pain.

What would you most like to change?
My office. It's dark and dingy and part of a building site right now. I've been there for 5 years after leaving a great office in the School of Computer Science. It's set to change next year as I move into the new UCD Science Centre!

The future applications of sensor technologies across sport, energy, healthcare, enterprise and the social web were showcased on November 21, 2013 at an event opened by the Minister for Jobs, Enterprise and Innovation, Richard Bruton T.D.

'The Applications of the Sensor Web: CLARITY 2012' Showcase Event took place at Clontarf Castle in Dublin.

The open day was attended by over 150 researchers, industry professionals and state agencies and the latest advances in the areas of adaptive sensing and information discovery were on show.

Pictured were Prof Barry Smyth, Director of Clarity with Minister Richard Bruton, Prof Mark Ferguson, Director General, SFI and the Rubicon robot which is designed to bring high-tech sensor technology to the high-street. Picture Jason Clarke Photography.

Are you a workaholic?
I don't think so but others will disagree. I am very productive but I try to finish work by 6pm on weekdays and do little over the weekend. However, a lot of my relaxation time is spent reading about science and technology and tinkering so it seems that I am always working…

What do you do to relax?
Run and read.

Do you like living in Dublin?
I live in Greystones actually and love it.

Are you married?
I'm divorced.

What plans have you for the future?
More of the same ;-)

Have you a message for educators?
Resist inertia and embrace change for the good.

Have you a message for policy makers?
Don't take short-cuts with our kids' education. Mistakes in education last a generation. Concretely, I think we need to look more carefully at prioritising certain subjects such as science and maths and perhaps even considering differential teacher pay rates to encourage the best and brightest to join the profession.

Chapter 6

Further Education & Lifelong Learning

Contents

		Page
1.	**Reform and Austerity - strange bedfellows** *Michael Moriarty*	220
2.	**SOLAS rises from the ashes of FÁS** *Brian Mooney*	222
3.	**It's all about People** *Paul O'Toole*	225
4.	**Professionalising teaching in Further Education and Training in Ireland** *Stan McHugh*	227
5.	**Becoming a Teacher: my experiences on the Professional Diploma in Education (FE)** *Margaret Lavelle*	229
6.	**A local perspective on the changing nature of Adult & FE Provision** *Joe Cunningham*	231
7.	**Digital Literacies for Life** *Paul Gormley*	233
8.	**Access and Widening Participation in Higher Education in Ireland** *Ann O'Brien and Imelda Byrne*	235
9.	**RPL and Professional Development in the FE sector** *Dr Cathal de Paor*	237
10.	**WHO's WHO** *Professor Michael Hayes*	239

Introducing the Further Education & Lifelong Learning Chapter

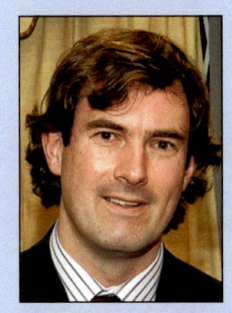

by Tony Hall, *Editor*

A characteristic theme in Irish education, and it has ostensibly always been the case, is that Irish education is like a perpetual motion machine, always moving and never quite settling into homeostasis or stillness. However, unlike such machines, there is considerable energy constantly being invested in Irish education - by students, teachers, parents, educators, policy makers, and key stakeholders. The further education, training and lifelong learning sector is, like the other parts of the great dynamic of Irish education also seeing significant change in the contemporary moment. The further education and lifelong learning sector has experienced considerable development in recent years, with the new further education and training authority, SOLAS, and the 16 new Education and Training Boards (ETBs).

The chapter begins with an article by Michael Moriarty, General Secretary of the IVEA on the challenges of reform in this, the apparent 'Age of Austerity'. Following on from this keynote article, Brian Mooney, Guidance Counsellor, Oatlands College Dublin, and Educational Columnist with the Irish Times, identifies key questions and issues for SOLAS, the new infrastructure to support further education and training programmes in the State. Paul O'Toole, Director General of FÁS, outlines in his article how structured delivery plans and constant, consistent and objective evaluation will help to support further education and training in an optimal way for all learners.

Stan McHugh, Consultant in Qualifications and Quality Assurance in Education and Training, and former Chief Executive of FETAC, discusses the changes to teacher education, and the professionalisation of teaching in the evolving further education and training sector in Ireland. Mr McHugh's article is complemented by Margaret Lavelle's article, which describes her experiences of becoming a recognised teacher in the sector, after completing the first year of NUI Galway's Professional Diploma in Education, Further Education (PDE (FE)). Joe Cunningham's article affords an insight – at the local level – into the changing nature of adult and further education provision. In his article on digital literacies for life, Paul Gormley, eLearning facilitator at NUI Galway and Chair of the Irish Learning Technology Association (ILTA), underscores the importance of digital literacy for all, in all aspects of our lives: education, leisure, communication etc. The article also provides an interesting insight into what technologies students are currently using to support their learning. Dr. Cathal de Paor, Director of CPD in the Faculty of Education, Mary Immaculate College discusses the key issue of recognition of prior learning (RPL) in lifelong learning; and the 'Who's Who' profile in Irish education is: Professor Michael A Hayes, President of Mary Immaculate College, Limerick.

Further Education & Lifelong Learning

Reform and Austerity make strange bedfellows

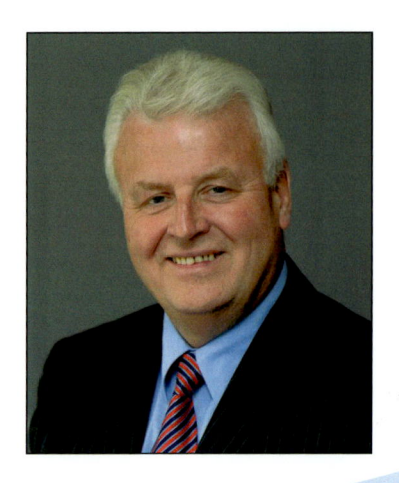

Michael Moriarty General Secretary
Irish Vocational Education Association (IVEA)

The very significant reform agenda of Minister Quinn, if implemented, could well revolutionise Ireland's education and training sectors.

The change agenda in the Further Education and Training sector, propelled by an ambitious and driven Minister, is taking place in an educational setting which is increasingly struggling from a significant resource deficiency and a worsening industrial relations scenario arising from on-going salary cuts and worsening conditions of service for VEC and school employees.

The on-going financial crisis and the consequential austerity programme have severely affected all sectors of Irish society. Although the education sector is seen as crucial to economic recovery and regeneration, it has, nevertheless, been subjected to annualised funding cuts as the Department of Education and Skills is allocated a reduced budget year on year. The consequential cuts have cascaded down to all parts of the education system, which have all taken a share of the imposed cuts in essential resources. Certainly we have long passed the point where cuts will not affect services; at all levels, the student and client services are in danger of being further eroded and diminished.

The very significant reform agenda of Minister Quinn, if implemented, could well revolutionise Ireland's education and training sectors. However the agenda could be derailed by education sector employees becoming increasingly angry and frustrated with their particular lot. The public sector has seen significant reduction in numbers, with salaries and other cuts made more painful by other indirect taxes. The stark choice for teachers and other staff is to accept the difficult medicine contained in the Haddington Road Agreement or to suffer a worse fate by the application of the provisions of the Financial Emergency Measures in the Public Interest Act (FEMPI) 2013. In a few short years, all has been transformed and the public sector has shown that it is paying dearly for the financial woes of the state.

In this context of austerity and cutbacks in essential resources, schools and colleges have tried to sustain a supportive, caring and positive educational environment, despite being stripped of a large number of middle management posts from the school staffing infrastructure. This process has placed a particular burden on the remaining post holders, as well as on school management.

The July 1st cuts in salary and allowances payments could have catastrophic consequences if, for example, teachers were to refuse to undertake substitution and supervision duties when schools re-open in September. We are at a crossroads, and we hope that the focus remains on the needs of the students in our care in these most difficult and unprecedented times.

Against this volatile and uncertain background we must view the many fine initiatives announced in recent times. The reform of the Junior and Leaving Certificate programmes and examinations are designed to end 'teaching to the test', which has been driven by the domination of the terminal examination as the only means of testing ability and knowledge. The proposed reform of the marking scheme and the overhaul of the CAO system are also to be welcomed.

There is more clarity about the reform proposals in the Junior Cycle, with the implementation of school-based short courses and school-based assessment, designed to enhance such attributes as critical thinking and team building, so as to boost self-learning and autonomy.

School self-evaluation is another initiative which seeks to follow the European strategy of devolving more autonomy to schools and fits into the school-based assessment proposals for Junior Certificate students. Indeed, much of the success of the Finnish school system has been attributed to the increased autonomy of local schools to devise their own educational programmes.

The Further Education and Training (FET) sector is being revolutionised through an extensive structural overhaul. The establishment of 16 Education and Training Boards (ETBs) from the ashes of the VECs, and the integration of the FÁS Training Centres into the ETB structure means that for the first time in decades, the delivery of education and training will be the responsibility of statutory authorities, the ETBs, under the guidance of SOLAS, which will have a strategic policy and funding role for the Further Education and Training sector. In effect, the FET sector is being mainstreamed, to stand shoulder to shoulder with First, Second and Third level sectors. This most significant enhancement of the FET sector underpins a major policy shift by government, which realises that Further Education and Training can be the springboard to restore Ireland's competitive edge by providing the necessary generic and industry-specific skills for jobseekers and other learners seeking to re-enter the workforce.

The parallel processes of structural reform and current austerity measures make for strange bedfellows. Certainly, the old maxim of doing more with less applies. But there is no doubt that the on-going austerity agenda will continue to diminish and erode service delivery in schools and other educational institutions. Minister Quinn certainly has no room for manoeuvre in this regard, and needs to focus on the positives which rest squarely within the realm of structural reform. In this context, he could certainly look at reforming the management structures within schools through engagement with the education partners, so that efficient and effective structures could be built on a framework defined by essential needs and functions. IVEA has been calling for such a process over the past few years, and we had hoped that the Minister's reforming zeal could be applied to such a project also.

The level and pace of reform being driven by Minister Quinn has to be admired. He is prepared to tackle any sacred cow that needs to be addressed. Let us hope that the on-going reductions in resources, both financial and staffing, will not outweigh the benefits of the reform agenda.

All that we in the sector do must be in the best interests of education and the students and clients of our schools and services. Perhaps all stakeholders need to commit to doing better with less, rather than more with less. But that is a tall order when the cupboard is long since bare.

SOLAS rises from the ashes of FÁS

Brian Mooney, *Guidance Counsellor, Oatlands College Dublin, and Columnist with The Irish Times*

For the new infrastructure to work, we may need a George Mitchell-type figure to mediate and knock heads together if necessary...

As President of the Institute of Guidance Counsellors for five years during the height of the Celtic Tiger years, I dealt with FÁS on a regular basis and in that period I often felt uncomfortable with what I regarded as a culture of entitlement and excess at senior management level.

Back in 2008 my views on FÁS were already in the public domain and I was invited onto the panel of 'Questions and Answers' on RTÉ to discuss them on Monday night, September 29. The Government Minister sitting alongside me was Mary Hanafin, and the question of the ongoing banking crisis was central to our discussions both on and off air. As we relaxed over refreshments following the programme, in the early hours of the morning, her phone rang summoning her to return to Government buildings. In the hours that followed that phone call - and similar ones to all members of the Cabinet that night - the social and economic destiny of Ireland was about to change profoundly, in ways none of us could ever have imagined.

In the five years that have intervened since that fateful night, FÁS chief executive Roddy Molloy resigned, various senior executives defended themselves against disciplinary actions in the Courts, and the FÁS brand became so politically toxic that its demise was inevitable. A whole new infrastructure is now being put in place to provide education and training of a vocational nature.

On January 25, 2013, the current Minister for Education and Skills published the Further Education and Training Bill 2013. The purpose of the Bill is to give effect to the Government decision to establish an education and training authority called **An tSeirbhís Oideachais Leanúnaigh agus Scileanna (SOLAS)** under the aegis of his Department. The main provisions of the Bill are to provide for the establishment of SOLAS, the dissolution of FÁS, and the transfer of the staff and property of the FÁS training division to the newly formed Education and Training Boards. SOLAS will, according to the Minister, facilitate more coherent integrated national and regional planning across the further education and training sector.

The second piece of legislation which the Government has introduced to complement SOLAS is the **Education and Training Boards Bill 2012.** It repealed nine pieces of legislation, and many statutory instruments, and replaced them with one consolidated Act. This Bill is the legislative basis for the new **"Local Education and Training Board"** system.

On July 1, 2013, thirty-three VECs ceased to exist and on the same day sixteen local Education and Training Boards opened their doors. All administrative and support services to schools and centres for education transferred to the new LETBs. In launching the new local education and training boards on that date, Minister Quinn said:

"Today marks a new era for education and training in Ireland. The new ETB's will strengthen locally managed education and enhance the scale of local education and training. This represents a major component of the public service transformation agenda. At a time when the need for training and re-skilling has never been more important, it is crucial to provide appropriate programmes and courses that offer students and learners the best opportunities to progress. We must do all of this while providing value for money to the taxpayer."

This major reform will reduce the number of Chief Executive Officers in line with the number of bodies and full year savings are estimated at €2.1m. The new configuration paves the way for exciting new provisions that will provide for the establishment of SOLAS, the dissolution of FÁS and the transfer of **training functions** to the newly formed Education and Training Boards.

The Further Education and Training Bill 2013 to provide for the establishment of SOLAS was enacted in July 2013. It is envisaged that SOLAS will be formally established before the end of the year. As part of the change, the Irish Vocational Educational Authority will change its name to **Education and Training Boards Ireland (ETBI)**. ETBI will represent the Education and Training Boards and promote their interests.

SOLAS will effectively become, for Vocational and Further Education, what the Higher Education Authority (HEA) is for the third level sector. It will exercise strategic leadership in the provision of further education and training.

In consultation with the new *"Local Education and Training Boards"* it will determine what further education and training programmes should be provided, allocate and advance funding, and carry out financial and quality assurance audits on **LETB's** and other bodies, including private sector course providers, for the provision of further education and training, funded by SOLAS.

There are important questions that need to be addressed in relation to the changes currently taking place. I have already raised these questions publicly as far back as February 2013, and am glad of the opportunity to do so again here.

- Do the teaching staff within the Further Education and FÁS training services have the skills to educate and train people to the high standards required by multinational and domestic employers, particularly in ICT, foreign language skills, international business, engineering and technology?
- Will those educated and trained within the new structures meet the employability needs of those who are thinking of creating jobs in the Irish economy?
- If the new ETB's do not deliver to these standards, will SOLAS gradually award a growing share of their budget to private-sector colleges and trainers?
- While it is important to flag the successful programmes currently on offer from both PLC's and FÁS in areas such as personal training, outdoor pursuits, accounting technicianship and access programmes to university, will the duplication and labour-market suitability of many courses currently on offer be addressed in the new regime?
- There are also some very successful institutions, e.g. Dublin colleges such as Coláiste Dhúlaigh, in Coolock, and Ballyfermot College of Further Education, have international reputations for the quality of their graduates. How can these progressive and productive colleges be supported within the new framework?
- The terms and conditions of employment of the teachers within the F Further Education sector are very different from those currently employed within FÁS training. Teachers in PLC colleges have contracts which currently see them on holidays for two weeks at Christmas and Easter, mid-term breaks and three months in the summer. FÁS trainers enjoy higher pay scales than teachers, but do not enjoy anything like the same holidays. How are these two groups of public servants to be integrated into a single service under the management of the ETB's?

Last month the Sunday Business Post reported that workers in FAS training centres are querying the fact that they are being **seconded** to the new LETB's, whilst the staff of the VEC's are being **transferred**. The FAS staff have quite rightly questioned where they will stand when the organisation from which they are being seconded (FAS) will cease to exist at the end of 2013.

A further function of SOLAS will be to support the systematic referral of jobseekers on the Live Register and in particular in consultation with the **National Employment and Entitlements Service (NEES)** to publicly provided further education and training programmes delivered by **LETB's** and to other providers, and to provide opportunities for those not on the Live Register to access further education and training courses.

The newly formed **NEES (National Employment Entitlements Service)** is made up of current **Department of Social Protection (DSP)** staff, plus the former **Placement Officers at FÁS**, who have now transferred into this new structure as **Case Officers**, as have the existing staff of **Community Welfare Officers**. The first one-stop-shop established under this new process opened in Sligo in October 2012. It is planned to open such offices throughout the country over the next two years.

There are questions also regarding this new service to unemployed persons.

- How do we ensure that these three distinct staff groups are sufficiently up-skilled to ensure that when they sit down with the hundreds of thousands of unemployed people, they are capable of identifying a suitable education or training pathway that meets their long-term interests and capacities?
- Many of the Placement Officers transferred from FAS are fully trained Guidance Counsellors, holding a NUI Maynooth qualification, but cannot exercise their guidance counselling skills with their unemployed clients, as they are only allowed to spend fifteen minutes with each person, engaged in what the DSP call's a profiling exercise.
- Will the Guidance Counsellors within adult-education guidance services, which currently operate within the existing VEC structure, be integrated into the new one-stop-shop services to provide a high level of guidance competency? If they were to be so integrated, would they be confined to a 15-minute session with clients thus making the exercise of their qualifications useless?
- If the Adult Education Guidance Service continues to operate within the LETB's providing a professional guidance counselling service to clients who turn up at its door, why should similar clients who access the NEES services be confined to a 15-minute profiling exercise, which may in no way clarify which course or programme of training is most appropriate for their individual circumstances?

Being honest at this stage about problems posed by the introduction of the proposed legislation is enormously important if we are to avoid another exercise in waste of public money. The Career Guidance issue is crucial because Ireland's employment crisis stems not only from a lack of jobs, but also from a lack of suitably qualified workers in key areas, both in high technology and in service industry skills.

For this new infrastructure to work, we may need a George Mitchell-type figure who will mediate between these new structures, knocking heads together if necessary, to create an environment of trust and joined-up thinking between these bodies. If this does not happen, we will be back where we started, with billions wasted every year, or the private sector may end up replacing a large part of the existing Further Education and FÁS training public sector structure.

Now that all of the legislative pieces are in place, FAS can be finally wrapped up. It is to be hoped that the many thousands of public servants who worked in FAS since its establishment in the late 1960s will not feel tainted by the cause and manner of its demise. The arrogance and hubris of a few at the top undermined the good work of the vast majority of its staff.

Let us hope that the lessons have been truly learnt and that the newly emerging structures will be given the political and administrative support necessary to deliver on behalf of those people whose employment prospects will be determined by its success or failure.

It's all about people

Paul O'Toole, *Director General, FÁS*

Making further education and training work better

Over the next five years we have a golden opportunity to ensure that people from all walks of life, all levels of educational attainment and all types of life and work experience increase the positive impact on their lives and job prospects through a new approach to further education and training (FET).

At present, there are profound changes underway to the manner in which FET will be planned and delivered in the future. Initially this process is concentrating on making changes to the institutional framework surrounding further education and training.

On the 1st July this year 16 new Education & Training Boards (ETBs) came into being. They replaced 33 former Vocational Education Committees (VECs) in a move that marked the passage of their eighty plus years of service into a new era. The new bodies will expand the traditional roles of VECs in secondary and further education through the acquisition of training provision as a responsibility. All of the existing FÁS Training Centres and their accompanying human and other resources will transfer to the ETBs in the coming months.

Quality and Qualifications Ireland (QQI) was established on 6 November 2012. The new Authority was created by an amalgamation of four bodies that had both awarding and quality assurance responsibilities: the Further Education and Training Awards Council (FETAC), the Higher Education and Training Awards Council (HETAC), the National Qualifications Authority of Ireland (NQAI) and the Irish Universities Quality Board (IUQB).

At time of writing, the legislation to establish Seirbhísí Oideachais Leanúnaigh Agus Scileanna (SOLAS), the new Further Education and Training Authority, is well advanced. Following the enactment of this legislation, SOLAS will be established and FÁS will be wound down. SOLAS will be responsible for the strategic planning, coordinating and funding of FET.

Together, these institutional changes represent a profound restructuring of the structures and processes which will guide and deliver FET opportunities into the foreseeable future.

The fundamental question is how will we ensure that these enormous structural changes deliver real strategic change which will benefit future generations of learners?
It is to this question that all actors in the world of FET must turn their attention.

The SOLAS legislation anticipates the need to develop a new strategic vision, purpose and direction for FET. SOLAS will be required to develop a proposed FET strategy and bring it to the Minister for Education & Skills in early course. It will also be required to develop a plan for SOLAS itself, to ensure that its role, responsibilities and deliverables are clear and agreed.

The world of FET has a myriad of programmes, courses, providers and customers of further education and training. The sector represents a very broad categorisation of learner interventions with, in my view, ill-defined parameters. This enables many activities to be classified as FET but it does not facilitate an agreed or structured approach to how the State manages its investment in this vital part of the educational firmament. This is important, because at a time of scarce resources and constantly expanding need and opportunity, we must optimise and combine the resources which are available to properly serve the people - the learners - to whom FET offers the best and sometimes only possibility to improve their lives from an educational, skills and employment perspective.

SOLAS will develop the new FET strategy for consideration by the Minister in the coming months. The expertise of the sector itself and the contributions of stakeholders such as providers, employers, the community education sector and others will be harnessed through an advisory group and consultative process. A comprehensive review of available research will be undertaken as will a consideration of best practice; both national and international.

SOLAS will be mindful of the need to explore and develop new approaches to improve FET but will not 'throw the baby out with the bathwater'. The sector already has excellent programmes and providers across the spectrum, delivering vital skills-driven, technical and vocational programmes while also addressing the very real challenges of adult literacy and numeracy and developing responses to the aims of social inclusion.

How to balance the real benefits of locally derived FET solutions to local circumstances while ensuring that national imperatives are met will be a key consideration.

One of the objectives of any new strategy must be to develop the appropriate measures of performance to inform future decisions. 'Appropriate' in this case means identifying and applying the correct assessment of performance and impact to programmes based on their specific purpose and objectives. Applying this to FET will plug a significant gap for the sector. The existing absence of a comprehensive range of measures to support an agreed strategy is, in my opinion, serving to hold the sector back from developing its full potential.

FET is sometimes described as the 'Cinderella' part of the education system. A new strategy, supported by the right measures of performance, will enable the sector to respond proactively, constantly evaluate and improve its performance and demonstrate, comprehensively, the value it provides.

Evidence based policy, supported by excellent research on (i) learner experiences and outcomes, (ii) the evolving skills needs of enterprise, (iii) the economy and the best ways to ensure social inclusion and equity, will be the hallmarks of a new approach to FET. The use of available resources must be optimised through making the right choices from the universe of FET possibilities.

To realise the opportunities that FET presents in the next five years means we must and will articulate a clear ambition for the sector. I will be supported by structured delivery plans and constant, consistent and objective evaluation, which will lead to better decision making. This can only benefit our learners, the economy and society.

Pictured at the launch of the MOMENTUM initiative (left to right): Michael Dempsey, Chairman, FÁS; Ciarán Cannon TD, Minister of State for Training and Skills; Eamon Gilmore TD, Tánaiste; Ruairí Quinn TD, Minister for Education and Skills and Paul O'Toole, Director General, FÁS.

Professionalising teaching in Further Education and Training in Ireland

Stan McHugh *Consultant in Qualifications and Quality Assurance in Education and Training*

Formal registration with the Teaching Council is required of teachers involved in Further Education

Since it was formally established in 2006, the Teaching Council has been gradually formalising the process by which teachers become recognised as "qualified professionals" in Ireland. The latest development in this regard is in respect of teaching and teachers in the Further Education Sector.

This article sets out (1) the recent evolution of the sector in Ireland, (2) the introduction of formal teaching qualifications and programmes, (3) issues arising for the sector and the key players involved.

The professionalisation of teaching in Further Education and Training

The Teaching Council was established on a statutory basis in 2006, and three years later set out the regulations that would formalise the professionalisation of teaching at Primary and Post Primary level in Ireland.

With regard to the Further Education Sector, formal registration with the Teaching Council under Regulation 5 is required of teachers involved in Further Education in "recognised schools" from the 1st of November this year.

In 2012, six programmes were accredited by the Teaching Council as professional/graduate diplomas, three at level 8 and 3 at level 9, and are being delivered since last September. Another two were accredited in May 2013, both at level 8, one of which is a concurrent degree over 4 years.

Current Issues

A number of issues are arising in the Further Education and Training Sector now that the professionalisation of teaching is being rolled out:

- The **Teaching Council's remit is currently restricted to Further Education in "recognised schools"**, which excludes many national programmes such as Youthreach and VTOS, the whole training sector and all private providers, all of whom are key players in the National Skills Strategy. Strategically, the boundaries of the Further Education Sector are being extended by the transfer of FÁS Training Centres to the control of the Education and Training Boards (formerly VEC's). This means that **the way the sector is officially defined is changing,** which in turn will have ramifications for the Department of Education and Skills and its statutory bodies with responsibilities for Quality Assurance in the sector - Quality and Qualifications Ireland (QQI) and SOLAS - and for the Teaching Council also.

As things stand, there will continue to be a **significant cohort of tutors, trainers and instructors** doing commendable work in delivering programmes at Levels 1 to 6 on the Framework **who will remain outside the remit of the Teaching Council.** They (and their learners) would benefit from being offered opportunities to further develop their professional competencies through teacher education programmes at Levels 6 and 7. These are currently available to a limited extent and in a relatively unstructured way. Could these or similar programmes be recognised as progression options to facilitate better development opportunities for this cohort and deeper implementation of the National Skills Strategy?

- To date many tutors, teachers and instructors have been **required to teach modules which have been outside their field of expertise.** Most have done so in a spirit of cooperation, and have gathered enough of the necessary knowledge skills and competence to "get by". Many have developed expertise in the new area. This approach is **not tenable into the future** from a quality perspective, and needs to be addressed by the provision of appropriate programmes to facilitate the necessary upskilling of personnel and through the Recognition of Prior Learning, if the sector is to successfully contribute to the National Skills Strategy.

- Of the eight programmes accredited by the Teaching Council to date, five are at Level 8 and three are at Level 9. Generally speaking, programmes at Level 9 develop competencies for **leadership/management roles.** In Teacher Education in FET, these roles involve mentoring and supervising student-teachers, and others cover broader roles such as programme development and evaluation, authentication and quality assurance, and overseeing the Recognition of Prior Learning procedures. There is a need in the sector for **programmes in all of these areas to be developed and accredited for experienced teachers.** The fact that programmes are at both levels 8 and 9 has shown up these issues in sharp relief, and warrant further exploration between the sector, the Teaching Council, and QQI, the body with responsibility for the National Framework of Qualifications.

- The Teaching Council has **different criteria for the recognition of qualifications for teaching in primary as opposed to post-primary schools.** These sectors cover levels 1 to 5 on the Framework. Yet in FET, which covers Levels 1 to 6, the same set of professional criteria are deemed sufficient to teach across all six levels. In practice very few if any teach at both level 1 and 6, and for good reason: the set of competencies required are very different, the former requiring high levels of pedagogical knowledge and skills, and the latter high levels of technical knowledge and skills. Is there a case to be made for developing separate programmes to match the requirements of the different levels? Could the solution be elective modules, including some in Special Education and Integrating Literacy for example, and others in advanced levels of subject expertise in areas which are particular to levels 5 and 6 in FET, such as animal grooming and the crafts?

- At the moment, if one is registered to teach in a post-primary school, one is automatically eligible to teach in FET. The corollary does not hold, however. This anomaly, while perhaps being understandable in the short run, needs to be addressed by the Teaching Council. The two sectors are very different in terms of learner age and profile, and in terms of module/subject areas. The history, structures, roles and evolution of the two sectors are quite different also, each valid in its own right. Could accredited bridging modules/programmes be at least part of the solution?

Concluding comments

As outlined above, the Further Education and Training Sector has successfully evolved from where it was in the early 1990's to centre stage today. The national and international social and economic environment has changed over that time also, and will continue to change. **The FET sector will have to change again and again** to both anticipate the future and to respond to emerging needs. In this context **it is essential that the professional competence of teachers also continues to evolve.** The issues raised here will need to be addressed by the relevant bodies and Higher Education providers if the programmes and systems put in place in recent years are to be improved further. It is in the national interest that they are.

Becoming a Teacher: my experiences on Professional Diploma in Education (FE)

Margaret Lavelle *Adult Education tutor, Ennis, Co. Clare*

I had been waiting for some time for an opportunity such as the NUIG Professional Diploma in Education, Further Education - PDE (FE)

Finally it arrived last year, and having just completed the first year of the 2-year programme, I am already looking forward to the second!

I began to teach adults in 2001 and was immediately bitten by the bug. Prior to this I was employed for 10 years in the ICT industry with various private companies. My work over the last 12 years has been very varied. I've mostly been employed by Co. Clare VEC Adult Education Services. It has involved various roles, from teaching literacy at FETAC Level 1 and 2 to co-ordinating and teaching several modules on a supervisory management programme at FETAC Level 6. I've also spent some time with NALA, the National Adult Literacy Agency, working with literacy learners on a one-to-one basis.

The learners I have met are eager to learn and grateful for the educational opportunity. They come from a wide variety of backgrounds and their journeys are an inspiration. I believe that they deserve to have the best teachers that they can get.

The group which undertook the NUIG course this year was made up of people who, like me, enjoy working in this sector. Everyone has their own experiences to share and this wealth of knowledge alone made the course worthwhile. We met for six intensive days over the academic year, we shared teaching resources, we blogged, we critiqued each other in micro-teaching and chatted over coffee in the college bar.

The course content has been very relevant to my teaching. The three main areas we studied were Teaching Practice, Psychology of Learning and Programme Design. With each subject I learned more and more about teaching and found myself constantly adjusting the way that I taught in the classroom, eager to apply and test what I had just learned.

I now understand so much more about the theory and practice of constructive alignment, formative and summative assessment, memory techniques, metacognition and the importance of reflection. Just like our NUIG group, adult learners bring a wealth of knowledge to each class and I can now appreciate the educational importance of tapping into that prior knowledge as well as making learning relevant to real life.

The journey has been a very valuable one. However there was a lot to learn, and regular assignments to complete. I haven't been the only one that has benefited - each of my learners has gained too. I feel that they have profited from the new knowledge and practices I have acquired. Their learning has also been helped by the fact that I was able to immediately apply new practices in the classroom or reflect on past experiences that I had while teaching.

I now feel that I have more of an impact on the learning in my classes. Feedback from the classes has been excellent - I am now much better at giving feedback, and so are they! And, YES, it has made my work easier and more fulfilling!

National Learning Network
Investing in People, Changing Perspectives

Kick-Starting Careers with

National Learning Network has a wide range of training and further education courses that can open the door to exciting new careers and employment opportunities. From business and computer skills through to graphic design, art, sport and recreation studies, National Learning Network has something for everyone.

So, whether a person has just left school or wants to return to education or the workforce following an illness or a set-back in life, National Learning Network can help them gain the qualifications and experience they need to kick-start their career.

Our success rate speaks for itself. In 2012, over 90 per cent of those who have completed our programmes moved on to employment or to further education and training.

Entry Requirements

National Learning Network specialises in providing training and further education to students who may require additional supports due to health conditions or difficult life circumstances.

Our training is individualised to meet each student's own abilities, talents, needs, goals and career plans. There are no fees or formal entry requirements for our courses– which have a continuous intake – but participants must be aged over 16 years.

Want to find out more?
Call us today on 1890 283 000 or visit www.nln.ie

Sandra's Story

Sandra Morrissey is a former student with National Learning Network in Tralee.

"My life has changed so much in the past five years. Today, I live in Cork city, where I study jewellery design. I'm really enjoying my life. Cork is such a vibrant city and I really love what I do. However, just five years ago, things were very different.

Back in 2008, I was in a very, very bad place. I had come from a troubled family background and I suffered from depression and severe anxiety. It had reached a point in my life where I didn't know who I was. I was really just existing; I certainly wasn't living.

Focus Programme

It was at this time that I heard about National Learning Network's Focus programme in Tralee. The Focus programme is specially designed for people who have experienced mental health difficulties. It provides students with the skills and confidence they need to gain greater independence, to plan further education and employment and to integrate more fully with their local community. It took a lot of courage, but I decided to enrol in the programme and it was one of the best decisions I ever made.

When I first started the Focus programme, I was quite simply terrified. But I knew that it was a place where I needed to be, so I stuck with it. It was such a warm, nurturing and non-judgmental environment that I soon learned to relax.

Throughout my time at National Learning Network, the team respected me and they challenged me, but I never felt under any pressure and I never felt like I was on my own. I didn't only receive support from the staff, all of the participants on the programme had their own personal battles and difficulties, but we were there for each other. I made friends for life on the Focus programme.

Exploring Career Opportunities

After a year on the Focus programme, I moved on to National Learning Network's Introductory Skills Training (IST) programme. In addition to developing my computer and presentation skills, IST enabled me to explore different career opportunities based on my own needs and strengths. I've always been creative and I love working with my hands, so I guess that jewellery design is the perfect choice for me!"

For more information on National Learning Network

A local perspective on the changing nature of Adult & FE Provision

Joe Cunningham, *Adult Education Officer, Laois & Offaly ETB*

The system is far from perfect but is moving in the right direction

The provision of relevant adult education programmes and services is more important than ever before in meeting the needs of those wishing to return to education to develop and update their skillsets. While the Education & Training Boards are ideally placed to meet these needs, there are many challenges for both student and provider.

A local perspective

Laois & Offaly ETB provide an integrated adult education service with progression opportunities for all students with due regard for their aptitudes, goals, and abilities. A key strength of our provision is the delivery and development of **core, transferrable skills** among students in the areas of communications, personal and interpersonal skills, and information & communications technologies, regardless of the chosen field of study.

These skills leave students best placed to adapt to changing work practices and shifts in employer requirements. We are also conscious, however, of the role of education as a mechanism for **personal growth** and as a method of **improving the self-esteem and ability of students** to better engage with the challenges and opportunities they encounter in life.

Progression routes exist from part-time to full-time programmes and our adult education guidance service, in conjunction with centre managers, works hard to ensure students can progress effectively between the varying education options available within the ETB as well as progressing into higher level courses where appropriate. To this end, we have developed **links with a number of Institutes of Technology** to facilitate progression to their programmes whereby students gain maximum exemptions for their chosen course based on their subject choice and results. In addition, we have recently been chosen by Limerick Institute of Technology (Limerick School of Art & Design) as an **Outreach Centre** for the delivery of their degree programme at Abbeyleix Further Education Centre. This will provide access to a degree course for students who otherwise would not be in a position to enrol for personal and financial reasons.

We work hard at **aligning our provision with the skill needs of enterprise** and are cognisant of FORFÁS research and the reports generated by the Expert Group on Future Skill Needs. As a result, our provision of the Science, Technology, Engineering, and Maths subjects has increased significantly.

The move to the Common Award System has been challenging for all FETAC providers, particularly delivering programmes that included existing modules and new components during the transition phase. As a group, the ETBs worked well together in writing, evaluating, and validating the new programmes at Levels 3-6. **Cross-moderation and continuous**

evaluation will be important going forward to ensure consistency in programme delivery and assessment.

The legislation giving effect to the new **Education and Training Boards** came into effect on 1 July and with it brings challenges and opportunities in equal measure. Along with the merging of administrative functions, the challenge of developing an integrated adult and further education service across two or, in some cases, three counties must be met head-on to ensure the best possible service to the communities we serve as a statutory provider.

The forthcoming legislation creating **SOLAS will give further education a clear identity and direction** but will also bring with it enormous challenges for Education and Training Boards in managing the Training Services section of the soon-to-be disbanded FÁS and providing a seamless transition for those enrolled on training programmes. There is no doubt that the funding model for the sector will change significantly in the coming years; something that is to be welcomed in the hope that we can move away from the 'silo' effect of individual programme budgets to a **multi-year allocation model** that identifies key targets and outcomes in response to both local and national needs.

The **public sector moratorium** has also adversely affected the sector; the **non-replacement of caretakers and administrative staff** in particular has put a huge strain on our ability to deliver a professional service. The use of work placements and internships, through the **TÚS programme and JobBridge** respectively, has certainly helped. However, the time invested by Centre Managers in constantly training and mentoring new staff is significant; time that should ideally be devoted to managing and developing education provision. In many cases the only recourse is to recruit staff through employment agencies and this has to be funded from a reducing non-pay budget, therefore compounding the problem.

Our **Adult Education Centres** have also seen The role of our Guidance and Information Service is key to ensuring that prospective students are placed on the programme or course that best meets their needs; the numbers accessing the service is increasing year on year. Having the necessary information, advice, and guidance available to support students in their decision-making is crucial, particularly in relation to progression options and career paths.

The need for personal counselling has increased dramatically in recent times. The recession has resulted in enormous financial and social pressures on those wishing to return to education and many students simply cannot cope with the pressures of combining and managing the home, personal, and educational challenges they are facing.

The **costs** associated with returning to education are preventing many prospective students from enrolling on courses and the perceived lack of consistency in financial supports and allowances across the further and higher education sectors is frustrating for both student and provider. Changes and cutbacks to grant income thresholds, childcare provision, and the cost of education allowance have a very real impact on the ability of prospective students to commit to education, even on a part-time basis. While there may be a case for reducing or removing a specific benefit or allowance on an individual basis, when viewed collectively **the policy changes remove the incentives and supports necessary to participate in education.**

The system is far from perfect but is **moving in the right direction.** The dedication of staff working in adult and further education is second to none and watching students grow in confidence and self-esteem as they progress in education is a reward in itself. While there are many challenges ahead, **an integrated approach** to the provision of both programmes and education supports will see the sector continue to deliver an effective service and contribute to the educational, economic, and social needs of society.

Digital Literacies for Life

Paul Gormley, *eLearning facilitator at NUI Galway and Chair of the Irish Learning Technology Association (ILTA)*

We all need to develop the skills and competencies to fully participate in an increasingly networked society

Education at all levels faces great opportunities and challenges in the face of rapid change. Some commentators have characterised this period as 'fruitful turbulence' in education as digital technologies create new social, cultural and collaborative learning opportunities.

Rapid change calls for new capabilities. These capabilities are increasingly referred to as 'Digital Literacies' which the European Union describes as *'the confident and critical use of ICT for work, leisure, learning and communication'*.

Why are digital literacies important?
In the 21st Century we all need to develop the skills and competencies to fully participate in an increasingly networked society, and to cope with rapid changes in work, education, family life and society in general. The changing nature of the workplace means that growing numbers of graduates are increasingly being employed in digital industries or professions that require them to be digitally literate.

Education has a huge role to play in supporting and driving the digital literacy agenda forward. As Minister for Education and Skills Quinn commented on May 30 2013 *'...the educational system must respond to national priorities in a coherent way to provide graduates with the skills and qualifications that are essential for Ireland's society and economic well-being'*.
How can education address this need?
First of all, we need to have an evidence-base to understand the future educational landscape. The Government projects that the **post-primary student population will increase at the following rate:**
2013: 170,000
2015: 181,000
2027: 208,000

The **demographic composition** of these students and how they access education will also change during this time. At present, the majority (79%) of full-time students in the Irish higher education system are recent school-leavers and aged 17 to 20 years of age. The Department of Education and Skills' lifelong learning supports for flexible learning has seen an increase of total undergraduate participation on part-time programmes from 7% in 2008 to 17% in 2013. Students can now access many courses online from anywhere in the world and at times that suit their increasingly busy lifestyles, and this trend is set to continue.

Secondly, we need to know **what is happening in the institutions where lifelong learning is occurring.** The Irish Learning Technology Association (ilta.ie) recently commissioned the '2013 Technology-Enhanced Learning Survey', Ireland's first nation-wide survey of Universities and Institutes of Technologies to provide a national snapshot of the lifelong learning digital literacies landscape.

The high-level findings of the survey shows **a rich diversity of supports** available to our students with all institutions employing virtual learning environments (e.g. Blackboard, Moodle, Sakai) which allow 24 x 7 access to learning content, and administrative information.

In a dynamically changing technological landscape, new learning technologies are being used within and outside of virtual learning environments (VLEs) to provide exciting opportunities for student communication and collaboration, student-generated multimedia content, and real-time live access to blended and distance learning courses through live online meeting rooms.

Which learning technologies are institutions currently supporting?

The 2013 survey shows the top three learning technologies in institutions were related to **assessment-based tasks** such as plagiarism detection (100%), online assessment submissions (82%) and online quizzes (82%). This was followed by leaning technologies that supported student-centred **collaborative activities**: lecture capture (53%), video and Web 2.0 communication and collaboration tools such as wikis (53%), online document sharing (47%), blogs (41%), and podcasting (41%).

Which learning technologies are students currently using in their learning?

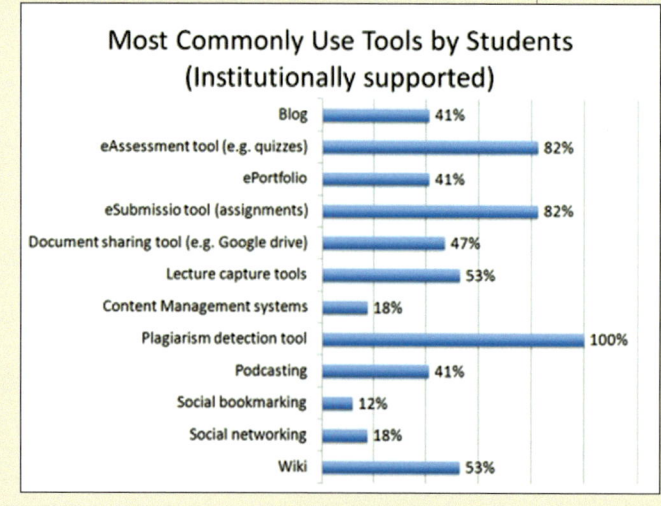

Most Commonly Use Tools by Students (Not Institutionally Supported)

- Blog: 65%
- eAssessment tool (e.g. quizzes): 24%
- ePortfolio: 12%
- Submission tools (assignments): 6%
- Document sharing tool (e.g. Google...): 71%
- Lecture capture tools: 29%
- Content Management systems: 0%
- Plagiarism detection tool: 0%
- Podcasting: 29%
- Social bookmarking: 29%
- Social networking: 53%
- Wiki: 29%

Most Commonly Use Tools by Students (Institutionally supported)

- Blog: 41%
- eAssessment tool (e.g. quizzes): 82%
- ePortfolio: 41%
- eSubmissio tool (assignments): 82%
- Document sharing tool (e.g. Google drive): 47%
- Lecture capture tools: 53%
- Content Management systems: 18%
- Plagiarism detection tool: 100%
- Podcasting: 41%
- Social bookmarking: 12%
- Social networking: 18%
- Wiki: 53%

The 2013 survey findings document **sharing** as the most popular learning technology tool (65%) followed by blogs (65%), social networking tools (53%) followed by a number of Web 2.0 web-based collaborative tools such as blogs, wikis, podcasting and social bookmarking.

Looking to the future

So how will this snapshot change when the survey will run again in 2015 and beyond? What technologies will institutions and students be using in 10 years time? This is very difficult to predict. After all, it's incredible to think that YouTube was launched as recently as 2005. However, what we CAN say with certainty is that the next 10 years will see rapid change, with new technologies replacing current ones, and an increasingly complex work, education and social landscape that we must all negotiate.

Therefore the digital literacies we promote today must equip us to cope and take advantage of these changes. This is an exciting challenge. We must develop a suite of capabilities that can be applied to a range of diverse contexts that we cannot envisage today. These capabilities must be developed and supported by the Government, business, community groups, educational institutions, teachers and learners together. Why? Because we are ALL lifelong learners.

Access and Widening Participation in Higher Education in Ireland

Ann O'Brien, *Director of Access, NUI Maynooth, (retired)*

Imelda Byrne, *Access Officer, NUI Galway*

The aim must be to create groups of educational achievers to act as role models in the community

From 1970 - 1990 Ireland experienced one of the fastest growth rates in higher education in Europe. The student numbers expanded from less than 20,000 to over 80,000 and the higher education institutions increased to more than 30. This educational expansion has continued to the current time with 196187 enrolments in higher education institutions in Ireland.

A number of policy documents in the early 1990s, including the Green Paper, Education for a Changing World (1992), heralded the need to improve participation in higher education by under-represented groups.

In 2001 the Report of the Action Group on Access to Third Level Education took account of developments and made recommendations with regard to students from socio-economically disadvantaged backgrounds, mature students and students with a disability. The Action Group made a total of 78 recommendations and also highlighted that there is a democratic, social, and economic imperative to widen access to higher education. The key recommendation of the 78 with regard to students from socio-economically disadvantaged backgrounds was to:

set up a National Office for Equity of Access to Higher Education to "…draw up policy proposals and to over see the implementation of the National Programme…"
The National Office for Equity of Access to Higher Education was established in August 2003. Since then the office has established an Advisory Group, produced a number of Action Plans, set targets for under represented groups and introduced a new funding model linked to student numbers from under represented groups.

Statistical research undertaken by Prof. Patrick Clancy has focused on an analysis of the student body in various colleges (Clancy: 1982, 1988, 1995, 1998, 2001). His research reiterated continually large differences between socio-economic groups in levels of participation in higher education.

The overall rate of admission to higher education in Ireland has risen from 20% in 1980 to 44% in 1998. Likewise most social groups experienced a progressive increase in the proportion moving on to higher education. It is clear that while all groups have increased participation rates since 1980 those in the lower socio-economic groups continue to be 'under-represented' in higher education.

Currently the profile of new entrants to higher education nationally among the targeted groups continues to grow; 21% socio-economic target groups, 15% mature and 6% with a disability

Third level Initiatives
The third level response was to appoint Access Officers with responsibility for access and equity issues. Particular groups are targeted: socio-economically disadvantaged school leavers, mature students, students with a disability

and those from the travelling and refugee communities. Most universities introduced access initiatives featuring the creation of links with designated disadvantaged schools that operate a range of activities to familiarise school students with higher education and raise aspirations. These include school visits on campus, tuition by university personnel or students, language days and the opportunity to experience the college experience with shadowing days. The development of special entry mechanisms such as The Higher Education Access Route (HEAR) and the Disability Access Route to Education (DARE) offers socio-economically disadvantaged and disability school leavers a direct entry route to the participating institutions. Mature student entry is also offered to those over 23 and first time entrants to higher education.

Comprehensive post-entry supports for these students have been developed to sustain them in their academic career. Some universities developed pre-entry access courses targeting both socio-economically disadvantaged students and mature students. Community Based Initiatives have also been established with the specific intention of attempting to have an educational impact on severely marginalised communities. The aim is to create a small yet increasing critical group of educational achievers to act as role models in the community and to build links between communities and higher education.

HEAR and DARE are national admissions programmes for under represented school leaver groups. The schemes have identified indicators of educational disadvantage experienced by applicants as a result of socio-economic status or disability. In the case of HEAR these indicators are independently verified and a rigorous process of screening applicants is undertaken. An Advisory Group for each indicator monitors and advises on issues related to the specific indicator and a quality assurance process is also in place. Likewise each DARE indicator is supported by an Advisory Group with skilled professionals. These expert groups contribute to the robustness of the indicators and the independence and transparency of the scheme.

The Access/Foundation courses have adapted the HEAR and DARE indicators to establish the eligibility of applicants. Currently the HEAR/DARE scheme is undergoing an independent evaluation

Issues
The numbers enrolled at HE from these under-represented groups form the basis for competitive allocation of all HEA Access Budgets and SAF (Student Assistance Fund) allocation since 2011. They are also a category in all HEI's Strategic Plans for which targets of over 20% of First Year Entrants have been set. More recently strategic dialogue relating to the National Strategy for Higher Education up to 2030 includes Access and Engagement as two domains to be incorporated in performance measurement of Higher Education institutions by the HEA.

However the Employment Control Framework and changes in the funding allocation model means that the capacity to service the level and diversity of programmes, student numbers and general demands for educational support services is exceeding its limit. More significantly the recent shift in policy direction of the National Office for Equity of Access to Higher Education from its original mandate of widening participation for under represented groups to labour market intervention administration, i.e. Springboard, is a cause for serious concern. At a time when strong support and advocacy for the under represented and vulnerable groups is most needed the resources of the office are directed to the vast administration of the Springboard programme.

The Social Dimension strand of the Bologna process requires higher education in member states to maintain Widening Participation as a key strategic objective.

In Ireland, in the absence of an environment which is responsive to the developmental needs and resources necessary to ensure growth and innovation, the Widening Participation agenda at higher education may find itself with no option but to reduce the number and range of programmes, student intake and new initiatives.

RPL and Professional Development in the FE sector

Dr Cathal de Paor, *Director of CPD, Faculty of Education, Mary Immaculate College Limerick*

Recognition of Prior Learning (RPL) takes account of the full range of an individual's knowledge, skills and competences

The **recognition of prior learning (RPL)** is now a major priority in the education and training sector in the European Union, with member states being urged to establish national systems by 2018 (European Commission, 2012). This reflects the increasing importance of the full range of an individual's knowledge, skills and competences – those acquired not only at school, university or other education and training institution, but also outside the formal system. There are also calls for greater use of the **recognition of prior certified learning.**

In Ireland, any individual has the right to apply for RPL for access, credit and/or exemptions in his/her education and training. The Qualifications (Education and Training) Act 1999 established **a firm legislative base for RPL,** and this was followed by the NQAI principles and guidelines (NQAI, 2005). However, the level of RPL activity can **vary widely between education providers,** in further education (EGFSN, 2011), as well as in higher education (FIN, 2011). Much work needs to be done in developing the use of RPL and this requires the involvement of a range of stakeholders, including providers, learners, qualification experts, and employers. In the case of programmes leading to professional qualifications, the relevant professional body will also have a role.

An example of such a professional qualification is that required for teaching in the Further Education sector. The year 2013 has been significant for this profession, given the introduction from 1 April of **a requirement for teachers wishing to register in this sector to have a Teaching Council approved teaching qualification** as well as other degree requirements (Teaching Council, 2009). These requirements stipulate that applicants should have either (1) a Level 8 degree or else (2) an ordinary degree (Level 7), together with an appropriate additional qualification or certified accreditation of prior learning. Such prior learning must be based on relevant experience in a workplace or instructional setting.

The inclusion of the RPL provision in the second option reflects the fact that, **given the vocational nature of many programmes in further education,** somebody aspiring to become a teacher in this sector may have relevant prior learning, which could be presented in conjunction with the Level 7 degree. One implication arising out of this is the need for **providers of FE teaching qualifications** in higher education institutions to **develop expertise in processing applications from such candidates.**

This provided a major part of the rationale for **the launch of a European project on RPL in Mary Immaculate College in January 2012.**

RiPLVET, *Recognition of prior learning in vocational education and training,* was **a**

Leonardo da Vinci partnership funded under the European Lifelong Learning Programme, and designed as a way of finding out more about the policy and practice of RPL in the professional development of practitioners for the further education and training sector in various European countries (www.riplvet.eu). The participating institutions were Mary Immaculate College (co-ordinator); City of Limerick Vocational Education Committee; University of Stirling, Oslo; Akershus University College of Applied Sciences, FLORIFORM-Formation Fleuriste, France; Gazi University, Turkey.

Therefore, the consortium represented both **providers of teacher education programmes,** as well as **providers of further education and training.**

The project examined the use of RPL across a range of roles in further education and training, including **teachers, trainers, and instructors in both state and private sector provision.** It also took place at a time of great change more generally in the sector here in Ireland, e.g. the establishment of a new Further Education and Training Authority, SOLAS *(Seirbhísí Oideachais Leanúnaigh agus Scileanna)*, and the lead-up to the establishment of 16 new education and training boards (ETBs).

A key finding from the project was that practice with regard to the use of RPL in the professional development of practitioners for the further education and training sector **varied greatly.** Secondly, while the RIPLVET project focused on just one specific domain, (staff development for the FE sector), it was clear that many of the issues and practices encountered were **relevant for other sectors and professional areas.**

Of particular interest was the **approach used in France,** which, in 2013 marked the tenth anniversary of its introduction of a national system of RPL across all education and training. Two separate routes can be distinguished.

The first, VAPP *(validation des acquis professionnels et personnels)* is for candidates wishing to **gain entry to a programme on the basis of their own personal and professional experience.** A second route enables candidates to obtain part, or all of an award, using one of two options. They may apply on the basis of their experiential learning *(Validation des acquis de l'expérience)*, in a process involving the support of a mentor, portfolio preparation, and interview with an independent jury. Or, the **second option is the recognition of prior certified learning.**

As stated, RPL is now a**n issue of major importance** in education and training in Ireland as well as in Europe. In accordance with the Qualifications and Quality Assurance (Education and Training) Act (2012), the newly-established Quality and Qualifications Ireland (QQI) has responsibility for addressing RPL as part of its work on Access, Transfer and Progression (ATP). Under the Act, **learners may also apply to QQI for awards where they meet established standards.**

QQI is currently engaged in consultation with stakeholders on a Green Paper on RPL, where it has highlighted various priorities, including the establishment of a comprehensive system of national reporting (QQI, 2013). Such a system will serve an important quality assurance function, and together with the other measures proposed can assist greatly in the development of a national system of RPL, one that enjoys the confidence and trust of all concerned.

The work recently commenced by QQI will be crucial in building capacity and in achieving progress in the use of RPL in all education and training. Alongside the national and European developments outlined above, small-scale projects such as RIPLVET can be a valuable way of learning about practice in other countries for specific domains, in this case, **staff development in the further education and training sector.** Such knowledge-sharing is very useful in a context of increasing co-operation and coordination across national boundaries, and at a time where similar European-wide challenges are being encountered.

WHO'S WHO

The WHO'S WHO Profile introduces people who are making an important contribution to education in Ireland today.

Meet Professor Michael A Hayes

POSITION: President, Mary Immaculate College, Limerick

Where did you grow up?
In Limerick.

What is your earliest childhood memory?
My parents and my twin sister.

How many siblings have you?
Six - one brother and five sisters (including two sets of twins!).

Where did you go to school/college?
St Munchin's College, Limerick; St Patrick's College, Maynooth; The London Institute of Psychosynthesis, University of London, University of Surrey.

To what extent did your education shape who you are today?
My own educational experience and in particular those who taught me and those with whom I studied in various institutions have had a profound effect on how I both see the world and how I am in the world.

What attracted you to work in teacher education?
I see education as a prime vehicle for personal growth and social cohesion. I see human flourishment as supported by education.

In what way do you consider yourself well suited to your current position?
I bring a rich international experience to my role as President which includes a strong grasp of strategic planning in the context of education and an understanding that students are at the centre of the educational enterprise and that policy develops from there. I have also held senior positions elsewhere in Higher Education.

What are the main responsibilities/ challenges of your job?
As President I am the CEO of the organisation and so it is my responsibility to ensure that the College's strategic plan is carried out. In the context of a changing landscape in Higher Education in Ireland, there are many challenges which include financial constraints in the current national fiscal environment as well as ensuring that the College meets the requirements outlined by the Higher Education Authority and the specific requirements set out for our teacher education programmes by The Teaching Council of Ireland.

How do you view the changes in initial teacher education and teaching practice?
All our education programmes are validated through our validating university and are designed to meet the requirements of The Teaching Council. In the last twelve months our programmes have been accredited by The Teaching Council. This means that these programmes will enable our graduates to enter the teaching profession with state of the art qualifications designed to meet the current needs of education in Ireland.

What impact will the professionalization of Further Education and Early Childhood teachers have on their respective sectors?
We have programmes designed for those who work in both these sectors and are committed with colleagues who work in these sectors to support the growing and important professionalization that is taking place. It is important that all who work in Further Education and Early Childhood settings are fit for purpose.

How important is Continuing Professional Development?
The health of any profession requires that those engaged professionally embrace life-long learning. Mary Immaculate College is committed to supporting teachers through various media – including blended learning approaches – in their continuing professional development.

What place has research in education?
All good teaching should be underpinned by relevant research. Mary Immaculate College is a teaching led institution underpinned by active researchers.

What does a typical workday involve for you?
Much of my day is packed by meetings of various kinds, from chairing meetings to meeting individual members of staff. I also do a lot of ambassadorial work on behalf of the College which includes welcoming visitors and going to external meetings.

What do you enjoy most about your work?
The people that I work with, my colleagues, and when I get the opportunity to engage with students.

What do you enjoy least about your work?
The pace of change.

What would you most like to change?
All institutions require processes of accountability and proper engagement in such processes is beneficial to the institution and to the public purse which funds the institution. However, at times some external requirements can appear constrictive to the work of an institution. I would change some of the external pressures and let the institution get on with its work.

Are you a workaholic?
Some might say that!

What do you do to relax?
I cook and I travel (when I can)

Do you like living in Limerick?
After 31 years out of Ireland and living in London, Limerick is a very different place but I have found nothing but welcome and support. Limerick, although small, has a rich history and a vibrant spirited people.

Are you married?
No

What plans have you for the future?
To do my job to the best of my ability

Have you a message for teacher educators?
Yours is a noble profession. Find time to remind yourself of what was your original motivation to enter the profession.

Have you a message for student teachers?
You are entering a wonderful profession and you will have the opportunity to change lives.

Have you a message for policy makers?
Always conduct a full impact assessment before any policy is implemented.

Afterword by Minister for Education & Skills Ruairí Quinn T.D.

Extract from Address by Minister for Education and Skills Ruairí Quinn at the MacGill Summer School on August 1, 2013

"Building one of the best education systems in the world, and accessible to all, is crucial"

Educators
If the curriculum must continue to adapt, to better prepare our young people to participate in the social, economic and cultural spheres of our society, then the same is true of those delivering the curriculum.

This is another area where considerable reforms are underway at present. The existing 19 teacher training centres have moved to become 6 centres of education. The centres will have the size and capacity to ensure that all of our teachers are trained to the very highest standards. And to ensure that we are constantly exploring and researching our education system – prodding it and poking it to find ways to improve it.

We have lengthened, by a year, the amount of time it takes to qualify as a school teacher – at primary and post-primary levels. That additional time will focus on developing the pedagogical skills of our teachers. Our educators must be instilled with the capacity to facilitate learning at all levels of our system.

From this year, it will be compulsory for all teachers to be registered with the Teaching Council. This will allow increasing professional standards to be set, and regulated.

Considerable reform is underway. So why are we making these changes?
As with the curriculum, we must be more ambitious in looking further into the future. We know that the quality of a teacher, more than any other factor, transforms and improves the educational outcomes for our children. But developing methods of communications are changing the relationship between educators and learners.

The experiences of all of our children, and particularly those with special needs, are being transformed by these changes. Just as mobile phones and computers have become ubiquitous over the last 20 years, the next 20 will see further transformations.

Even looking back 5 years, who would have predicted the rapid shift from desktop and laptop computers, to mobile and tablet device domination. With Google glasses and Apple watches currently being talked about, it is safe to assume that we have little idea what the technologies of the 2030s will look like.

It seems equally safe to assume that these technologies will certainly be used by us regularly, if not even embedded within us. In such an exciting context, it frustrates me that we remain in patterns of the past, simply seeking to replicate in our classrooms what is already being disregarded in our workplaces.

We must develop the abilities of our educators to adapt, to experiment, and to embrace all modes of communication to inspire and connect with our young people. Schools and colleges must be more accountable – to their communities, rather than to the Department.

And a culture of self-reflection, and continuing improvement, must be fostered in each classroom. If continuously improving the quality of our educators is our aim, then we must also explore how to make the profession increasingly attractive. In the past, a conservative system of promotions developed, where teachers were appointed to posts of responsibility. Some contained no additional responsibility, most were simply filled by the longest serving teachers in the schools.

In 20 years' time, we need to have developed a system where teachers are promoted to management positions that involve genuine responsibilities. Their promotion should be based on the quality of their work, and their capacity and ambition to become leaders.

The creation last month of 16 local Education and Training Boards, to replace 33 VECs, allows us to develop better management and support structures than we currently have in place. Over time, I expect the Education and Training Boards will take on a greater role in areas like HR, technical support, or the management of capital projects.

This will leave school leaders free to focus on the management of teaching and learning in their schools – becoming leaders of education instead of administrators.

Infrastructure
I've spoken little of the future of further and higher education in Ireland. When considering the infrastructure of the future, both elements are essential. The creation of SOLAS, to oversee the 16 new Education and Training Boards, will be completed later this year.

Replacing FÁS and the 33 VECs.
And providing us with an opportunity to completely rebuild the further education and training sector. Reinventing apprenticeships that will give first-class opportunities to students.

And ensuring that further education and training is a realistic, relevant offering that will provide people with opportunities to learn throughout their lives.

The Irish University and Technological sectors will also transform over the coming years. They have already begun to explore and embrace the reconfiguration of the third level landscape which I have published this year.

The creation of college clusters will ensure that unnecessary duplication and inefficiencies can be driven out of the system. And the prospect of Technological Universities will help reinforce the structural links between enterprise and the technological sector.

These structural changes in further and higher education will be firmly embedded, over the course of the next two decades. And more will need to be done to overhaul the student experience. To make sure that these sectors, as well as delivering for our economy, deliver for their students.

The trends towards part-time study, online courses, and life-long learning, will no doubt persist. We are continuing to invest in the construction of new schools and colleges, despite our economic difficulties. During the lifetime of this Government, that investment will amount to considerably more than €2bn. All around the country, prefabs are being replaced with permanent classrooms – the rental bill for prefabs has been cut in half since I first raised concerns about this issue. And the quality of our new school buildings always amazes me.

For those of you without young children, it is difficult to describe how different many of our schools are to those that we remember from our own time. Wide corridors where children's artwork is proudly displayed, bright, airy classrooms with groups of young people working collaboratively, whiteboards, computers and tablets - these are all common features of the new schools we construct.

Two years ago, we held a design competition for post-primary schools, and three of the winning designs will be constructed. New designs which completely reimagine how the physical building of a school can influence the learning inside that school.

Already, in our newer schools, I have seen wonderful examples of shared sporting facilities – used by children during that day, and by the whole community outside of school hours, throughout the week. And we are currently running an ideas competition for primary schools.

So that, without having to design a complete school, we can access the ideas and the energy of Irish architects – harnessing their talents to explore how we can build schools that become centres of fun and learning in the lives of our children.

But the future could be even more exciting. Will we need, in 20 years' time, children to gather in one physical building in order to receive their education? Even if we do, will they need to be separated into classrooms, or could new models emerge.

We all now assume open plan offices to be the norm in workplaces, but as we speak, that model is changing in many companies. In offices such as Google's, we can see the creation of discrete spaces for different purposes, stimulating the energies and the ideas of all those who work there.

I have no doubt that even more interesting 'spaces' will exist in our schools and colleges in 20 years. Regardless of the structure of the buildings, surely we can see a future where these facilities are genuine community resources.

Spaces where parental involvement in education is encouraged.
Where all of the community gather for celebrations of sport, music and the arts.
Where parents and the wider community can educate, and be educated by, our children.
Much more than buildings - beating hearts for our communities – filled with life, love and learning.

Conclusion
Children entering pre-school this year will mostly leave school in 2028. With reshaped opportunities in further and higher education, most of them will leave full-time education between 2029 and 2032. There is little time to prepare them for the dramatically changed environment into which they will enter. We can't afford to waste any of it.

www.education.ie/en/Press-Events/Speeches/2013-Speeches/SP13-08-01.html#sthash.MChcZjbO.dpuf

Index

A
access *5, 7, 10, 11, 41, 54, 71, 75, 76, 92, 105, 108, 109, 110, 111, 112, 116, 133, 144, 152, 156, 157, 158, 161, 162, 169, 178, 185, 193, 198, 212, 218, 223, 224, 231, 233, 234, 235, 236, 237, 238, 243*
Adoption Authority of Ireland *17, 46*
After School Scheme *11*
Aistear *16, 17, 18, 19, 31, 33, 35, 36, 37, 44*
allowances *50, 51, 63, 65, 69, 121, 144, 165, 168, 235, 246*
An Comhairle um Oideachas Gaeltachta agus Gaelscolaíochta (COGG) *83, 117, 118*
anti-bullying *54, 76, 90, 91, 92, 124, 146*
assessment *4, 18, 36, 37, 61, 66, 97, 98, 99, 100, 101, 103, 106, 107, 108, 109, 110, 114, 132, 166, 167, 196, 197, 206, 210, 235, 240, 243, 246, 248, 254*
Association of Childhood Professionals (ACP) *39*
Association of Management of Catholic Secondary Schools *83, 120*
Association of Secondary Teachers, Ireland (ASTI) *9, 69, 104, 108, 121, 133, 136, 137, 140, 141, 142, 143, 145, 149, 151, 187, 204*
Association of Trustees of Catholic Schools *120*
Atlantic Philanthropies *18, 150*
austerity *50, 93, 186, 232, 233, 234, 235*
'A 2020 Vision for Education' *82, 136, 137*

B
ballot *9, 51, 52, 121, 133, 136, 137, 140, 141, 144, 145, 186, 204*
Barnardos *4, 15, 16, 139*
Boards of Management *iii, iv, 52, 62, 120, 122*
Boland, Tom *144, 145, 146*
Breslin, Gerry *55*
Broderick, John *144, 196*
Brown, Margaret *2, 19, 20*
Browne, Carmel *35, 66*
Browne, Professor James J. *vii, 145, 152*
budget *3, 9, 21, 30, 38, 42, 63, 66, 70, 104, 105, 112, 134, 147, 172, 172, 184, 185, 213, 226, 234, 237, 246*
bullying *10, 54, 75, 76, 90, 91, 92, 124, 146, 148, 173*
Byrne, Clive *82, 83, 88, 103, 137*
Byrne, Imelda *219, 235*

C
Cannon, Ciarán *115, 116, 226*
Catholic Schools Partnership *54, 58, 74, 120*
Childcare Education Training Support (CETS) *10, 11*
child protection *3, 32, 51*
Children's Referendum *3, 7, 9, 12, 13*
Children's Research Network *17, 18*
Chinese *101, 112, 129, 130, 190, 190, 191, 191*
Church of Ireland College of Education *41, 45, 166*
civic engagement *149, 199*
Coláiste Chiaráin *83, 96, 97, 98*
Coláiste na Coiribe *vi, 83, 104*
Community Childcare Subvention (CCS) *10, 11*
Computers in Education Society of Ireland (CESI) *109*
Confucius Institute of Ireland *115, 116*
continuing professional development (CPD) *3, 17, 39, 60, 61, 62, 106, 107, 108, 122, 124, 125, 156, 158, 196, 197, 233, 251*
continuum of teacher education *44, 46, 78, 188, 189*
contract *24, 25, 36, 50, 128, 173*
Cork Institute of Technology *xi, 41, 166, 189*
Council of Europe *113, 114*
Craughwell, Gerry *55*
crèches *8, 24, 34, 35, 37, 38, 41, 43*
Croke Park Agreement *50, 51, 75, 133, 141, 184, 186*
Croke Park II *8, 51, 121, 136, 136, 137, 140, 141*
Crowley O'Sullivan, Joan *82, 141*
Cummins, Denis *144, 145, 164*
Cunningham, Joe *218, 231*
cutbacks *9, 54, 65, 75, 121, 133, 147, 234, 246*
cyberbullying *48, 49, 90, 91*

D
Daly, Dr Mary *2, 22, 23*
debt *171, 213*
DEIS *101, 102, 103, 157*
denominational *59, 72, 79, 88, 134*
de Paor, Dr Cathal *218, 219, 237*
Department of Children and Youth Affairs (DCYA) *5, 9, 10, 18*
Department of Education and Skills *18, 25, 43, 54, 58, 60, 66, 70, 71, 73, 74, 75, 76, 92, 97, 100, 106, 114, 117, 122, 123, 124, 132, 135, 143, 146, 151, 155, 161, 205, 221, 228, 234, 241, 247*
Department of Social Protection *11, 38, 162, 224*
digital literacies *218, 219, 233, 234*
digital tools *110*
disadvantage *31, 32, 165, 236*
Drumm, Fr Michael *54, 58, 63, 74*
Dublin City University (DCU) *59, 165, 178, 185, 188, 192*
Dublin Institute of Technology *xi, 162, 197*
Dublin VEC *192, 193*
Dundalk Institute of Technology *164*
Dún Laoghaire Institute of Art, Design and Technology (IADT) *xi*

E
Early Childhood Ireland (ECI) *6, 17, 18, 23, 28, 30, 33, 34, 35, 36, 37, 38, 41, 43, 44, 45*
Early Childhood Care and Education (ECCE) *16, 21, 22, 24, 31, 37, 38, 39*
Economic and Social Research Institute (ESRI) *32, 42, 55, 72, 123, 161, 169, 172*
Edco *119, 126*
Educate Together *59, 68, 72, 73, 77, 78, 130*

Education and Training Boards *5, 13, 176, 233, 235, 236, 237, 241, 246, 252, 256*
Education at a Glance *5*
education centre *20, 60, 61, 62, 97, 107, 129, 130, 138, 203, 245*
Enterprise Ireland (EI) *13, 176, 177, 221, 226*
equality *56, 65, 76, 77, 78, 80, 115, 120, 158, 170*
Erasmus *147, 168, 171*
EU Kids Online *76, 77*
European Commission *150, 179, 182, 237*
European Universities Association (EUA) *179*
evaluation *3, 31, 32, 33, 48, 61, 65, 74, 75, 96, 97, 103, 109, 114, 115, 116, 117, 118, 122, 175, 233, 235, 240, 242, 246, 250*
exam *102, 103, 105, 108, 109, 119, 124, 132, 144, 154, 170, 207*

F

family *23, 25, 30, 31, 38, 40, 42, 43, 67, 78, 83, 87, 135, 146, 170, 172, 191, 210, 214, 230, 244, 247*
FÁS *2, 13, 14, 24, 25, 176, 182, 232, 233, 235, 236, 237, 238, 239, 240, 241, 246, 256*
Feeney, Chuck *150*
fees *11, 22, 24, 25, 38, 101, 104, 135, 169, 172, 177, 185, 207, 208, 244*
Fennelly, Dr Ken *34, 56*
Ferguson, Prof Mark *203, 207, 208, 209, 211, 216*
FETAC *13, 22, 31, 33, 39, 44, 171, 175, 233, 239, 243, 245*
First Communion *45*
First Reconciliation (Confession) *45*
Fitzgerald, Frances *8, 20, 26, 28, 34, 35, 38, 39, 76, 92*
Fleming, Dr Mary *144, 188, 191*
Forfás *114, 231*
fourth level *1, 6, 208, 217, 218*
free pre-school year *22, 24, 37, 38, 39*
funding *8, 12, 13, 24, 25, 35, 37, 41, 64, 65, 66, 69, 70, 79, 89, 101, 131, 161, 169, 172, 176, 179, 181, 182, 183, 185, 192, 194, 197, 217, 218, 219, 221, 222, 223, 226, 227, 234, 235, 237, 239, 246, 249, 250*
further education *1, 2, 5, 13, 44, 69, 174, 175, 176, 212, 232, 233, 234, 235, 236, 237, 238, 239, 241, 242, 243, 244, 245, 246, 251, 252, 254, 256*

G

Gaeilge *83, 101, 102, 116, 184, 191*
Gaelscoileanna *54, 117*
Gaeltacht *49, 175, 187, 214*
Gallagher, Michael *vi, 34, 35, 50, 178*
Gallagher, Seán *82, 108*
Galway Education Centre *97, 129, 130, 130, 203*
Galway-Mayo Institute of Technology (GMIT) *147, 164, 174*
Going to Big School *16, 31*
Gormley, Paul *218, 219, 233*
graduate education *205*
grants *12, 104, 135, 172, 184, 206, 207*
Green Shoots *14*
Growing Up in Ireland *17, 28, 72, 73*
Gunning, Irene *2, 3, 4, 14*

guidance counsellor *x, 133, 134, 156, 219, 222*
guidelines *4, 34, 36, 44, 56, 58, 59, 74, 78, 91, 92, 101, 110, 111, 114, 115, 117, 118, 146, 148, 149, 202, 222, 251*
Gurría, Angel *5*

H

Haddington Road Agreement *8, 9, 49, 51, 52, 141, 144, 187, 227, 234*
Hall, Dr Tony *vi, vii, 3, 35, 83, 145, 203, 219*
Hannon, Cliona *144, 156*
Halpin, Dr Attracta *vii*
Hammond, John *82, 83, 84*
Hayes, Prof Michael A. *218, 239*
Hayes, Prof Noirín *25*
Healthy School Lunches *53*
Hegarty, Diarmuid *144, 168*
Heinz, Dr Manuela *144, 188, 190*
Help My Kid Learn *2, 29*
HETAC *13, 22, 182, 201, 239*
Hibernia College *183, 189 201, 203*
Higgins, Michael D. *179, 190, 205, 207*
higher education *5, 11, 12, 13, 19, 55, 109, 158, 159, 160, 161, 164, 165, 166, 168, 169, 170, 171, 172, 174, 175, 176, 177, 178, 180, 181, 182, 183, 189, 193, 194, 195, 196, 197, 207, 211, 212, 217, 218, 219, 221, 222, 224, 232, 237, 239, 242, 246, 247, 249, 250, 251, 253, 253, 256, 257*
Higher Education Authority (HEA) *12, 55, 159, 160, 165, 168, 178, 180, 181, 182, 189, 207, 237, 253*
Holmes, Trevor *144, 180*
Horizon 2020 *203, 205, 212*
Hpat *152*
Hume, Carmel *35, 60*
Hunt Report *150*

I

inclusive education *5, 44*
Incredible Years *18*
increments *51, 52, 120, 121, 133, 140, 141, 145, 187, 200, 204*
induction *48, 49, 60, 61, 92, 156*
inequality *5, 32, 156, 192*
Information and communications technology (ICT) *75, 90, 91, 96, 103, 104, 105, 110, 111, 117, 119, 122, 123, 124, 125, 126, 151, 177, 182, 190, 205, 220, 224, 226, 237, 243, 247*
initial teacher education (ITE) *46, 118, 191*
Institutes of Technology Ireland (IoTI) *145, 164, 169*
international *11, 22, 23, 42, 44, 55, 56, 58, 61, 65, 77, 87, 108, 113, 120, 124, 128,143, 146, 148, 160, 163, 164, 165, 167, 168, 169,171, 174, 175, 176, 177, 179, 185, 189, 190, 191, 192, 194, 195, 197, 202, 210, 217, 218, 219, 221, 222, 223, 224, 227, 237, 240, 242, 253*
Internet safety *110*
Irish Federation of University Teachers (IFUT) *107, 172, 185*
Irish Higher Education Quality Network (IHEQN) *168*
Irish language *79, 97, 131, 132, 144*
Irish National Teachers' Organisation (INTO) *126*
Irish Primary Principals' Network (IPPN) *vi*

Irish Research Council (IRC) *13, 216, 217, 218, 218, 219*
Irish Vocational Education Association (IVEA) *220*

J
JC2.0 *82, 96*
Jennings, Mike *144, 170, 185, 213*
Joint Managerial Body *83, 121*
Joint Oireachtas Committee *76*
Judge, Bernie *82, 83, 132*
Junior Cycle for Teachers (JCT) *83, 92, 93*
Junior Cycle reform *iv, x, 83, 88, 89, 102*

K
Kelly, Ferdia *82, 82, 120*
Kenny, Enda *12, 21, 36, 49, 150, 193*
Kenny, Orla *2, 26*
Keogh, Daire Dr. *45*
Kids' Own *26, 27*
King, Pat *82, 83, 90, 122, 127, 128*
Kinsella, Dr Stephen *213*
Kirk, Bernard *82, 83, 115, 116*
Kirk, Dr Pádraig *82, 83, 92, 93*

L
Labour Relations Commission (LRC) *123*
language and literacy *5*
Laudet, Dr Claire *145, 194*
Lavelle, Margaret *218, 229*
Layte, Richard *18, 28*
Leaving Certificate *10, 54, 103, 111, 124, 128, 131, 132, 144, 166, 167, 170, 170, 175, 192, 205, 235*
Letterkenny Institute of Technology *35, 76*
lifelong learning *1, 45, 163, 233, 233, 234, 247, 252*
Limerick College of Further Education *30*
Limerick Education Centre *124*
literacy *3, 4, 10, 16 17, 19, 43, 56, 57, 58, 74, 96, 97, 98, 101, 103, 104, 105, 115, 117, 118, 122, 132, 202, 233, 240, 242, 243, 247*
Literacy and Numeracy Strategy *iii, 60, 101*
Logan, Emily *71, 140*
Logue, John *174*
Lonergan, John *11*
Lynch, Áine *vi, 2, 31, 34, 39*

M
MacLaren, Dr Iain *144, 182, 183*
Malone, Dr Rose *144, 172*
Malone, Noel *82, 83, 96*
Marino Institute of Education (MIE) *xi, 41, 166, 189*
Martin, Archbishop Diarmuid *45, 63*
Mary Immaculate College *11, 55, 180, 198, 203, 233, 251, 252, 253, 254*
Matthews, Deirdre *82, 83, 100*
McHugh, Stan *xiii, 218, 219, 227*
McLaughlin, Sharon *34, 35, 76*
McManus, Bridget *89*
massive open online course (MOOC) *175*

Meehan, Dr Eucharia *202, 203, 204*
mental health *31, 42, 48, 80, 81, 82, 83, 84, 146, 148, 158, 173, 208, 210, 211 244*
mentoring *4, 47, 48, 179, 190, 194, 212, 228, 232*
merger *161, 164, 165, 181, 217*
Merriman, Brian *2, 17, 18*
Modern Languages in Post-Primary Education *82, 113*
Mooney, Brian *i, viii, 218, 219, 222*
Moore, Jim *82, 83, 136, 137*
Morgan, Dr Mark *34, 72*
Moriarty, Michael *137, 218, 219, 220*
Mulvey, Kieran *123*
Murray, Margaret *2, 29*
music education *41*

N
National Adult Literacy Agency (NALA) *29*
National Association of Principals and Deputy Principals (NAPD) *88, 95*
National College of Ireland *xi, 166*
National Council for Curriculum and Assessment (NCCA) *92, 94*
National Council for Special Education (NCSE) *71, 74, 75*
National Development Plan (NDP) *113*
National Employment and Entitlements Service (NEES) *224*
National Framework of Qualifications (NFQ) *145, 160, 161*
National Induction Programme for Teachers (NIPT) *46*
National Learning Network *2, 68, 73, 244*
National Parents' Council Primary *vi, 39*
National Parents' Council Post-Primary *vi*
National University of Ireland (NUI) *vii, 149, 150, 178*
National University of Ireland, Galway (NUIG) *vii, 149, 191, 229*
National University of Ireland, Maynooth (NUIM) *149, 164, 174*
newly qualified teachers (NQTs) *34, 46*
Ní Mhóráin, Muireann *82, 83, 117*
numeracy *3, 4, 10, 43, 56, 58, 74, 75, 98, 103, 115, 117, 118, 122, 132, 202, 240*
Nunan, Sheila *48, 49, 50, 63, 76, 136, 137, 144*

O
obesity *28*
OECD *3, 9, 12, 19, 20, 22, 23, 32, 61, 82, 92, 142, 170*
O'Brien, Ann *218, 235*
O'Connell, Dr Joe *82, 124*
O'Connor, Deirdre *34, 64*
Ó Cualáin, Stiofáin *vi, 82, 83, 104*
O'Driscoll, Cat *144, 145, 192*
Ó Foghlú, Seán *95*
O'Mahony, Conor *6*
Ombudsman *85, 154, 192*
Ó Ruairc, Tomás *87*
O'Sullivan, Bernadette *82, 138*
O'Sullivan, Professor Mary *144, 198*
O'Toole, Paul *218, 225*

P

parents *4, 6, 8, 9, 11, 16, 17, 18, 19, 21, 23, 24, 25, 26, 28, 29, 30, 31, 32, 33, 34, 35, 36, 38, 40, 41, 43, 45, 52, 53, 54, 59, 66, 68, 71, 72, 73, 74, 75, 76, 77, 79, 83, 85, 86, 87, 88, 89, 90, 91, 92, 102, 103, 105, 106, 108, 109, 110, 112, 113, 114, 118, 120, 126, 131, 134, 135, 136, 139, 140, 146, 150, 151, 152, 154, 155, 170, 173, 175, 177, 184, 206, 210, 233, 253, 257*
pastoral care *132, 133, 134*
patronage *9, 53, 68, 72, 73, 77, 78, 79, 88*
personal wellbeing *82, 83, 124, 126*
Piesse, Dr Amanda *144, 194*
policy *5, 13, 18, 19, 25, 28, 30, 31, 32, 42, 43, 46, 50, 54, 56, 58, 59, 70, 71, 76, 77, 79, 85, 90, 91, 92, 94, 96, 120, 127, 128, 131, 132, 136, 146, 147, 148, 150, 151, 161, 165, 168, 179, 182, 183, 193, 202, 203, 204, 213, 214, 218, 219, 222, 230, 233, 235, 240, 246, 249, 250, 252, 253, 254*
Post-Primary Education Forum (PPEF) *136*
Physical Education (PE) *58, 101, 153, 159, 212, 213*
points *13, 14, 19, 54 77, 120, 123, 128,144, 152, 153, 154, 159, 165, 166, 167, 170, 179, 187, 208, 222*
post-primary education *82, 83, 92, 113, 136*
Post-Primary Languages Initiative (PPLI) *113, 114*
Preparing for Life (PFL) *17*
Prevention and Early Intervention Programme (PEIP) *17, 18*
primary education *9, 45, 49, 70, 71, 79, 88, 96, 97, 106, 127, 150, 151, 201, 201, 212*
primary principals *vi, 34, 50, 52, 65*
Prime Time *8, 17, 34, 35, 38*
principals *3, 4, 6, 8, 10, 48, 49, 60, 63, 64, 65, 66, 74, 79, 82, 83, 84, 87, 93, 97, 102, 103, 106, 107, 109, 112, 117, 118, 125, 135, 138, 140, 147, 148, 149, 156, 201, 203*
professional development *16, 17, 39, 44, 60, 61, 76, 84, 92, 97, 99, 100, 106, 107, 122, 123, 124, 125, 129, 131, 146, 155, 159, 196, 205, 213, 214, 232, 251, 252, 254*
Professional Development Service for Teachers (PDST) *83, 93, 108, 109, 141*
Professional Diploma in Education (ITE) *187, 188, 191, 219, 229*
Professional Diploma in Education (FE) *187, 188, 191, 219, 229*
Professional Diploma in Mathematics for Teaching (PDMT) *214*
Project Maths *91, 130, 214*
Promethean *48*
protest *69, 112, 227*
public sector *14, 63, 101, 113, 121, 133, 136, 141, 183, 186, 187, 188, 234, 238, 246*
pupil-teacher ratio *90, 120*
'Put Education First' *63, 106*

Q

Quality and Qualifications Ireland (QQI) *158, 159, 174, 239, 241, 252*
Quinn, Marian *25*
Quinn, Ruairí *3, 6, 7, 11, 37, 38, 55, 66, 68, 72, 76, 77, 79, 88, 89, 92, 98, 100, 101, 106, 108, 109, 113, 114, 116, 120, 144, 149, 164, 165, 169, 180, 181, 185, 190, 240, 255*

R

recognition of prior learning (RPL) *219, 237*
Redmond, Billy *34, 35, 46*
referendum *8, 17, 20, 21, 23, 26, 27, 54, 188*
reform *4, 9, 10, 50, 74, 75, 77, 97, 99, 100, 102, 103, 108, 109, 113, 116, 120, 140, 159, 160, 161, 166, 167, 169, 171, 172, 181, 188, 232, 233, 234, 235, 237, 255*
religion *48, 77, 78, 79, 113, 120*
Robinson, Prof Ken *83, 138, 140*
role models *6, 44, 141, 235, 236*
Royal Irish Academy (RIA) *166, 178, 179*
RTE *27, 34, 37, 38, 43, 68, 77, 111, 144, 236*
Ruddock, Karen *82, 113*
rural schools *56*
Ryan, Emer *112*
Ryan, Mary *2, 30*
Rynn, Joe *2, 10, 11*

S

science education *44, 191*
Science Foundation Ireland (SFI) *xiii, 202, 203, 207, 208, 209*
school self evaluation (SSE) *3, 35, 48, 60, 65, 74, 75, 96, 97, 100, 103, 104, 109, 114, 115, 116, 117, 118, 122, 235*
school inspection *36*
school principals *iii, 60, 73, 93, 111, 121*
Scoilnet *122, 123, 124*
Shannon, Dr Geoffrey *2, 3, 32*
Sherlock, Seán *203, 204, 206, 211, 212*
Síolta – The National Quality Framework for Early Childhood Education *16, 17, 18, 31, 33, 34, 44*
Small Schools Initiative (SSI) *56*
Smyth, Prof Barry *202, 203, 215, 216*
social network *99*
Social, Personal and Health Education (SPHE) *87, 110*
SOLAS *5, 13, 176, 232, 233, 235, 236, 237, 238, 239, 240, 241, 246, 252, 256*
special educational needs *51, 75, 86, 137, 191*
standardised tests *60*
Stanley Letter, 1831 *35*
Start Strong *8, 9*
St. Patrick's College Drumcondra *35, 189*
St Vincent de Paul *159, 193*
strategy *3, 14, 19, 31, 43, 48, 50, 53, 58, 74, 115, 122, 125, 130, 131, 148, 160, 161, 164, 174, 185, 217, 218, 221, 222, 223, 225, 228, 235, 239, 240, 241, 242, 250*
students *4, 5, 7, 9, 12, 24, 28, 34, 49, 55, 56, 57, 58, 59, 69, 76, 88, 89, 90, 91, 92, 94, 97, 98, 99, 100, 102, 103, 104, 105, 106, 107, 108, 109, 110, 111, 112, 113, 114, 115, 116, 117, 118, 119, 122, 123, 124, 125, 126, 127, 128, 131, 132, 142, 143, 144, 146, 147, 148, 150, 151, 152, 153, 154, 155, 156, 158, 159, 161, 163, 165, 166, 167, 167, 168, 169, 170, 171, 172, 173, 174, 175, 176, 177, 179, 181,182, 183, 185, 188, 190, 191, 192, 193, 194, 195, 198, 202, 203, 205, 206, 207, 208, 209, 210, 211, 211, 213, 214, 218, 220, 221, 233, 235, 237, 244, 245, 246, 247, 248, 249, 250, 253, 254, 256*
student welfare and support *132*
'Super Options' *96, 97*
SUSI *159, 206, 207, 209*
Synod Board of Education *56*

T

Tallaght West Childhood Development Initiative (CDI) *17*
Teaching Council *13, 14, 56, 58, 60, 61, 62, 92, 101, 108, 201, 202, 204, 228, 241, 242, 251, 253, 255*
Teacher Education Section (TES) *46, 141*
teacher induction *47, 78*
Teachers' Union of Ireland (TUI) *107, 126, 131, 132*
teaching religion *35, 64, 65, 99*
technological university *11, 160, 178, 179, 180, 181*
technology *10, 11, 12, 13, 49, 55, 79, 82, 84, 90, 104, 105, 111, 117, 122, 123, 124, 125, 125, 126, 158, 159, 160, 161, 169, 172, 173, 176, 178, 178, 179, 180, 181, 182, 183, 185, 189, 193, 194, 196, 203, 205, 211, 217, 218, 221, 223, 224, 225, 226, 229, 230, 233, 237, 238, 245, 247, 248*
The Gathering *175*
third-level *12, 121, 131, 159, 165, 169, 173, 176, 180, 181, 185, 189, 192, 208, 209, 229*
transitions *4, 19, 95*
Trinity Access Programmes (TAP) *156, 157*
Trinity College Dublin *11, 28, 42, 55, 164, 179, 203, 220, 229*
Tuffy, Joanna *38*
Tyndall National Institute *148, 213, 215*

U

Union of Students in Ireland (USI) *145, 174, 192*
United Nations (UN) Convention on the Rights of the Child *17*
Universities Bill *154, 155*
University College Cork (UCC) *11, 20, 55, 111, 162, 163, 180, 192, 194, 195, 203, 227*
University College Dublin (UCD) *11, 55, 93, 96, 129, 130, 162, 163, 164, 165, 173, 176, 178, 180, 181, 185, 188, 190, 192, 194, 203, 211, 217, 229, 230*
University of Limerick (UL) *11, 55, 111, 155, 159, 164, 165, 177, 178, 180 183, 185, 198, 203, 212, 212, 213, 226, 227, 228*
university ranking *144, 180*

V

'Value for Money' *34, 56*
van Turnhout, Jillian *14*
van Vught, Prof Frans *150, 151*
VEC *24, 25, 44, 63, 97, 106, 107, 206, 207, 211, 234, 238, 243*
voluntary secondary schools *96, 97, 134, 135*

W

Waldron, Dr Fionnuala *34, 35, 42*
Walsh, Dr Anne *vi*
Walsh, Marijka *15*
Walsh, Dr Padraig *144, 145, 160*
Wang, Prof Liming *115, 116, 144, 176*
Ward, Noel *34, 35, 79*
Waterford Institute of Technology (WIT) *xi, 166*
wellbeing *16, 31, 82, 96, 97, 138, 139, 140*
Who's Who *16, 17, 46, 48, 49, 93, 96, 97, 155, 159, 212, 213, 216, 217, 229, 229, 232, 233, 253*

Wolfe, Toby *2, 8, 9*
Wright, Alan *105, 112*